SYNTAX and SEMANTICS

VOLUME 14

SYNTAX and SEMANTICS

VOLUME 14
Tense and Aspect

Edited by

Philip J. Tedeschi

Department of Hospital Administration
School of Public Health
University of Michigan
Ann Arbor, Michigan

Annie Zaenen

Center for Cognitive Science
Massachusetts Institute of Technology
Cambridge, Massachusetts

ACADEMIC PRESS
A Subsidiary of Harcourt Brace Jovanovich, Publishers
New York   London   Toronto   Sydney   San Francisco

ACADEMIC PRESS, INC.
111 Fifth Avenue, New York, New York 10003

United Kingdom Edition published by
ACADEMIC PRESS, INC. (LONDON) LTD.
24/28 Oval Road, London NW1 7DX

LIBRARY OF CONGRESS CATALOG CARD NUMBER: 72–9423

ISBN 0–12–613514–2

PRINTED IN THE UNITED STATES OF AMERICA

81 82 83 84   9 8 7 6 5 4 3 2 1

To the memory of Michael Bennett

CONTENTS

Aspect and Quantification   31

LAURI CARLSON

Aspect and Voice: Some Reflections on Perfect and Passive   65

BERNARD COMRIE

On the Definition of the Telic–Atelic (Bounded–Nonbounded) Distinction   79

ÖSTEN DAHL

Aspectual "Skewing" in Two Australian Languages: Mara, Nunggubuyu   91

JEFFREY HEATH

Remarks on *Noch* and *Schon* in German   103

J. HOEPELMAN AND C. ROHRER

Aspect Theory and Georgian Aspect   127

DEE ANN HOLISKY

A Unified Temporal Theory of Tense and Aspect   145

MARION R. JOHNSON

Aspect, Markedness, and t_0 177

HENRY KUČERA

LIST OF CONTRIBUTORS

Numbers in parentheses indicate the pages on which the authors' contributions begin.

DAVID ARMSTRONG (1), *Department of Classics, University of Texas at Austin, Austin, Texas 78712*

MICHAEL BENNETT* (13), *Department of Linguistics, University of Pittsburgh, Pittsburgh, Pennsylvania 15260*

LAURI CARLSON (31), *Department of Linguistics, Massachusetts Institute of Technology, Cambridge, Massachusetts 02139*

BERNARD COMRIE (65), *Department of Linguistics, University of Southern California, Los Angeles, California 90007*

ÖSTEN DAHL (79), *Department of Linguistics, University of Stockholm, S-106 91 Stockholm, Sweden*

JEFFREY HEATH (91), *Department of Linguistics, Harvard University, Cambridge, Massachusetts 02138*

J. HOEPELMAN (103), *Institut für Linguistik, Romanistik, 7 Stuttgart 1, Keplerstrasse 17, West Germany*

* Deceased.

xiii

DEE ANN HOLISKY (127), *Department of Linguistics, The University of Chicago, Chicago, Illinois 60637*

MARION R. JOHNSON (145), *Department of Anthropology, University of Western Ontario, London, Ontario N6A 5C2, Canada*

HENRY KUČERA (177), *Department of Slavic Languages, Brown University, Providence, Rhode Island 02912*

ALEXANDER P. D. MOURELATOS (191), *Department of Philosophy, University of Texas at Austin, Austin, Texas 78712*

C. ROHRER (103), *Institut für Linguistik, Romanistik, 7 Stuttgart 1, Keplerstrasse 17, West Germany*

CARLOTA S. SMITH (213), *Department of Linguistics, University of Texas at Austin, Austin, Texas 78712*

PHILIP J. TEDESCHI (239), *Department of Hospital Administration, School of Public Health, University of Michigan, Ann Arbor, Michigan 48109*

FRANK VLACH (271), *School of Philosophy, University of New South Wales, Kensington, New South Wales 2033, Australia*

† Present address: 5000 N. 13th Street, Arlington, Virginia 22205.

PREFACE

Although all linguists are occasionally confronted with the problem of accounting for natural language phenomena that are dependent on tense and/or aspect, the topic has not received very much systematic attention from linguists. Treatments of tense and aspect have tended to fall into two categories: language-specific studies that did not attempt to address questions of general theoretical interest and more philosophical studies that frequently did not pay sufficient attention to natural language phenomena. The development of a formal semantics for natural language that has taken place over the last 10 years was, of course, bound to cause some change in this picture. Tense and aspect, however, were not among the areas first affected by this development (despite important exceptions like the work of Hans Kamp and several European linguists), and the advances in formal semantics often remain unknown to linguists who are more oriented toward the study of specific languages.

When we organized the Symposium on Tense and Aspect held at Brown University in January 1977, one of our aims was to contribute to a narrowing of the gap between formal semanticists and language-oriented linguists. The interest shown by the participants and the stimulating discussions that ensued encouraged us to pursue this aim a bit further by presenting this volume on the subject. This volume contains several papers that were presented at the conference as well as several invited papers that make the volume more representative of the work currently done in this area.

Although this collection of papers illustrates the fact that we are very far from a general theory of time-related phenomena in natural language, on the positive side, it also shows that it has become possible to discuss these phenomena in a systematic manner.

The chapters in this volume may be viewed as falling into several groups. One group (by Armstrong, Carlson, Holisky, and Mourelatos), takes as a point of departure Vendler's or Kenny's four-way aspectual typology and discusses improvement of this aspectual typology together with the similarity between the count–mass distinction for nouns and the perfective–imperfective distinction for predicates. The illustrations come from languages as diverse as Ancient Greek, Finnish, Georgian, and English. Another group of chapters concentrates on the English progressive, an area in which much systematic work based on model-theoretic semantics has been accomplished during the last few years. This group includes the chapters by Bennett, Vlach, and Tedeschi. Also using the model-theoretic approach, Hoepelman and Rohrer develop an analysis for the adverbs *noch* and *schon* in German. Johnson and Smith both use the ideas of Reichenbach as the starting point for their analyses. Johnson develops a Montague-style interval-based semantics for Kikuyu; Smith presents an account of temporal anaphora in English.

Whereas the preceding three groups of chapters have all been influenced in an interesting way by philosophers' views on tense and aspect, a fourth group of chapters presents a more linguistic approach. Included here, are the contributions of Kučera—investigating the use of the markedness analysis for Czech—and Comrie—arguing for a correlation between the passive voice and the perfective aspect. Dahl's chapter considers the distinction telic–atelic under both its more philosophical and its more linguistic guises, thus providing a bridge between the two approaches. Heath's chapter, more purely linguistic, represents an important caveat to the students of tense and aspect as systems by showing the interaction between these categories and other categories of language.

We hope that this volume will help to convince linguists that frameworks elaborated by philosophers can be used in interesting ways in the study and analysis of natural languages. Further, we hope that the more philosophically oriented will be convinced that the applications of general theories of tense and aspect to specific natural languages are not trivial.

We have the agreeable duty of thanking several people for their help, both in the organization of the Symposium and in the compilation of this volume: We thank, first, the participants of the Symposium, who cheerfully ignored the horrors of a New England winter ice-storm and kept up animated discussions in underheated rooms; second, faculty and students of the Department of Linguistics, as well as several administrators, at Brown University for practical help and hospitality, especially James Wrenn, M. Glicksman, and Polly Jacobson; and most of all, we thank the referees who helped us select first the abstracts and papers for the conference and later the papers for this volume: Arthur Abramson, Emmon Bach, Gregory Carlson, Nick Clements, Elan Dresher, John Grima, Ken Hale, Alice Harris, Norbert Hornstein, Hans Kamp, Lauri Karttunen, William Ladusaw, John McCarthy, James McCawley, Nicholas Ostler, Barbara Partee, Joachim Schindler, Neil V. Smith, Alan Timberlake, and Calvert Watkins. A special note of thanks is due to Elisabet Engdahl whose encouragement and help at all stages was instrumental to the entire project. Finally, we would like to thank the previous and the present editors of the Syntax and Semantics series, Jerry Sadock and Stephen Anderson, for their collaboration.

SYNTAX and SEMANTICS

VOLUME 14

THE ANCIENT GREEK AORIST AS THE
ASPECT OF COUNTABLE ACTION

DAVID ARMSTRONG

1. INTRODUCTION

Ancient Greek is a more interesting field for the study of perfective–imperfective contrast than is the modern language, as its verb paradigm is much more elaborate and complex, and the two principal stems, still called (in an inconvenient memorial to the theories of ancient grammarians) "aorist" (perfective) and "present" (imperfective), are remarkably fertile in contrasted forms. Indicatives, subjunctives, optatives, infinitives, participles, and imperatives exist in present and aorist from Homer onward, and in all three numbers (singular, dual, and plural) where number is possible. Two further tense systems are elaborated, "future" and "perfect" (these are also conventional terms). The "future" is a kind of subjunctive in origin, and develops a few modal forms (infinitive, optative, participle) by analogy. The "perfect" is an aspectually problematic tense, much like "perfects" in Western languages in general, a combination stative and phase marker. It develops a few extra forms in fifth-century and later Greek, and becomes more complex in meaning, but is basically confined, for most purposes, to a simple system of indicative, infinitive, and participle. Aspectual contrast in Ancient Greek is therefore mainly expressed by aorist and present stems. The influence of this con-

1

trast extends also into the future passive, which allows a certain extent of distinguishing between aoristic and present-like markers, but not the future active, which is more or less felt as aspectually neutral. None of the future forms turned out to be relevant to the present study.

2. THE AORIST

The nature of this all-important aspectual contrast between present and aorist stems in Ancient Greek, a thorny and much-discussed problem, appears to be significantly illuminated by the theory discussed by Mourelatos (this volume), in which count quantifiability is basic to perfectivity and to event predication. The test to be applied is a simple but obvious one: examining the regular behavior of the tense stems throughout the moods with (a) adverbs of cardinal count, 'once', 'twice', 'thrice', and so on, which ordinarily, when used as adverbs, define a verbal predication as count quantifiable; and (b) with adverbs of indefinite frequency count, 'always', 'countless times', 'once a day', 'twice a year', and so on. Everyone who has studied Ancient Greek knows that the phrase ''single act'' is frequently used to explain the behavior of the aorist stem. Everyone who knows the language well knows that 'twice' and 'three times' and other expressions of definite count commonly take aorist stem, in apparent contradiction of this rule, as do many other adverbs that imply definite limits of repetition. He also knows that 'always' and the other expressions in (b) regularly take present stem. But as count quantifiability has not yet been proposed as basic to perfectivity in the literature of Ancient Greek grammar, neither rule has received more than casual observation.

Questioning a dead language for the co-occurrence of adverbs with the aspects is difficult, as to get results in a reasonable amount of time means reliance on the accuracy of lexicons and concordances, and the results themselves are *ex silentio,* in the sense that, if a given adverb does not co-occur in extant literature with a certain aspect, that is not a very scientific assurance that it cannot, especially in a literature of which so small a part survives. For this reason, and because it is a general feeling among scholars who know the modern and ancient languages that present and aorist aspect operate more or less the same way in both, I have once or twice appealed to the opinions of Modern Greek speakers as to what is and is not grammatical. But basically the evidence for this study comes from examining, as well as the current state of lexicography permits, the surviving body of Classical Greek to the end of the fourth century B.C. for the syntax of all the adverbs of cardinal count and some of those of frequency count. Some other adverbs of frequency count are not relevant to the present study. For example, *pollakis* 'often' (formed from *poll-*

'many' and *akis* 'times') might be expected to, and does, co-occur with either aspect, according to whether it happens to be felt as 'often' or 'a certain number of times'. Besides some papyrus and epigraphic texts my survey is deficient mainly for Aristotle and Xenophon, for whom complete lexicons do not yet exist. I believe the fairly large body of writing examined is enough to provide significant results.

2.1 Co-occurrence Restrictions

It will be seen that the aorist turns out to be the regular tense with adverbs of cardinal count, and the present with adverbs of frequency count. The "perfect" is capable of co-occurring with either kind of adverb at various periods of its development (although there is no period at which it ever co-occurs with such adverbs as 'once a day', it is found from Homer's day with 'always' and from the late fifth century with 'once', 'twice', and so on). The perfect is felt as primarily stative in early Greek, and so can co-occur with such adverbs as 'always'. Perfects of a resultative nature, with a sort of kinship to the aorist, begin appearing with adverbs of cardinal count from about 450 B.C. on and become increasingly frequent with such adverbs as the perfect becomes in many verbs a mere equivalent of the aorist, a process completed in Hellenistic times (from about 300 B.C. on). Thus the usage of the perfect with these adverbs is a reflection of its original kinship with presents as a stative and its developing relation with the aorist as a resultative,[1] and is omitted from the present study.

Regular usage of the adverbs of cardinal count *hapax* 'once', *dis* 'twice', *tris* 'three times', *tetrakis* 'four times', *etc.*, can be shown as follows:

(1)   ἅπαξ   ἐν τῇ ζωῇ μειχθῆναι   ἀνδρὶ ξείνῳ . . .
                                                         HERODOTUS 1.191.1
     hapax *en tēi zoēi* ***meichthēnai*** (aor.) *andri xeinoi*
     '*that* **once** in her life she **slept with** (aor.) a foreigner'

---

[1] Greek "perfects" present (see Mourelatos, this volume) a very similar problem to "perfects" in modern European languages, including English, and some of the same logical difficulties discussed in Comrie (1976 pp. 52ff) and the various authors mentioned in John Lyons (1977, pp. 714–716). The peculiar history of the Greek perfect, mostly stative in Homer and developing a much wider resultative use in the fifth century B.C. and later, is brilliantly described in J. Wackernagel (1920, V.1. pp. 166–171) and in more detail in his earlier work (1904). *All* the adverbs I discuss in this paper are found, consequently, at some period of Greek, co-occurring with perfect stem. I follow not only Comrie and Lyons but several scholars who have tried to discuss aspect in the classical languages (cf. J. Gonda, 1962, p. 53) in feeling that the nature of this tense is a separate issue from perfective and imperfective aspect properly so-called.

(2)   δὶς τῷ αὐτῷ ποταμῷ οὐκ ἔστιν ἐμβῆναι.
                                                    HERACLITUS B91
       dis toi autoi potamoi ouk estin embenai (aor.)
       'It is not possible **to step** (aor.) **twice** into the same river.'

(3)   ἐὰν ἕλωνται   τρὶς ἐφεξῆς τὸν βίον τοῦτον . . .
                                                    PLATO *Phaedrus* 248b
       ean helontai (aor.) *tris ephexes ton bion touton*
       'if they **choose for themselves** (aor.) **thrice** in succession the same
       life'

The following show the standard contrast between this regular usage, adverb of cardinal count + aorist, and the regular usage with adverbs of frequency count like *aei* (also spelled *aiei* and *aien*) 'always' and its equiva-
lents, which regularly co-occur with present stem.

(4)   κρεῖσσον γὰρ εἰσάπαξ θανεῖν
       kreisson gar eisapax thanein (aor.)
       ἢ τοὺς ἁπάσας ἡμέρας πάσχειν   κακῶς.
                                                    AESCHYLUS, *Prometheus* 750f
       e tous hapasas hemeras paschein (pres.) *kakos*
       'It is better **to die** (aor.) **once** for all than **to suffer** (pres.) evil
       through all time.'

(5)   ὅμοιον   δὲ τοῦτο ἅπαξ τε εἰπεῖν   καὶ ἀεὶ λέγειν . . .
                                                    ZENO B1
       homoion de touto hapax te eipein (aor.) *kai aei legein* (pres.)
       'It is the same **to say** (aor.) this **once** and **to say** (pres.) it **always**.'

   The following example shows regular usage with such phrases of frequency count as 'once a year', 'twice a day', 'every year'.

(6)   ἐθύομεν   πεντάκις τῆς ἡμέρας.
                                                    MENANDER 4.166 (Mein.)
       ethuomen (pres.-stem impf.) *pentakis tes hemeras*
       '**We sacrificed** (pres.-stem imperfect) **five times a day**.'

This squares with the fact that Modern Greek speakers identify the following as ungrammatical:

(7)   *ἔγραψε   δύο ψορὲς τὸ χρόνο.
       **egrapse* (aor.)   *duo phores to chrono.*
       He wrote (aor.) **twice a year.**

The imperfect is required instead.

2.2 Problematic Cases

Very many examples of the usages illustrated in (1)–(6) can be given from all periods of Greek. It is possible also to discover cases in which adverbs of cardinal count co-occur with present stem, and of frequency count with aorist stem. The consensus of most scholars, grammarians, and lexicographers about these cases is that the aspect of the verb either alters the sense of the adverb or becomes consistent with it because of a special situation made clear by the context. These exceptions can be grouped into five main categories, in the first four of which, in my opinion, the sense of the adverb is altered, with only the fifth involving a special situation.

1. *Nikao* 'conquer' and its synonyms may co-occur in present stem with adverbs of cardinal count listing four or more athletic victories.

2. In fifth-century and later Greek *dis* 'twice' co-occurs with present stem in the sense 'again' or 'over again.'

3. In fifth-century and later Greek *dis kai tris* 'twice and thrice' is used with present (never aorist) stem in the meaning 'over and over'.

4. Indefinite repetition of an action itself internally countable ('always doing something three times') requires adverb of cardinal count + present stem.

5. Once in Homer, but, as far as I can discover, not elsewhere in Ancient Greek, *aei* 'always' co-occurs with aorist stem in what ancient and modern commentators identify as the unusual sense 'on each occasion'.

2.2.1 NIKAŌ

Nikaō 'conquer' and 'be victor' (cf. LSJ s.v.) frequently appears in the imperfective stem as an event predication, where aorist would be expected (so also, e.g., *eutucheō* 'obtain/be the possessor of good fortune'). However, it is resistant to this usage with adverbs of cardinal count except in lists of athletic victories totaling four or more [Pindar *Olympians* 7. 81–86; *IG* 4. 561. 5 (Argos), 5 (1). 213 (Laconia), *etc*.]. With victories scored once, twice, or three times the aorist seems to be regular. The ordinary usage of the verb's imperfective stem seems enough to explain this anomaly, but there seems a possibility that in at least some of the examples the large numbers are taken as the equal of 'many times' or 'often'. Only this verb and its synonyms seem to co-occur in imperfective stem with adverbs of cardinal count in their proper sense.

2.2.2. DIS

From the mid sixth century B.C. we find *dis* 'twice' construed as 'again' (a recognized usage; cf., e.g., Slater, *Lexicon to Pindar*, Berlin 1969, s.v. δίς sub fin.).

(8)   δὶς γὰρ ἀνηβᾶν   οὐ πέλεται πρὸς θεῶν
                                                                        THEOGNIS, 1009f

    dis gar anēban (pres.) *ou peletai   pros theōn*
    'for **to be young** (pres.) **twice** (i.e., **again**) is not given us by the gods'

In all the not unusual cases of *dis* + present stem in Ancient Greek, it is generally agreed that the present aspect dictates a different lexical translation, 'again' or 'over again', so that the adverb is no longer one of cardinal count.

2.2.3. DIS KAI TRIS

Similarly, from the fifth century on we find *dis kai tris* 'twice and thrice', *tris tetrakis* 'thrice and four times', and similar expressions construed as 'over and over' (frequency count).

(9)   ἐξαλείφοντες   δὶς καὶ τρίς
                                                                        ARISTOPHANES *Peace* 1181

    exaleiphontes (pres.) *dis kai tris*
    '**rubbing out** (pres.) names **twice and thrice** [i.e., **over and over**]'

Here again the present aspect of the verb changes the meaning of the adverb from cardinal to frequency count.

2.2.4. INDEFINITE REPETITION

This is almost all that can be discovered in the way of apparent exceptions to the rule that adverbs of cardinal count take aorist and of frequency count present stem verbs, always leaving the perfect *hors concours*, except for one example, apparently not elsewhere paralleled, in Homer of an adverb meaning 'always' + aorist stem. The usage is most unusual; a medieval scholiast thinks it impossible; and a great modern scholar comments that the meaning of 'always' must be changed to 'each time' if the grammar is to be correct. Modern Greek speakers identify the following as equally as ungrammatical, in normal usage, as example (7):

(10)   πάντοτε ἔγραψε
    pantote   egrapse (aor.)
    'he **always wrote** (aor.)'

but agree that a context might just possibly be created in which, changing the sense of *pantote* (Hellenistic and Modern Greek 'always') to 'each (and every) time', the phrase might be intelligible.

Ancient Greek *aei* (*aiei, aien*) 'always' has, from the mid fifth century B.C. on, an occasional idiomatic sense when used with a participle 'at any given time' (e.g., *hoi aei kratountes* (pres.) 'those ruling (pres.) at any given time'). In this sense, though the vast majority of usages are with present-stem participle, it now and then appears with an aorist participle (Eur. *Hecuba* 1182; Demosthenes *Midias* 131). But in its normal sense 'always, continually' it seems to take aorist only at *Iliad* 21.263 (Aesch. *Prometheus* 163 is not an example, as *aei* does not modify the verb). Jebb mentions this passage in attempting to defend the emendation of *aei* + aorist stem by Arndt into Sophocles *Philoctetes* 1140: "Nauck objects that with αἰέν we ought to have the pres. inf. λέγειν. But αἰὲν εἰπεῖν = 'to assert *on each occasion*'—the aor. inf. marking the moment of the assertion [Sir Richard Jebb (Ed.), *Sophocles: Philoctetes,* 179, ad loc.]".

Jebb's proposed translation of *aei* + aorist stem as 'on each occasion' tallies remarkably with the feeling of Modern Greek speakers cited earlier. He goes on to cite *Iliad* 21.263 as an example. I cannot find any other comparable example in Ancient Greek. The context immediately following the line is worth giving, in translation:

(11)   So **always** (*aei*) the flood of the river **overtook** (*kichēsato,* aor.) Achilles, swift though he was; for gods are stronger than men. And **as many times** (*hossakis*) as swift godlike Achilles tried (*hormēseie,* aor.) to stand against him . . . **so many times** (*tossakis*) **would** the great flood of the heaven-fed river **hit** (impf.) his shoulders from above.

                                                                Iliad 21.263–269

Given that it is Homer's continual manner to gloss one statement of a fact with another, as here he does by giving a shorter and longer version of Achilles' contest with the Scamander, it appears certain from the context that in Homer's mind also was the meaning 'on each occasion'. Not only is this the one appearance of such usage in epic and as far as I can tell in Classical Greek (no one since Jebb prints Ardnt's emendation of *Philoctetes* 1140, which is implausible for other than grammatical reasons), but the medieval scholiast Eustathius comments irritatedly that either Homer means by the aorist indicative the imperfect indicative or the syntax is impossible.[2]

---

[2] *Lexicon d. Frühgriechischen Epos* (Göttingen, 1955–), fasc. 2, col. 284 (s.v. ἀεί, αἰεί, αἰέν), lines 52–56, citing this line as unique usage, with Eusthatius' comment. The old Firmin Didot lexicon (*Thesaurus Linguae Graecae,* Paris, 1865) s.v. ἀεί tried to refute Eustathius' comment (vol. 1.1, col. 727 a and d), but in my opinion the examples there given are not relevant.

I might mention here an apparent example of *tris* + imperfective stem which occurs twice

2.2.5. Adverbs of Cardinal Count with Present Stem

I can group here a few examples of disguised frequency count in which an adverb of cardinal count appears with present stem for an immediately obvious reason. The phrase *hapax legomenon* (pres.) 'once read' (Late Greek) is common among scholars to denote a word found only once either in Greek literature or in a given author; so also *dis* and *tris legomenon*. As the participle is present tense, this seems anomalous till you realize that the literature or the author is conceived of as a permanent entity in which the word is found 'once', not on one single reading, but as often as anyone looks for it. Such situations of disguised frequency count occur regularly when what is in question is actions, themselves internally capable of count, that are indefinitely repeated; in such situations it is not the internal count ('doing this three times') but the frequency of the multiple action itself ('always doing this three times', 'doing this three times every year', and so on) that dictates the choice of aspect:

(12)   Τεθνηκόσιν γὰρ ἔλεγεν, ὦ μόχθηρε σύ,
        tethnekosin gar elegen, o mochthēre su,
        οἷς οὐδὲ τρὶς λέγοντες   ἐξικνούμεθα.
        hois oude tris legontes (pres.) *exiknoumetha*

Aristophanes Frogs 1175f.

'Well, he was talking to the dead, you wretch, whom we can't reach even by **calling** (pres.) them **three times**.'

What Aristophanes is describing is a ritual action which is itself threefold but is performed an indefinite number of times ('calling them three times every time we call them'). Similar examples can be found elsewhere (*Odyssey* 12.22 ('all men die once'), Herodotus 1.185, Menander *Epitrepontes* 533f).

---

in Homer. In general, in Homeric Greek, sentences that would appear in later prose and poetry in the hypotactic form 'saying (pres. participle) this, he left (aor.)' appear in the paratactic form 'he was saying (impf. ind.) this and left (aor.)':

> (the wrath of Achilles) which **hurled** (*proiapsen*, aor.) the souls of many mighty men to Hades, and **made** (*teuche*, impf.; i.e., 'making') the men themselves prey to dogs . . .
>
> <div align="right"><i>Iliad</i> 1. 3f</div>

Twice in Homer this usage appears with adverbs of cardinal count (*Il.* 8. 169f, 11. 462f):

> thrice he *debated* (*mermerixe*, aor.) in mind and heart, thrice from the Idean mountains Zeus *thundered* (*ktupe*, impf.)
>
> <div align="right"><i>Il.</i> 8. 169f</div>

But it seems obvious enough that the second 'thrice' means, in this poetic usage, 'each time' and is a frequency count; once more, the aspect influences the meaning of the adverb, not the other way round. The usage is more commonly found with two aorists, for example, *Odyssey* 11. 206–208.

Finally, there is one striking and familiar example which I think is in every way the exception that proves the rule, showing how unusual a situation it takes to call forth an adverb of real cardinal count with an imperfective (like Mourelatos's from the Santa Claus song): the title of Menander's play Δὶς 'Εξαπατῶν (*Dis Exapatōn*, pres. participle), 'The Man Who Deceives (pres.) Twice'. I might take refuge in 'again' or 'over again' for the meaning of *dis* here, as in my second category of exceptions, but the real explanation is more interesting.

We know from the fragments of the play that the double deception was part of the action. If the aorist participle which would normally be used (*Dis exapatēsas*) came into Menander's mind, he rejected it for two different reasons at once. First, the aorist of the verb 'to deceive' can only imply completed or successful—not, like the present, attempted—deception. We may therefore say that such a title would lack dramatic suspense; the present implies "you are about to see a man putting over deceptions twice—will he succeed?" A second and even more compelling reason is that the perfective aspect inherent in the aorist would imply, without further qualification, that the deceptions are already over before the actions begin (a *dis exapatēsas* would be a man who ALREADY has succeeded in two deceptions).

It appears, then, that only in the case of a title covering the whole unfolding action of a play do we find a plausible situation for a definite cardinal count of actions + perfective.—Or at least so I suppose, as I am relying on personal observation plus the incomplete lexicons of Bonitz and Sturz for Aristotle and Xenophon, two writers famous for drawing elegant distinctions and creating unusual syntactical situations. But so does Ancient Greek in as a whole, beside whose sensitivity and elegance in the use particularly of imperfect (present-stem) versus aorist indicatives similar usages in the Hellenistic, Byzantine, and Modern languages, not to mention Latin, seem rather cut-and-dried and over-obedient to rules. That, I think, makes it clear that, basically, cardinal count is a function of the aorist as the tense of event predication, as the exceptions turn out to be so few and so comparatively easy to explain. Similarly, though I have checked only a limited number of adverbs of frequency count (*aei, pantote* 'always'; also *muriakis, apeirakis* 'countless times', and all such expressions as 'once a day', 'twice a year'), the evidence seems to me conclusive that frequency count is basically a function of the present.

3. NEGATIVE RESULTS

Two negative results of great interest appear. First, it is a more widely permissible usage in Greek to substitute a "historic present" indicative for aorist indicative in narration (less often for imperfect indicative) than in almost any other language where historic presents are allowed. The historic present may be substituted, for example, for one verb and not the other verbs in the same sentence, or used and not used several times inconsistently in the same paragraph. But it is apparently NOT an option (this has not been noticed in any of the standard grammars) to substitute historic present for aorist indicative when the historic present would co-occur with an adverb of cardinal count like *hapax, dis, tris, etc.* Evidently, the adverbs of cardinal count divide and count occurrences to an extent that cancels the permissibility of this substitution, extensive and random elsewhere.

Second, ancient Greek has only a past tense aorist indicative, which, like the past imperfect indicative, is augmented as a marker of past time. But this indicative has a wide range of uses which imply present time; that is, it is used whenever a speaker wants to imply perfective action in present time, and the augment and the secondary personal endings (common to past tenses and the optative, as opposed to the primary endings of present and future tenses and the subjunctive) are treated as irrelevant.[3] The most puzzling of these substitutions and the most resistant to logical explanation is the so-called "empiric" or "gnomic" aorist, expressing a proverbial truth or a truth of general experience. Such uses of the perfective are not yet well explained in Greek or in any other language. However, it is noted in at least one standard grammar that although the "gnomic" aorist co-occurs with such adverbs as *te* (Homeric: 'generally'), *pollakis* 'often', *ēdē* 'before now', it does not co-occur with *aei* or any other expression of universality.[4] My own researches appear to confirm this. It seems this may be part of the logic of gnomic perfectives in general; but for the present I will confine myself to noting that the gnomic aorist, like other usages of the aorist, obeys our hypothesis by resisting co-occurrence with adverbs that ought a priori not to appear.

4. CONCLUSIONS

If countability, as opposed to indefinite frequency or indefinite continuation, is basic to event predication, the evidence of Ancient Greek goes to show that this distinction really is reflected in the usage of perfective (aorist) and imperfective (present) stems throughout the moods. The simplicity of this function in the aorist, which presents countable items (events), compared to the complex uses of the imperfective stem (ongoing

---

[3] See Smyth (1956, Sects. 1930–1941, pp. 431ff.), Schwyzer-Debrunner (1950, Vol. 2, pp. 282–286).

[4] See Schwyzer-Debrunner (1950, Vol. 2, Par. 9).

activity, indefinitely repeated actions, unfulfilled attempts or intentions) is a contrast apparently reflected in morphology, where the relatively simple aorist forms can be contrasted with a wide variety of present forms. I believe both usage and morphology support the view of those grammarians who feel that the aorist is marked and the present unmarked;[5] and although the idea that the marking is for count, and represents a distinction essentially similar to that in the noun-field between sortals (*cup of tea*) and mass nouns (*tea*), where sortals are countable and mass nouns not, is still somewhat new, nonetheless, the simple tests I have applied seem to justify it.

There are further and more complicated questions that must be answered to establish the aorist's logic as the tense of event predication. Such evidence would come from a complete study of the behavior of verbs in Ancient Greek whose present and aorist stems articulate distinctions that are made in English lexically, with two different verbs: for example, *peithein* (pres.) 'persuade, try to persuade' versus *peisai* (aor.) 'convince'; or *iasthai* (pres.) 'treat' as opposed to *iasasthai* (aor.) 'cure'— both excellent examples of what Gilbert Ryle calls "task verbs" versus the related "achievement verbs," but articulated by contrasting two aspects of the same verb in Greek. Also, we need to examine in Vendler's manner what seem to be permitted adverbs with one stem, but not the other stem, of the same Greek verb. Aristotle gives us one precious example (which Kenny did not fail to note)[6] of an actual speaker of Ancient Greek offering a formal analysis of such usage:

(14)   For while we may *become* pleased (*hēsthenai,* aor.) 'quickly' (*tacheōs*), we cannot *be* pleased (*hēdesthai,* pres.) 'quickly', not even by comparison to another person, while we can walk (*badizein,* pres.) or grow (*auxesthai,* pres.) or the like 'quickly'. So, it is possible to change state *into* pleasure 'quickly' or 'slowly'; but to be realizing this state—I mean be pleased (*hēdesthai*)— 'quickly' is impossible.

ARISTOTLE Nicomachean Ethics 10.3 (1173a35ff)

I feel convinced that questioning our present body of texts on such points will make the hypothesis that the aorist is the tense of countable action, and therefore of event predication, all the more secure.

---

[5] There is an excellent survey of discussions of Ancient Greek aspect, together with a review of aspectual studies in many other languages, in Gonda (1962, pp. 7–53). I have treated it as established that the aorist and present stems in Greek are in fact perfective and imperfective, as does Comrie (1976, pp. 17–22); there are still writers on classical grammar who resist this solution, as does Gonda himself, but their arguments seem to me negligible.

[6] Anthony Kenny (1963, p. 177, n. 1).

ACKNOWLEDGMENTS

I would like to thank A.P.D. Mourelatos and the various members of my graduate seminars in Platonic and philosophical Greek at the University of Texas, Austin, in 1975 and 1976—especially Steve Strange and Miriam Galston—for help and criticism of earlier versions of this study, which developed out of work done in designing presentations of Greek grammar for philosophy graduate students. This work was financed by a grant from the National Endowment for the Humanities in June–July 1975.

REFERENCES

Comrie, B. (1976). *Aspect: An Introduction to the Study of Verbal Aspect and Related Problems.* Cambridge: Cambridge University Press.

Gonda, J. (1962). *The Function of the Rgvedic Present and Aorist.* The Hague: Mouton.

Kenny, A. (1963). *Action, Emotion and Will.* New York: Humanities Press.

Lyons, J. (1977). *Semantics., Vol. 2* Cambridge: Cambridge University Press.

Schwyzer-Debrunner. (1950). *Griechische Grammatik.* Munich: Beck.

Smyth, H. (1956). *Greek Grammar.* Cambridge, Mass.: Harvard University Press.

Wackernagel, J. (1904). *Studien über die Griechischen Perfektum,* Göttingen: Officina Academica Dieferichiana.

Wackernagel, J. (1920). *Vorlesungen über Syntax.* Basel: Birkhäuser.

OF TENSE AND ASPECT: ONE ANALYSIS

MICHAEL BENNETT

1. INTRODUCTION

Bennett 1977 presents an analysis of the present perfect and the present progressive tenses that was proposed by Glen Helman. Almost everyone initially finds the analysis to be mysterious—a "logician's trick." Further, the proposal appears to be subject to some rather obvious objections. My purpose here is to both explain and defend the analysis. Because of limitations of space, I will assume an acquaintance with the earlier paper. It sketches the intellectual history that led to the Helman analysis and defines several of the terms that are used here.

2. HELMAN'S ANALYSIS

We represent time by the set of positive and negative real numbers. This choice reflects a number of metaphysical intuitions: (*a*) time is linearly ordered; (*b*) time is infinite both ways; (*c*) time is DENSE (given any two moments of time, there exists another moment of time that lies between them); and (*d*) if a set of moments of time has an upper bound (lower bound), then it has a least upper bound (greatest lower bound). We

13

Syntax and Semantics, Volume 14
Tense and Aspect

do not represent time by the rational numbers because they fail to have this last property. We take an INTERVAL of time to be a connected set of moments of time (no gaps) that has both a least upper bound and a greatest lower bound. Certain intervals, namely the unit sets, correspond to moments of time.

We have in mind a framework similar to that in Montague 1973, where a translation relation holds between analysis trees for English sentences and formulas of intensional logic. The proposal is that we consider the more general notion of a formula of intensional logic being true with respect to an interval of time and not just to a moment. However, translations corresponding to analysis trees for English sentences will be designed in such a way that they can be true only with respect to moments of time. Nevertheless, intervals of time will play a role in defining the truth conditions for such sentences.[1]

The leading idea of Helman's suggestion is to distinguish in some way the intervals of time that represent occurrences of performances from the intervals of time that represent occurrences of activities. Let us say that activities are represented by OPEN intervals (no endpoints) and that performances are represented by CLOSED intervals (two endpoints). It is important to note that BOTH performance verb phrases and activity verb phrases can be true of individuals at both open and closed intervals—that is, individuals can be in the extension of either kind of verb phrase with respect to either kind of interval of time. The way in which the two kinds of verb phrases are distinguished will be explained in what follows. We give (1) as the truth condition for **Jones has left.**

(1)   **Jones has left** is true at interval of time I if and only if I is a moment of time, and there exists an interval of time I' (possibly a moment) such that I' is a closed interval, $I' < I$, and Jones is in the extension of **leave** at I'.

The analysis requires that there exist a past interval of time at which Jones is in the extension of **leave.** One intuition motivating this analysis is that if Jones is in the extension of **leave** at an interval I, then the event of Jones's leaving is regarded as starting at the beginning of I, taking place during I, and finishing at the end of I. This reflects our intuition that the

---

[1] This is a simple but misleading way of putting what I really have in mind. More precisely, the translation of an English sentence expresses a TIME-INDEPENDENT proposition. The value of such a proposition for a world–interval (point of reference) will be the truth-value of the sentence relative to the world in question and a FIXED moment of time; the fixed time being the moment of utterance that is supplied by the context of speech. This effect is created by introducing the *now*-operator into the translation of every English sentence. See Bennett (1976, Section 12). So it IS possible for the translation to be true at an interval of time that is not a moment after all.

truth condition should involve some past INTERVAL of time during which Jones is leaving and eventually completes this act. The requirement that the past interval be closed reflects the intuition that the present perfect tense always describes a performance; the perfect aspect indicates a completion.

We give (2) as the truth condition for **Jones is leaving.**

(2)   **Jones is leaving** is true at interval of time I if and only if I is a moment of time, and there exists an interval of time I' such that I' is an open interval, I is included in I', and Jones is in the extension of **leave** at I'.

The requirement that I' be an open interval reflects the intuition that the present progressive always describes an activity. Condition (2) has the consequence that **Jones is leaving** neither implies **Jones has left** nor implies, in effect, **Jones will have left,** as there is no guarantee that Jones is in the extension of **leave** with respect to a CLOSED interval. In other words, the truth of **Jones is leaving** gives no guarantee that a performance of leaving has, or will have, taken place.

Although (1) and (2) involve the performance verb phrase **leave,** it is intended that the same analyses would be given if we shifted to an activity verb phrase.

Activity verb phrases are distinguished from performance verb phrases by requiring that the former satisfy the following closure condition: If an activity verb phrase is true of an individual at an interval I, then it is true of that individual at every CLOSED subinterval of I.[2] The intention here is, roughly, that every ''part'' of an activity is a performance; as soon as the action of walking has started, an act of walking has occurred. We do not impose this condition on performance verb phrases. This requirement explains why **Jones is walking** implies **Jones has walked.** Suppose **Jones is walking** is true at I which is a moment of time. Then there exists an open interval of time I' such that I is included in I' and Jones is in the extension of **walk** at I'. But given these conditions and the fact that time is taken to be the real numbers, there exists a closed interval of time I'' that is a subinterval of I' such that $I'' < I$. Given the condition imposed on activity verb phrases, Jones is in the extension of **walk** at I''. From this it follows that **Jones has walked** is true at I.

Activity verb phrases also seem to satisfy a condition that is something like the inverse of the closed subinterval condition: If an activity verb phrase is true of an individual at every moment in an interval I (open or

---

[2] This requirement, and the others that will be given, can be imposed by introducing a sentential operator into the intensional logic and adding some meaning postulates. In this case we add a sentential operator C to the logic such that $C\phi$ is true at I if and only if ϕ is true at every closed subinterval of I.

closed), then it is true of that individual at I. This condition, which we might call the UPWARDS CLOSURE condition, ensures, for example, that **John ran continuously for an hour** implies **John ran for an hour.** Again, we should not impose such a condition on performance verb phrases.

It is necessary to impose the following condition on activity verb phrases and performance verb phrases alike: If a verb phrase is true of an individual at an interval I, then it is true of that individual at every OPEN subinterval of I. Intuitively every ''part'' of either an activity or a performance is itself an activity. However, it is not so easy to give simple examples of entailments that depend on this condition. I will provide the following examples without detailed discussion. We need the open subinterval requirement on performance verb phrases to ensure that **Jones walked to the store without stopping in ten minutes yesterday** implies **Jones was walking to the store yesterday.** (The phrases **in ten minutes** and **without stopping** are serving to exclude the possibility that the performance occurred in an instant or over a staggered sequence of instants.) The open subinterval requirement is needed for activity verb phrases so that **Jones walked without stopping for ten minutes yesterday** implies **Jones was walking yesterday.** (Again, the phrases **for ten minutes** and **without stopping** are serving to exclude the possibility that the performance occurred in an instant or over a staggered sequence of instants.)

3. TERMINOLOGY AND ONTOLOGY

I am unhappy with the terminology STATIVE, ACTIVITY, PERFORMANCE, for classifying verb phrases. The last two expressions suggest that the agent is a conscious being. We need terminology that is neutral in this respect.[3] However, I am even more unhappy with the often-used alternatives: STATIVE, PROCESS, EVENT. STATIVE is fine. But PROCESS is too broad as it covers some performances (cf. *the process of disintegrating*). Most of all, I dislike EVENT. We do not say *in the event of building a house;* but we do say *in the event of John's building a house.*

This raises the ontological question of how to analyze generic events. I think they should be analyzed as PROPOSITIONS: functions from world–intervals (ordered pairs consisting of a possible world and an interval of time) to truth-values.[4] Montague (1969) gives essentially this analysis; it is

---

[3] I am now beginning to favor the already existing terminology: STATIVE, ATELIC, TELIC. But, although this terminology is perfect for sorting out the verb phrases, it is NOT useful for classifying the metaphysical entities whose occurrences are being represented by open and closed intervals. Here we are still stuck with ACTIVITY and PERFORMANCE.

[4] Just what kind of proposition is less clear. If English sentences express only time independent propositions (see Note 1), they do not naturally express propositions that represent GENERIC events in Montague's sense. Nor do they naturally express propositions that repre-

just twisted around. He analyzes generic events as functions from possible worlds to sets of one-place sequences of moments (or, more generally, intervals) of time. What about generic activities and performances? These are PROPERTIES OF INDIVIDUALS: functions from world–intervals to sets of individuals. This is just a variation on the analysis of experiences in Montague 1969. There Montague analyzed generic experiences as functions from possible worlds to sets of two-place sequences of persons (individuals) and moments (or, more generally intervals) of time.

Is there a difference between the activity of building a house and the performance of building a house? YES. But let me state the difference as in Montague 1969, since it is easier. The activity of building a house is a function from possible worlds to two-place sequences of individuals and open intervals of time. The performance of building a house is a function from possible worlds to two-place sequences of individuals and closed intervals of time. Generic states are also properties of individuals; following Montague (1969), they are functions from possible worlds to two-place sequences of individuals and MOMENTS OF TIME.

It might be wondered what is the intension of **build a house.** It is something like the "union" of the activity of building a house and the performance of building a house. I say "something like" because maybe there is more in the intension that just the "union." Maybe the intension includes half-open intervals, for example. In any case, give the intension of **build a house,** we can extract both the activity and the performance.

I hope that the connection between the linguistic (and semantic) enterprise in Montague 1973 and the metaphysical enterprise in Montague 1969 is beginning to emerge.

4. SOME METAPHYSICAL JUSTIFICATION

Everyone initially finds our way of distinguishing activities and performances to be subliminal. What difference can an endpoint make? What is needed is some intuitive motivation for the structure—some metaphysical justification.

The proposal is that occurrences of activities be represented by open

---

sent INDIVIDUAL events in Montague's sense; see Montague (1969, p. 177). I am not quite sure what to make of Montague's distinction.

How do these ontological issues relate to syntax? How do we talk about events in English? We should consider the syntactic constructions called GERUNDIVE and DERIVED nominals (cf. Chomsky 1970). Gerundive nominalization transforms **Edison invents the phonograph** into **Edison's inventing the phonograph.** Does the latter DENOTE the proposition EXPRESSED by the former? If so, the related derived nominal, **Edison's invention of the phonograph,** should denote the same proposition. But just how the syntax and semantics of derived nominals would accommodate this intuition is a complete mystery.

intervals and occurrences of performances by closed intervals. Is this choice arbitrary? Could we switch things around and represent activities by closed intervals and performances by open intervals? I believe that there is a reason why we cannot. My intuition is that an activity cannot be represented by a moment of time; activities must have some "body." However, it does seem that a performance can be represented by a moment of time; a performance can be PUNCTUAL. These intuitions are reflected by our choice. A nonempty open interval is always an infinite set of times. [We exclude the empty open interval; (t, t) is not among the intervals at which sentences are evaluated.] However a closed interval can correspond to a moment of time; just consider the unit set $[t, t]$, for any moment of time t.

There are other intuitions that motivate our representation. A performance has a starting point and a finishing point. But intuitively an activity does not. Otherwise there would be a "part" of the activity (an endpoint) that is not flanked on both sides by more of the activity. By representing an activity by an open interval, we capture the intuitive condition that at any point in the activity, the appropriate sentence in the present progressive is true.[5]

I have just argued that there is a difference between an activity and a performance—the former has some "body" and the latter can be punctual. But how is this to be reconciled with the closed subinterval condition imposed on activity verb phrases? What is the difference between an individual being in the extension of **walk** with respect to an open interval as opposed to being in its extension with respect to a closed interval? In

---

[5] Mourelatos (this volume) makes the intriguing observation that the derived nominals corresponding to activity verb phrases differ from those corresponding to performance verb phrases. We naturally get COUNT noun phrases for performance verb phrases.

(i)   **John built a house last year**

(ii)   **there was a building of a house by John last year**

However, we naturally get MASS noun phrases for activity verb phrases.

(iii)   **John ran yesterday**

(iv)   **there was some running by John yesterday**

This suggests that we are on the right track to represent performances with "countable" sharp-edged entities (closed intervals) and activities with "measurable" entities whose edges are "vague" (open intervals).

There is even a semantic similarity between the activity–performance verb phrase distinction and the mass–count noun phrase distinction. The extensions of mass nouns, like **gold,** are closed under physical composition. That is, given any subset of the set of all quantities of gold, there exists a quantity of gold in the set which is the mereological sum of the members of the subset. Activity verb phrases satisfy a similar condition: the upwards closure condition mentioned in Section 2.

other words, what is the difference between an activity of walking and a performance of walking? My reply is short; I think we understand this difference as well as we understand the difference between an activity and a performance generally.

The open and closed subinterval conditions on activity verb phrases suggest that an activity consists of both that activity as well as performances. Does this make any sense? I think so. This is an instance of describing the same thing in two different ways. Suppose we have before us an occurrence of the event of John's walking to the store. Then we have before us some walking. Let this activity be represented by an interval of time, I. We can view this activity in two different ways. First, we can "divide up" I into contiguous performances of walking. This is because every closed subinterval of I (and this includes every moment in I) represents a performance of walking. But we can also "divide up" I into contiguous portions of the activity of walking. This can be stated more mathematically: We can almost "cover" I with a family of open intervals that are disjoint from one another. (We cannot strictly "cover" I in this way, for there will remain a finite number of scattered points that have been left out.)

5. TWO COMMON OBJECTIONS

It has been suggested that the open and closed subinterval conditions on verb phrases are incorrect. For example, on these conditions, **John built a house in one month last year** implies **John is building a house** is true for any time during that month, excluding the last moment. It is argued that this should not follow, as John was not engaged in the activity of building a house throughout that month. After all, there were lulls and gaps when he was not working.[6] I believe that our analysis can be refined to reflect these intuitions.

[6] Consider a time during the month when John is asleep in his bed. Suppose we are asked *What's John doing these days?* We can truthfully answer *He is building a house.* I believe that this example should be explained as a use of the present progressive in a nonreportive sense. We mean by the reply something like: John is frequently engaged in the activity of building a particular house.

The previous example involves a performance verb phrase. But consider the following example from Vlach (this volume) which involves an activity verb phrase. John is sitting in a theater during intermission and someone asks *Is someone sitting there?* while pointing to the empty seat next to John. John answers *Yes,* as his girlfriend has only momentarily repaired to the lobby. My intuition in this case is that STRICTLY the answer is *No.* The questioner knows this just by observation. But he or she is USING the question to communicate another: **is that seat taken.** The question used might not have the same meaning as the question intended.

We can represent an occurrence of a performance, not simply by a closed interval, but by a union of closed intervals.[7] This leads to a generalization of our previous notion of truth; sentences are to be evaluated with respect to unions of intervals, and not just intervals. A union of intervals of time, of course, might not be a connected set of moments of time; there might be gaps. John's building a house might look like this:

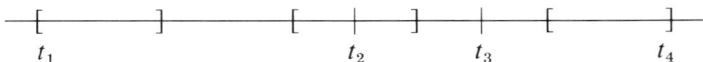

The closed intervals represent periods of work, and the gaps indicate periods of rest. John starts to build a house at t_1 and he finishes building it at t_4. At t_2 he is building a house, but not at t_3. This analysis still retains a form of the open subinterval condition on performance verb phrases. If a performance verb phrase is true of a union of closed intervals, then it is true of every open, CONNECTED subinterval of that union. The refined analysis gives us the following truth conditions for the present perfect and the present progressive.

(3)   **Jones has left** is true at union I of intervals of time if and only if I is a moment of time, and there exists a union I' of closed intervals of time (possibly a moment) such that $I' < I$, and Jones is in the extension of **leave** at I'.

(4)   **Jones is leaving** is true at a union I of intervals of time if and only if I is a moment of time, and there exists a union I' of intervals of time such that I' is an open, connected interval, I is included in I', and Jones is in the extension of **leave** at I'.

The present perfect and the present progressive are given the same analyses even with activity verb phrases. It is necessary to allow activity verb phrases to be true of unions of intervals because, in the case of verbs of motion, there is an entailment relation between a performance verb phrase and the corresponding activity verb phrase; for example, **John walked to Rome last year** entails **John walked last year** (see Bennett, 1976, Section 15).

The refined analysis also retains a form of the open and closed subinterval conditions on activity verb phrases. If an activity verb phrase is true of a union of intervals, then it is true of every open and closed, CONNECTED subinterval of that union.

I believe that the analysis just sketched gives a more natural solution to

---

[7] In essence, this was proposed by Richard Montague (1969, p. 150); see also Bennett (1977, Note 7).

the "gaps problem" than the proposals of Dowty (1977) and Vlach (this volume); for their solutions involve rejecting subinterval conditions.

What is the truth condition for **John built a house in one month last year?** Does **in one month** measure just John's working hours or does it measure the length of time from the moment he started to the moment he finished, counting all the breaks? My intuition is that we mean the latter. This sets the stage for noticing that there is a difference between the refined analysis and the unrefined one. **John built a house in one month last year** does not imply **John was building a house last year** on the refinement. This is because the one-month long union of closed intervals might be a union of moments of time with intervening gaps. This is the logically possible case where John builds the house in instantaneous spurts.

Another common objection to our analysis of the present progressive is that it does not account for the reading of **John is running** that asserts what John habitually does, or what he frequently does. I agree that I have not accounted for such readings of the present progressive; this is the problem of analyzing nonreportive readings (see Bennett 1977). The fact that I do not have an analysis of the nonreportive readings (reading?) of the present progressive is not an objection to the proposed analysis of the reportive reading of the present progressive. This fact merely indicates that there is more to be done.

I wish to make some speculative remarks about the nonreportive readings of the present progressive. First, I am inclined to believe that, just like the nonreportive readings of the simple present, the analysis can involve adverbs of frequency.[8] For example, we might use **John is running** with the nonreportive sense **John is frequently running.** The truth condition for the latter sentence is something like the following:

(5)   **John is frequently running** is true at interval of time I if and only if I is a moment of time, and there exists an interval of time I' (possibly constrained in some way by the context) such that I is included in I' but is not an endpoint for I', and John is in the extension of **run** with respect to a CLOSED interval of time MANY times each α in I', where α is some measure of length of time, like *week*, which is vague.

I believe that (5) also is the truth condition for a nonreportive reading of **John runs,** namely **John frequently runs.** Intuitively there is no logical difference between the present progressive and the simple present on a nonreportive reading; **John runs** and **John is running** seem to share the same nonreportive readings. If the preceding remarks are correct, then at

---

[8] Adverbs of frequency are discussed in Bennett and Partee (1972, Section 4.2).

least some of the nonreportive readings of the present progressive receive an analysis that is distinct from the one I have proposed for the reportive present progressive.

6. "BARE" PLURALITY AND GENERIC READINGS

Nonreportive readings are often signaled by instances of "bare" plurality, occurrences of plural common noun phrases without quantifiers.[9]

(6)   **John is building houses**

(7)   **John is building some houses**

Sentence (6) is most naturally read in a nonreportive way, and (7) in a reportive way. The sentences differ logically in that intuitively (6) implies (8) whereas (7) does not imply (9).[10]

(8)   **John has built houses**

(9)   **John has built some houses**

The verb phrase **build houses** functions like an activity verb phrase, but **build some houses** is a performance verb phrase. The fact that we get an entailment in the nonreportive case is predicted by the truth conditions we suggested for such readings in Section 5.

(10)   **John is often building houses** is true at interval of time I if and only if I is a moment of time, and there exists an interval of time I' (possibly constrained in some way by the context) such that I is included in I' but is not an endpoint for I', and John is in the extension of **build a house** with respect to a closed interval of time SEVERAL times each α in I', where α is some measure of length of time, like *month,* which is vague.

---

[9] The terminology is Chomsky's (1975). The same phenomenon occurs with mass noun phrases.

(i)   **John shoveled snow for an hour**

[10] Does **John is building houses** imply **John has built houses?** Could not the progressive sentence be true at a time when John is in the middle of constructing his first house? I think so. Is not the present perfect sentence false at this time? I do not think so. Suppose John agrees to build houses every day from April 1 to September 1. On April 3 he is building houses—he is engaged in a certain activity. Has he not already engaged in the activity? Is it not true on April 3 that John has built houses? If someone denied that **John has built houses** is true on April 3, then I would argue that they cannot maintain that **John is building houses** is true on April 3.

As was suggested in Section 5, **John often builds houses** would get EX-
ACTLY the same truth condition. The corresponding present perfect sentence has (11) as its truth condition:

(11)   **John has often built houses** is true at interval of time I if and only if
        I is a moment of time, and there exists an interval of time I' such
        that $I' < I$, and **John often builds houses** is true at I'.

It is clear from these conditions that **John is often building houses** (and
John often builds houses) implies **John has often built houses**.

A notorious case of "bare" plurality involves a "bare" plural in subject
position (cf. Chomsky, 1975).

(12)   **beavers build dams**

(13)   **dams are built by beavers**

It is usually overlooked that (12) and (13) have readings in common, for
example,

(12')   **occasionally a beaver builds a dam**

(13')   **occasionally a dam is built by a beaver**

where (12') and (13') are logically equivalent.[11] Rather, the discussion has
usually contrasted (12) and (13) by focusing on the "generic" reading of
(12), the reading that concerns all members of the species **(the beaver
builds dams).** This might be analyzed as follows:[12] **(necessarily?) all members of the species beaver are disposed to (occasionally?) build a dam.** We
are not inclined to give (13) a generic reading because dams do not form a
species. As Chomsky (1975, p. 89) notes, we give (10) a reportive reading
that is false: All dams are things that have been built by a beaver.

Chomsky (1975, p. 81) suggests that simple examples involving "bare"
plurality show that "syntactic structures are not a projection of the semantics" and that "even a principle of compositionality is suspect." He
goes on to say that these examples suggest that

---

[11] However, Chomsky is quite aware of this (cf. Chomsky, 1975, p. 80, Note 11, and p. 89,
Note 32).

[12] Generic sentences are not analyzed uniformly: **lions are mammals** DROPS the disposition
condition:

(i)   **all members of the species lion are mammals**

Carlson (1977, p. 65) notes that **lions have manes** ADDS a restriction to males only:

(ii)   **all male members of the species lion are disposed to have a mane** we cannot expect linguistic theory to associate syntactic and semantic rules very closely. There may well be interesting correlations between the class of formal structures generated and the expressions of an appropriate ''broader-minded logic,'' but it seems doubtful that these correlations can be reduced to a point-by-point correlation among rules [p. 102].

Of course this is an implicit challenge of Montague grammar (as well as other theories) and an argument for Chomsky's ''absolute thesis of autonomy of syntax''—roughly, a thesis to the effect that syntax should be studied independently of semantics.

Why are examples involving ''bare'' plurality supposed to show this? Two of Chomsky's examples involve the verb phrase **have wheels** (p. 81). He points out that **unicycles have wheels** is true if each unicycle has A WHEEL, whereas **each unicycle has wheels** is true if each unicycle has SOME WHEELS. Chomsky says of the first example that ''plurality is, in a sense, a semantic property of the sentence rather than the individual noun phrase in which it is formally expressed.'' He concludes:

We cannot simply assign a meaning to the subject and a meaning to the predicate (or to a sentence form with a variable standing for the subject), and then combine the two. Rather, the meaning assigned to each phrase depends on the form of the phrase with which it is paired [p. 81].

Apparently Chomsky believes that the evidence favors studying syntax independently of semantics, for his view suggests that it will be very difficult to construct a framework where the two work hand-in-hand. Developing the areas independently of one another will lead to simpler theories in both cases; however, the resulting theories will not reflect each other in a simple way (cf. Chomsky, 1975, p. 100).

I completely agree with Partee (1975) that the issue cannot be decided in the absence of explicit formal developments of the competing alternatives, and that, so far as can be seen, there is nothing essential to Montague grammar that would preclude a description of the ''bare'' plurality phenomenon. In fact, Carlson (1977) has already attempted to accommodate ''bare'' plurality in Montague grammar. In my view, neither Chomsky nor Carlson has paid enough attention to the transformational character of the phenomenon. Further, they have not emphasized an intimate connection between ''bare'' plurality and aspect. Indeed, I advocate a return to the approach initiated by David Dowty (1972; Sections 2.6 and 3.4). I wish to sketch some moves in this direction.

I believe that there are at least two processes that create ''bare'' plural count noun phrases. One of them is a meaning-preserving transformation which I will call PLURAL **some** DELETION. It applies to sentences and deletes one or more occurrences of the plural **some**.

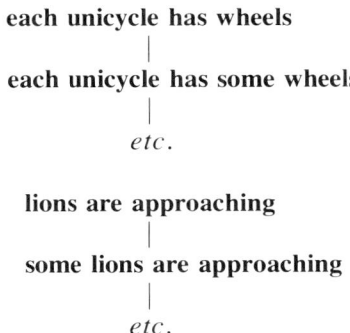

each unicycle has wheels

|

each unicycle has some wheels

|

etc.

lions are approaching

|

some lions are approaching

|

etc.

The other is a meaning–preserving transformation which I will call PLU-RAL SWEEP.[13] As I have not studied this transformation carefully, I have only the most general ideas about how it works. (I suspect that, as is usual with transformations, it will still be difficult to describe its operation precisely even after a careful study.) Roughly, it applies to a sentence and is triggered by either a plural term, such as **all men** or **many men,** or an adverb of frequency. Basically it sweeps from left to right transforming singular indefinite descriptions into ''bare'' plural count noun phrases, but it can delete or transform many other kinds of constructions.

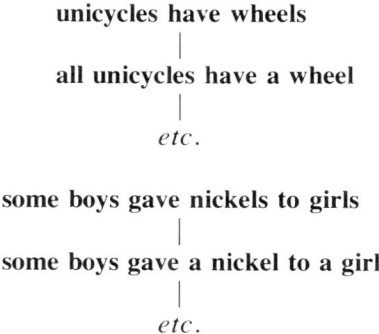

unicycles have wheels

|

all unicycles have a wheel

|

etc.

some boys gave nickels to girls

|

some boys gave a nickel to a girl

|

etc.

One question is whether or not the sweep is obligatory once it gets started. In some instances this seems to be the case. Is the following a proper application of PLURAL SWEEP (where the input sentence is assumed to have a reportive reading in which **some boys** has wider scope than **a girl**)?

---

[13] Long ago (summer of 1974), Barbara Partee convinced me that there exists some syntactic process like PLURAL SWEEP.

some boys gave nickels to a girl

|

some boys gave a nickel to a girl

|

etc.

I am inclined to say that this is not a proper application because the output does not have the reading of the input.

The connection between "bare" plurality and aspect is the following: PLURAL SWEEP can be triggered by an adverb of frequency. This is why "bare" plurality often indicates a nonreportive reading.

John builds houses

|

occasionally John builds a house

|

etc.

boys give girls pictures of horses

|

sometimes a boy gives a girl a picture of a horse

|

etc.

frequently boys kiss the girls that love them

|

frequently a boy kisses the girl that loves him

|

etc.

PLURAL SWEEP can play a role in the derivation of a sentence with a generic reading:

lions have tails   (ellipsis)

|

lions are disposed to have tails   Plural Sweep

|

all lions (members of the species lion) are disposed to have a tail

|

etc.

Both PLURAL **some** DELETION and PLURAL SWEEP apply to sentences. It is in this sense that "bare" plurality is a global or "semantic" property of sentences.

7. DURATIVE ADVERBIAL PHRASES

Adverbial phrases, such as **for one year** and **from 12:00 to 1:00,** are closely connected with the constructions we have considered so far. Roughly, they combine with iterative constructions to form performance verb phrases.

(14)   **John built houses for one year**

(15)   **John was building houses for one year**

These sentences share a nonreportive reading where **for one year** is serving to indicate the duration of the iteration of John's building a house. Sentence (15), but not (14), has a second reading, the reading in which John was engaged in the activity of BUILDING HOUSES FOR ONE YEAR. This second reading results from applying the progressive aspect to the performance verb phrase **build houses for one year.**

Let us shift to the present tense.

(16)   **John builds houses for one year**

(17)   **John is building houses for one year**

Neither (16) nor (17) allows a reading like the one shared by (14) and (15). Sentence (16) forces a reading such as: John occasionally (builds houses for a year). And we can now see that (14) can have such a reading as well. Sentence (14) has a reading like the second reading mentioned for (15). This is confirmed by our intuition that (17) does not imply: **John has built houses for one year.**

Now let us shift to the corresponding reportive construction.

(18)   * **John built a house for one year**

(19)   **John was building a house for one year**

Sentence (18) is ungrammatical on a reportive reading (although it allows a nonreportive one). It is inappropriate to apply **for one year** to **build a house** if the verb phrase is not given an iterative interpretation. Sentence (19) has a reportive reading, but its truth condition is somewhat nonstandard: (It is true just in case **John is building a house** is true at every moment within a past interval that measures one year.[14]

---

[14] This truth condition is similar to the original Montague–Scott analysis of the present progressive (see Bennett, 1977). Another example that requires a similar analysis is:

(i)   **John has been here for an hour**

This is true if **John is here** is true at every moment in the last hour. Occasionally we do use a stative verb phrase in the present progressive.

(ii)   **John is being silly**

Here, it seems that the Montague–Scott analysis is correct after all.

So far we have just considered constructions involving a performance verb phrase. As far as I can see, the situation is much the same if we shift to an activity verb phrase.

(20)   **John ran for one hour**

(21)   **John was running for one hour**

However (20), unlike (18), allows a reportive reading. Possibly this is because the reportive reading for (20) is equivalent to the nonreportive reading: **John ran continuously for one hour.** If the reportive reading of (21) is analyzed along the same lines as that of (19), then the reportive reading of (21) is NOT equivalent to the reportive reading of (20). For (20) might be true and (21) false. Suppose John ran for EXACTLY one hour. Then, at the moment he stopped, **John is running** is false. But the reportive reading of (21) implies that at the last moment of the hour **John is running** is true. However, it is the case that (20) and (21) share nonreportive readings.

Vlach (this volume) considers the following example. Suppose Max sold cars for one week only, and had lunch every day that week from 12:00 to 1:00. We have the intuition that **Max was selling cars for a week** is true but that **Max was selling cars from 12:00 to 1:00** is false. Vlach takes this example as evidence that the subinterval condition does not hold generally for such sentences. I wish to dispute this claim. I believe that the first sentence IMPLIES the second, on a certain reading, and that in the given situation, the second sentence is true. The first sentence asserts Max's selling a car occurred with a certain frequency over a period of one week [cf. the previous discussion of (15)]. But if something performs a certain act with a certain degree of frequency over a period of time I, then that entity performs that act with that degree of frequency over any subinterval of I. So the second sentence, on a certain reading, is true. Why do we have an initial intuition that the second sentence is false? The second sentence involves a durative adverbial phrase that describes a much shorter period of time, an hour in contrast to a week. This adverbial phrase leads us to give a reading to the second sentence that asserts that Max's selling a car is occurring at a much higher frequency than that asserted by the first sentence. This, in turn leads us to consider the second sentence to be false in the situation described.

ACKNOWLEDGMENTS

At the Symposium on Tense and Aspect, held at Brown University on January 14 and 15, 1978, I read part of Bennett 1977. Here I give further motivation for the analysis. I am especially grateful to Emmon Bach and Barbara Partee. Most of this chapter is an effort to answer their questions. I am also responding to several points raised by Frank Vlach in his interesting paper (included in this volume). Both Werner Saurer and Richmond Thomason generously read an earlier version of this chapter and offered helpful advice. I am also grateful to Greg Carlson and Hans Kamp whose comments prompted me to clarify various parts of the chapter.

REFERENCES

Bennett, M. (1978). Demonstratives and indexicals in Montague grammar. *Synthese* **39**, 1–80, Reidel, Dordrecht.

Bennett, M. (1977). A guide to the logic of tense and aspect in English. *Logique et Analyse* **20**, 491–517, Centre national Belge de recheches de Logique, Louvain, Belgium.

Bennett, M. (1900). A guide to the logic of tense and aspect in English. *Logique et Analyse.*

Bennett, M., and Partee, B. (1972). *Toward the logic of tensé and aspect in English.* System Development Corporation, Santa Monica, Calif. (Available from the Indiana University Linguistics Club).

Carlson, G. (1977). *Reference to Kinds in English.* Unpublished doctoral dissertation, University of Massachusetts, Amherst.

Chomsky, N. (1970). Remarks on nominalization. [Reprinted in N. Chomsky (1972), *Studies on Semantics in Generative Grammar,* The Hague: Mouton. Pp. 11–61.]

Chomsky, N.: (1975). Questions of form and interpretation. *Linguistic Analysis,* **1**, 75–109.

Dowty, D. (1972). *Studies in the Logic of Verb Aspect and Time Reference in English.* Doctoral dissertation, University of Texas at Austin (Published in *Studies in Linguistics,* No. 1, Department of Linguistics, University of Texas at Austin)

Dowty, D. (1977). Toward a semantic analysis of verb aspect and the English 'imperfective' progressive. *Linguistics and Philosophy,* 1, 45–77.

Montague, R. (1969). On the nature of certain philosophical entities. *The Monist* **53**, 161–194. [Reprinted in R. Thomason, 1974. Pp. 148–187.]

Montague, R. (1973). The proper treatment of quantification in ordinary english, in Hintikka *et al.* (eds.), *Approaches to Natural Language.* D. Reidel, Dordrecht, 1973. Pp. 221–242. [Reprinted in R. Thomason (1974). Pp. 247–270.]

Partee, B. (1975). Comments on Fillmore's and Chomsky's Papers. In R. Austerlitz (Ed.), *The Scope of American Linguistics.* Lisse: The Peter De Ridder Press. Pp. 197–209.

Thomason, R. (Ed). (1974). *Formal Philosophy: Selected Papers of Richard Montague.* New Haven: Yale University Press.

ASPECT AND QUANTIFICATION[1]

LAURI CARLSON

1. INTRODUCTION

In this chapter, I shall apply model-theoretic semantics, in particular, the variety of it known as Hintikka's *game-theoretical semantics,* to the analysis of temporal aspect.[2]

The chapter is structured as follows: In Section 2, I introduce a binary feature system for the description of inherent verb aspect and give a model-theoretic interpretation to the features. In this section, the conceptual framework of game-theoretical semantics remains implicit, as the distinctions made primarily concern the initial assignment of truth of atomic sentences in given periods of history.

In Section 3, I show how atomic truth definitions interact with recursive clauses of interpretation of quantified noun phrases to predict aspectual properties of quantified sentences. In this section I introduce and define

---

[1] This represents an excerpt from a planned chapter of my Helsinki dissertation. For reasons of space, about half of the chapter (mostly material relevant to Section 2 here) has been left out. Unavoidably, this has made the argumentation in places rather thin. I refer to Carlson (in preparation) for fuller detail. The present discussion should make the outlines of my approach clear, however.

[2] See the works by Hintikka, Saarinen, and Carlson listed in the References.

31

Syntax and Semantics, Volume 14
Tense and Aspect

an important cross-categorial semantic property of PARTITIVITY. Partitivity not only distinguishes semantically mass nouns from count nouns, but it is also operative in verb aspect. This claim is substantiated by showing its role in the curious effects of noun phrase character on the temporal aspect of a sentence.

The empirical material in this chapter comes from English, but similar distinctions and explanations apply in Finnish.[3] Indeed, I suspect that the findings reported here represent universal properties of natural language systems of aspect. Another, and secondary, concern is whether such universals turn out to be specific to human language faculty or due to some more general, presumably just as innate, capacity of concept formation.

2. VERB ASPECT

2.1 Preliminaries

First of all, I wish to distinguish clearly what I call TEMPORAL ASPECT from other modifications usually associated with verbs. I restrict the term "aspectual" to properties of sets of periods which essentially involve the concept of (initial, internal, final) subperiod.[4] Likewise, I call an operation on sets of periods aspectual only if its values involve periods overlapping with periods it applies to.

Operations in the temporal domain which are defined in terms of relations of temporal order (before, after) I call TENSES, whatever their morphology. To take an example, the English perfect comes out as a tense; theoretically, it might be an aspect at the same time. As the example indicates, the definitions of aspect and tense are not intended as exclusive. In fact, it is quite likely that languages have expressions for mixed temporal operations.[5]

Finally, I want to exclude from aspect proper any morphological modifications of verbs that perform no operation at all in the temporal domain. One may imagine, for example, a marker of intentionality, forcefulness, or the like.

---

[3] Of course, there are also differences, but the deeper similarities far outweigh superficial divergences.—Particularly interesting evidence for the claims of Section 3 comes from the use of the Finnish partitive case both as a partitive quantifier and as a progressive aspect marker (see Carlson in preparation).

[4] For definitions, See Note 7.

[5] These characterizations of tense and aspect seem to come close to the intention of Comrie (1976, Section 0.1). For mixed temporal operations, see Chapter 4.

2.2 The Structure of Time

The aspectual features defined in this chapter are primitive in the following sense. They are formulated on only very weak assumptions about the underlying structure of time. Specifically, I shall only assume that time is BACKWARDS LINEAR.

Stronger assumptions such as infinity, density, continuity, and existence of a metric are not used. Insofar as the reconstruction of central aspectual distinctions on such minimal assumptions is possible, we may infer that the relevant contrasts are independent of these stronger assumptions of time.

This result is interesting in its own right. What is more, it makes it possible to vary the articulation of time with respect to one and the same actual course of events, without loss of major aspectual distinctions. For instance, one may move from continuous real time to a division of time in terms of indivisible moments of distinguishable length; perhaps in terms of members of some important succession of events. Observe that in this case, time is at most countably infinite and its natural topology is discrete.

It is my impression that such variable articulation of time is a central part of our common-sense conceptualization of time, and should be incorporated in any adequate theory of natural language time reference. The theory of aspect outlined in Section 2 of this chapter suggests that central aspectual distinctions can indeed be defined in a way consistent with variable assumptions about the structure of time.

I do not want to claim that the aspectual features defined in this chapter exhaust the inventory of aspectual distinctions available in human languages. For one thing, the present distinctions are QUALITATIVE: They only refer to order properties of time, not to its metric. It is quite likely that languages make further distinctions of metrical character. An aspectual operation meaning "for a short time" is a plausible candidate.[6]

2.3 Truth Definition

The models of time considered in this study are BACKWARDS LINEAR TENSE LOGICAL FRAMES.[7] A temporal frame becomes a model of, say, En-

---

[6] Finnish and Russian have such aspectual operations (cf. Finnish derivational suffix -hta- in *levähtää* 'rest for a short while' from *levätä* 'rest'; Russian *po-* in *pospat'* 'sleep for a short while' from *spat'* 'sleep').

[7] More precisely, let τ be a linearly ordered set of points of time. Any order-connected subset T of τ is an INTERVAL of time; if T is a unit set, call T an INSTANT; otherwise, T is EXTENDED. A TEMPORAL FRAME is a set F of functions h from τ to a set of possible instantaneous states of affairs ζ. Members of F are called HISTORIES. F is BACKWARDS LINEAR if for all h, h' in F,

glish aspect when English temporally qualified expressions are interpreted on it. The interpretation functions I am contemplating are definitions of TRUTH OR FALSITY OF A SENTENCE S OF A LANGUAGE L IN A
PERIOD P OF A HISTORY H, WITH RESPECT TO A TEMPORAL FRAME F.[8]

An important feature of the truth definitions I set out to constrain is that
they are NOT TOTAL, that is, not everywhere defined between the set of all
sentences of L and all periods of a frame F. What aspect features will do is
specify in exactly WHICH TYPE of period the truth or falsity of sentences
of a given aspect type is defined, as well as impose certain global conditions on the temporal range of a sentence (the set of periods in which it is
true). A sentence will prove unacceptable or used in some marked way if
it is forced to have truth value with respect to a period in which its truth is
not defined.

The null step of a recursive truth definition is an assignment of truth to a
set of (relatively) simple "atomic" sentences. The makeup of the sentences that are considered atomic naturally depends on the depth of analysis. For the present purposes, I treat as atomic any simplex sentence
whose main verb is in the simple (nonprogressive) present tense, which
does not contain any temporal adverbials, and whose noun phrases either
occupy predicative position or are proper nouns or pronouns.

These restrictions largely leave the aspectual properties of atomic sentences dependent on the inherent aspectual character of the main verb
(phrase). Following tradition, I may sometimes loosely speak of aspectual
properties of verbs. Strictly, however, aspect is a property of a whole sentence.

In the beginning stages of the investigation, I shall cheat a little and
choose examples of aspect types more freely, not restricting the choice to
simple (atomic) examples. Ultimately, the aspectual properties of such

---

If $h(t) = h'(t)$ for some t in τ, then $h(t') = h'(t')$ for all t' in τ earlier than t.
That is to say, if two histories coincide at some point, they coincide at all earlier times (i.e.,
share a past).

Any restriction of a history h to an interval T is a PERIOD P of h. If T is an instant, P is a
MOMENT of h, else P is an EXTENDED period. An interval T is earlier than another interval T'
if each member of T is earlier than each member of T'. A period P of history h is earlier than
another period P' of h if the domain of P is earlier than the domain of P'. Let "$<$" stand for
"is earlier than." If $P = P_1 \cup P' \cup P_2$ and $P_1 < P' < P_2$, then P' is a SUBPERIOD of P;
  If $P_1 \cup P_2 \neq \emptyset$, then P' is PROPER;
  If $P_1 = \emptyset$, then P' is INITIAL;
  If $P_2 = \emptyset$, then P' is FINAL;
  If $P_1 = \emptyset$ iff $P_2 = \emptyset$, then P' is INTERNAL.
See Rescher and Urquhart (1971) for another formulation.

[8] The generalization of the truth definition of declarative sentences to appropriate analogous conditions for other sentential moods (imperatives, questions) is not difficult in the
game-theoretical framework (see Carlson 1976 for an outline).

examples are derived from the interaction of recursive clauses of interpretation with the underlying atomic assignments.

Note that the concept of truth given here lets the truth or falsity of a sentence in a period depend on which history the period is considered a part of. (Recall that in branching time, one and the same course of events may be part of a number of different histories.) If nothing more is said, nothing stops two histories from materially coinciding most of the time while being everywhere different in terms of truth assignments.

Fortunately, most atomic sentences of English (or any other natural language) are HISTORY INDEPENDENT; in particular, the future course of history will not affect the truth of a sentence in a given period. There are exceptions, such as sentences involving words like *forthcoming, terminal, predict, prevent, bring about*. But, except for such cases, atomic truth assignments can be given directly with respect to periods. History independence is largely carried over to complex sentences by recursive clauses of interpretation, again with exceptions in future-referring operations. These considerations ensure that histories that share a past will also have a more or less similar past in terms of the language at hand.

2.3. Why Have a Taxonomy of Aspect?

In making aspectual classifications, one often finds that the aspectual nature of a given verb is not quite hard-and-fast; with some stretching of imagination, a verb can be switched from its most natural aspect class to another. This has made people doubt the usefulness of aspectual classifications in the first place. It is said that aspectual distinctions only codify our "real world knowledge"; and that, moreover, they distort this knowledge in postulating discrete classes where there is in fact only a continuum of cases.

I wish to contend both claims. First, there are cases where aspectual classifications are quite stable, and can justly be considered criterial for the application of a predicate. The inherently stative NOUNS are a case in point.

There is a qualitative difference. I think, between the well-formedness of

(1)   *That tree is being a pine.*

and

(2)   *That tree is suffering from drought.*

There are inherently momentaneous verbs like *notice:* The following sentence:

(3)   *I noticed it for a while.*

can at best describe an iterative event, short of redefining the meaning of the verb. There are inherently extended ones, too:

(4)   *I waited.*

surely implies

(5)   *I waited for some time.*

however short the time.

Second, as the reader may have noticed, there are SYSTEMATIC ways of changing the interpretation of a verb so that it changes its aspectual class. One such operation is to move from a semelfactive sense of a verb to an ITERATIVE sense, as may happen in (3). Another such operation is to move from "be NP" to "act like (or so as to be) NP"—perhaps the best move available in (1).

Insofar as such switches of meaning are indeed discrete, systematic, marked, and predictable from the basic sense of a verb, one would want to describe them as such. This involves among other things determining what the unmarked case is.

Moreover, the question of aspectual taxonomy is not set aside by pointing out that the unmarked classification of a particular word may depend (as it clearly does in many cases) on our common-sense beliefs of what is usually the case or what is empirically possible. For one can still ask, in WHAT FORMAT such real world knowledge enters our conceptual and linguistic representations. Aspectual taxonomies, even where not immutable, can be psychologically real if they are the proper way of describing how real world information is ARTICULATED in our conceptual system. The prediction of a discrete taxonomy is that such information is indeed codified as a finite set of (binary) distinctions. One can imagine psychological tests that would bear on this question, for example, by analogy with tests that show that consonant perception is categorial rather than continuous. The evidence adduced in this chapter is linguistic. It indicates that a discrete classification is adequate for the representation of central linguistic intuitions about aspect. However, being itself discrete in character, it does not suffice alone to rule out alternative approaches.

2.5 A Taxonomy of Inherent Aspect

My strategy in this section is the following. Instead of setting out a ready-made taxonomy of aspect types, I shall first single out three pretheoretic grammatical criteria for aspect type, and elucidate their interrelations by means of an array of examples. On the basis of the examples, I define three theoretical constraints on interpretation, or semantic features if you like. Their interaction with principles of interpretation of the criterial expressions will account for the observed combinatory properties.

Three grammatical criteria offer themselves as relatively clear-cut and theoretically significant:

1. Momentaneous adverbials of time with the simple tenses.[9] Momentaneous time adverbials include *at once, at that (very) moment, at 8:30,* as well as temporal adverbial clauses which themselves have momentaneous aspect.
2. The progressive aspect.
3. Durative adverbials of time with the simple tenses. Durative adverbials are those which answer to the question *how long.* Examples are *(how) long, for a while, from one to ten o'clock, all day (long).*

To see that these criteria cross-classify English verbs, consider the following Examples, (6)–(8). Remember that I need not show that any of the (marked) examples are unconditionally unacceptable. Most of them are quite admissible with a secondary interpretation, most likely iterative, habitual, dispositional, ingressive, or "act as if" sense, or can be understood as part of a lively narrative, plot, or an instruction. Others can be conceived of by more exotic imaginative effort.

The fact remains that there is a DIFFERENCE between the marked examples and the corresponding unmarked ones (corresponding either by having the same main verb or by exhibiting the same construction). The difference may be one of ACCEPTABILITY, MEANING of the main verb, and/or range of appropriate contexts of USE. Hence conceivable but quite artificial contexts into which even the worst examples could just about be fitted do not constitute counter examples, but rather supporting evidence for my claims. Concepts can be stretched in many areas of meaning, with no detriment to the fundamental difference between the marked and unmarked cases.

The exclamation mark before a sentence indicates a marked case in my sense.

(6) a. *At that point I hit him.*
     b. *I noticed it at once.*
     c. *Just when the light went on, he blinked.*
     d. *He was a full-grown man when I was born.*
     e. *At that point I remembered the rule.*
     f. *At that point he closed the door.*

---

[9] I call a sentence of form

(i)   [$_N$ . . . [$_{Aux}$Tense *be ing*] . . .]

a sentence in PROGRESSIVE ASPECT, and the PROGRESSIVE FORM of

(ii)   [$_S$ . . . [$_{Aux}$ Tense] . . .],

Whereas (ii) is a sentence in the SIMPLE (present or past) tense, and the SIMPLE FORM of (i) (cf. Chomsky 1957).

g. *He lost the tournament when he missed that ball.*
h. *The dog attacked me at once.*
i. *At that point, the plane took off from the ground.*
j. *At seven o'clock, the caravan stood in its old place.*
k. *!He ran a mile at that moment.*
l. *!She grew restless at eight o'clock in the evening.*
m. *!Right now, I write my aspect paper.*
n. *!The children played when I returned.*
o. *!At sunrise, I walked eastward.*
p. *!You don't use the right word now.*

(7)   a. *!At that point I was hitting him.*
b. *!I was noticing it at once.*
c. *!Just when the light went on, he was blinking.*
d. *!He was being a full-grown man when I was born.*
e. *!At that point I was remembering the rule.*
f. *At that point he was closing the door.*
g. *He was winning the tournament when he missed that ball.*
h. *The dog was attacking me when the owner intervened.*
i. *At that point, the plane was taking off from the ground.*
j. *At seven o'clock, the caravan was standing in its old place.*
k. *He was running a mile at that moment.*
l. *She was growing restless at that point.*
m. *Right now, I am writing my aspect paper.*
n. *The children were playing when I returned.*
o. *At sunrise I was walking eastward.*
p. *You aren't using the right word now.*

(8)   a. *!For a while, I hit him.*
b. *!I did not notice it long.*
c. *!For a minute, he blinked.*
d. *He was a full grown man from the year 1900 on.*
e. *I remembered the rule for two days.*
f. *!He closed the door too long.*
g. *!He won the tournament all the time.*
h. *!The dog attacked me for quite a while.*
i. *!The plane didn't take off from the ground that long.*
j. *The caravan stood in its old place for days.*
k. *!He ran a mile for four minutes.*
l. *!I almost wrote my aspect paper too long.*
m. *!She grew anxious from early evening on.*
n. *The children played for a while.*
o. *I walked eastward for three hours.*
p. *You used the wrong word throughout the discussion.*

TABLE 3.1. SENTENCE CLASSES

Class	Example sentences	Momentaneous adverbials	Progressive aspect	Durative adverbials	Class name
I	(a)–(c)	+	–	–	Momentaneous
II	(d)–(e)	+	–	+	Stative
III	(f)–(i)	+	+	–	Achievement
IV	(j)	+	+	+	Dynamic
V	(k)–(m)	–	+	–	Accomplishment
VI	(n)–(p)	–	+	+	Activity

The examples fall into six classes, as illustrated by Table 3.1.

I have tabulated the grammatical criteria, giving a "+" if members of the class pass the test WITHOUT ANY COMMENT, and a "−" otherwise. At the right you find mnemonic names for the six classes, matching those of Vendler (1967) when possible.

Recall that Vendler recognizes only four types. In the present finer taxonomy, his class "achievement" splits into the two classes—Classes I (my MOMENTANEOUS) and III (my ACHIEVEMENT proper). An intermediate Class IV (for which I coined the name DYNAMIC) is recognized between Vendler's classes "stative" and "activity" sharing properties of both.[10]

2.6. Definitions of Aspect Features

I did not choose the particular grammatical criteria at random, but with a quite specific theory of aspectual distinctions in mind. The criteria have been chosen so as to match the theoretical distinctions as closely as possible. Nevertheless they should not be construed as operational definitions of the distinctions. The claim is only that if these particular tests fail in a particular case, there is some systematic explanation why they do. With this proviso in mind, I give the following correspondences.

2.6.1. POINT

I construe the simple tenses of English so that they will not change the aspect of a sentence at all. Therefore the applicability of point adverbials to an atomic sentence in the simple present or past is an indication that the sentence is evaluated (true or false) at points of time (moments of history).

This constitutes the first aspectual feature POINT (WISE EVALUATED).

[10] Inherently dynamic verbs are rare in English, probably because of the progressive aspect. Sentences in progressive aspect have the features [+ point + ext + cont], that is, they are dynamic. The dispositional interpretation provides more examples (cf. Section 2.7).

Technically, aspect features can be construed as conditions on aspectual adequacy on interpretations of a language in temporal frames. For the feature POINT, I have the following definition:

(C.point)   An interpretation I of a language L in a temporal frame F is aspectually adequate only if:

An atomic sentence S of L has feature [+ point] iff S has a truth value at moments of F.

In the lexical entries of certain words (notably verbs, nouns, and adjectives), there is, I assume, a specification of its unmarked aspectual features. If aspect is a criterion of application of a word, its aspectual features may be primitive. In most cases, however, a word's aspect is predictable from other properties of its meaning. It may happen that a word is not fully specified with respect to some aspectual features by any semantical rule. For instance, a number of verbs seem to vacillate between the classes momentaneous and accomplishment. As was already mentioned, the aspectual properties of an atomic sentence will be a fairly direct function of the feature specification of its main verb (phrase).

2.6.2. EXTENDED

Following Dowty (1977) in essential respects, I construe the progressive aspect of English in such a way that it only applies to verbs evaluated (true or false) in extended periods. This leads to the second aspectual feature EXT(ENDED), whose model-theoretic definition is

(C.ext)   An interpretation I of a language L in temporal frame F is aspectually adequate only if:

An atomic sentence S of L has feature [+ ext] iff S has a truth value with respect to extended periods of F.

2.6.3. CONTINUOUS

Durative adverbials will be construed as (parametrized) universal quantifiers over subperiods of a given period. A necessary condition for their applicability is the following condition of continuity, definitory of a third aspectual feature CONT(INUOUS):

(C.cont)   An interpretation I of a language L in a temporal frame F is aspectually adequate only if:

If an atomic sentence S of L has the feature [-cont], then the following holds of it:

If S is true in periods P, P', and P'', and $P' \neq P \neq P''$, then $P \cup P' \cup P''$ is a period only if P is a moment and $P' = P''$.

Condition (C.cont) says in effect that accomplishments, achievements, and momentaneous sentences cannot hold in overlapping or contiguous periods. The only exception is that an achievement is allowed to hold at some unique climactic moment contained in a period that that achievement extends over.[11]

Three independent properties can define eight disjoint classes. In the case at hand, two putative classes, for which both features [point] and [ext] assume negative value, are empty by the definitions of the aspectual features. A sentence in these classes would never be true nor false, as all periods are either moments or extended. This leaves six classes, corresponding to the Classes I–VI of Table 3.1. In virtue of the correspondences just given, the binary values in Table 3.1, from left to right, give the values of features [point], [ext], and [cont], respectively, for the Classes I–VI.

In Sections 2.7, 2.8, and 2.9, I give a brief summary of my treatment of the simple present, the progressive, and the durative adverbials. For reasons of space, detailed arguments have to be omitted. A perceptive reader can derive many of them himself from my assumptions. They are given explicitly in Carlson (in preparation) where a detailed account of the Examples (6a)–(8p) can be found.

2.7. The Simple Present

The simplest theory of the simple present is, of course, that it has no semantic effect whatsoever. This is my theory of the English simple present. Whatever asymmetries verbs of different aspect types exhibit with respect to the simple present are derived, I maintain, from their inherent aspect combined with various practical constraints on use.

This theory can only be maintained when it is embedded in the context of a number of supplementary, but independently motivated, assumptions. I shall single out four sorts of such assumptions.

First, the period of evaluation of a sentence in the simple present may be, but need not be, the period of utterance of that sentence. Beside its DEICTIC use to point to a period of utterance,[12] the simple present serves as the unmarked member of the tense system of English. This property of the simple present comes out in the so-called historical present.[13] It is also involved when a sentence in the simple present is interpreted with respect

---

[11] Further conditions on achievements specify the position of the climactic moment [whether final (6g), initial (6h), or internal (6i)].

[12] Sometimes, period of UPTAKE is meant, for example, in written messages.

[13] See Kiparsky (1968) for an interesting discussion of the historical present.

to some constructed or imaginary sequence of events: This includes the use of the simple present in commands, plots, and instructions. The use of simple present on the simplest theory requires one to match the period of truth of the sentence with a period of evaluation. There are obvious practical constraints on such matching when the period of utterance dictates the period of evaluation. Such constraints are absent in other uses of the present tense; hence the greater range of the simple present on such uses. As a striking extreme case, the PERFORMATIVE use of sentence defines its own period of evaluation. The match of period of utterance and period of truth could not be more perfect; accordingly, the simple present is one of the hallmarks of a performative sentence.

Second, the period of evaluation of a sentence in the simple present is not always a moment, but may vary in extent. I have dubbed this insight JESPERSEN'S PRINCIPLE, with reference to the following quote from Jespersen (1923): "In practice, 'now' means a time with appreciable duration, the length of which varies greatly accordingly to circumstances [p. 258]." This option seems to be involved in the use of simple present in habitual sentences. Such sentences seem true or false of longer periods only.

Third, the articulation of the WHOLE TIME DOMAIN varies from context to use to another. This point has been made already in Section 2.2. Not only can the interpretation of "now" vary from an indivisible moment to periods of varying extension, the very definition of an indivisible moment may change according to need and circumstance. I propose to call this principle of variability the CHRONOLOGY PRINCIPLE.

Fourth, in addition to variation in major interpretational parameters such as those just given, there is a limited number of additional rules of secondary semantic interpretation. Independent of considerations particular to the simple present, sentences in English can have a range of well-defined derived senses, registered in so many additional rules of semantic games.

A common property of such rules is that they reduce the truth of a sentence on the relevant secondary sense to the truth of the same sentence in its basic primary sense in periods related in a systematic way to the period of evaluation. Moreover, in their temporal effect, these rules are aspectual in the sense defined in Section 2.1.

The following is a reasonably complete list of rules relevant to Examples (6)–(8).

1. Rule of iterative interpretation
2. Rule of habitual interpretation

3. Rule of dispositional interpretation
4. Rule of ingressive interpretation

The rule of iterative interpretation applies to practically any sentence to pluralize it—that is, to form a sentence that is true in any period in which the same sentence is true several times in its semelfactive sense. It is obvious from this description that the result of the pluralization will be a sentence of the activity type.

In English, iterative interpretation need not leave any morphological trace. In Finnish, iteration is marked in the morphology of the verb.[14] The situation is quite analogous to the linguistic variability of plural marking in nouns.

The rule of habitual interpretation adds a modal or counterfactual condition over and above iterativity: A habit is assumed to be upheld in a range of favorable counterfactual circumstances even if accidentally broken. Aspectually, habits come out as activities.

In contrast, the rule of dispositional interpretation construes sentences as descriptions of DYNAMIC conditions in which one is able to disposed to realize the same sentence in a primary manifest sense. Accordingly, it is somewhat odd to predicate a habit of moments of time, whereas a disposition may be pointwise valid. Beside the aspectual difference, the intensional implications of dispositions differ from those of habits: A habit may or may not involve a disposition, but a disposition need not be manifested in a habit.

Finally, the rule of ingressive interpretation applies to sentences of continuous aspect to single out the first moment of a maximal period in which the same sentences are true in their continuous sense. An example of an ingressively understood activity is Sentence (60).

One further derived sense of ambivalent status has been mentioned: the dynamic interpretation of states which imputes a state a flavor of manifest or even intentional activity. Such a nuance is felt, for example, in (7d). It is somewhat unclear whether such an interpretation is conventional enough to deserve a semantic rule. It might be enough to derive it as a conversational implication of a misuse of the progressive. The intensional conditions on applicability of the progressive discussed in what follows predict in any case that such a violation will give a stative sentence a dynamic flavor.

Taken together, the four assumptions discussed go a long way toward

---

[14] This is exemplified by the contrast between *välähtää* 'flash once' and *välähdellä* 'flash repeatedly'.

saying what need be said in order to accommodate the surface variability of examples such as (6) to the simplest theory of the simple present.

The rationale for the choice of momentaneous adverbials as a test for pointwise sentences can now be appreciated more precisely. Insofar as such an adverbial really succeeds in pinning down an indivisible moment, only sentences with the aspectual feature [+ point] can be associated with it.

2.8. The Progressive Aspect

Because the applicability of the progressive aspect will depend on the aspect type of the whole sentence which it applies to, and because this in turn may be a function of the subject of the sentence, the progressive is an operation on sentences, not on verbs or verb phrases.

My analysis of the progressive aspect is in many essential respects similar to that of Dowty (1977). The leading idea of this treatment is that, in its temporal aspect, the progressive is a PARTITIVE operation in the time domain.[15] As a first approximation, this means that the progressive form of a sentence is true in periods that are proper internal subperiods of the temporal range of the corresponding simple sentence. One may think of the progressive operation as a function that takes as an argument the set of periods in which the simple form of a sentence is true and returns as its value another set of periods, each member of which is an internal part of some period in the argument set. The value of the function is a set of periods in which the progressive form of the same sentence is true.

There is a notorious problem with this sort of characterization, known as the imperfective paradox. It is that the progressive form of a sentence can be true in a period of a history h while the simple form of the same sentence never becomes true in h. As Dowty points out, however, if the truth of a progressive sentence S in a period P of history h is allowed to depend on the truth of the simple form of S in superperiods P' of a number of alternative possible continuations h' of P, the imperfective paradox is accommodated. The main problem of Dowty's analysis concerns the appropriate choice of such alternative continuations.

Another paradox of the progressive suggests a direction in which the solution to this problem can be sought. It is also possible for Sentences (9) and (10) to hold at the same moment while the corresponding simple sentences exclude each other in each future of that moment.

---

[15] Not surprisingly, therefore, it is frequent for languages to transfer locative and partitive operations from the object domain to the expression of progressive aspect. English and Finnish provide examples.

(9)   *The carpenter was drilling a hole through the board.*

(10)   *The drill was bending double under the pressure.*

In Carlson (in preparation), I define and motivate an analysis of the intensional conditions of the progressive which construes (9) and (10) as true simultaneously only when seen from the different POINTS OF VIEW of the carpenter in (9) and, say, some partial physical theory in (10).

There are more nontemporal conditions on application of the progressive aspect. Vlach (this volume) argues persuasively that the progressive is not a pure aspect in English. What the progressive form of a simple sentence picks out is periods of some dynamic condition or activity manifesting or bringing about whatever the simple sentence describes. This condition seems to be laid bare in the "act as if" implications of progressive statives. As a result of this condition, progressive sentences will belong to the aspect class dynamic. With the help of such intensional conditions of truth of the progressive form over and above the temporal core idea, Dowty's analysis can be maintained even in the face of Vlach's criticisms (this volume).

The importance of the temporal aspect of the progressive comes out clearly in the suggestion of temporariness of the progressive form. In particular, when the choice of the progressive form over the simple form makes no difference to intensional conditions of truth, this suggestion of the progressive stands out in bare outline. An example of this is the pair (6j)–(7j).[16] The temporal aspect of the progressive makes it a suitable test of extendedness of a sentence. Moments of time do not have proper internal subperiods. Therefore the progressive form of a pointwise but nonextended sentence (momentaneous or stative) will fail by definition.

2.9. Durative Adverbials

The promissory note of Section 2.6 connected the applicability of durative adverbials to the aspectual feature [cont]. At first blush, the definition of continuity looks overly restrictive. It does not allow one and the same accomplishment, achievement, or momentaneous event to repeat itself without an intervening pause. I believe, however, that the reader will find it hard to find a cut-and-dried counterexample to it once he takes care to keep all the essential participants of such events constant.

The best evidence for the definition is, however, that it gives intuitively

---

[16] This is by no means the only indication that the temporal facet of the progressive is indispensable. For one thing, the temporal core idea is essential for an explanation of the use of the partitive case in Finnish to express progressive aspect (cf. Note 2).

correct results when it interacts with other rules of semantic interpretation. The rules that interest us here are the rules for durative adverbials.
An intuitively appealing approach to durative adverbials is to think of
them as some sort of MEASURE of time. Think for instance how one would
go about assessing the truth of

(11)   *He ran for four minutes.*

say, in an athletic event. What happens is that some sufficiently fine PAR-
TITION (or perhaps just COVER) of the period of four minutes in terms of its
proper subperiods is chosen, and the truth of

(12)   *He runs.*

is ascertained in each member of it.[17]

An essential feature of my treatment is that the choice of partition or
cover is left to be determined by various pragmatic considerations. For
the purposes of the semantic theory of aspect, it does not matter how the
division is made in each particular case, as long as it is finer than the period "measured."

Note that, although extensive measurement of time can be construed as
a special case of the operation just described, the description was NOT
metric in itself. Only qualitative topological concepts were involved. Thus
the present analysis of durative adverbials does not import any additional
assumptions of the structure of time over and above Section 2.2. And it is
true that, in ordinary practice, less stringent methods of partitioning are
used than extensive measurement.

One consequence of the present approach is that the truth of (11) is not
dependent on any particular distribution of truth of (12) over subperiods
of the four minutes in (11). The choice of unit is left to the users of language to decide on.

This notion of the pragmatic variability of the choice of "measure" introduces a new parameter of vagueness to natural language temporal reference. Let us call it the MEASURE PRINCIPLE.

One prediction of the measure principle is that the conditions of truth of
a sentence like

(13)   *I worked all the time.*

are not at all as unambiguous as those of a stative sentence like

(14)   *I was in my room all the time.*

In (14), the only available partition by subperiods of whatever is referred

---

[17] For the definitions of partition and cover, see, for example, Kelley 1955.

to by *the time* is the set of all moments of that time. In (13), there is more leeway. Sentence (13) may be found true on a rough partition, but false on a more pedantic one. This seems to be exactly how things ought to be intuitively.

The reason for the unapplicability of durative adverbials in noncontinuous verbs is now apparent. The durative adverbial looks for a sequence of overlapping or contiguous periods, in each of which the sentence without the adverbial is true. Such periods can only be found, in virtue of (C.cont), for sentences marked [+cont].

The particular way of interpreting durative adverbials I have proposed gains interesting theoretical support when partitivity, a further semantic distinctive property, is defined. Let me now proceed to do so in Section 3.

3. ASPECTUAL PROPERTIES OF QUANTIFIED SENTENCES

3.1 Partitivity

Recall that, in Sections 2.6 and 2.9, applicability of durative adverbials was construed as a function of the aspectual feature of continuity. I recognize three classes of continuous verbs: states, dynamic verbs, and activities. States were distinguished from the other two classes by being true only pointwise, whereas the other two were extended (activities exclusively so).

In this section, I shall argue for another important aspectual property that distinguishes extended continuous verbs from the other classes. It is a special case of a more general cross-categorial referential distinction, which may be called, in honor of the ingenious Swedish grammarian Adolf Noreen,[18] the property of PARTITIVITY. In nominal reference, partitivity is the semantical distinction corresponding to the syntactic distinction of countability. Noncount nouns are semantically partitive, whereas count nouns are not. Cross-categorial application of the partitivity property is, I shall claim, involved in certain curious correlations and analogies between noun and verb reference.[19]

What is partitivity anyway? The immediate connotation of the term is that some sort of divisibility is involved. Intuitively, a portion of some partitive substance—for example, water—can be divided into parts each

---

[18] Noreen (1903).
[19] See Carlson (in preparation) for fuller argumentation.

of which is also water. In temporal reference, the analogy is close: A sustained stretch of, say, working, can be divided into a number of smaller stretches of working.

This seems to be the intuition behind several writers' characterization of activity verbs by means of some closure condition over subintervals of intervals in the temporal range of a sentence of the activity type. A particularly popular simple definition of such divisibility is called by Bennett and Partee (1974) the SUBINTERVAL PROPERTY:

> Subinterval verb phrases have the property that if they are the main verb phrase of a sentence which is true at some interval of time I, then the sentence is true at every subinterval of I including every moment of time in I. Examples of subinterval verb phrases are: *walk, breathe, walk in the park, push a cart* [p. 17].

It seems obvious to me that literally taken, the subinterval property is all too strong. (For arguments, see, for example, Taylor 1977.) It is interesting to observe that the exactly analogous result is arrived at by Quine (1960) concerning the semantics of mass terms. As Quine points out, it is false of most partitive substances that every part of such a substance is also that substance; for example, there are parts of water too small to count as water.

In Carlson (in preparation), I investigate various putative characterizations of divisibility and their adequacy as definitions of partivity. My conclusion is that there is no simple perfectly general definition of partitivity in terms of divisibility. At best, one can hope to define some disjunction of interesting properties (such as atomic structure, infinite divisibility, and mixture structure), a member of which is satisfied by each partitive predicate.

However, it appears that an important inverse property of ADDITIVITY holds unconditionally of mass terms and extended continuous verbs alike, and alone goes a long way toward establishing an essentially divided structure to the extensions of such terms. This property of additivity is none other than Quine's principle of cumulative reference: the sum of a number of portions of water is always water.[20] It follows from additivity alone that, except for bizarre special cases, most members of the extension of a partitive substance are divisible into further members of its extension. It may well be that this is enough for a general definition of partitivity. However, I reserve the possibility of supplementary downward characterizations of divisibility.

The existence of important analogies between reference in the object domain and in the temporal domain has long been recognized.[21] My explanation of these analogies starts from the hypothesis that the parametrized

---

[20] See Quine (1960, p. 91).

[21] See, for example, Allen (1966), Taylor (1977), Mourelatos (this volume).

referential distinction of partitivity effects a division of predicates of each domain into two classes, the partitive and the nonpartitive. This distinction can be characterized in model-theoretical terms. It involves at least the referential closure condition of additivity, approximated by

(A)   Any subset of the extension of a partitive predicate P that satisfies formal conditions of membership of P is a member of the extension of P.

Let me first briefly explain the relevance of (A) for the domains of nominal and temporal reference.

3.2. Partitivity in the Object Domain

There is ample linguistic and extralinguistic evidence for the semantic analysis of the countability distinction in terms of the partitivity property. Here I can only point out some of the major themes. One of the conspicuous contrasts between count and noncount nouns is their respective quantifier systems. Count nouns admit of numerals and take specific singular quantifier words (e.g., *a/an, each, every*), which do not apply to noncount and plural nouns. Correspondingly, plural and noncount nouns allow measure phrases, but singular count nouns do not. A related characteristic of noncount nouns is that they "admit of more and less," as the ancient Greeks characterized matter in contrast to the individuating principle.[22] In modern terms, expressions of comparison and measurement are applicable to noncount and plural nouns but not to singular count nouns.

An investigation of the respective logics of the operations of counting and measuring reveals the underlying semantic motivation of these grammatical constraints.[23] The concepts of comparative order and additivity are the two essential components of the THEORY OF EXTENSIVE MEASUREMENT.[24] A basis of quantitative comparison of a class of objects and a method of combining them into more similar objects are the two essential components of the theory of extensive measurement. These components are halfway provided for by partitivity. A method of combining objects into new ones is guaranteed by (A), and a starting point for quantitative comparisons is implicit in the part–whole relations induced by (A).[25]

Conversely, it can be shown that the operation of counting is practica-

[22] See for example, McMullin (1963).

[23] I am not claiming that the grammatical countability distinction is definable in terms of the semantic concept of partitivity. On the contrary, I do not believe it is.

[24] See, for example, Helmholtz (1930), Hempel (1952), Krantz *et al.* (1971).

[25] One can go on to argue, on the basis of Piaget's findings on the development of the concept of quantity, that the part–whole relation constitutes the developmental starting point of quantitative comparison. See Piaget (1941, 1952, 1968), and Carlson (in preparation).

ble only in a domain of nonadditive objects. Consider the problem of counting some partitive material, say water or rice. The obvious reason why water is not counted is that we do not know what to count. The parts already counted may again be divided into a larger number of smaller parts, in virtue of partitivity. If we have infinite divisibility, there is no end to the count. Furthermore, even where a finite upper bound to the number of minimal parts of a substance exists, there is often vagueness about the exact number, due to difficulties in individuation. Finally, and most strikingly, partitivity drastically reduces the utility of counting. In some cases, the number of objects that satisfy a given noncountable noun can be ascertained (say, rice). The fact remains that the number of such objects bears only a very indirect relation to the usual uses of the cardinal number of a set. For a given number of minimal objects that satisfy a noncountable noun, there is an exponentially related number of other overlapping objects that also satisfy the same noun, in virtue of additivity. Hence the number of ALL objects that satisfy a noncountable noun bears no linear relation to important global properties of the collection (e.g., weight, volume, divisibility).

The paradox of counting the noncountable can be put in the form of a dilemma. If all objects that satisfy a noncountable noun can be counted at all, their number is worthless. Two conditions are needed for a practicable numerical estimate: (a) the objects counted should be more or less equal in relevant respects; and (b) they should exhaust the totality without overlap. In other respects, the choice of unit is immaterial. But this, in turn, is nothing other than a rough description of MEASURING a substance!

Consider next the fact that plurals of count nouns share many properties with noncount nouns. It can be shown independently that plural nouns pick out (nonnull and nonunit) subsets of the extension of their singular. It is possible to give an approximate explanation of the parallelism by a direct application of the definition on the extension of a plural noun. That extension, being roughly the power set of the extension of the singular noun, satisfies straightforward additivity relative to unions: The union of any subset of it is a member of it. Plural nouns thus turn out to be partitive with respect to the natural choices of values of the parameters of partitivity. The details of the explanation are somewhat more complicated, but this gives a fair approximation of it.

3.3. Partitivity in the Temporal Domain

The foregoing observations suggest that partitivity is indeed the essential semantic distinction between singular count nouns and noncount or plural nouns. If my generalization of partitivity into temporal reference is valid, one would expect arguments applicable in one domain predictably apply in the other domain. Moreover, one can form specific expectations about the interaction of the two domains.[26]

Before proceeding to substantiate one class of such expectations, let me spell out the partitivity property for the temporal domain.

(A.temp)   If a sentence S is true in each member of a set of periods $\mathscr{P}$, and the union of $\mathscr{P}$ is a period P, then S is true in P.

I now add a further condition of aspectual adequacy of interpretation functions:

(C.part)   An interpretation I of a language L in a temporal frame F is aspectually adequate only if:

If a sentence S has the feature [+ part], it satisfies (A. temp).

The following redundancy rule concerning aspectual feature specifications connects (C.part) to the rest of the feature system:

(R.part)   If a sentence has the features [+ ext] and [+ cont], it also has the feature [+ part].

3.4 Aspect and Nominal Reference

It has often been observed that the choice of subject and certain other NP complements of a sentence has an effect on its aspect.[27] Examples are

(15) a. *A guest arrived.*
      b. *The guest arrived.*
      c. *Some guest arrived.*
      d. *Every guest arrived.*

(16) a. *Water came in.*
      b. *The water came in.*
      c. *Some water came in.*
      d. *All the water came in.*

(17) a. *Guests arrived.*
      b. *The guests arrived.*
      c. *Some guests arrived.*
      d. *All the guests arrived.*

[26] Nominalizations of verbs represent one such area of interaction. See Mourelatos (this volume) for interesting observations.
[27] See, for example, Allen (1966), Heinämäki (1974), Verkuyl (1972).

(18) a. *The toad caught a fly.*
     b. *The toad caught the fly.*
     c. *The toad caught some fly.*
     d. *The toad caught every fly.*

(19) a. *The goat ate grass.*
     b. *The goat ate the grass.*
     c. *The goat ate some grass.*
     d. *The goat ate all the grass.*

(20) a. *The toad caught flies.*
     b. *The toad caught the flies.*
     c. *The toad caught some flies.*
     d. *The toad caught all the flies.*

(21) a. *We pedaled over a bridge.*
     b. *We pedaled over the bridge.*
     c. *We pedaled over some bridge.*
     d. *We pedaled over every bridge.*

(22) a. *We passed through snow.*
     b. *We passed through the snow.*
     c. *We passed through some snow.*
     d. *We passed through all the snow.*

(23) a. *We pedaled over bridges.*
     b. *We pedaled over the bridges.*
     c. *We pedaled over some bridges.*
     d. *We pedaled over all the bridges.*

Examples (15)–(17) exemplify the aspectual effect of the referential properties of the subject; Examples (18)–(20) owe their aspectual differences to choice of object; and in Examples (21)–(23) the character of a directional adverbial affects the aspect of a movement verb.

These are among the most typical effects. The exact range of aspectually relevant complements is unknown. But I believe that there are no interesting generalizations concerning that range independently of otherwise motivated properties of interpretation of particular sentences. That is, there is little independent insight to be gained from listing the admissible aspectual changes in terms of aspect type before and after appending complements of various types. If I am right, all such effects will come out as side effects of otherwise motivated rules of interpretation.

The task of characterizing the aspectual effect of nominal complements can be divided into two subtasks. The first subtask concerns the underlying predicate-argument structure of a given sentence (in our terms, the structure of the atomic sentences that emerge in the game connected with a given sentence).[28] For instance, naturally enough, an instrumental object of a transitive activity verb does not influence aspect in the way an "essentially affected" object does. Thus compare the following sentences:

(24)   *I used the axe for a while to fell the tree.*

(25)   *I felled the tree for a while with the axe.*

These near-synonymous sentences differ in acceptability because of the different roles the object NP plays in each case. The classification of complements in terms of semantic role (or "deep case") is relevant here. For instance, one may want to distinguish between effected and affected direct objects in the light of contrasts like

(26)   *I wrote the book for hours.*

(27)   *I read the book for hours.*

The result object of (26) makes it an accomplishment, whereas the object of (27) does not change aspect. Observations of this sort point to the fact that the inherent aspect type of a verb is to a large extent a function of its nontemporal meaning (including the semantic roles of its arguments). I shall not go into the general problem of determining that function.

The second subtask is to determine, given specifications of inherent aspect of atomic sentences and rules of interpretation of quantified noun phrases, the aspectual properties of quantified sentences such as (15)–(23). My thesis is that the aspectual properties of quantified sentences are an automatic consequence of the interaction of rules of quantification with inherent aspect. No specific rules of aspectual projection are needed to account for the interaction of nominal reference with aspect. Clearly, this is the simplest and most desirable theory of aspectual projection. In the following sections, I shall try to substantiate this thesis.

3.5. Quantifier Rules

Testing with temporal adverbials, we find that all of the examples in (15), with singular count noun phrase subject, are noncontinuous. Examples (15a)–(15b) are understood as momentaneous; Example (15d) might be an accomplishment as well, depending on whether the guests arrived in a group or not. In contrast, (16a) seems continuous; (16c) seems ambiguous; whereas (16b) and (16d) are noncontinuous unless iterated. Sentences

[28] See also Verkuyl (1972, pp. 96–98). Verkuyl's work represents an interesting attempt to solve the first subtask. His treatment of the second subtask assumes specific rules of aspectual projection.

in (18) and (21) seem to behave like those in (15), whereas (17), (19), (20), (22), and (23) follow the model of (16).

How are these intuitions accounted for? Note first that the contrasts are not statable directly in terms of the grammatical count–noncount distinction. Some sentences with count subjects are nondurative (15a), some durative (17a); some with noncount subjects are durative (16a), others are not (16d). A better fit is gotten by a direct application of the definition of partitivity to the crucial noun phrases. Compare for instance *water* to *a guest*. The sum of a number of portions of water is still water, but the fusion of a number of individuals each satisfying the NP *a guest* is not a guest, whatever it may be. In contrast, the union of a number of objects properly described by *guests* is another such object.

In view of such considerations, one might be tempted to write feature-spreading rules telling one to transfer the partitivity feature of a subject, object, or other relevant complement to the whole sentence. Thus a sentence with a partitive noun object such as (16a) would be correctly predicted to be partitive too. However, such a simplistic classification of noun phrases accompanied with rules of feature projection fails to capture the logic of the situation. What is more, the approach proves to be completely superfluous.

First, note that it is not all that clear how to apply the partitivity property to all noun phrases: think of, for example, *the water, my friends, most of it, a little water*. Moreover, the classificatory approach fails to differentiate between *water,* and *some water.* For obviously whatever is water is some water and vice versa; thus *some water* should behave aspectually just like *water.* Yet there is a difference in aspectual preferences between (16a) and (16c). It is here that the interaction of recursive clauses of quantifier interpretation comes to its right. For, although taken out of context *water* and *some water* apply to exactly the same objects, they differ in their interaction with sentential environment.

These properties come out when quantifier phrases are interpreted in their sentential context. In earlier publications, game-theoretical rules of contextual interpretation of English quantified noun phrases have been proposed, including rules for the singular quantifiers *a/an, the, some,* and *every.*[29]

---

[29] See the literature referred to in Note 1. What the game-theoretical rules of interpretation do syntactically is to reduce a given English sentence step by step to a number of simpler English sentences. Semantically, the rules recursively associate to each pair of a sentence S of a language L and a model W for L a two-person zero-sum game $G(S, W)$. The players of the game can be thought of as the proponent of S and its opponent. S is true in W if the proponent of S has a winning strategy in the game $G(S, W)$. For the concepts of the mathematical theory of games, see, for example, Luce and Raiffa (1957) or Owen (1968).

Let me repeat some of these rules here in a somewhat simplified form.

(G.an)   When the game has reached a sentence S of form
            $X-[_{NP} \, a/an \; N]-Y$,
            the proponent of S may choose an individual, let it be called
            "A," and the game is continued with respect to
            A is a/an N, and $X-A-Y$.

(G.the)   When the game has reached a sentence S of form
            $X-[_{NP} \, the \; N]-Y$,
            the proponent of S may choose an object A while the oppo-
            nent of S chooses an object B, whereupon the game is contin-
            ued w.r.t.
            A is/are (a/an) N, and $X-A-Y$, and if B is/are (a/an) N,
            then B, is/are A.

(G.every) When the game has reached a sentence S of form
            $X-[_{NP} \, every \; N]-Y$,
            the opponent of S may choose an individual, say B, and the
            game is continued w.r.t.
            if B is a/an N, then $X-B-Y$.

(G.some)   When the game has reached a sentence S of form
            $X-[_{NP} \, some \; N]-Y$,
            the proponent of S may choose an object, say A, and the
            game is continued w.r.t.
            A is/are N, and $X-A-Y$.

The predeterminer *all*, a universal quantifier over partitive domains, commands a rule analogous to the interpretation of durative adverbials. The comparison is better put the other way around: Durative adverbials turn out to be simply a special case of partitive universal quantifiers. The game rule (G.all) is motivated by observations like the following. When one says

(28)   *All the ground was speckled with leaves.*

one does not mean that there were absolutely no bare spots (that is even excluded by the meaning of *speckled*), only that there were no bare spots big enough to break a pattern of speckles. This is quite analogous to the way in which I construed durative adverbials.

This analogy will allow one and the same game rule (G.all) apply to interpret both occurrences of *all* in

(29)   *All the water flows all the time.*

—surely a desired result.

The game rule for *all* is something like

(G.all)   When the game has reached a sentence S of form
            A is/are N, and $X-all$ $A-Y$,
            where A is the syntactic head of *all,* the opponent of S may
            choose any member of some contextually determined partition
            (cover) of A, say he chooses B, and the game is continued
            w.r.t.
            if B is/are N, then A is/are N and $X-B-Y$.

The game rules introduce new logical constants into the game, along with auxiliary conjuncts and conditions—notably, *and, if,* and the copula *be*. I shall not write out the game rules for these expressions here. Roughly, sentences conjoined with *and* are tested sequentially from left to right; the proponent of the conjunction wins the game if he gets to the end of the sequence without losing a single subgame. *If* invites the opponent of the main clause to try and vindicate the conditional clause. If he is successful, the proponent of the hypothetical has to defend the main clause.

The interpretation of *be* is an interesting chapter of natural language semantics. For the present purpose, it is enough to say that it ambiguously represents the operations of identity, membership and class inclusion. The last interpretation is relevant in copular sentences with partitive subject.

3.6. Ordering Principles

A powerful property of rules of interpretation in Hintikka's game-theoretical semantics is that they are in the main intrinsically unordered. Given a particular sentence and the set of game rules, there is usually a large number of different game possibilities, depending on the order in which different game rules are applied. For instance, the quantifier rules given earlier are essentially context free, interpreting in themselves one quantifier at a time paying no attention to their environment.

If nothing more could be said, we would expect sentences with several quantifiers to be multiply ambiguous. And indeed, this is often the case, as is well known from examples like

(30)   *There is an answer to every question here.*

However, natural languages have means of reducing such ambiguity. Syntactic precedence and dominance relations are one way. Thus (31)

(31)   *There is an answer here which satisfies every question.*

is not ambiguous in the way (30) is.

Such syntactic principles are registered by the general ordering principles (O.command) and (O.precede).

(O.command) If a constituent C commands another constituent D but not vice versa, a game rule must not be applied to D before a game rule has been applied to C.

(O.precede) If a constituent C precedes another constituent D (in temporal or left-to-right order), a game rule must not be applied to D before a rule has been applied to C.

When these principles come into conflict, (O.command) usually overrides (O.precede), which is somewhat weaker anyway.

Another important means of reducing scope ambiguities is lexical multiplication of synonymous quantifiers which have different scope preferences. It seems to be characteristic of the way in which natural language manages scope relations that scope preferences are in a sense LOCAL: They typically resolve scope preferences between specific pairs of operators. In particular, such piecewise preferences need not always add up to a unique preferential linear ordering of operators in a given sentence. Different principles may conflict in some cases; in others, the order of operators may be left underdetermined. The result is exactly the kind of twilight world our intuitions of operator scope seem to describe.

Lexical ordering principles governing the order of specific quantifier words and other types of operators have been registered elsewhere (see Note 1). Among such preferences is the tendency of *some* to take larger scope than negation, whereas *every* gives way to *not;* *the* tends to go before several other quantifiers, whereas *an* gives way to them.

Recall now that durative adverbials are in themselves quantifiers of a sort. It is hence to be expected that certain preferences govern the order of interpretation of temporal adverbials and quantified noun phrases, too. Such preferences play a role in explaining the different aspectual properties of sentences exemplified by (15)–(23).

3.7. Games with Aspect

The first thing to determine in order to account for the aspectual properties of the Examples (15)–(23) is the inherent aspect of the atomic sentences underlying them. For this purpose, consider

(15) e. *Annie arrives.*

(16) e. *Nick comes in.*

(18) e. *Sylvester catches Tweety.*

(19) e. *Sylvester eats Tweety.*

(21) e. *Sylvester pedals over Harvard Bridge.*

(22) e. *David passes through Tennant Creek.*

These examples are atomic in the sense of Section 2.3. All of them are noncontinuous—some seem momentaneous, others are achievements or accomplishments.

Let us now look at the semantic game associated with (15a). Assume that the past tense of (15a) has been interpreted by a rule not relevant to the present concern. Next, (G.an) is applicable. The proponent of (15a) has to search for an appropriate individual. Let us assume he comes up with Annie and proceeds to defend the sentence

(15) f. *Annie is a guest, and Annie arrives.*

After an application of a rule for *and,* the game ends with one of the conjuncts of (15f). The first conjunct is an auxiliary sentence produced by (G.an); it is not relevant here. The second conjunct is nothing else than (15e).

On considering the strategies that the players have at their disposal in this game, we find, not surprisingly, that (15a) is true in any period in which (15e) or some variant of it with a different (or differently interpreted) subject noun, is true. The quantifier move by (G.an) preserves type of period of evaluation, as it only serves to pool together periods in which different variants of (15e) are true severally.

As a confirmation of this expectation, consider what happens if a durative adverbial is appended to (15a) to yield

(15) g. *A guest arrived all the time.*

The result is quite awkward. With some imagination, one may think of a series of iterated arrivals—that is, to interpolate a move by the rule of iterative interpretation after the interpretation of the adverbial so as to construe (15a) as continuous.

Notice that it seems practically obligatory for the guest to be a specific one on this reading; that is, (G.an) has to be applied before the rule (G.all) and the rule of iterative interpretation. In order to describe repeated arrivals of different guests, one takes recourse to the plural and uses (17a) instead.[30]

What is the reason for this curious restriction? It turns out to be a special case of a more general ordering principle of English concerning the order of interpretation of NONPARTITIVE AND PARTITIVE QUANTIFIER PHRASES. Consider

(32)   *All the water was poured into a bottle.*

It is hard to understand (32) to say that some quantity of water was partitioned into a number of different bottles. If that is the intent, one again takes recourse to the plural:

(33)   *All the water was poured into some bottles.*

The generalization is that a nonpartitive (singular count) quantifier takes right of way over a partitive (noncount or plural) quantifier. Let us dub this ordering principle (O.part). As expected, (O.part) also surfaces in plural cases. It is more natural to say in English

(34)   *Unicycles have wheels.*

than

(35)   *Unicycles have a wheel.*[31]

if mention is made of the defining property of unicycles. Recall now that durative adverbials as well as the rule of iterative interpretation in my reconstruction involve partitive quantification. The expectation is, then, on the basis of (O.part), that (15g) and sentences like it tend to have only the reading where the individual quantifier goes first.

3.8. Partitive Examples

For comparison, consider Example (16c). Watch what happens when a durative adverbial is attached to it:

(16)   f. *Some water came in all the time.*

The result is intuitively impeccable. Comparison with (16e) shows that the partitive subject has managed to turn an achievement into the activity sentence of (16a). Note, however, that although (16f) is a DESCRIPTION of

[30] This observation is due to Verkuyl (1971, p. 4).
[31] The examples (34)–(35) are Noam Chomsky's (Class lectures, MIT, 1978).

a process of water seeping in, it is itself no longer an activity sentence after the addition of the temporal adverbial, but an accomplishment.

These are the intuitions that await explanation. If I am right, the explanation is already there: One only has to apply game rules in their appropriate order.

The key to (16f) is the observation that the unstressed existential quantifier *some* generally gives way to universal quantifiers. For instance, the sentences

(36)   *Some water was poured into all the bottles.*

(37)   *Every bottle contained some water.*

are naturally understood so that different water went into each bottle. It is hard to take (36) and (37) as describing the fate of some specific amount of water. [*Some* would allow that interpretation, and *this* would decide in favor of it, if added before *water* in (36)–(37).]

Let us now look at the adverbial *all the time* more closely. From the predeterminer *all*, it is seen that the ambiguous noun *time* is here meant to have partitive extension. We already know how to interpret the quantifiers *the* and *all* in such contexts, so let us just apply rules to (16f).

After an application of (G.the), we have something like

(16)   g. *T is time, some water came in all T, and if T' is time, then T' is T.*

What the conditional sentence of (16g) does is to ensure the contextual uniqueness of the period of time referred to by *the time* in (16f). Every choice of a period T' available in the context must be part of the proponent's choice of period T.

Let me ignore the uniqueness condition in the sequel.

The next move comes by (G.all):

(16)   h. *If T'' is time, then T is time and some water came in at T''.*[32]

T'' is a member of a partition of T into smaller periods of time.

After detaching the auxiliary clauses, we are left with the main assertion

(16)   i. *Some water came in at T''.*

The temporal adverbial takes us to consider the truth of

(16)   j. *Some water comes in.*

with respect to the period T''. Now it is time to apply (G.some) to *some water,* with the result

---

[32] The preposition *at* is inserted by a minor adjustment rule.

(16)   k. *W is water, and W comes in.*

The first conjunct of (16k) is an atomic auxiliary clause, and the second conjunct is of form (16e), that is, an atomic sentence of noncontinuous aspect.

We have now reached the end of the game connected with (16f) without encountering any difficulties along the way. An inspection of the players' strategies in the game shows that (16f) is true if there is a way of splitting the period picked out by *the time* in (16f) into a number of overlapping or contiguous smaller periods, in each of which some or other amount of water comes in. And this is of course intuitively what (16f) says.

Let us think of the logic of this account. The activity nature of (16a), shown by the well-formedness of (16f). is based on the fact that a process of water seeping in can be divided, on account of the partitivity of water, into a series of overlapping or contiguous entries of distinct volumes of water. Thus the partitivity property of water figures in the account, but enters it only indirectly. The verb *come in* always stays noncontinuous.

Let me clear up a putative counterexample to the present account. Consider the sentence

(38)   *The man cleaned up a large area all day long.*

Intuitively, *a large area* may well be additive—that is, the sum of contiguous large areas is itself always a large area. Yet (38) is not well-formed meaning that someone was occupied with an increasing area all day long. And this possibility is indeed ruled out by the ordering principle (O.part) discovered earlier. In order to give precedence to *all day,* one has to revert to a partitive object, for example:

(39)   *The man cleaned up large areas all day.*

For contrast, let us finally consider the game connected with Sentence (16b), incremented by a durative adverbial:

(16)   l. *The water came in all the time.*

Intuitively, (16l) could be understood as a description of an iterated event, for example, a series of failures in an experiment of dam building. There is an ambiguity about the water involved: Either one and the same amount of water came in each time, or, possibly, fresh water was involved in the repetitions. This ambiguity depends on the order of application of (G.the) on *the water* and (G.all) on *all the time.*

What is noteworthy about (16l) is that it does not bring to mind a smooth process of water seeping through. Whence these subtle intuitions? Let us consider the game possibilities open in (16l). If the interpretation of *the water* is fixed first, we end up with a sentence of form

(16)   m. *W came in all the time.*

where *W* names an individual portion of water. As is familiar from (15g), a sentence like (16m) will not do unless a special rule of interpretation, most likely the iterative rule, intervenes.

The other play possibility, which starts from the durative adverbial, most naturally invokes the Chronology Principle introduced in Sections 2.2 and 2.7. The Chronology Principle allows time to be articulated, instead of by a clock, by, say, a series of successive experiments in dam building. In that case, the partition of the period of experimentation meant by *the time* may simply be the set of the experiments themselves. *The water* will, in each experiment, pick out the water used in the experiment. Note that, without this rearticulation, it would be hard to see what contextually unique portions of water *the water* could pick for each value of *all*.

It seems that the game we have just described is a live option: A frustrated experimenter in dam building can quite well utter (16l) meaning nothing else than what a more detached observer would express by

(16)   n. *The water came in every time.*

Amusingly enough, we have an explanation why (16l) sounds a little exaggerated as compared with the more sober version (16n). In (16n), objective articulation of time is preserved: the individual quantifier *every* serves to single out the set of experiments. In (16l), one has to look away from everything except the all-important experiments in order to accept the partitive quantifier.

The essential contrasts exhibited by Examples (15a), (16a) and (16b) are duplicated by the rest of the Examples (15)–(23). The reader is invited to try the game rules on other examples and figure out their aspectual properties. It should become clear in this process that the at first curious correlations between verb aspect and nominal reference are completely straightforward consequences of what is known of the aspect of atomic sentences on one hand and the logic of natural language quantification on the other hand. And that is what I set out to show in this part of the chapter.

ACKNOWLEDGMENTS

I am very thankful to my friends Annie Zaenen, Nicholas Ostler, David Nash, and Jane Simpson for the invaluable help and guidance they have given to me in my research, and for the patience they have shown in doing so.

REFERENCES

Allen, R.L. (1966). *The Verb System of Present-Day American English*. Mouton: The Hague.

Bennett, M., and Partee, B. (1972). *"Toward the logic of tense and aspect in English."* System Development Corporation, Santa Monica, Calif. (Available from the Indiana University Linguistics Club.)

Bunt, H. (1976). The formal semantics of mass terms. In F. Karlsson (Ed.), *Papers from the Third Scandinavian Conference of Linguistics*. Turku.

Burge, T. "Mass terms, count nouns, and change. *Synthese,* **31,** 459–478.

Carlson, L. (1976). Languages games and speech acts. In F. Karlsson (Ed.), *Papers from the Third Scandinavian Conference of Linguistics*. Turku.

Carlson, L. (in preparation) *Reference and Cross-Reference in Natural Language*.

Carlson, L., and Hintikka, J. (1979). Conditionals, generic quantifiers, and other applications of subgames. In F. Guenthner and S.J. Smith (Eds.), *Formal Semantics and Pragmatics for Natural Languages*. Dordrecht: D. Reidel.

Chomsky, N. (1957). *Syntactic Structures*. The Hague: Mouton.

Comrie, B. (1976). *Aspect*. Cambridge University Press.

Dowty, D. (1977). Toward a semantic analysis of verb aspect and the English 'imperfective' progressive. *Linguistics and Philosophy,* **1,** 45–77.

Heinämäki, O. (1974). *Semantics of English Temporal Connectives*. Unpublished doctoral dissertation, University of Austin, Texas.

von Helmholtz, H. (1930). *Counting and Measuring*. New York: Van Nostrand.

Hempel, C. G. (1952) *Fundamentals of Concept Formation in Empirical Science*. Chicago: University of Chicago Press.

Hintikka, K.J.J. (1968). Language-games for quantifiers. In N. Rescher (Ed.), *Studies in Logical Theory*. Oxford: Basil Blackwell. [Reprinted with revisions as Ch. III of J. Hintikka (1973), *Logic, Language-Games and Information,* Oxford: Clarendon Press.

Hintikka, K.J.J. (1974). Quantifiers vs. quantification theory. *Linguistic Inquiry,* **5,** 153–177.

Hintikka, K.J.J. (1975). On the limitations of generative grammar. In *Proceedings of the Scandinavian Seminar on Philosophy of Language*. Department of Philosophy, University of Uppsala, Uppsala.

Hintikka, K.J.J. (1976a). Quantifiers in logic and quantifiers in natural language. In S. Körner (Ed.), *Philosophy of Logic*. Oxford: Basil Blackwell.

Hintikka, K.J.J. (1976b). *The Semantics of Questions and the Questions of Semantics* (Acta Philosophica Fennica Vol. 28, No. 4). Amsterdam: North-Holland.

Hintikka, K.J.J. (1977). Quantifiers in natural language, some logical problems II. *Linguistics and Philosophy,* **1,** 153–172.

Hintikka, J., and Carlson, L. (1977). Pronouns of laziness in game-theoretical semantics. *Theoretical Linguistics,* **4,** 1–29.

Hintikka, J., and Saarinen, E. (1975). Semantical games and the Bach–Peters Paradox. *Theoretical Linguistics,* **2,** 1–20.

Jespersen, O. (1923). *The Philosophy of Grammar*. London: Allen and Unwin.

Joos, M. (1968). *The English Verb: Forms and Meaning*. Madison: University of Wisconsin Press.

Karlsson, F. (Ed.) (1976). *Papers from the Third Scandinavian Conference of Linguistics*. Turku.

Kelley, J.L. (1952). *General Topology*. New York: Springer Verlag.

Kiparsky, P. (1968). Tense and mood in Indo-European syntax. *Foundations of Language* **4**, 30–57.

Krantz, D.H., Luce, R.D., Suppes, P., and Tversky, A. (1971). *Foundations of of Measurement*. New York: Academic Press.

Luce, R.D., and Raiffa, H. (1957). *Games and Decisions*. New York: John Wiley & Sons.

McMullin, E. (Ed.) (1963). *The Concept of Matter in Greek and Medieval Philosophy*. Notre Dame: University of Notre Dame Press.

Moravcsik, J., and Gabbay, D. (1973). Sameness and individuation. *Journal of Philosophy*, **70**, 16, 513–526.

Noreen, A. (1903). *Vårt Språk*. Lund.

Owen, G. (1968). *Game Theory*. Philadelphia: Saunders Co.

Piaget, J., and Inhelder, B. (1941). *Le Developpement des quantités chez l'infant*, Neuchatel: Delachaux & Niestle.

Piaget, J. (1952). *The Child's Conception of Number*. New York: Humanities Press.

Piaget, J. (1968). *The Development of Memory and Identity*. Barre, Mass.: Clark University Press.

Poutsma, H. (1921). *The Characters of The English Verb and The Expanded Form*, P. Groningen: Noordhoff.

Quine, W.V. (1960). *Word and Object*. Cambridge, Mass.: MIT Press.

Rescher, N., and Urquhart, A. (1971). *Temporal Logic*. Vienna and New York: Springer Verlag.

Saarinen, E. (1977). Game-theoretical semantics. *The Monist*, **60**, 3, 406–418.

Saarinen, E. (Ed.) (1979). *Game-Theoretical Semantics*, Dordrecht: D. Reidel.

Taylor, B. (1977). Tense and Continuity. *Linguistics and Philosophy*, **1**, 199–220.

Vendler, Z. (1967). Verbs and times. In Z. Vendler, *Linguistics and Philosophy*. Ithaca: Cornell University Press.

Verkyul, H.J. (1972). *On the Compositional Nature of Aspects*. Dordrecht: D. Reidel.

Ware, R. (1975). "Some bits and pieces, *Synthese*, **31**, 379–393.

ASPECT AND VOICE: SOME REFLECTIONS ON PERFECT AND PASSIVE[1]

BERNARD COMRIE

1. INTRODUCTION

In an earlier publication (Comrie, 1976, pp. 84–86), I noted in passing, on the basis of observations by Indo-European scholars supplemented by my own, that there are certain correlations between aspect and voice, in particular between perfect (resultative) aspect and passive voice, that are manifested in a number of languages by forms that combine together expression of perfect aspect and of passive voice. The aim of this chapter is, first, to elaborate in more detail the theoretical basis of these correlations (Section 2); and, second, (in Section 3) to look at data from two further languages, Modern Eastern Armenian and Nivkh, that provide empirical support for these correlations and for the theoretical approach outlined in Section 2. The data are almost entirely from other linguists' accounts of these languages. The chapter attempts, therefore, not to present new material, nor even to offer a primary analysis of old material, but rather to show how such material, already given a primary analysis by other linguists, can be integrated into a general account of correlations between aspect and voice.

[1] This work was supported by a grant from the Social Science Research Council, London, for the investigation of the linguistic typology of the non-Slavic languages of the Soviet Union.

65

2. CONCEPTUAL FRAMEWORK

2.1. Aspect

The aspectual distinctions with which I shall be concerned in this chapter are a subset of those discussed in Comrie 1976, and I shall use the same terminology as in this earlier work. In addition, I shall retain the notational device used in Comrie 1976 of having an upper case initial letter for formal aspectual (or temporal/aspectual) categories in individual languages, and a lower case initial for conceptual aspect or time distinctions irrespective of any particular language. Where, however, I refer to a language-specific form by citing its morphological form, I shall use a lowercase initial, to preserve consistency of transcription, as there can be no confusion with language-independent concepts here [e.g., the -ɣəta form in Nivkh (Section 3.2)].

The aspectual categories most relevant to the present discussion are perfect, imperfective, and prospective. By PERFECT, I mean that a given form describes a state that is the result of an earlier situation by giving expression to the earlier situation: For instance, the English sentence *John has broken the cup* relates a present state (the fact that the cup is broken) to an antecedent cause (the fact that John broke the cup), and does so by using a form of *break the cup,* which in itself refers to the antecedent situation rather than to the resultant state, which latter is inferred from the use of a form with perfect meaning (*have* plus Past participle). The PROSPECTIVE is the inverse of this: A state is related to some subsequent situation, such that the seeds of this subsequent situation are already present in the earlier state, by giving expression to the subsequent situation; for instance, the English sentence *John is going to break the cup* relates a present state (John's state of mind, or more generally the state in which he is at present) to a subsequent situation (John's breaking of the cup), and does so by using a form of *break the cup,* so that the antecedent state has to be inferred from the use of a form with prospective meaning (*be going to* plus verb). In the IMPERFECTIVE, reference is to a single situation, which is viewed as ongoing, as if one were positioning oneself internal to the situation as a whole, with the possibility of looking both backward and forward at the rest of the situation; English examples would be *John is breaking the cup, John breaks cups, John loves Mary.*

These three conceptual aspects are independent of tense, so that, for instance, in addition to *John has broken the cup,* which relates a present state to a past situation, one can have in the perfect *John had broken the cup,* relating a past state to an even earlier situation, and *John will have broken the cup,* relating a future state to a situation preceding that future state (though without specifying the temporal location of that situation relative to the present moment). Similarly, one can have, in the prospective: *John was going to break the cup, John will be going to break the cup;* and in the imperfective: *John used to break cups, John will be breaking cups, etc.*

Although these aspectual distinctions are, in principle, independent of tense, in practice certain close correlations are found between these aspects and various tenses. Each of the three aspects contains an element of relative tense: In the perfect, one's viewpoint of the situation is from a later point, where its result is felt, so that the perfect has much in common with relative past tense; in the prospective, one stands as it were within a state and looks forward to some situation whose seeds are already contained in the state, so that the prospective has much in common with relative future tense; and, as the observer's vantage point for the imperfective is within the situation, this aspect has much in common with relative present tense. And often in language one finds relative tense, in the absence of any specific indication of the point to which the tense is relative, being interpreted as absolute tense, that is, with the present moment as reference point. Thus perfect relates through this chain to the past tense, especially perfective past (where imperfectivity is excluded). Well-known illustrations of this as a historical development are to be found in the Romance languages, for instance French, where an original distinction between the form *j'ai acheté* with perfect meaning ('I have bought') and *j'achetai* with perfective past meaning ('I bought') has been lost in the spoken language with the Perfect form encroaching to take over both meanings: *j'ai acheté* 'I bought' and 'I have bought'. In German, a similar development has gone even further, with the form *ich habe gekauft,* originally having perfect meaning ('I have bought'), becoming the only form with past tense meaning, irrespective of aspect, in certain varieties of the language (i.e., 'I have bought', 'I bought', 'I was buying', 'I used to buy'). In the same way, imperfective is linked through this chain to present tense, and prospective to future tense. Indeed, even further links are possible with the prospective, insofar as it expresses the potential of a future situation, and is therefore related to modal distinctions, such as potentiality, irrealis.

The correlations I shall be outlining in Section 2.3 have their basis in correlations between aspect and voice. But because there are also the correlations between aspect and tense, in many instances one finds correlations between tense and voice, these correlations being mediated (perhaps diachronically) by aspect. Because of this, one may use the cover-term tense-aspect, where the distinction between tense and aspect is irrelevant or where a given form combines tense and aspect specification.

2.2. Voice

The discussion of voice in this chapter is based on the following assumptions. I assume that the lexical representation of a given predicate will specify how many arguments that predicate takes, and provide a characterization of each argument independent of alternative ways of expressing that argument in derived syntax. Corresponding to a given set of lexical arguments of a predicate, there may be more than one way of encoding these arguments in surface syntax (or, more generally, derived syntax), and the difference among these various encodings is a difference in voice. In this chapter, I am concerned with a relatively restricted set of argument combinations, so that the discussion can be reduced to the following. I shall be concerned primarily with one-place and two-place predicates. The single argument of a one-place predicate (or at least, of most one-place predicates) may be symbolized by S. The two arguments of a two-place predicate may be symbolized as A and P: the argument A is, for the majority of predicates, agentive (e.g., with the predicate 'kill'), though in individual languages a number of nonagentive arguments are usually assimilated to this class (for instance, *John* in English *John saw Bill*); the argument P is, for the majority of predicates, patient of that predicate. Thus the classification of lexical arguments corresponds closely to, although it is not identical with, a classification into semantic roles (agent, patient, *etc.*).

In most languages, one finds that, from the viewpoint of derived syntax, a single noun phrase from among the arguments of a predicate is singled out for preferential treatment—preferential in that, for instance, it alone undergoes a number of syntactic rules such as movement rules, agreement rules, *etc.* (the precise range of such rules characterizing a single noun phrase varies considerably from language to language). This noun phrase we shall call the SUBJECT of the sentence. More generally, the notion of "subject" can be viewed as a weighting of ROLE-RELATED PROPERTIES (in particular, agentivity) and REFERENCE-RELATED PROPERTIES (such as topicality, definiteness), such that the subject is relatively high on both these scales (see, further, Keenan, 1976, and, for a more critical approach, Foley and Van Valin, 1977). However, as we have dealt with role-related properties under the lexical representation of the predicate, in our discussion of voice we may concentrate on reference-related properties. Just as lexical arguments do not correspond exactly to case-roles, although they can be regarded as grammaticalizations of case-roles, so too the notion of subject (concentrating on reference-related properties) does not correspond exactly to the notion of topic (theme), although it can be regarded as a grammaticalization thereof. Thus subjects, as identified by language-specific behavior (amenability to movement rules, triggering of agreement, *etc.*), are typically agentive, and are typically thematic, but there is no requirement that they should be so.

As already indicated, I regard voice as a relationship between the set of lexical arguments and the set of surface syntactic arguments, in the latter case paying particular attention here to subjects. In the case of one-place predicates, the S is usually the subject of the sentence. (Exceptions would be, for instance, impersonal passives of the type Latin *curritur*, literally '(it) is-run', that is, 'running takes place', with no S. I do not discuss such examples further here, and in the discussion that follows "passive" should be taken to mean "personal passive.") With two-place predicates the situation is rather more complex, as in principle the subject properties could characterize either A or P, or be distributed between them; moreover, the terminology in this area (with such terms as active, passive, and antipassive; ergative, and accusative) is confused and unstandardized. Because in this chapter, I am concerned solely with the distribution of subject properties relative to A and P, I need in fact only to make a two-way distinction: (*a*) reference-related properties characterize A; (*b*) (at least some) reference-related properties characterize P. Type (*a*) we shall abbreviate as active-accusative (more fully, active-accusative-antipassive), as it subsumes these three types (more accurately: it includes accusative actives and all antipassives); Type (*b*) we shall abbreviate as passive-ergative, as it subsumes ergative and passive. Differentiation of the types grouped together here is discussed, for instance, in Comrie (1978), and the simplified set of distinctions made here is maintained solely because these are the only distinctions relevant to the present topic, namely correlations between aspect and voice. To summarize even further the brief discussion of this section, we can say that the active-accusative implies A-orientation, whereas the passive-ergative implies P-orientation.

[To amplify these statements somewhat for clarification: The term passive is usually used where a marked (morphologically complex and/or contextually restricted) voice with P-orientation contrasts with an unmarked voice with A-orientation (or at least, a greater degree of A-orientation). The term antipassive indicates a marked voice with A-orientation contrasting with an unmarked voice with P-orientation (or at least, a greater degree of P-orientation). An unmarked voice with (at least, some) P-orientation is ergative. An unmarked voice with A-orientation is active and accusative. Variation in terminology consists primarily in relaxing the condition of markedness, so that ergative would be subsumed under passive, for instance, because of the P-orientation.]

2.3. Aspect and Voice Correlations

In language in general, there seems to be a marked bias toward A-orientation, to having A as subject in derived syntax—that is, a preference for active and accusative syntax rather than for passive and ergative syntax. However, under certain conditions, this bias can be either weakened (increased incidence of P-orientation) or further strengthened (even lower incidence of P-orientation). One such set of conditions is aspect. The present section will establish a general explanatory framework for this claim. As I am concerned primarily with A-orientation versus P-orientation, I shall restrict the discussion for the most part to two-place predicates.

With the perfect, one is interested in a state resulting from an earlier situation, and, as I am restricting the discussion to two-place predicates, one may therefore ask the question: To which of the two participants is the resulting state primarily attributed, that is, is the state A-oriented or P-oriented? With some sentences with perfect meaning, either A-orientation or P-orientation is equally likely; an example is *John has hit Bill,* where the point at issue may be either Bill's state after having been hit or John's state (e.g., the fact that he has broken his thumb) after hitting Bill. With most two-place predicates, however, in particular those that, lexically, describe a change in state [e.g., 'kill', 'melt', (transitive), 'move' (transitive)], the state is attributed primarily to P. Suppose one takes sentences of the type *John has killed Bill, John has melted the ice, John has moved the chair,* and suppose one wishes to ascertain whether or not these sentences are (at least potentially) true. Suppose, moreover, that the only test one is allowed to carry out is to observe the state before and after the putative change of state takes place, but not to observe directly whether or not the change of state takes place. If one were to examine John, then, whether or not he has done any of these things, it is quite likely that there would be no ascertainable change in him. On the other hand, if one were to examine Bill, the ice, or the chair, then one would notice a marked change in the state of Bill (he would be dead), or the ice (it would be water), or the chair (it would be in a different place). Thus the resultant change of state is attributed primarily to P, rather than A, in the perfect. Given this, one might expect the perfect to favor P-orientation, that is, that the perfect would be more likely than other aspects to correlate quite highly with passive-ergative. Given the relationships between perfect, past perfective, and past, one would also expect to find correlations between past perfective and passive-ergative, between past and passive-ergative.

The prospective introduces precisely the opposite correlation. If one takes sentences like *John is going to kill Bill* or *That falling rock is going to hit Bill,* then one is attributing a certain potential to John or to the falling rock, rather than to Bill. Although *John is going to kill Bill* might serve to indicate Bill's state as a potential victim, it is much more likely to be used to inform of John's state of mind. More generally, potentialities are more likely to be attributed to A than to P, so that we would expect prospective, future, potential, and irrealis to favor A-orientation, to correlate with active-accusative. In fact, I have very few examples where an active-accusative prospective/future/potential/irrealis contrasts with passive-ergative elsewhere. McConvell (1976, p. 192) notes that in the Australian language Yukulta, which has basically ergative case-marking, the accusative system (antipassive) is used in the nonpast irrealis. I suspect that the apparent rarity of such examples is due to the following factors: (*a*) because language is biased toward A-orientation anyway, a contrast between A-orientation in the prospective and P-orientation elsewhere is less likely than a contrast between basic A-orientation and P-orientation in the perfect; (*b*) in most of the world's languages that have been most fully studied to date, a well-developed distinct prospective (future, potential, irrealis) is much less common than a well-developed perfect (past perfective, past)—it is perhaps significant that the only example I have been able to give is from an Australian language: in many Australian languages, the basic tense-aspect distinction is future/irrealis versus nonfuture/realis, so that further investigation of Australian languages might well uncover more such examples.

Imperfective aspect occupies an intermediate position: If one is observing a situation internally to that situation, then in principle one could orient oneself either to A or to P, though given the overall tendency of language to favor A-orientation one would expect the result to be predominance of A-orientation. One of the subdivisions of imperfective aspect, however, namely habitual aspect, might be expected to lead to some increase in the level of A-orientation, given that referring to a habitual occurrence—where no instance of the occurrence need be taking place at the moment of speaking—is in some ways akin to a potential mood.

In the discussion of data in Section 3, I shall be concerned primarily with the contrast between P-orientation in the perfect and A-orientation elsewhere.

3. DATA

3.1. Armenian (Modern Eastern)

The data I will examine from Modern Eastern Armenian (i.e., the variety of Armenian currently spoken in Soviet Armenia) are almost all taken from the excellent summary of voice in Armenian by Kozinceva (1974). Of the various tense-aspects in Armenian, I shall restrict myself to those forms that relate to past situations (including, where appropriate, subsequent results of past situations). Three such tense-aspects in Armenian are the Imperfect, the Aorist, and the Perfect, each of which exists in the active and passive. In the examples in Table 4.1, *Ašot* is a proper name, which occurs with the definite article -*ə*/-*n*; *namak* means 'letter', giving with the definite article *namakə* 'the letter' (in the examples, I follow the convention tacitly adopted by Kozinceva of having an indefinite direct object, 'a letter', in the active, but a definite subject, 'the letter', in the passive, to provide more natural sentences); most verb forms are periphrastic, consisting of the auxiliary verb 'to be' (e.g., *e* 'he is', *er* 'he was') and a participle (e.g., Present *grum* 'writing', Past *grel* 'having written'), although the Aorist is a finite verbal form; in the passive, the verb stem takes a suffix -*v*, while the agent is either unexpressed or, less commonly, constructed as an oblique form, for instance the dative (which takes no definite article) with the postposition *koɣmicʰ*.

On the basis of these forms, there is no particular correlation between aspect and voice, rather, they are two independent dimensions in the Armenian verbal system. However, Armenian has another set of forms with perfect meaning, the so-called Resultative, formed from the Resultative participle in -*ac* and the auxiliary 'be'. Although both the Perfect and the Resultative have perfect meaning, they are not completely synonymous. In particular, the Perfect combines perfect meaning with perfective meaning, that is, refers to a state resulting from a single event that took place in the past, whereas the Resultative can combine perfect meaning freely with other aspectual parameters. An example cited by Kozinceva (1974, p. 85) will illustrate this:

(1)   *Srčaranum hačax drvac   er ʒʲi cxaxot.*
      café-in   often placed-Resultative was free tobacco
      'In the coffee house free tobacco was often laid out.'

The sense of this sentence is that, as a regular phenomenon, free tobacco could be found lying about in the coffee house, as a result of someone having put it there; in other words, one has a habitual past result of a prior action. If one were not to use the Resultative, then the appropriate tense-aspect would be the Imperfect (communicating the habituality, though losing the idea of result of a previous action), not the Perfect.

TABLE 4.1. Active and Passive in the Past Tense in Armenian

	Active	Passive
Imperfect	Ašotə namak er grum.	Namakə grvum er Ašoti koymic^h.
Aorist	Ašotə namak grec^h.	Namakə grvec^h Ašoti koymic^h.
Perfect	Ašotə namak e grel.	Namakə grvel e Ašoti koymic^h.

Even where both Perfect and Resultative are possible, they differ slightly in meaning, in that the Resultative places more emphasis on the result, whereas the Perfect places somewhat more emphasis on the cause: Compare the examples k^hnac e 'he has fallen asleep' or 'he is asleep' versus k^hnel e 'he has fallen asleep' (but not 'he is asleep'), cited by Fairbanks and Stevick (1958, p. 227). In some cases, the Resultative indicates a state that is difficult to relate explicitly to a cause, for example, (Kozinceva, 1974, p. 85):

(2)   *Petrosə aramarvac   er   pajk^{h}ari*
        Petros   despise-Passive-Resultative was   fighting
        ənkerneric^h.
        companions-by
        'Petros was despised by his fellow combatants.'

Conceivably, the verbal form in -*ac* should be defined as a stative, with perfect meaning as one of the submeanings of stative meaning. For present purposes, however, only -*ac* forms with perfect meaning are relevant. Overall, one can thus say that perfect meaning is more prominent in the Resultative than in the Perfect: As far as aspect and voice are concerned, the Perfect does not differ from other tense/aspects, whereas the Resultative shows precisely the kind of correlation between perfect aspectual meaning and passive voice that one would anticipate.

The Resultative can be formed from both intransitive and transitive verbs. With intransitive verbs, the voice is of course active, the one argument of the intransitive verb functioning as subject (e.g., *Ašotə bezarac e* 'Ašot has become tired, Ašot is tired'). With transitive verbs, the only productive, reasonably frequently occurring construction with the Resultative is in the passive, with the suffix -*v*, as in the following example (Kozinceva, 1974, p. 83):

(3)   *K^{h}ayak^h-* ə   *šrǯapat* -*v*   -*ac*   *e*
        city   the surround-Passive-Resultative is
        (*t^{h}šnamu koymic^h*).
        enemy by
        'The city has been surrounded (by the enemy).'

In Modern Eastern Armenian, then, one has good evidence for the correlation between perfect aspect and passive voice: There is a form with perfect meaning (the Resultative) which, when formed from transitive verbs, appears only in the passive.

Before leaving Armenian, there are two less central uses of the Resultative of transitive verbs that should be examined—one apparently somewhat restricting the aspect–voice correlation, the other strengthening it further. A few transitive Resultative participles survive in Modern Eastern Armenian in active form and with active meaning (e.g., *xmac* 'drunk' from *xmel* 'to drink', *kardacʰac* 'well-read' from *kardal* 'to read'). However, these are not serious exceptions to the general correlation, as the phenomenon is restricted to a few verbs, and, moreover, these Resultative participles have been lexicalized, with meanings more specific than the combination of the meaning of the Resultative with the lexical meaning of the verb—thus *xmac* means 'drunk, inebriated', and not just 'having had something to drink', and *kardacʰac* means 'well-read', not just 'having read'. Interestingly enough, for translations of these Armenian forms, English also offers items that are, formally, Past participles of transitive verbs (*drunk, well-read*), which in English usually have P-orientation, but in these items refer exceptionally to the agent of the action of drinking or reading. Moreover, the state of being drunk (i.e., inebriated) or of being well-read (as opposed to just read) is clearly predicatable of A rather than P, that is, of the person who has drunk or read a lot rather than of the things he has drunk or read. In other words, pragmatically, given the lexical specialization of *drunk* and *well-read*, one would expect A-orientation.

The second deviation from the most usual construction with the Resultative participle of transitive verbs is for the Resultative participle to be in the active form (without *-v*), but still to function as a passive, as in the following example cited by Kozinceva (1974, p. 84), with the transitive Resultative participle *kaxac* from *kaxel* 'to hang' (transitive):

(4)   *Bajcʰ lvacʰkʰi tʰokʰicʰ kaxac*   *e miajn jerku*
         but   washingline-on hang-Resultative is only   two
         hin toprak.
         old sack
         'But on the washing-line only two old socks have been hung.'

The possibility of such examples in Modern Eastern Armenian, even though they are rare, emphasizes further the correlation between perfect meaning and passive voice: The correlation is so strong that forms with perfect meaning (i.e., the Resultative) are interpreted as passive even in the absence of passive morphology, where from a formal viewpoint the Resultative participle is active.

3.2. Nivkh

Nivkh, also known as Gilyak, is a language isolate spoken near the mouth of the River Amur and on Sakhalin Island in the Soviet Far East. The verb form of interest here is that with the suffix -ɣəta, and the data derive exclusively from Nedjalkov *et al.* (1974). In the majority of instances, this suffix expresses a state resulting from a preceding situation, that is, has perfect meaning. (There are also some predicates where -ɣəta indicates a state not (necessarily) resulting from a previous situation, for example, *člə ma*-ɣəta-*d'* 'the sky is clear' [(Nedjalkov *et al.,* 1974, p. 243). Compare the discussion of the Armenian sentence (2).] Where the verb to which -ɣəta is attached is intransitive, then the state is attributed to its S, and this noun phrase functions as subject—for example, *anaq yo-d'* 'the iron rusted', but *anaq yo*-ɣəta-*d'* 'the iron has rusted (and is now rusty)'. The interesting cases are where the verb is transitive.

If one looks first at verbs taking just one object, then one finds that there are a few examples where A remains subject of the -ɣəta form, as in the following (Nedjalkov *et al.,* 1974, p. 245):

(5)   *Andx pʰrə-nə   -d' if yim   -d'.*
        guest come-Future   he find-out
        'He found out that the guest would come.'

(6)   *Andx pʰrə-nə-d' if yim-*ɣəta-*d'.*
        'He has found out/knows that the guest will come.'

Usually, however, the state is attributed to the P, which functions as subject of the -ɣəta form, in which case A is obligatorily omitted. In Nivkh, there is a simple morphological test for direct object status that can be applied in the presence of a certain subset of verbs, although noun phrases are not themselves case-marked for subject, direct object, or indirect object. Certain verbs change their initial consonant when accompanied by a direct object, which must immediately precede the verb; such verbs have up to four distinct initial consonants, depending on the final segment of the direct object. The following two examples illustrate the use of -ɣəta to indicate a state resulting from a previous situation with change of voice (Nedjalkov *et al.*, 1974, p. 236):

(7)   *Umgu   t'us   tʰa   -d'.*
      woman meat roast
      'The woman roasted the meat.'

(8)   *T'us   řḁ-ɣəta-d'.*
      'The meat has been roasted.'

In (7), *t'us* 'meat' is direct object of the verb, which therefore has the initial *tʰ*-. In (8), *t'us* is no longer direct object of the verb (in fact, it is subject), and this is shown by a different initial consonant on the verb, namely *ř̥*-.

With some verbs, either of two objects may appear as subject in the -ɣəta form (Nedjalkov *et al.*, 1974, p. 240):

(9)   *If   kʰuva   nux   tʰə   -d'.*
      he thread needle insert
      'He inserted the thread into the needle.'

(10) *Kʰuva nux tʰə-ɣəta-d'.*
      'The thread has been inserted into the needle.'

(11) *Nux kʰuva ř̥ə-ɣəta-d'.*
      'The needle has had the thread inserted into it.'

In (9), the direct object *nux* immediately precedes the verb and, since this verb shows the *ř̥* ~ *tʰ*- alternation, we have initial *tʰ*-. In (10), the other object *kʰuva* has been made subject; *nux* remains direct object, and therefore the verb, now with the suffix -ɣəta, still has initial *tʰ*-. [Note that initial *ř̥*- rather than *tʰ*- in (8) therefore cannot be attributed directly to the presence of -ɣəta, as (10) shows that the initial mutation to *tʰ*- is compatible with -ɣəta.] In (11), *nux* is made subject; words ending in a vowel do not trigger the mutation of *ř̥*- to *tʰ*-, so initial *ř̥*- in the verb of (11) provides no evidence of the grammatical relation of *kʰuva*.

The Nivkh data presented are very similar, in terms of the correlation between aspect and voice, to those presented earlier for Armenian, despite the immense economic and cultural gap between traditional Armenian society and traditional Nivkh society. However, Nivkh does present one interesting new twist to the aspect–voice correlation, and this stems from a particularly rigid interpretation of perfect aspectual meaning. In Nivkh, the result that emanates from the preceding situation must be an ascertainable change of state in the entity to which that property is attributed. In the examples presented so far this has not been apparent, as all these examples could be translated reasonably literally into other languages with a special form to indicate perfect aspect. In certain cases, however, this restriction means that Nivkh sentences with the -ɣəta form have a rather different meaning from their literal translations into, say, English, as with the following example cited by Nedjalkov *et al.* (1974, p. 237):

(12)   *Arak   ra -   ɣəta-d'.*
         vodka drink

One might imagine that (12) means 'the vodka has been drunk', and certainly this sentence is possible in English, the result of the situation of vodka-drinking being, for instance, the presence of empty bottles or glasses, or the inebriation of the guests. However, if one says *The vodka has been drunk* in English, one is not attributing an ascertainable result of vodka-drinking to the vodka in question: Indeed, (barring application of surgical techniques in any case unavailable in traditional Nivkh society), the fact that vodka-drinking has taken place is ascertained from the state of entities other than the vodka (e.g., the bottles, the guests). In Nivkh (12) cannot be used this way. However, (12) is not excluded in Nivkh, rather it is possible with the meaning 'some of the vodka has been drunk' (sc. but some remains)—by comparing the vodka before and the quantity of vodka that remains, one CAN ascertain from the vodka alone that some of it has been drunk. This interpretation is a natural consequence of the restrictive meaning of the -ɣəta form in Nivkh.

In this chapter, I am arguing that correlations between aspect and voice, and specifically between perfect aspect and P-orientation (e.g., passive voice), are not purely mechanical correlations, to be handled in a purely formal way, but rather that these correlations stem from features of the semantics and pragmatics of the aspectual and voice categories involved. The Nivkh data provide striking confirmation of the basic soundness of this approach. There is no rigid mechanical correlation between aspect and voice in Nivkh, because some transitive verbs take -ɣəta but with retention of A as subject, and some passives in -ɣəta have more restricted meanings than any corresponding active [e.g., (12)]. Change in voice and restriction in meaning are dictated not by formal properties of the sentences concerned, but rather by the general constraint that changes in state expressed by the -ɣəta form must be ascertainable changes of state in the entity to which they are attributed (i.e., the subject). In (6), 'he has found out/knows that the guest will come', the only ascertainable change of state is in the A of the main clause (his knowledge has expanded)—it makes no sense to ask if an ascertainable change of state has been undergone by P, here an embedded sentence. In (8), 'the meat has been roasted', and (12), '(some of) the vodka has been drunk', the ascertainable change of state has taken place in P, and this therefore appears as subject. In (10) and (11), respectively 'the thread has been inserted into the needle' and 'the needle has had the thread inserted into it', there is an ascertainable change of state in both the thread (it is now in the needle, whereas before it was not) and the needle (it now contains a thread, whereas before it did not), and so either of these two noun phrases can function as subject of the -yəta form.

4. CONCLUSIONS

In this chapter, I have tried to present a semantic-pragmatic explanation for correlations between aspect and voice, especially between perfect aspect and passive voice. Some of the idiosyncrasies noted in the relations between aspect and voice in Modern Eastern Armenian and in Nivkh, although quite exceptional from the viewpoint of a formal aspect–voice correlation, find a natural explanation in terms of this semantic-pragmatic approach.

REFERENCES

Comrie, B. (1976). *Aspect: An Introduction to the Study of Verbal Aspect and Related Problems*. London and New York: Cambridge University Press.

Comrie, B. (1978). Ergativity. In W.P. Lehmann (Ed.), *Syntactic Typology: Studies in the Phenomenology of Language*. Austin and London: University of Texas Press. Pp. 329–394.

Fairbanks, Gordon H., and Stevick E.W. (1958). *Spoken East Armenian*. New York: American Council of Learned Societies. (Reissued in 1975 by Spoken Language Services, Ithaca, New York.)

Foley, W.A., and Van Valin, R.D. (1977). On the organization of "subject" properties in Universal grammar. In *Berkeley Linguistic Society 3*. Department of Linguistics, University of California, Berkeley. Pp. 293–321.

Keenan, E.L. (1976). Towards a universal definition of "Subject." In C.N. Li (Ed.), *Subject and Topic*. New York and London: Academic Press. Pp. 303–333.

Kozinceva, N.A. (1974). Zalogi v armjanskom jazyke. In A.A. Xolodovič (Ed.), *Tipologija Passivnyx Konstrukcij: Diatezy i Zalogi*. Leningrad: Nauka. Pp. 73–90.

McConvell, P. (1976). Nominal hierarchies in Yukulta. In R.M.W. Dixon (Ed.), *Grammatical Categories in Australian Languages*. Canberra: Australian Institute of Aboriginal Studies. Pp. 191–200.

Nedjalkov, V.P., Otaina, G.A. and Xolodovič, A.A. (1974). Diatezy i zalogi v nivxskom jazyke. In A.A. Xolodovič (Ed.), *Tipologija Passivnyx Konstrukcij: Diatezy i Zalogi*. Leningrad: Nauka. Pp. 232–251.

ON THE DEFINITION OF THE TELIC–ATELIC (BOUNDED–NONBOUNDED) DISTINCTION

ÖSTEN DAHL

1. TERMINOLOGY

In many discussions of aspect and related categories, a semantic distinction is made which is exemplified by the verb phrases in Columns A and B:

A	B
sing	*make a chair*
ride a bicycle	*go to London*
write	*write a letter*
write letters	
work	*kill the President*

It is observed that the verb phrases in Columns A and B behave differently in several respects. Thus, the A verb phrases combine with adverbial phrases such as *for two hours,* whereas the B cases take, instead, adverbial phrases such as *in two hours:*

(1)   *I sang for two hours/*in two hours.*

(2)   *I wrote a letter *for two hours/in two hours.*

79

Syntax and Semantics, Volume 14
Tense and Aspect

Further, a sentence containing an A verb phrase with the main verb in the present progressive tense will entail the corresponding sentence with the verb in the perfect future, whereas this is not the case for the B verb phrases. Thus, (3) entails (4), whereas (5) does not entail (6).

(3)   *I am singing.*

(4)   *I will have sung.*

(5)   *I am writing a letter.*

(6)   *I will have written a letter.*

Intuitively, the semantic difference is that the B verb phrases contain a reference to a "terminal point," where the action or process comes to an end, whereas the A cases do not.

The distinction between the cases in the A and B columns, which was formulated by Aristotle (Kenny, 1963; Taylor, 1977), has subsequently been "rediscovered" and renamed several times. As a result the terminology is chaotic. I give the following list of some of the terms that have been used, without claiming that I have found them all.[1] When a pair of terms is associated with a specific author, I give the reference to that author within parentheses.

A	B
energeia	kinesis (Aristotle)
imperfective	perfective
cursive	terminative
irresultative	resultative
durative	nondurative
nonpunctual	punctual
nonconclusive	conclusive
nontransformative	transformative
noncyclic	cyclic (Bull, 1963)
atelic	telic (Garey, 1957)
nonbounded	bounded (Allen, 1966)
activity	accomplishment (Vendler, 1967)
activity	performance (Kenny, 1963)
nepredel'nyj	predel'nyj [Russian]
nicht-grenzbezogen	grenzbezogen [German]

Part of the explanation for this terminological confusion is that aspect-

---

[1] The list is an expansion of a list given in S.-G. Andersson 1972.

ologists differ as to whether they recognize one or two distinctions. There are thus two positions, which I shall refer to as the "Western" and the "Eastern" view, respectively, since these names correspond—very roughly—to the geographical distribution of their adherents. Thus, whereas the "Eastern" view dominates in the Slavic world, most of the adherents of the "Western" view either belong to the philosophical tradition emanating from Aristotle or are non-Slavic linguists who have tried to apply concepts from Slavic aspectology to their own languages. Whereas the "Westerners" recognize one distinction only, the adherents of the "Eastern" view claim that two distinctions must be made, one of which would distinguish (7) on the one hand, from (8) and (9), on the other, whereas the other would distinguish (7) and (8) from (9).

(7)   *I was writing.*

(8)   *I was writing a letter.*

(9)   *I wrote a letter* (taken to imply *"I finished it"*).

2. THE T PROPERTY AND THE P PROPERTY

Typically, the terms that were listed are used to refer to the first distinction, whereas the second distinction is named differently, if it is named at all. For instance, S.G. Andersson 1972, which is a recent exposition of the "Eastern" view, refers to the first feature as "Grenzbezogenheit" and to the second as "Erreichung/Nicht-Erreichung einer Grenze." We shall here use the terms "the T property" and "the P property," respectively, for the two purported concepts. I say "purported" because, as we shall see, it is not clear what the concepts are and if they can really be kept apart. Let us now turn to the definitions that have been proposed for the T and P properties. As was the case with the terms, the definitions given vary from author to author. The following are two alternative definitions of the T property taken from recent works:

A situation, process, action, *etc.* or the verb, verb phrase, sentence, *etc.* expressing this situation, *etc.* has the T property iff

(DEFINITION 1, S.G. Andersson 1972) it is directed toward attaining a goal or limit at which the action exhausts itself and passes into something else.

(DEFINITION 2, Comrie 1976) it leads up to a well-defined point behind which the process cannot continue.

Given any of these definitions, the P property could then be defined in the following way:

A situation, process, action, *etc.* has the P property iff it has the T property and the goal, limit, or terminal point in question is or is claimed to be actually reached.

Before returning to the problems with these definitions, we shall make a few general remarks. To start with, we shall note that there is a definite logical relation between the two purported properties—if something has the P property, it also has the T property. In other words, the P property entails the T property. This means that there are only three possible combinations of the properties, as illustrated in Table 5.1. The critical cases, which motivate the distinction between the two properties, are those in the upper right-hand box, that is, such sentences as (8), where the goal or terminal point—the letter being finished—is referred to although it is not claimed that it is actually attained.

At least one possible way of looking at the perfective–imperfective opposition in Slavic and other languages is that verb phrases that do not have the T property are always imperfective, whereas verb phrases that have the T property are perfective or imperfective according to whether they have the P property or not. Thus, S.G. Andersson (1972) claims: "Die tatsächliche Erreichung und die tatsächliche Nichterreichung der Grenze sind Inhaltsmerkmale des perfektiven bzw. des imperfektiven Aspekts im Russischen [p. 62]."

Therefore, the counterpart of (8) in the Slavic languages—for example, the Russian sentence (10)—is in the imperfective aspect, as it does not have the P property. This, of course, is in accordance with the view that the perfective aspect is the marked member of the opposition.

(10)   *Ja pisal pis'mo.*

Adherents of the "Western" view, on the other hand, tend to analyze (8) as being derived from (9) by applying a "progressive operator." This solution is more natural for a language like English, where (8) is in fact grammatically more complex than (9).

TABLE 5.1. Combinations of the T Property and the P Property

	not-T	T
not-P	*I was writing.*	*I was writing a letter.*
P	(does not occur)	*I wrote a letter.*

3. PROBLEMATIC CASES

I shall now turn to some of the problems connected with the definitions. The first problem is: What should the purported properties be regarded as properties of? In the literature, we find the concepts applied to at least the following: sentences, verb phrases, verbs as lexical items, verb forms, situations, and processes.

The most popular alternative at present would probably be to say that they apply primarily to processes (situations) and secondarily to the verb phrases or sentences that express these processes. However, there is a difficulty with this. Seeing John sitting at his desk, we may answer the question *What is he doing?* by using either (11) or (12).

(11)   *He is writing.*

(12)   *He is writing a letter.*

Both these sentences can thus be said to describe the same situation. Nevertheless, (12) is said to have the T property, whereas (11) does not. Thus, the T property cannot be a property of a situation or process per se: It comes only as the result of describing the situation, that is, subsuming it under a concept of a situation (process), or in extensional terms, under a class of situations (processes). In other words, the T property (and also the P property) must be regarded as applying primarily to situation (process) concepts or classes, according to whether an indication of a goal or limit is included in the criterial properties of the members of this class or not. (In the same way, the same object may be described by a mass concept or a count concept—we may say of the same thing *This is gold* and *This is a nugget*.) A linguistic expression, whether it be a sentence, verb phrase, or verb, will be said to have the T or P property iff it expresses a concept with the property in question. As we shall see later, this formulation is not without its problems, but we shall ignore them for the time being.

The second point to be discussed pertains to the terms "goal," "result," "limit," "terminal point," and "end-state" which appear in the definitions of both the T and the P properties. It is not often pointed out that one cannot equate all these without further discussion.[2] Any process that comes to an end has a terminal point. This terminal point may be defined by a certain state-of-affairs, as when the coming into being of the chair defines the terminal point of the making of the chair. But the terminal point may also be defined, for example, by indicating some other mea-

---

[2] But see, for example, E. Andersson (1977, p. 118) and Johanson (1971, p. 228) for discussions of the problems involved.

sure (e.g., *This car has run 20,000 miles*). In these cases. an "end-state" cannot be defined independently of the action: We can understand what it means for a chair to exist without referring to how it comes into being, but we cannot understand what it means for a car to have a certain mileage without referring to the process of running.

In all the cases mentioned, we must distinguish "potential (intended or probable) terminal points" from "actually achieved terminal points," and accordingly, among linguistic expressions, between "indicators of potential terminal points" and "indicators of actual terminal points":

(13)   a. *John is studying* **for a bachelor's degree.**   (potential, i.e., intended result)
       b. *John has completed* **a bachelor's degree.**   (actually achieved result)

(14)   a. *I am going to France* **for two months.**   (potential duration)
       b. *I traveled in France* **for two months.**   (actual duration)

(15)   a. *I am staying* **until he returns.**   (potential temporal limit)
       b. *I stayed* **until he returned.**   (actual temporal limit)

Some languages are more systematic than English in distinguishing indicators of actual and potential terminal points. Thus, Swedish uses different prepositions in the translations of (14a)–(14b).

(14)   a'. *Jag reser till Frankrike* **på** *två månader.*

(14)   b'. *Jag reste i Frankrike* **i** *två månader.*

It is even possible to construct a sentence that contains both kinds of terminal point indicators, as in the admittedly nonoptimal Sentence (15):

(15)   *Han har suttit inne på två år i sex veckor.*
       'He has been serving a two-year sentence for six weeks.'

We can see that the distinction between indicators of potential and actual terminal points corresponds to the distinction between the T and P properties (although a sentence may have one of these properties without there being an overt indicator of a terminal point). This distinction will also play a crucial part in the further discussion.

Having established the difference between "potential" and "actual" terminal points, our next question is: How potential may a potential terminal point be? Saying that "a process leads up to a terminal point" or "has built into it a terminal point" may be interpreted as involving one or more of the following conditions:

(16)   There is a terminal point *t* such that
   a. if *t* is reached, the process cannot continue.
   b. *t* will be reached in the normal course of events (= if nothing unexpected intervenes).
   c. *t* will be reached in all possible courses of events.

Accepting (c) would make the T and P properties collapse, and that cannot be what the authors cited want. We can therefore leave (c) out of the discussion, although the wording of the definitions does not exclude it. Condition (b) is more interesting. Consider the sentence-pair (17)–(18).

(17)   *John is building a house.*

(18)   *John is trying to build a house.*

It seems that (b) is entailed by (17) but not by (18)—that is, (17) but not (18) says that we can expect the house to be finished. We also see that (17) does not entail (19), although (18) entails (20).

(19)   *John will have built a house.*

(20)   *John will have tried to build a house.*

It is therefore tempting to include (b) in the definition of the T property. However, we shall see that there are cases that fulfill (b) that are still problematic.

At the beginning of this chapter, we presented two classes of verb phrases, which were said to differ in their "behavior" in at least the following two ways:

(21)   a. The A class took *for*-phrases whereas the B-class took *in*-phrases.
   b. In the A cases, the present progressive entailed the future perfect.

Normally, these or similar "tests" have been taken as criteria for what is a T verb phrase and what is not. In an earlier version of this chapter, I referred to them as "behavioral tests" for the T property. What I was interested in was whether there were any cases in which these "behavioral tests" gave different results than the definitions quoted earlier. I claimed that if such cases could be found, we must conclude that the "behavioral tests" did not really test the T property but something else. To this the following objection can be made (G. Carlson, personal communication). Behavioral tests like these should be regarded as means for getting rid of vaguenesses in the definition, that is, as criteria for deciding the unclear cases. Thus, there will not be any contradiction in saying, for example, that a VP by the definition appears to have the T property but fails to do so by the behavioral tests. However, there are alternative ways of looking at the relations between (21) and the definitions given earlier. For example, (21a)–(21b) may be viewed as observed facts to be explained and the definitions as part of the explanation (i.e., as characterizations of the general semantic property distinguishing the two classes). In that case, a contradiction or an apparent contradiction between (21) and a definition shows that there is something wrong with the definition—either it is wrong or so vague that it cannot be properly applied. In fact, even on Carlson's view, an apparent contradiction shows at least that the definition is not satisfactory. The question, then, is if it can be amended and how.

Let us now turn to the problematic cases. Consider the following sentence:

(22)   *The submarine moved toward the North Pole.*

Sentence (22) describes a process, "moving toward the North Pole," that has a well-defined potential terminal point, namely, the point in time when the submarine reaches the North Pole. This would thus seem to be a point at which the process will "exhaust itself" and "pass into something else" and "beyond which it cannot continue." In other words, the process appears to have the T property as defined. In addition, at least given the assumption that the North Pole is stationary, Condition (16b) is fulfilled (the submarine will reach the North Pole under normal circumstances). However, if we try to apply the behavioral tests, the results are not what we would expect. Thus, the sentence can be expanded with a *for*-phrase rather than an *in*-phrase:

(23)   *The submarine moved toward the North Pole for two hours.*

Similarly, (24) entails (25).

(24)   *The submarine is moving toward the North Pole.*

(25)   *The submarine will have moved toward the North Pole.*

I have chosen this example, because it is a very clear one as to its semantic interpretation.[3] But there are several other classes of examples that

[3] There is in fact another reason for choosing this kind of example. Garey (1957, p. 106) defines "telic verbs" as "a category of verbs expressing an action tending towards a goal." Ironically, the verb phrase *tend towards a goal* fails the "tests" for the T property ("telicity") used by Garey himself.

may be slightly less unambiguous but still provide reasonably clear examples of verb phrases (sentences) that suit the definitions but fail the behavioral tests of the T property.

At least one example has already been mentioned, namely, (13a). It seems to meet the definition—there is a well-defined terminal point, John's prospective degree—but in the tests it behaves like a non-T example, it takes a *for*-phrase, as can be seen in (26), and has the entailment (27).

(26)   *John studied for a bachelor's degree for two years.*

(27)   *John will have studied for a bachelor's degree.*

We can contrast this with *complete a bachelor's degree,* which takes an *in*-phrase—see (28)—and which does not have the corresponding entailment—(29) does not entail (30).

(28)   *John completed a bachelor's degree in two years.*

(29)   *John is completing a bachelor's degree.*

(30)   *John will have completed a bachelor's degree.*

The crucial difference between *study for a bachelor's degree* and *complete a bachelor's degree* is that the first contains an unequivocal indicator of a potential terminal point, whereas *a bachelor's degree* in the latter is normally taken to be an actual terminal point (notable exception: progressive tenses).

Further cases in point are examples of a construction that is not very frequent in English but that is systematically exploited in some other Germanic languages. I am referring to sentences like (31) (from Verkuyl, 1972) and (32), which are Dutch and Swedish, respectively:

(31)   *Katinka breide aan een trui.*
         Lit. 'Katinka knitted at a sweater.'

(32)   *Katinka stickade på en tröja.*   [= (31)]

In these sentences, the goal, and, presumably, the potential end-point of an activity are indicated by a prepositional phrase. Compare (31)–(32) with (33)–(34), which contain the same verbs with direct objects:

(33)   *Katinka breide een trui.*
         'Katinka knitted a sweater.'

(34)   *Katinka stickade en tröja.*   [= (33)]

The semantic difference seems to be that whereas the terminal point in the sentences with prepositional phrases is unequivocally potential, it is preferably interpreted as actual in the direct object construction.[4] As for the behavioral tests, we see that (31)–(32) behave like non-T sentences, whereas (33)–(34) behave like T-sentences. We see once more that the tests distinguish those verb phrases that contain indicators of actual terminal points (in the nonprogressive tenses) from those that do not.

If this is generally the case, the motivation for keeping apart the T and P properties in the theory of verbal aspect becomes considerably less well motivated. It may be questioned whether the T property is really relevant for aspectology at all. Is there any way to save the situation? It may of course be that the definitions are faulty and have to be remedied. It might be possible to find a reformulation of the T-property that would exclude the troublesome cases. One could, for instance, suggest that what is relevant is really some stronger form of goal-directedness. However, such an attempt to find a reformulation is faced with the following dilemma. If we want to say, as does for instance Andersson (1972, p. 41), that the German sentence (35) differs from (36) by having the T property ("Grenzbezogenheit"), and interpret this to mean that (35) "eine gbz. Handlung bezeichnet" whereas (36) does not, what are we to say of the English sentence (37), which is the natural translation of (36) and maybe also of some uses of (35)?

(35)   *Er baute ein Haus.*

(36)   *Er baute an einem Haus.*

(37)   *He was building a house.*

At least for Comrie (1976), sentences of this type are the paradigm examples of "sentences which describe telic situations." (Comrie's first example is *John is making a chair*).

Sven-Gunnar Andersson (personal communication) suggests the following way out. We should distinguish two classes of VPs: One class contains verb phrases that include in their semantic description an indication

---

[4] The interpretation of sentences such as (31)–(32) presents a problem, because, although it is clear that the final goal of the activity is indicated by the propositional phrase, it is not clear that the agent mentioned is the one who is supposed to attain it. Another example is a better illustration of this:

(i)   *Arbetarna byggde på ett hus.*
        'The workers worked on a house.'

        (lit. 'The workers were building at a house')

Sentence (i) does not exclude the possibility that the workers in question are there only temporarily and will soon be replaced by someone else.

of a limit or a result-state which can be realized and remain potential. The other class contains VPs that either lack indications of end-points or where the end-point is only potential. I think this is a way to save the suggested classification of VPs: Notice, however, that it means that we abandon the idea of a one-to-one correspondence between classes of VPs and classes of situations (or even classes of classes of situations). Under this proposal, we do not distinguish VPs as to whether they express situations with certain properties, but rather as to whether they can, in some context, express such situations. Notice also that it is the P property that is relevant in the end, as the crucial property of the first class of VPs is whether they can ever have this property.

As Greg Carlson points out (personal communication), there is the following difficulty in the definition of the P property. If we take the definition as it stands, the VP *built a house* would have the P property in (38) but not in (39), as only (39) has the entailment ''A house came into existence.''

(38)   *John built a house.*

(39)   *John possibly built a house.*

Intuitively, there is no aspectual distinction between (38) and (39), and they also both have Russian translations with the perfective aspect:

(38′)   *Ivan postroil dom.*

(39′)   *Vozmožno, čto Ivan postroil dom.*

This seems to show that if the definition of the P property is to be useful in aspectology, we have to apply it to ''unembedded'' or ''extensional'' cases of VPs. But this, in fact, throws further doubt on the distinction between the T and P properties, because it allows for ''potentiality'' also in the P property. In particular, if we claim that (39) in fact has the P property, by relating it to (38), on what grounds are we then claiming that a sentence such as (37), which was quoted as a paradigm example of the combination [+ T, − P], cannot be treated in the same way?

My personal opinion is that it may not be worthwhile to go on and try to refine the definitions of the properties we have been talking about in this chapter. Rather, a better understanding of the problems will be obtained by developing an adequate explicit semantics which takes account of aspectual distinctions. In particular, things may become clearer if we consider, not only the meanings of various forms, but also how these meanings have to be derived. For example, it may be argued that (36) and (37) are derived in quite different ways although they seem to mean more or less the same. Thus, (36) should probably be analyzed in accordance with the "Western" view cited earlier, that is, by the following steps:

1. Start from the verb *build*, which does not contain any indication of a terminal point.
2. Add the actual point indicator *a house*, yielding *build a house*.
3. Apply the progressive operator, yielding *be building a house*.
4. Convert this into the past tense, yielding *was building a house*.

A verb phrase like the German *baute an einem Haus*, on the other hand, could be derived in the following way:

1. Start from the verb *bauen* (no terminal point indicated).
2. Add the potential terminal point indicator *an einem Haus*, yielding *an einem Haus bauen*.
3. Convert this into the past tense, yielding *an einem Haus baute*.

The crucial difference would thus be that in the first case, we go via a verb phrase with the P property, that is, *build a house*. It is not quite unproblematic how to extend this kind of analysis to other examples, but at least it may be a possible approach.

ACKNOWLEDGMENTS

I am indebted to Sven-Gunnar Andersson and Greg Carlson for commenting upon an earlier version of this chapter, which, as a result of their comments, has been revised fairly thoroughly. However, they should not be blamed for the shortcomings of the final version.

REFERENCES

Allen, R.L. (1966). *The Verb System of Present-Day American English*. The Hague: Mouton.
Andersson, E. (1977). *Verbfrasens struktur i svenskan. En studie i aspekt, tempus, Tidsadverbial och Semantisk Räckvidd*. Åbo: Åbo Akademi.
Andersson, S.-G. (1972). *Aktionalität im Deutschen: Eine Untersuchung unter Vergleich mit dem Russischen Aspektsystem*. Uppsala: Acta Universitatis Upsaliensis.
Bull, W.E. (1963). *Time, Tense, and the Verb: A Study in Theoretical and Applied Linguistics, with Particular Attention to Spanish*. (University of California Publications in Linguistics 19).
Comrie, B. (1976). *Aspect*. Cambridge: Cambridge University Press.
Garey, H.B. (1957). Verbal aspect in French. *Language, 33* 91–110.
Johanson, L. (1971). *Aspekt im Türkischen*. Uppsala: Acta Universitatis Upsaliensis.
Kenny, A. (1963). *Action, Emotion, and Will*. London and New York: Humanities Press.
Taylor, B. (1977). Tense and continuity. *Linguistics and Philosophy, 1*, 199–220.
Vendler, Z. (1967). *Linguistics and Philosophy*. Ithaca, New York: Cornell University Press.
Verkuyl, H.J. (1972). *On the Compositional Nature of the Aspects*. Dordrecht: D. Reidel.

ASPECTUAL "SKEWING" IN TWO AUSTRALIAN LANGUAGES: MARA, NUNGGUBUYU[1]

JEFFREY HEATH

1. GENERAL

This chapter presents data from two Aboriginal languages spoken on the western coast of the Gulf of Carpentaria in northern Australia. In Mara, verbs show two formally independent aspectual systems, one of which also undergoes semantic skewing in environments where aspect as such is neutralized. In Nunggubuyu, a system of "nominal aspect" preserves an aspectual character only in certain environments, and is generally subject to full or partial semantic skewing in combination with other grammatical categories. This chapter thus focuses on the interaction of aspect with the "environment."

---

[1] My fieldwork between 1973 and 1976 was supported by the Australian Institute of Aboriginal Studies. A grammar-text-dictionary volume on Mara has been completed and will hopefully be published in Australia. A grammar-text-dictionary volume on Nunggubuyu is in preparation. The grammars will compensate for the sparse exemplification in this brief chapter, and will describe additional details and "irregularities" not treated here.

Syntax and Semantics. Volume 14
Tense and Aspect

2. MARA VERBAL ASPECT

A simple Mara verb form has the shape PRF-(RDP-)ASP-ROOT-SFF. (Many verb complexes also include a preposed verb particle, so that this simple verb form functions as an auxiliary.) The symbol PRF includes pronominal subject- and object-markers, and sometimes other prefixes. The symbol RDP represents a reduplicative morpheme, indicating prolongation or repetition and compatible only with certain ASP and SFF categories. We are mainly concerned with ASP and SFF.

Basically, ASP represents a binary opposition between DUR (durative) and NONDUR (nondurative); the markedness relationship suggested by these labels is manifested both formally and distributionally. For several verbs, DUR is formed by a stem-initial consonantal change: $y \rightarrow j$, $w \rightarrow b$, etc.[2] For some others, a special DUR prefix is added, hence -nbu- becomes -gu-nbu-. In some of these latter cases, the prefix is actually a frozen reduplicative morpheme (formally distinct from RDP; hence -yaga- becomes -jaga-yaga- (note $y \rightarrow j$ as well). A few verbs have no DUR–NONDUR opposition; this is true mainly of roots beginning in m (we indicate in what follows that most of these roots, in compensation, have especially elaborate suffixal aspect systems). Some verbs roughly express the DUR–NONDUR opposition by root-suppletion (e.g., -ya- / -miŋn-), but in these cases the distribution of the two roots does not exactly coincide with that of DUR and NONDUR forms of regular verbs, and there may even be a partial DUR–NONDUR opposition overlain on one or both of the roots (hence -ya- in -ya-/-niŋu- forms NONDUR -ya- and DUR -ja- by $y \rightarrow j$).[3]

The system of suffixes (SFF) involves tense, aspect, and other categories. Negation is expressed by the preverb *ganagu* (past or present actual) or *ŋula* (past potential, future, imperative), but the presence of one of these preverbs also requires modifications in suffixation. Suffixes distinguish PUN (punctual) from NONPUN (nonpunctual) in the past positive and future positive. The complete set of suffix oppositions, in combination with negative preverbs and the curious third person pres-

---

[2] Thus -yarawu-/-jarawu- 'to take dogs hunting' and -waru-/-baru- 'to defecate'. Another alternation is Ø versus g before a vowel, hence -alu- / -galu- 'to hold'. In theory, we could consider these alternations to represent either lenition ($j \rightarrow y$) or hardening ($y \rightarrow j$). There is no purely phonological argument for either analysis. The bulk of the morphological and morphophonemic data point to the hardening analysis, hence taking y, w, and Ø as basic (though not necessarily "underlying").

Many verb roots function only as Aux's and thus cannot be translated, hence the omission of glosses in some examples.

[3] Without going into details, we can say that the suppletive pairs tend to use only one root with each suffix category, but there are many exceptions to this generalization.

TABLE 1. MARA SUFFIXAL AND PREVERBAL OPPOSITIONS

(1) X-ROOT-PaPun	past punctual positive
(2) X-ROOT-PaCon	past continuous positive
(3) X-ROOT-Pot	past potential positive
(4) ŋula X-ROOT-Pot	past potential negative
(5) ganagu X-ROOT-Pot	past/present negative
(6) wa-X-ROOT-Pr$_3$	present/evitative positive (3rd, 3rd → 3rd)
(7) X-ROOT-Pr$_{1-2}$	present/evitative positive (other persons)
(8) X-ROOT-Pr$_3$	future indefinite positive
(9) X-ROOT-FutPun	future punctual positive
(10) X-ROOT-FutCon	future continuous positive
(11) X-ROOT-Imper	imperative positive
(12) X-ROOT-Desid	desiderative positive
(13) ŋula X-ROOT-FutPun	future/imperative negative

ent/evitative prefix *wa-* is shown in Table 1 (where -X- represents PRF-RDP-ASP- or PRF-ASP-).

Suffixal labels like "PaPun" and "Pr$_3$" represent formal categories only, and in some cases it is difficult to choose a meaningful label.[4] For example, "Pot" occurs in present and past negative forms (potential or actual), and in the past potential positive, but not in present or future potential positive forms; its distribution thus involves not only mood but also tense and negativity. Similarly, the label "PR$_3$" for one form is chosen because it occurs in Combination (6), whose normal function is to express present tense (positive) for third person subject (if transitive, the object must also be third person). However, the label "PR$_3$" is misleading, as Combination (6) can also be evitative (a "lest . . . " clause warning of an undesirable event or circumstance which can be averted by appropriate action), and we find it also in Combination (8) (future indefinite positive) for all pronominal categories (not just third). As a general comment about the verbal system of Mara, it is difficult or impossible to find a single core meaning (*Grundbedeutung*) for a particular morpheme. Because each morpheme (and each morpheme slot) is part of an overall functional system, the essential principle is that the "basic" or "underlying" meaning of each morpheme (if it can be ascertained at all) is skewed in different contexts to maximize its FUNCTIONAL COMPLEMENTARITY to other morphemes. In other words, the overall system of oppositions in the verb complex makes sense, though the distribution of individual elements in it often seems chaotic and bizarre.

Thus the *ŋula* versus *ganagu* opposition (not found in English, for example) is motivated functionally by the absence of affixal oppositions in

[4] To simplify the labels, Con (continuous) is used here instead of NonPun (nonpunctual).

Combinations (4) and (5). The presence of *wa-* in Form (6) (through -X-here already contains a specific third person pronominal prefix) is motivated by the fact that it permits an opposition between Forms (6) and (8) (present/evitative versus future indefinite) for third person subject (and object). Because the present/evitative for other pronominal persons—Combination (7)—has a suffix (PR_{1-2}) distinct from that of Combination (8)[(Pr_3), though here not restricted to third person], Combination (7) has no need of a morpheme like *wa-*.

Notice that aspectual alternations in the suffix system occur in the past positive—(1) versus (2)—and future positive—(9) versus (10). Actually, for most verbs the FutPun and FutCon suffixes are indistinguishable (*-y*), so Combinations (9) and (10) are identical and there is no suffixal aspectual opposition in the future forms. (For the remaining verbs, including the most important stems beginning in a nasal and thus lacking a DUR–NONDUR stem-initial alteration, the FutPun and FutCon suffixes are again both *-y* but the preceding vowel undergoes a shift $a \rightarrow i$ in the FutPun only, hence /*-ma-y*/ $\rightarrow$ /*-mi-y*/ $\rightarrow$ *-mi-∅* FutPun versus *-may-y* FutCon.)

For the majority of verbs, then, the suffixal aspect system boils down to Pun versus NONPUN (= Continuous) in the past positive. In many of these paradigms there is no clear evidence as to which of the two forms is unmarked. However, there are some defective paradigms where only one past positive form occurs; thus "eat" has only the single past positive form *-ya-ḷi* (usually *-ja-ḷi* in DUR form). This cannot be explained as a phonological merger, and the suffix *-ḷi* here is definitely a PaCon (not PaPun) ending in other paradigms. Hence, on grounds of defective distribution, we take the PaPun form as marginally more marked than the PaCon form. (In addition, normally only the PaCon form can co-occur with true reduplication, -RDP-, though this is to be expected on semantic grounds.)

It remains to describe the interaction between the DUR–NONDUR stem-initial aspectual opposition (not shown in Table 1) and the remaining morphemes (shown in Table 1). The basic point, again, is that the uses to which the DUR–NONDUR opposition is put are best interpreted in terms of functional complementarity to the rest of the system, rather than by trying to extract a common feature in all DUR forms, distinguishing them as a class from all NONDUR forms. I argue that we must contextualize the analysis of the meaning of the stem-initial opposition—in other words, that the labels DUR and NONDUR are oversimplified and arbitrary.

First, let us examine how DUR and NONDUR operate in the past positive and future positive (where aspect is also expressed, at least potentially, by the PUN–NONPUN suffixal opposition). Here we get a maximal paradigm of three combinations for each tense, consisting of the partial intersection of two binary oppositions. The combinations that occur are: (*a*) NONDUR stem-initial with PUN suffix; (*b*) NONDUR stem-initial with NONPUN suffix; and (*c*) DUR stem-initial with NONPUN suffix. The combination of DUR with PUN does not occur. Note that these distributional data justify our decisions to label DUR and PUN as the respective marked forms in their own paradigmatic oppositions.

In careful speech (for example, in short utterances produced by informants in elicitation sessions), the (*b*) combination does not occur. Instead, the two oppositions (stem-initial and suffixal) line up exactly, so that NONDUR implies PUN and DUR implies NONPUN. But in casual speech, as for example in narrated texts, the (*b*) form is quite common. Although the suffixal PUN–NONPUN opposition remains stable from one style to another, the stem-initial DUR–NONDUR opposition shows a clear markedness asymmetry, with the marked DUR stem-initial becoming progressively less common (even with the NONPUN suffixes) as we move from careful to casual speech. Even in the most casual speech, the DUR stem-initial can occur (and does so commonly), but at this level it must be clearly justified semantically; for example, it is regular with true reduplication (RDP) in all styles. But in aspectually ambiguous forms DUR becomes uncommon in casual speech and it often replaced by its unmarked counterpart NONDUR.

Consider, for example, the root -ŋa- 'to see'. This happens to be one of the roots that forms the DUR by a special prefix, here -mi-. The PaPun suffix is -ji, the PaCon -ni. Hence, in careful speech, we get ŋa-na-ji (NONDUR PUN) and ŋa-mi-na-ni (DUR, NONPUN), which correspond to French *je l'ai vu* and *je le voyais*, respectively, except that ŋa-mi-na-ni is rather more common than *je le voyais*. In more casual speech, ŋa-mi-na-ni tends to be replaced by ŋa-na-ni (NONDUR, NONPUN) except that ŋa-mi-na-ni can still be used when the durative quality is clearcut or foregrounded. All three forms can be glossed 'I saw him' and contain 1Sg → 3Sg prefix ŋa-.

As mentioned earlier, for many roots the FutPun and FutCon suffixes are not distinct. For these paradigms the only aspectual opposition in the future is formed by stem-initial DUR versus NONDUR: 'I will see him' can be DUR ŋa-mi-na-y or NONDUR ŋa-na-y. Some other roots have distinct FutPun and FutCon endings, but generally lack the DUR–NONDUR opposition, so we again get a binary overall opposition: Auxiliary -ma- with 1Sg → 3Sg prefix has future forms ŋa-mi-∅ (PUN) and ŋa-ma-y (NONPUN). In careful speech, the DUR–NONDUR opposition for 'will see' is semantically identical to the PUN–NONPUN opposition for future forms of -*ma-;* in casual speech, however, the probability of the NONDUR form in the first case greatly increases, whereas the respective probabilities of the PUN and NONPUN forms in the second case remain stable.

For roots like 'to eat' which have defective paradigms lacking a PaPun form, the only past positive form (PaCon, here -*ya-ḷi*) can still form a binary DUR–NONDUR opposition (*ŋa-ja-ḷi* versus *ŋa-ya-ḷi*, both 'I ate it'); in this case the type *ŋa-ja-ḷi* (DUR) is more common and less restricted.

Hence, although many verbs have less than the maximal ternary opposition in the future, and some in the past as well, nearly all verbs end up with at least a binary aspectual opposition in both the past and the future.

However, in other environments the DUR–NONDUR opposition is used in other ways. Note that in Table 1, Form (5) is the negative for both past and present tense, though these tenses are clearly distinguished in the positive. As it happens, the DUR–NONDUR opposition is called into action here, splitting Form (5) into a past form (NONDUR) and a present form (DUR). Thus from -*na-* (DUR -*mi-na-*) 'to see' we get *ganagu ŋa-na-yi* 'I did not see him' but *ganagu ŋa-mi-na-yi* 'I do not see him'. Even in emphatically durative contexts, such as 'We never used to eat parrots [a tabooed food]', informants avoided using DUR with past negatives. Hence what was initially presented as a purely aspectual stem-initial DUR–NONDUR opposition here functions as a tense opposition (a pragmatic categorization).

Similarly, in Table 1, Combinations (6) (third person) and (7) (other persons) are labeled "present/evitative positive." The evitative, it will be recalled, is a "lest . . ." clause specifying an undesirable event or condition which can be avoided by appropriate action. To keep this formally distinct from the present positive, the DUR–NONDUR opposition is used, with DUR marking the present positive and NONDUR the evitative. Hence we get present positive *wa-'-mi-na-ja* 'He sees him and *ŋa-mi-na-jini* 'I see him' versus evitative positive *wa-'-na-ja* 'lest he see him'[5] and *ŋa-na-jini* 'lest I see him' (root -*na-* "to see," DUR -*mi-*, Pr_3 -*ja*, Pr_{1-2} -*jini*). Because the evitative can be used freely with statives as well as event verbs, there is no natural association between it and nondurative aspect; the use of NONDUR stem-initials with the evitative can only be explained as a device to keep evitative distinct from present (aspect neutralized to save a more important mood opposition).

In those remaining cases where the DUR–NONDUR opposition is unnecessary and undergoes neutralization, normally the unmarked NON-

---

[5] The symbol ' represents the (complete) phonological elision of 3Sg (intransitive) or 3Sg → 3Sg pronominal prefix -*wu-*.

DUR form is found; hence we get NONDUR initials (regardless of meaning) in the following Table 1 combinations: (4) (past potential negative), (11) (imperative positive), and (13) (future/imperative negative). The one exception is the desiderative, Form (12), a rare and specialized form translatable "hopefully" (and requiring preverb ŋariwa). The use of the DUR initial with this form can be explained by noting that the -Desid suffix is simply a perturbation of the -Pr₃ ending, and the form as a whole thus seems to be built on the present positive form (which always takes DUR).

It seems, then, highly doubtful that we can extract a single common feature that distinguishes DUR from NONDUR semantically across all environments. Rather, it appears that the meaning of the opposition is skewed to fit the particular functional requirements of each environment, and where it can fulfill no useful function the opposition is neutralized. Indeed, explaining this as "skewing" of a basically aspectual opposition (which "becomes" a tense opposition or whatever in given environments) gratuitously assumes that the durative/nondurative sense seen in the past and future positive (but even there with additional stylistic skewing) is logically prior to the other contextualized senses. I would argue that the search for a "unified" analysis of this opposition is a fundamentally misguided research strategy, and that the details we have provided make sense in functional terms even without discovering invariant semantic properties of each morpheme.

3. NUNGGUBUYU NOMINAL (AND VERBAL) ASPECT

Our principal concern in this language is with nominal aspect, but we begin with a brief outline of verbal aspect as well. As in Mara, there is a complex interaction between prefixal and suffixal systems, and it is even more difficult in Nunggubuyu to determine invariant meanings for particular forms. There are again two negative particles, wa:ṛi (= Mara ganagu) and yagi (= Mara ŋula). Also as in Mara, there is a binary prefix opposition which I call simply A versus B, but in Nunggubuyu this is tightly fused with the pronominal prefixes rather than with the stem-initial (in most cases, if you allow a no-holds-barred generative phonological analysis, the B form turns out to be, in deep structure, the same as the A form with an additional morpheme -wan- interspersed with the other pronominal morphemes). There is only a limited similarity between the A–B opposition and the Mara DUR–NONDUR opposition in fine details of distribution, with A being roughly correlated with the Mara NONDUR. The Nunggubuyu suffix system is only roughly comparable to that of Mara:

The Mara PaCon and Pot are combined into a single category (PaCon); the FutPun suffix (rather than Pot) is used in the present negative; there is a special FutNeg suffix which spills over into the evitative (where it competes with the true Evit suffix). The confusion between FutNeg and Evit suffixes causes no difficulties because there is an obligatory Evit enclitic suffix -*magi* which keeps evitative and future negative distinct. In Table 2, the numerals represent suffixal and preverbal oppositions and the subcategories [such as (2a)] represent the interaction of these oppositions with the A–B prefixal opposition.

Although the mechanical details at the level of individual morphemes and morpheme slots differ greatly from Nunggubuyu to Mara, the overall system of oppositions is fairly similar. Without going into the Nunggubuyu system in detail, it should be apparent that the need for contextualization of semantic analysis of these morphemes is even clearer than in Mara. I can see no hope for a "unified" analysis of the meaning of the A–B opposition, nor of such suffixal categories as FutPun (which occurs in the future punctual positive and in the present negative, but not in the future negative, for example). Contextualization and functional complementarity are far more important for understanding this system than is the isolation of a *Grundbedeutung* for each component morpheme.

Unlike Mara, Nunggubuyu also has a system of what we might call (with reservations) "nominal aspect." Every noun in this language belongs to a particular noun class (adjectival nouns "agree" with a given noun or referent in particular contexts). For human nouns, there is only one form of the noun-class prefix (NC), so the only opposition is presence versus absence of the prefix, and for these nouns it normally is present in all syntactic environments except in vocatives. For nonhuman nouns,

TABLE 2 NUNGGUBUYU SUFFIXAL AND PREVERBAL OPPOSITIONS

(1) PRF$_A$-ROOT-PaPun	past punctual positive
(2) a. PRF$_A$-ROOT-PaCon	past continuous positive
b. PRF$_B$-ROOT-PaCon	past potential positive
(3) *wa:ri* PRF$_B$-ROOT-PaCon	past negative
(4) *yagi* PRF$_B$-ROOT-PaCon	past potential negative
(5) a. PRF$_A$-ROOT-FutCon	present positive
b. PRF$_B$-ROOT-FutCon	future continuous positive
(6) PRF$_B$-ROOT-FutPun	future punctual positive
(7) *wa:ri* PRF$_B$-ROOT-FutPun	present negative
(8) *yaga* PRF$_A$-ROOT-FutNeg	future negative
(9) PRF$_A$-ROOT-Evit-*magi* FutNeg	evitative positive
(10) *yagi-magi* PRF$_A$-ROOT-Evit FutNeg	evitative negative

TABLE 3 Nunggubuyu noun-class Prefixes

(A) Human:		MSg/MDu na-		FSg/FDu ŋara-		Pl(3+) wara-
(B) Nonhuman:	NA	NGARRA	ANA	MANA		WARRA
PUN	yi:-	yi:-	a-	ama-		wa:-, wara-
NONPUN	na-	ŋara-	ana-	mana-		wara-

however, there are two forms for the prefix, which we may call PUN and NONPUN. If the absence of the prefix is also considered (as it must be for this type of noun), we have a three-way opposition. Our task is, then, to see how these oppositions behave in different morphosyntactic environments. The actual forms are shown in Table 3; we omit discussion of the semantic value of the nonhuman NC categories and will label them simply as ANA, MANA, *etc.*

The first rule for when to use the PUN versus NONPUN nonhuman prefixes (and when to omit the prefix) is this: In a negative clause, or in the protasis ("if . . .") of a conditional construction, the prefix must be present and it must take the NONPUN form. Thus the stem ŋargu 'wallaby' always takes the form ana-ŋargu (never *a-ŋargu or *ŋargu) in these environments, regardless of case category or other co-occurring categories. This rule overrides all other rules.

In other environments (i.e., in positive nonprotasis clauses), as a temporary approximation we may formulate the following rules for nonhuman nouns: (*a*) omit the NC prefix with instrumental case suffix -*miri;* (*b*) use PUN prefix with other nonzero case suffixes (Ablative -*wala,* Allative-Dative -*wuy,* Relative-Genitive -*yiñuŋ,* and others); and (*c*) use NON-PUN prefix with the zero Nominative case (used regularly for subject and direct object). Hence the common forms in positive clauses are ŋargu-*miri* 'by means of wallaby', *a-*ŋargu-*wala* 'from the wallaby' (likewise *a-*ŋargu-*wuy* 'to the wallaby,' *etc.*), and Nominative *ana-*ŋargu. Note that if this rule were strictly adhered to, the distribution of PUN and NONPUN prefixes (and absence of prefix) would be entirely determined by case marking and the positive versus negative opposition, and there would be no justification for considering this to be nominal aspect.

However, the distribution rule for positive clauses is actually more complicated. In particular, there are a fair number of textual examples of the type *ana-*ŋargu-*wuy* 'to the wallaby' with NONPUN prefix plus a nonzero case marker. Moreover, the type *a-*ŋargu and even prefixless ŋargu occur in Nominative function, showing that the NONPUN prefix is not obligatory here.

The first of these exceptions, the occurrence of *ana-ŋargu-wuy* along-side of *a-ŋargu-wuy,* is perhaps the only clearly aspectual opposition between NONPUN and PUN. The less common form, *ana-ŋargu-wuy,* occurs normally in passages describing habitual activity over a long term, as in 'We used to go (hunting) for (lit. 'to') wallabies'. It is not so much the plurality of 'wallabies' here as the frequentative aspect of the clause that encourages the use of *ana-* in place of *a-* here; nonhuman nouns are not ordinarily marked for number, and the NONPUN prefix is not regularly chosen in contexts where multiplicity but not frequentative aspect is found. (Here "frequentative" is not a formal verbal category as such; the verbs in question are usually continuous in form, often with reduplication.)

The second type of exception, the occurrence of *a-* or zero instead of NONPUN *ana-* in the Nominative, seems to have two sources. First, the omission of the prefix (*ŋargu*) tends to occur when the noun is introduced for the first time, so that the semantic features (Saussure's *valeur*) of the noun are foregrounded; for example: 'We went along, and there we found a wallaby'. Once the noun has been introduced, or is otherwise contextually "present," subsequent forms of the noun are usually in the NONPUN form (*ana-ŋargu*).

The type *a-ŋargu* in the Nominative usually represents a pseudo-Nominative. In Nunggubuyu, certain case suffixes tend to be omitted if the speaker feels this will not make the sentence ambiguous; hence in *nuru-ya-ŋgi a-ŋargu-wuy* 'We went to the wallaby' the Allative–Dative ending *-wuy* can be omitted (*nuru-ya-ŋgi a-ŋargu*) and the addressee can deduce the particular case category of the noun from the context. In this example the logical possibilities are Allative-Dative and Ablative, but, because the Ablative suffix is not omitted in this way, the addressee will easily identify *a-ŋargu* as Allative–Dative. The high-frequency Relative–Genitive suffix *-yiñuŋ* is also frequently omitted in this fashion: *wuru-yambi:-na a-ŋargu-yiñuŋ* 'They are talking about wallabies' can be easily shortened to *wuru-yambi:-na a-ŋargu.*

Note that in the event that the NC of the Allative–Dative or Relative–Genitive noun coincides with that of the subject or object, the choice of PUN prefix (*a-ŋargu* instead of NONPUN *ana-ŋargu*) helps the addresses decode the utterance, as PUN is associated with (underlying) nonzero case suffixes. Whereas *ana-ŋargu* is a good Nominative form, *a-ŋargu* is not and its occurrence tips the addressee off to the fact that it represents a truncated nonzero case form. Hence, with no overt nonzero case suffix, the PUN–NONPUN opposition has important case-disambiguating functions which have little or nothing to do with aspect.

It is clear, then, that the "meaning" of the PUN–NONPUN (or PUN–NONPUN–zero) opposition in Nunggubuyu NC prefixes cannot really be understood by extracting a single common underlying feature for each category. Perhaps by taking the aspectual opposition (punctual versus nonpunctual) as "basic," we could explain the generalization of NON-PUN in negative environments by noting that the same kind of neutralization occurs in verbal aspect (as Table 2 shows, negative forms make no aspectual distinctions). However, the various specializations of the prefix oppositions in other environments cannot be understood by invoking general principles. Instead, we must consider the distributional adjustments as reflecting the functional interaction of nominal aspect with other grammatical systems (case marking, discourse reference), each system having been bent or twisted to compensate for deficiencies in the others.

4. CONCLUSION

This is a data paper, but some theoretical remarks are in order. First, it is noteworthy that, whereas in many languages (e.g., Russian) aspect is neutralized in favor of the durative (continuous, imperfective) form rather than the punctual (perfective) form, and this pattern also occurs in Nunggubuyu NC prefixes and past tense verbs, we also find examples of the opposite. In Mara, it is the NONDUR stem-initial that is generalized in negative (and imperative positive) forms. Similarly, the Nunggubuyu negative present and the Mara negative future suffixes are identical to suffixes that elsewhere have specifically punctual value.

More generally, the attempt by Friedrich (1974) to establish the universally unmarked value of the punctual (perfective) member of a binary aspectual opposition is not supported by our data. Indeed, as we have seen, Mara verbs have two formally independent aspectual oppositions (stem-initial and suffixal); in one of these (DUR–NONDUR) Friedrich's analysis works, but in the other we find the opposite markedness polarity (PUN–NONPUN).

Addressing broader issues, the framework advocated here (emphasizing the contextualization of semantic analysis and the notion of functional complementarity) is not compatible, in my view, with the general approach to morphological description (and to most of linguistic theory) developed by Jakobson and currently dominant in American linguistics. In "Shifters, Verbal Categories, and the Russian Verb," Jakobson (1957) attempted to analytically isolate the various domains of grammatical categories (tense, aspect, *etc.*) from one other in order to be able to perform neat structuralist analyses of the elements within each domain. To justify this segmentation of domains from one other, he appealed to the components of the speech event and the narrated event, arguing that each grammatical domain focuses on one component or relationship among components. This framework, however, seriously misrepresents and underestimates the web of interactions among categories within and across domains, and leads to the unfortunate propensity of linguists to seek invariant distinctive features for each formal unit independent of context. (Of course, Jakobson has to note interdomain interactions involving contextual neutralization, as these are the prime evidence for markedness asymmetries, but the broader import of such interactions was not fully recognized.) I hope that the publication of data such as those in this chapter will help to expose the inadequacies of this structuralism and will point linguists toward what Martinet (also criticizing Jakobson) called "realistic discrimination" (1962 p. 11).

REFERENCES

Friedrich, P. (1974). On aspect theory and Homeric aspect. *International Journal of American Linguistics* (Memoir 28) **40.**

Jakobson, R. (1957). Shifters, verbal categories, and the Russian verb. Cambridge, Mass.: Harvard University, Russian Language Project. [Reprinted in R. Jakobson (1971), *Selected Writings, 2,* The Hague: Mouton.] Pp. 130–147.

Martinet, A. (1962). *A Functional View of Language.* London: Oxford University Press.

REMARKS ON *NOCH* AND *SCHON* IN GERMAN[1]

J. HOEPELMAN

C. ROHRER

1. INTRODUCTION

In König 1977 an attempt is made to give a unified treatment of the German adverbs *schon* 'already' and *noch* 'still'. It is postulated that *noch* and *schon* may combine, on the one hand, with a sentence to form another sentence; in this case we have a temporal interpretation. On the other hand, they may combine with an abstract and a member of various categories such as verb phrase, noun phrase or adverb, to make a sentence (König, 1977, p. 185). In the latter case *schon* and *noch* are said to introduce a scale of comparison between the denotata of the syntactical elements mentioned above, which are then somehow ranked as marginal members. For the temporal use of *noch* and *schon* König has the following simple semantics (we have slightly changed his notation):

(1) $V_{i,w}((noch(p))) = t$ iff there is some j, $j < i$, such that, for all k, $j \leq k \leq i$, $V_{k,w}(p) = t$. $V_{i,w}((noch(p))) = f$ iff
   a. $V_{i,w}(p) = f$, and
   b. there is some $j < i$ such that $V_{j,w}(p) = t$.

[1] This work was written under DFG Project RO-245/8, "Tempus und Aspekt auf logischer Grundlage." We wish to thank the unknown referees and, in particular, Professor E. König for helpful comments and examples.

103

(2) $V_{i,w}((schon(p))) = t$ iff
   a. $V_{i,w}(p) = t$, and
   b. there is some j, $i < j$, such that $V_{j,w}(p) = t$.

   $V_{i,w}((schon(p))) = f$ iff
   a. $V_{i,w}(p) = f$, and
   b. there is some j, $i < j$, such that $V_{j,w}(p) = t$.

In (1) and (2) i, j, k are variables ranging over moments of time, and $<$ is the relation "earlier than" (König, 1977, pp. 182–183).

Graphically:

(3)

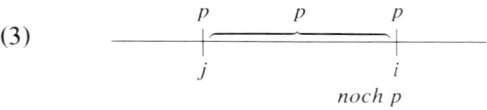

(4)

With this semantics König rejects a suggestion of Doherty 1973, where a time or period of p's NOT being the case is taken into consideration as well. In König's rendering:

(5)   *noch* P: phase$_1$(S), phase$_3$(not-S)
        A: phase$_2$(S)
  schon P: phase$_1$(not-S), phase$_3$(S)
        A: phase$_2$(S)

Here "P" means "presupposition of *noch/schon* S" and "A" "assertion of *noch/schon* S." Graphically:

(6)

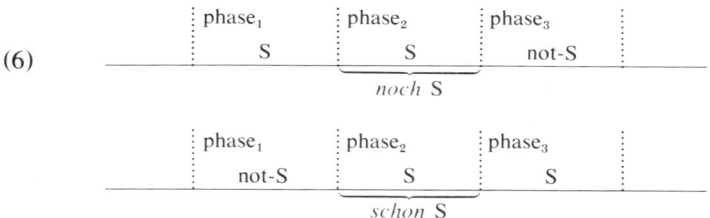

Although—as will be seen—Doherty's analysis of the temporal use of *noch* and *schon* is not adequate, we will argue, first, that an analysis that is more like hers is needed to account for certain phenomena in the use of *noch* and *schon* and, second, that—at least at this stage of the investigation—one has to assume the existence of at least two temporal expressions *noch* and *schon*. We do not preclude, of course, the possibility that a unifying treatment for these uses, and, moreover, for the numerous non-temporal uses of *noch* and *schon* can be given.

In addition, we will give a semantics for the German expression *nicht mehr*. *Nicht mehr* plus *schon* and *noch* varies in acceptability, as does *nicht* plus *schon* and *noch*. These phenomena are not considered by König (1977) and we will try to explain them by our semantics.

2. CO-OCCURRENCE RESTRICTIONS

2.1 *Noch*

Consider the following sentences:

(7)   *Hans schlief noch.*
        'Hans was still sleeping.'

(8)   **Die Bombe explodierte noch.*
        'The bomb was still exploding.

(9)   *Hans aß noch.*
        'Hans was still eating.'

(10)   **Hans kam noch an.*
        'Hans was still arriving.'

Sentences (7)–(10) indicate that in investigating the semantics of *noch* we have to take into consideration a classification of verbs such as that proposed, for example, by Vendler (1967). *Schlafen* (to sleep) and *essen* (to eat) can be classified as ACTIVITY VERBS (see Vendler, 1967, pp. 302ff.; Dowty, 1972, pp. 19ff.; Hoepelman, 1978). One of the semantic properties of activity verbs is that they denote a period during which the subject of the verb has a certain property. That the semantics of *noch* in one of its uses is connected with periods—and not with moments—of time is indicated by the unacceptability of sentences (8) and (10). In these sentences we find the verbs *explodieren* 'to explode' and *ankommen* 'to arrive', which can be classified as ACHIEVEMENTS, verbs denoting a property of the subject (or a relation between subject and object) that obtains at one moment. This, of course, is in accordance with the semantics given by König, reproduced here in (1). However, if it were only periodicity, and the fact that a certain property ϕ can be truly said to hold of a person/thing at a moment t' before the moment t° of speaking, we could not explain why Sentence (11) is not acceptable.

(11)   *Hans hat noch gegessen.
         'Hans has still eaten.'

The present perfect in German is a phenomenon that is relatively unexplored in formal semantics, but one plausible approximation in the framework of a tensed predicate logic would be to say that the present perfect, as in

(12)   Hans hat gegessen.
         'Hans has eaten.'

indicates that AT THE MOMENT OF SPEAKING the subject of the sentence, Hans, has the property that he ate at some earlier time.[2] The present perfect, thus understood, is durative—that is, true during a period of time, because, if we suppose the earlier-than relation to be at least a dense ordering of the set of moments of time, there is a period of time T between the moment in the past at which Hans ate (i.e., strictly speaking eats) and the moment of speaking such that, at each moment t of T, (12) is true at t.

Nevertheless, (11) is unacceptable, at least on one reading. There is another reading of noch which makes (8) and (10) acceptable. In this reading noch can be replaced by doch noch 'finally', and we get the sentences:

(13)   Die Bombe explodierte doch noch.
         'The bomb finally did explode.'

(14)   Hans kam doch noch an.
         'Hans finally did arrive.'

(15)   Hans hat doch noch gegessen.
         'Hans has finally eaten.

The following sentences are acceptable as well:

(16)   Die Bombe explodierte noch um elf.
         'The bomb exploded as late as 11:00.'

(17)   Hans kam noch um elf an.
         'Hans arrived as late as 11:00.'

(18)   Hans hat noch um elf gegessen.
         'Hans ate as late as 11:00.'

However, noch in (8), (10), and (11) cannot be replaced by noch immer 'still':

---

[2] In the face of the acceptability of a sentence like (68), one could add to these conditions the following: "and belongs to a certain fixed domain of discourse at the moment of speaking."

(19)　　*Die Bombe explodierte noch immer.*

(20)　　*Hans kam noch immer an.*

(21)　　*Hans hat noch immer gegessen.*

Sentences (19)–(21) are all unacceptable. On the other hand, in (7) and (9) we CAN replace *noch* by *noch immer*. Sentences (22) and (23) are perfectly normal.

(22)　　*Hans schlief noch immer.*
　　　　'Hans was still sleeping.'

(23)　　*Hans aß noch immer.*
　　　　'Hans was still eating.'

So we seem to have at least two uses of *noch* as a sentential operator: one that can be replaced by the emphatic *doch noch* and one that can be replaced by *noch immer*.

We also have the *noch* that occurs in expressions like *noch um elf*, as in (16), (17), and (18), in which it can neither be replaced by *doch noch* nor by *noch immer* (not even if we change the order of words). Thus, Sentence (24) means neither (25) nor (26).

(24)　　*Noch 1978 bestieg Franz den Mont Blanc.*
　　　　'As late as 1978 Franz climbed the Mont Blanc.'

(25)　　*1978 bestieg Franz doch noch den Mont Blanc.*
　　　　'In 1978 Franz finally climbed the Mont Blanc.'

(26)　　*1978 bestieg Franz noch immer den Mont Blanc.*
　　　　'In 1978 Franz was still climbing the Mont Blanc.'

(The combinations *doch noch 1978* and *noch immer 1978* are not possible at all.)

The first reading of *noch*—as *noch immer*—we will call durative and render by $noch_1$. The second reading—*doch noch*—we will call punctual. It will be rendered by $noch_2$. In this chapter we will mainly be concerned with these two uses of *noch*, considered as sentence-forming operators on sentences.

2.2 *Schon*

Schon seems to have several readings as well. The following sentence:

(27)　　*Als die Oper anfing schlief Hans schon.*
　　　　'When the opera began, Hans was already sleeping.'

seems to entail that Hans was sleeping before the opera began. But Sentence (27) does not have the same meaning as Sentence (28).

(28)   *Die Oper fing an und schon schlief Hans.*
          'The opera began and already Hans was sleeping.'

Sentence (28) entails that the beginning of the opera coincided with the beginning of Hans's sleep.

On the other hand, (29) is unacceptable if we take *schon* in the same reading as in (27).

(29)   *Als die Oper anfing explodierte die Bombe schon.*

In a sentence like (29) *schon* is interpreted as in (28), and there seems to be no difference in meaning—at least not with regard to the TEMPORAL elements of the sentences—between (29) and (30).

(30)   *Die Oper fing an und schon explodierte die Bombe.*

So we will distinguish two expressions: *schon*$_1$ (durative) and *schon*$_2$ (punctual).

2.3 Negation

Noch and *schon* are both somehow connected with negation, as can be seen from the following sentences:

(31)   *Hans schlief noch nicht.*

(32)   *Die Bombe explodierte noch nicht.*

(33)   *Hans aß noch nicht.*

(34)   *Hans kam noch nicht an.*

(35)   **Hans schlief noch nicht mehr.*

(36)   **Die Bombe explodierte noch nicht mehr.*

(37)   **Hans aß noch nicht mehr.*

(38)   **Hans kam noch nicht mehr an.*

(39)   **Hans schlief schon nicht.*

(40)   **Die Bombe explodierte schon nicht.*

(41)   **Hans aß schon nicht.*

(42)   **Hans kam schon nicht an.*

(43)   *Hans schlief schon nicht mehr.*

(44)   *Die Bombe explodierte schon nicht mehr.*

(45)   *Hans aß schon nicht mehr.*

(46)   *Hans kam schon nicht mehr an.*

2.4 Present Perfect

Finally *schon* is normal in combination with the German present perfect:

(47)   *Hans hat schon gegessen.*
         'Hans has already eaten.'

(48)   *Die Bombe ist schon explodiert.*
         'The bomb has already exploded.'

A restriction must be placed on (48), however. We will return to this later.

2.5 Explanation

We want to explain this behavior of *noch* and *schon* with past tense and present perfect, with durative and nondurative verbs and with *nicht* and *nicht mehr*, if possible in such a way that a link can be made with other uses of *noch* and *schon* as well. König (1977) has examples like the following, among many others (p. 183):

(49)   *Carlisle liegt noch in England.*
         'Carlisle is still in England.'

(50)   *Dumfries liegt schon in Schottland.*
         'Dumfries is already in Scotland.'

(51)   *Paul ist noch gemäßigt.*
         'Paul is still moderate.'

(52)   *Peter ist schon radikal.*
         'Peter is already radical.'

There are also examples of sentences that seem to involve a double comparison: In (53) and (54), a military rank is compared with other ranks and at the same time the age at which one—according to some norm—has this rank:

(53)   *Peter ist schon Offizier.*
         'Peter is already an officer.'

(54)   *Paul ist noch Offizier.*
         'Paul is still an officer.'

We propose to bring at least some order in the quite disparate properties of *schon* and *noch* by introducing two models, $\mathfrak{A}$ and $\mathfrak{A}_s$, where $\mathfrak{A}$ might be called the real model and $\mathfrak{A}_s$ the model of the speaker. Moreover we introduce a designated world, e, the "world of expectation" of the speaker. The value that a sentence ϕ can get in $\mathfrak{A}_s$ will then depend on a comparison between the value(s) ϕ gets in the real model in the real world at certain times and the values ϕ gets in the speaker's model in his world of expectation at the same times.

That temporal *noch* and *schon* have something to do with the expectations of the speaker (and in some cases of the hearer) may be illustrated by a few examples. Imagine the following dialogue:

(55)   A: *Peter war schon um 8 im Büro.*
          'By 8 o'clock P. was already in his office.'
        B: *Was heißt "schon"? Er war **noch** um 8 im Büro, er hatte die ganze Nacht gearbeitet.*
          'What do you mean "already"? He was **still** in the office, he worked all night long.'

In this example, A's expectation is that Peter arrives in his office after 8:00 (i.e., normally Peter arrives after 8:00), and B explains to A that in fact Peter was in his office much longer than was to be expected.

It is not always the case that the use of *noch* or *schon* in a sentence is in accordance with the point of view of the SPEAKER. In certain cases the speaker may accomodate to the (supposed) point of view of the hearer, or to some "social" or "generally accepted" point of view. Consider the following dialogue on the telephone:

(56)   A: *Kann ich Hans sprechen?*
          'Can I talk to Hans?'
        B: *Nein, er ist schon gegangen.*
          'No, he has already left.'

For B, the moment of Hans's departure is perhaps not at all earlier than expected. In fact, when Hans left, B may have thought "Geht er jetzt erst" ('Does he finally leave'), because Hans left later than usual. Thus, in using *schon*, B adopts A's point of view.

That *schon* has something to do with expectations also emerges from the following examples in which verbs are used that express, among other things, the contrary of an expectation. It is unnatural and one needs a quite artificial context to use such verbs with *schon*.

(57)   *. . . und an der nächsten Ecke, da verlor ich schon meinen Geldbeutel.*
          '. . . and on the next corner, I lost my wallet already.'

The oddness of (57) can be explained by the fact that the "I" seemed to expect the loss of his wallet, which makes the use of the word *verlieren* problematic. Another example of this is the famous joke about Göring:

(58)   A (to Göring): *Der Reichstag brennt!*
                      'The Reichstag is burning!'
       Göring: *Was? Schon!*
               'What? Already!'

The joke implies that Göring expected the Reichstag to burn, or perhaps even that he planned it.

We could, of course, get a similar effect with *noch*. Suppose that Göring for some reason wanted a brief, small fire in the Reichstag. Then the following dialogue brings out that he knew about the fire and expected (planned) it to be extinguished:

(59)   A (to Göring): *Der Reichstag brennt!*
       Göring: *Was? Noch!*
               'What? Still!'

3. FORMAL SEMANTICS

3.1 *Noch*₁

More formally, we propose the following semantics for $noch_1$.

Let $\mathfrak{A}$ be a model—the "real model"—$(T, W, <)$, where T is a set of time points, W a set of worlds, $<$ the relation "earlier than" on T ($<$ is a strict simple ordering, which we assume to be at least dense).

Let $\mathfrak{A}_s$—the "speaker's model"—be $(T, W', <, s)$, where T and $<$ are as before, $W' = W \cup \{e\}$, e is a designated member of W'—the speaker's "world of expectations"—and s is the speaker. To keep things simple we will assume that there is just one speaker.

Let g be an assignment of values to expressions of the formal language we are dealing with. As we are dealing with $noch_1$ as a supposed sentence-building operator on sentences we do not have to go beyond the framework of a propositional logic and we let g be an assignment of values from the set $\{0,1\}$ to proposition letters. An expression like $[\phi]^{\mathfrak{A},i,j,g}$ denotes the value assigned to an expression ϕ in a model $\mathfrak{A}$, relative to a world i and a time j by an assignment g. Let us assume that we have a propositional language L_1, of which the expressions are evaluated in the model $\mathfrak{A}$, and a language L_2 which differs from L_1 only in the fact that, in addition to the expressions of L_1, L_2 contains the propositional operators $noch_1$ and

$schon_1$. The expressions of L_2 are evaluated in $\mathfrak{A}_s$. Moreover we have the condition that for any $i \in W$ and for any expression ϕ of $L_1 = [\phi]^{\mathfrak{A}_s, i, j, g} = [\phi]^{\mathfrak{A}, i, j, g}$.

Then we have for $noch_1$:

(60) $[noch_1 \, \phi]^{\mathfrak{A}_s, i, j, g} = 1$ iff
        $(Vx) \, (Vy) \, (y < x < j \, \& \, (Az) \, (y < z \leqslant x \to [\phi]^{\mathfrak{A}_s, e, z, g}$
        $= 1) \, \& \, (Au) \, (x < u \leqslant j \to [\phi]^{\mathfrak{A}_s, e, u, g}$
        $= 0) \, \& \, (At) \, (x < t \leqslant j \to [\phi]^{\mathfrak{A}_a, i, t, g} = 1))$

In (60), V is the existential quantifier and A the universal one; $\leqslant$ is the relation "$<$ or $=$"; ϕ is an expression of L_2. Informally we may explain (60) as follows: A sentence like

(61)   *Hans schläft noch.*

where *noch* is interpreted as $noch_1$, is true for a speaker s at a moment j in a world i in the situation sketched in the following diagram:

3.1.1 CO-OCCURRENCE WITH THE PAST TENSE

If we have a sentence in the past tense, and assume that the German past tense can tense-logically be rendered by the propositional tense-operator P with its usual semantics (we adapt our languages L_1 and L_2 to this feature), then it is easy to see that in the formal language the order of the operators "$noch_1$" and "P" should be be "$P \, noch_1 \, . \, . \, .$" and not "$noch_1 \, P \, . \, . \, .$". The latter semantically leads to

(63) $[noch_1 \, P \, \phi]^{\mathfrak{A}_s, i, j, g} = 1$ iff
        $(Vx) \, (Vy) \, (y < x \leqslant j \, \& \, (Az) \, (y < z \leqslant x \to [P\phi]^{\mathfrak{A}_s, e, z, g}$
        $= 1) \, \& \, (Au) \, (x < u \leqslant j \to [P\phi]^{\mathfrak{A}_s, e, u, g}$
        $= 0) \, \& \, (At) \, (x < t \leqslant j \to [P\phi]^{\mathfrak{A}, i, t, g} = 1))$

Graphically:

However, if the ordering on T is transitive and connected—as a strict simple ordering is—than if ϕ is true at any past moment, $P\phi$ is true at all following moments, so that the picture reflects a contradiction in the

$$(65) \quad \mathfrak{A}_s \quad e \quad \underset{\underbrace{\qquad P\phi \qquad}}{\underset{}{\rule{0pt}{0pt}}} \quad \underset{\underbrace{\qquad \neg P\phi \qquad}}{\underset{}{\rule{0pt}{0pt}}}$$

model of the speaker, which we should not allow if we attach any value to having at least halfway normal speakers.

3.1.2 CO-OCCURRENCE WITH PRESENT PERFECT

This phenomenon is related to the unacceptability of one reading of a sentence like

(11)   **Hans hat noch gegessen.*
         'Hans has still eaten.'

As was pointed out before, the German present perfect indicates, among other things, the present property of someone/thing of whom a sentence in the past tense holds—that is, (66) entails (67).

(66)   *Hans hat gegessen.*
         'Hans has eaten.'

(67)   *Hans ist einer der aß.*
         'Hans is somebody who ate.'

It is intuitively clear that, with a strict simple ordering of T, in the same way as we had before with the past tense, if someone ate at some time in the past, he has eaten ever since.

Here again we have a good opportunity to illustrate the link between *schon* and the expectations of the speaker. The following example:

(68)   *Beethoven hat neun Symphonien geschrieben.*
         'Beethoven has written nine symphonies.'

is a normal sentence. Everyone knows that Beethoven is dead, and (68) gives no indication that its speaker has doubts about this. This is in contrast to

(69)   *Beethoven hat schon neun Symphonien geschrieben.*
         'Beethoven has already written nine symphonies.'

which indicates that the speaker thinks that nine symphonies are quite a few, considering Beethoven's age, or the time of the year or whatever, at the moment of speaking. In other words, the speaker expected Beethoven to complete his nine symphonies at some later time than the time of speaking. This again—at least in connection with our usual set of beliefs

—entails that the speaker thinks that Beethoven is still alive, as we usually don't expect dead composers to write symphonies.

A second property of the German present perfect, at least in connection with verbs like *essen* 'to eat', seems to be the expression of the end of the action. If Hans has not finished eating, one can not say of him

(70)   *Er hat gegessen.*
        'He has eaten.'

Now suppose

(66)   *Hans hat gegessen.*

is true, at some time j in some world i. Then Hans finished eating at a time j' before j and he was eating before j'. Moreover, at all moments j'' between j' and j, (66) is true as well. On the other hand, during the period before j', at which Hans was eating, (66) is not true.

We will not consider in depth the representation of the German present perfect in a formal language. Let it suffice to say that in a predicate logic the difference between a sentence like *Hans aß* 'Hans was eating', in the German simple past, and (66) can at least partially be explained by assuming that in *Hans aß* a sentence representing *Hans ißt* 'Hans is eating' is in the scope of the past-operator, and that in (66) a sentence of the form *Past-operator (er ißt)* is in the scope of an element representing the name *Hans*. As the past-operator should not occur in the scope of *noch,* the interpretation of (11) as $noch_1 (Hans (P(er \, i\beta t)))$ should be rejected, as can be seen from the following.

As a diagram illustrating the German present perfect we get:

(71) $\mathfrak{A}_i$

      Hans eats   *Hans finishes eating* *Hans doesn't eat*

        not: *Hans hat gegessen*   *Hans hat gegessen*

If we complete this picture in the same way as (62), but now for

(11)   *Hans hat noch gegessen.*

interpreted as indicated earlier, with *noch* having wide scope, we get

(72) $\mathfrak{A}_s$ e *Hans ißt*   *Hans hat gegessen* *Hans hat nicht gegessen*

       $\mathfrak{A}$ i *Hans ißt*   *Hans hat gegessen* *Hans hat gegessen*

       $\mathfrak{A}_s$ i (Hans hat $noch_1$ gegessen)

                        y x j

We see that, under the proposed semantics, *Hans hat gegessen* is first true in the expectation world of the speaker and then false, contrary to the normal meaning of the German present perfect. This may suffice as an indication why (11) in one of its readings is unacceptable.

In the same way in which we investigated the order of the operators P and $noch_1$, $noch_2$, we can investigate the order of the future-tense operator F and $noch_1$ and $noch_2$. It is immediately clear, that "$F\ noch_1\ .\ .\ .$" poses no problems.

However, "$noch_1\ F\ .\ .\ .$" leads to the following picture:

$$(64')\quad \mathfrak{A}_s\quad e$$

$$\mathfrak{A}\quad i$$

$$\mathfrak{A}_s\quad i$$

Under the given conditions on $<$, a situation like this should not obtain, as $F\phi$ has to be true at x and $\neg(F\phi)$ thereafter. If $F\phi$ is true at x, then there will be a v, with $x < v$, such that ϕ is true at v. Because we assume $<$ to be a dense ordering on T, there has to be a v' with $x < v' < v$, at which $F\phi$ is true. But $\neg(F\phi)$ is also true at v'. So, as in the case of the order "$noch_1$ $P\phi$," the order "$noch_1\ F\phi$" leads to a contradiction in the speaker's world of expectations.

3.1.3 *NICHT MEHR*

We have seen that *nicht mehr* 'anymore' in connection with *noch* is unacceptable, for example:

(35)   **Hans schlief noch nicht mehr.*

A sentence like

(73)   *Ich arbeite nicht mehr.*
         'I am not working anymore.'

seems to mean

1. *Ich habe gearbeitet.*
   'I have been working.'
   'I worked.'

2. *Ich arbeite nicht.*
   'I am not working/I don't work.'

We think that yet another element is involved.

3. *Ich werde eine Zeitlang nicht arbeiten.*
   'I will not work for some time.'

A sentence like

(74)   *Hans schreibt nicht mehr.*
         'Hans doesn't write anymore.'

clearly indicates that Hans's activities as a writer came to an end for the time being. In the same way, the following sentence:

(75)   *Danzig liegt nicht mehr in Deutschland.*
         'Danzig is no longer in Germany.'

means

1. *Danzig lag in Deutschland.*
   '*Danzig was in Germany.*'

2. *Danzig liegt nicht in Deutschland.*
   'Danzig is not in Germany.'

3. *Danzig wird eine Zeitlang nicht in Deutschland liegen.*
   'Danzig will not be in Germany for some time.'

Hence the following semantics for *nicht mehr*, taken as a propositional operator (we introduce *nicht mehr* in L_1 and L_2):

(76) $[nicht\ mehr\ \phi]^{\mathfrak{A}^*,i,j,g} = 1$ iff
         $(Vx)\ (x < j\ \&\ [\phi]^{\mathfrak{A},i,x,g} = 1\ \&\ (Vy)\ (j < y\ \&$
         $(Az)\ (j \leq z < y \rightarrow [\phi]^{\mathfrak{A},i,z,g} = 0)))$
         where $\mathfrak{A}^*$ is $\mathfrak{A}$ or $\mathfrak{A}_s$.

Graphically:

(77) i *Ich arbeite* — *Ich arbeite nicht mehr* — *Ich arbeite nicht*
                  x j y

Apparent counterexamples to this semantics are sentences like the following:

(78)   A: *Glaubst du, daß Johann noch kommt?*
            'Do you think Johann will turn up yet?'
         B: *Nein, der kommt bestimmt nicht mehr.*
            'No, he won't come anymore.'

(79)　*Beethoven vollendete die 10e Symphonie nicht mehr.*
　　　'Beethoven didn't complete the Tenth Symphony.'

Nicht mehr in (78) and (79) does not indicate that Johann came at some earlier time, or that Beethoven was about to finish his Tenth Symphony once more. We think that (78) and (79) can be understood as dealing with the possibility of Johann's coming and Beethoven's finishing his Tenth Symphony. Notice that (80) and (81) are synonymous with (78) and (79), respectively, but that (82) is not synonomous with (73):

(80)　A: *Glaubst du, daß Johann noch kommen kann?*
　　　　　'Do you think that Johann is still able to come?'
　　　B: *Nein, der kann bestimmt nicht mehr kommen.*
　　　　　'No he is certainly not able to come.'

(81)　*Beethoven konnte die 10e Symphonie nicht mehr vollenden.*
　　　'Beethoven wasn't able to complete his Tenth Symphony anymore.'

(82)　*Ich kann nicht mehr arbeiten.*
　　　'I can't work anymore.'

Seen in this way, we can say that *der kommt bestimmt nicht mehr* in (78) means that

1. It was possible for him to come at an earlier moment.
2. It is not possible that he comes now.
3. It will not be possible for him to come for some time.

Likewise we could say that (79) means that

1. It was possible for Beethoven to complete his Tenth Symphony.
2. Then, at some later time, it was not possible for him to complete his Tenth Symphony.
3. It was not possible for him to complete his Tenth for some time afterward.

Now, $[noch_1 \ nicht \ mehr \ \phi]^{\mathfrak{A}_s,i,j,g} = 1$ entails that we have that for some $x < j$: $[nicht \ mehr \ \phi]^{\mathfrak{A}_s,e,x,g} = 1$ and for all (and so for some) $z, x < z < j$: $[nicht \ mehr \ \phi]^{\mathfrak{A}_s,e,z,g} = 0$. It is easy to see that these two conditions lead to a contradiction in $\mathfrak{A}_s$ with respect to e under the conditions on $<$ given previously, which may explain the unacceptability of *$noch_1$ nicht mehr ϕ*. On the other hand, *noch nicht* is a completely acceptable combination, as in a case like (33') which we assume has *$noch_1$*:

(33')　*Hans ißt noch nicht.*

We will not write out the full truth-condition for $noch_1$ *nicht P* according to the given semantics, and just draw the picture for (33'):

(83)

A contradiction does not obtain.

3.2. $Noch_2$

For $noch_2$ (*doch noch*) we propose the following semantics:

(84) $[noch_2 \, \phi]^{\mathfrak{A}_s, i, j, g} = 1$ iff
$(\mathrm{V}x) \, (x < j \, \& \, [\phi]^{\mathfrak{A}_s, e, x, g} = 1 \, \& \, (\mathrm{A}z) \, (x < z \leqslant j \rightarrow$
$[\phi]^{\mathfrak{A}_s, e, z, g} = 0) \, \& \, [\phi]^{\mathfrak{A}, i, j, g} = 1)$

Graphically:

(85)

It is easy to see that the sentences we rejected for their semantical unacceptability with $noch_1$ are unacceptable in the same way with $noch_2$.

3.3. $Schon_1$

For $schon_1$ (durative) we propose:

(86) $[schon_1 \, \phi]^{\mathfrak{A}_s, i, j, g} = 1$ iff
$(\mathrm{V}x) \, (\mathrm{V}y) \, (y < j < x \, \& \, (\mathrm{A}z) \, (y < z \leqslant x \rightarrow$
$[\phi]^{\mathfrak{A}_s, e, z, g} = 0) \, \& \, (\mathrm{V}t) \, (x < t \, \& \, (\mathrm{A}w) \, (x < w < t \rightarrow$

$$[\phi]^{\mathfrak{A}_t,e,w,g} = 1)) \;\&\; [\phi]^{\mathfrak{A},i,y,g} = 0 \;\&\; (\mathrm{V}s)\;(j < s < x \;\&\;$$
$$(\mathrm{A}u)\;(y < u < s \rightarrow [\phi]^{\mathfrak{A},i,u,g} = 1)))$$

Graphically:

(87)

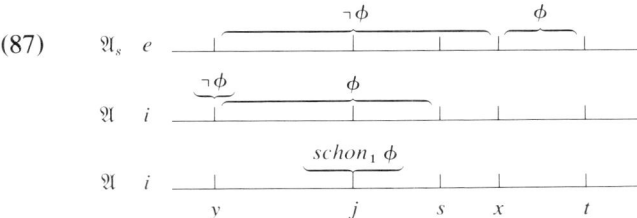

3.4 *Schon₂*

For *schon₂* we will have:

(88) $[schon_2\,\phi]^{\mathfrak{A}_s,i,j,g} = 1$ iff
     $(\mathrm{V}x)\;(\mathrm{V}y)\;(y < j < x \;\&\; [\phi]^{\mathfrak{A}_s,e,x,g} = 1 \;\&\; (\mathrm{A}z)$
     $(y < z < x \rightarrow [\phi]^{\mathfrak{A}_s,e,z,g} = 0) \;\&\; [\phi]^{\mathfrak{A},i,j,g} = 1 \;\&\;$
     $[\phi]^{\mathfrak{A},i,y,g} = 0))$

Graphically:

(89)

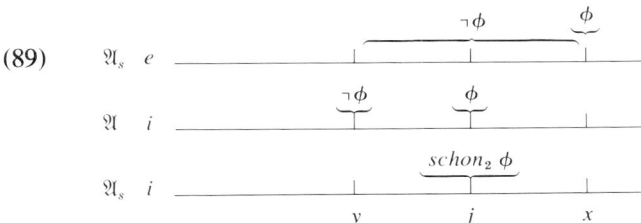

3.5 Co-occurrence Restrictions

Let us now investigate the semantical effects of the combinations *schon nicht* and *schon nicht mehr*. Of these combinations, the former is unacceptable, and the latter completely normal, as is shown by the following sentences:

(41)   **Hans aß schon nicht.*

(45)   *Hans aß schon nicht mehr.*

With *schon*$_1$ we have the following picture corresponding to the formal semantics, which we will not write out:

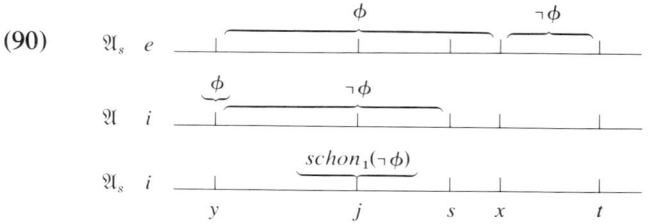

(90)

We compare (90) with the picture we get for $[schon_1 \ (nicht \ mehr \ \phi)]^{\mathfrak{A}_s,i,j,g} = 1$:

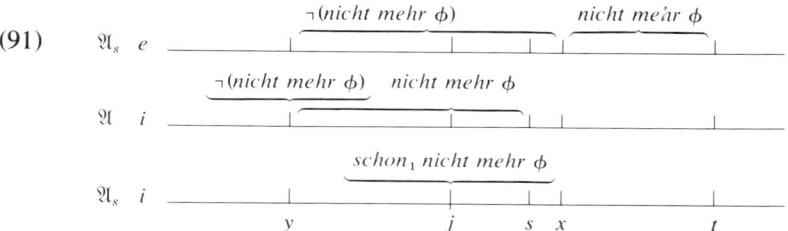

(91)

It is easy to see that, if we have a situation as sketched under (90), then, according to the semantics of *nicht mehr*, we also have a situation as sketched under (91)—that is, *schon*$_1$ ($\neg \phi$) implies *schon*$_1$ (*nicht mehr* ϕ). The reverse is not true. The same goes for *schon*$_2$. We might say that the German language has *schon nicht mehr* as a preferred expression, covering *schon nicht* as well. It should be noticed that in Russian, for example, the combination *uže ne* (lit: 'already not,' i.e., 'no longer') is quite common:

(92)   *On uže ne reb'onok.*
        (*Er ist schon kein Kind mehr.*)
        'He is no longer a child.'

This indicates that it is indeed no SEMANTICAL anomaly that renders *schon nicht* unacceptable.[3]

---

[3] Regarding Russian we remark that the given method of evaluating the truth-value of sentences for a speaker with regard to a world of expectations could be applied to certain semantical phenomena of aspect-forming in Russian. A sentence like

(i)   *Ja postojal tam čas.*
        'I stood there for an hour.'

In contradistinction to *noch*₁ and *noch*₂, the operators *schon*₁ and *P* can occur in the order "*schon*₁ *P* . . ." as well as in the order "*P schon*₁ . . ." we have graphically:

(93)

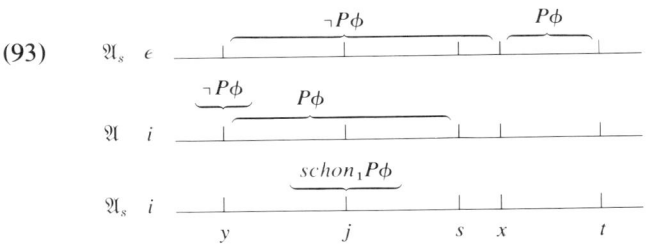

In a dense ordering of *T* it is possible to have ¬*P*ϕ true at *x* and during a period immediately preceding *x* (in $\mathfrak{A}_s$ with respect to *e*), and to have *P*ϕ true during a period immediately following *x*, because for any *w* with *x* < *w*, however close to *x*, there can be a *w'* between *x* and *w* (i.e., in the past of *w*), such that, at *w'*, ϕ is true. This is the kind of situation that obtains when we combine *schon*₁ with the German present perfect in such a way that *schon*₁ is interpreted as having the rest of the sentence in its scope, that is, if we interpret the in any reading acceptable Sentence (94) as (95).

(94)   *Hans hat schon gegessen.*
         'Hans has already eaten.'

(95)   *Schon*₁ (*Hans hat gegessen*)

The diagram for (95) will look like (96), which should be compared with (91):

(96) $\mathfrak{A}_s$ *e*

         ¬(*Hans hat gegessen*)   *Hans hat gegessen*

         ¬(*Hans hat gegessen*)

         Hans hat gegessen

         $\mathfrak{A}$ *i*

         *schon*₁(*Hans hat gegessen*)

         $\mathfrak{A}_s$ *i*

              y   *j*   *s*   *x*   *t*

---

indicates that the duration of an hour is shorter than was expected by the speaker. Conversely,

(ii)   *Ja prostojal tam čas.*
         'I stood there for an hour.'

indicates that one hour was longer than the speaker expected.

Diagram (96) once more indicates that for a more precise treatment we need a notion of "relevant interval," as by *Hans hat schon gegessen* it is generally not implied that we are in the first period in history that *Hans hat gegessen* is true.

On the other hand, the order "*schon₂* P . . ." leads to problems ("*P schon₂* . . ." does not, as the reader can easily verify):

(97)

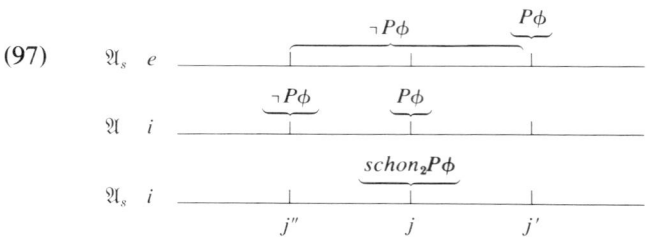

Under the given ordering on T it is impossible to have $P\phi$ true at a moment j' and $\neg P\phi$ true during an interval immediately preceding j' (in $\mathfrak{A}_s$, with respect to e). This means that if we have a sentence like

(98)   *Hans ist schon angekommen.*

it should not be interpreted as if *schon₂* has the rest of the sentence in its scope.

The combinations "*F schon₁* . . ." and "*F schon₂* . . ." do not lead to problems, but "*schon₁ F* . . ." and "*schon₂ F* . . ." do:

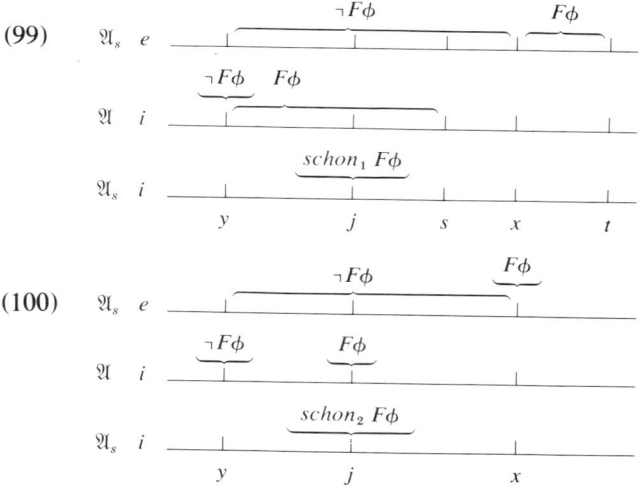

Under the given ordering on T and the usual semantics for the future-operator F, to have $F\phi$ true at a moment k (with respect to a model and a world) and $\neg F\phi$ true at a moment k' before k — a situation we have in both (99) and (100) — is impossible.

The combinations *schon schon φ*, *schon noch φ*, *noch schon φ* and *noch noch φ* do not seem to occur in German. In our semantics expressions like these are undefined, because evaluating an expression like *schon schon φ* in 𝔄 depends on evaluating *schon φ* in 𝔄.

However, in 𝔄 we evaluate only expressions of L_1, in which the operators *schon* and *noch* do not occur.

4. CO-OCCURRENCE WITH *UND* AND *ODER*

Native speakers of German do not seem to have clear intuitions about the semantics of *schon* and *noch* in connection with connectives like *und* and *oder* (*and, or*). For example, they find it hard to tell whether

(101)   *Opa hört und sieht noch.*
         'Granddad still hears and sees.'

allows them to say

(102)   *Opa hört noch und er sieht noch.*
         'Granddad still hears and still sees.'

and vice versa.

This is perhaps not so surprising, considering the complexity of the semantics of *noch* and *schon*. The truth definition for *noch* makes it possible for a sentence of the form *noch p & noch q* to be true in 13 different situations and for a sentence of the form *schon p & schon q* to be true in 144 situations, if we assume that in world *e* the tautologies of classical two-valued logic hold. Under this assumption, formulae of the following forms are valid in L_2:

(103) $noch_1 p \ \& \ noch_1 q \rightarrow noch_1(p \lor q)$
         $noch_1 \lnot p \rightarrow \lnot noch_1 p$
         $noch_1(p \rightarrow q) \rightarrow (noch_1 p \rightarrow noch_1 q)$
         $schon_1 \lnot p \rightarrow \lnot schon_1 p$
         $schon_1(p \rightarrow q) \rightarrow (schon_1 p \rightarrow schon_1 q)$

Some formulae that are not valid, although they do not seem implausible at first sight, are the following:

(104) $noch_1(p \lor q) \rightarrow (noch_1 p \lor noch_1 q)$
         $(noch_1 p \lor noch_1 q) \rightarrow noch_1(p \lor q)$
         $noch_1(p \ \& \ q) \rightarrow (noch_1 p \ \& \ noch_1 q)$
         $(noch_1 p \ \& \ noch_1 q) \rightarrow noch_1(p \ \& \ q)$
         $noch_1(p \ \& \ q) \rightarrow noch_1(p \lor q)$
         $noch_1 p \rightarrow noch_1(p \lor q)$

The same formulae with $schon_1$ replacing $noch_1$ again are not valid.

As an example of why these formulae not valid, consider the following diagrams for $noch_1(p \; \& \; q)$ and $noch_1(p \vee q)$.

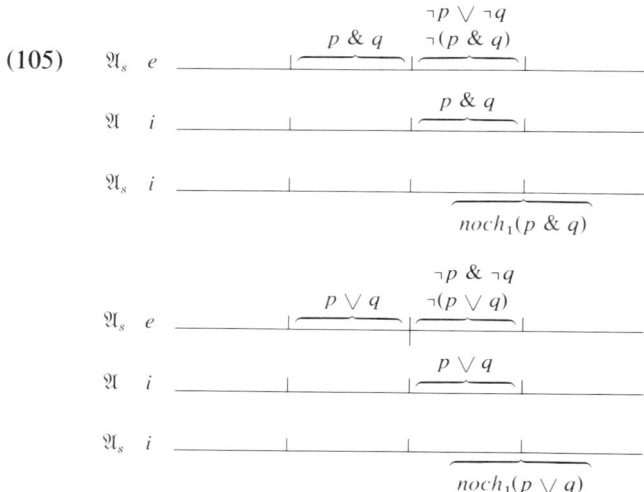

(105)

$noch_1(p \; \& \; q)$

$noch_1(p \vee q)$

We see that under a classical semantics for e neither sentence is implied by the other.

5. NONTEMPORAL *NOCH* AND *SCHON*

It is quite difficult to give a unified semantics for all uses of *noch* and *schon,* if only because—as König points out (1977, pp. 182ff.)—*schon* and *noch* seem to belong to various syntactical categories. In any case *noch* and *schon* seem to compare positions in an ordering in the real world with positions in the ordering in a world of expectation, or of norms.

We will not try to give a formal semantics for the nontemporal uses of *noch* and *schon,* and, instead, will just make a few intuitive remarks. In the first place, it should be noticed that we consider *noch* and *schon* in expressions like

(106)   *noch um elf . . .*
         'as late as 11:00 . . .'

(107)   *schon um elf . . .*
         'already at 11:00 . . .'

as essentially nontemporal, that is, as the same *noch* and *schon* that we encounter in sentences like

(108)   *Noch im Gefängnis brachte er verschiedene Leute um.*
          'Even in jail he killed several persons.'

(109)   *Schon an der nächsten Haltestelle stieg er aus.*
          'He got out at the next stop already.'

Let us assume that a sentence like

(53)   *Peter ist schon Offizier.*
          'Peter is already an officer.'

compares the age at which Peter got the rank of officer with the age at which people normally get this rank—that is, with the age at which Peter was to be expected to get this rank. The picture we get intuitively is

(110) $\mathfrak{A}_s$ e

          not: *Peter ist Offizier*   *Peter ist Offizier*

          not: *Peter ist Offizier*

          Peter ist Offizier

          $\mathfrak{A}$ i

          Peter ist schon Offizier

          $\mathfrak{A}_s$ i

          Peter's age: 18   20   25

Of course the structure of (110) is the same as the structure given for temporal *schon*$_1$, the only difference being that the ordered elements are Peter's ages and not the moments of time.

6. CONCLUSIONS

In contrast to previous works on *schon* and *noch,* we have handled the following main points:

1. The interaction of *schon* and *noch* with tense forms (especially preterite, present perfect and future) has been considered in a formal semantics.[4]
2. We have established a link between a verb classification in the spirit of Z. Vendler and different meanings of *schon* and *noch.*
3. The behavior of *schon* and *noch* under negation, as well the iteration of these operators, has been investigated.

[4] French grammarians distinguish two uses of the French equivalent of *schon* (*déjà*): (*a*) *déjà* modifying the action; and (*b*) *déjà* modifying the time at which the action takes place (see, e.g., R. Martin 1971, p. 260). This distinction of two functions correlates nicely with the distribution of tense forms. A formal reconstruction of this distinction has been presented at the colloquium on aspect organized by J. David and R. Martin in Metz, May 1978.

4. Possible extensions of the semantics for temporal *schon* and *noch* to nontemporal uses have been considered.[5]

Finally we remark that it may be interesting to investigate connectives like *aber* 'but', *sondern* 'but', *trotzdem* 'nevertheless', *doch* 'yet', *etc.* by means of semantical systems such as the ones proposed in this chapter.

REFERENCES

Doherty, M. (1973). "Noch" and "schon" and their presuppositions. In F. Kiefer and N. Ruwet (Eds.), *Generative Grammar in Europe.* Dordrecht:D. Reidel.

Dowty, D. (1972). *Studies in the Logic of Verb Aspect and Time Reference in English.* Doctoral dissertation, University of Austin, Texas.

Gabbay, D., and Rohrer, C. (1978). *Relative tenses: The interpretation of tense forms which occur in the scope of temporal adverbs or in embedded sentences.* Mimeograph, University of Stuttgart.

Hoepelman, J. (1978). The treatment of activity verbs in a Montague-type grammar. In F. Guenthner and C. Rohrer (Eds.), *Studies in Formal Semantics.* Amsterdam: North-Holland.

König, E. (1977). Temporal and non-temporal uses of "noch" and "schon" in German. *Linguistics and Philosophy,* **1,** 171–198.

Martin, R. (1971). *Temps et Aspect.* Paris: Klincksieck.

Rohrer, C. (1977). *How to define temporal conjunctions. Linguistische Berichte,* **51** 77 1–11.

Vendler, Z. (1967). *Linguistics in Philosophy.* Ithaca: Cornell University Press.

[5] Many uses of *schon* and *noch* are left unexplained. In a letter, Professor E. König pointed to a few examples. Whereas Sentences (i) and (ii) are acceptable, Sentences (iii) and (iv) are not.

(i)   *Ich fuhr noch am gleichen Tage ab.*
         'I departed still on the same day.'

(ii)   *Noch in der gleichen Stunde trat er zurück.*
         'He abdicated still the same hour.'

(iii)   **Noch am nächsten Tag fuhr ich ab.*
         'I departed still on the next day.'

(iv)   **Noch um Punkt 11 Uht trat er zurück.*
         'At exactly 11:00 a.m. he still abdicated.'

We assume that examples like these can be handled in connection with interval-restricting time adverbials like *am gleichen Tag* 'on the same day' and *heute* 'today' (cf. Rohrer, 1978; Gabbay and Rohrer, 1978). The uses of *schon* and *noch* in these examples seem to be what we called nontemporal in Section 5—that is, they serve to express the different placings of an entity in two different worlds on a scale, which in the above cases happens to be determined by the time adverbials *heute, am gleichen Tag, etc.*

ASPECT THEORY AND GEORGIAN ASPECT

DEE ANN HOLISKY

1. INTRODUCTION

The aspect system of Modern Georgian is unquestionably a well-motivated one. In some languages, like English, expression of the category of aspect is primarily lexical (see Vendler, 1967; Dowty, 1972), whereas in others, like Slavic or Indo-European, aspect is expressed by inflectional and derivational morphology. In Georgian, both covert-lexical and overt-morphological aspect marking are utilized in an explicit, regular way, making it an excellent language for research into the interaction between them. Study of this interaction is the main objective of this chapter.

Section 2 will deal with three shortcomings of traditional treatments of aspect, as background to the primary details of the general framework for this analysis. In Section 3, five overt aspect oppositions found in Georgian are presented, with discussion of the covert aspect types to which each opposition is restricted. Section 4 contains conclusions about the Georgian system, and Section 5, some general implications.

2. BACKGROUND

Aspect has been a relatively neglected area of linguistics, and a certain confusion typifies much of the existing discussion. There are at least three important factors contributing to this confusion.

127

Syntax and Semantics, Volume 14
Tense and Aspect

2.1. Terminology

The term "aspect" has almost as many definitions as there are linguists who have used it; the same can also be said about terms for specific aspects—"perfective," "inceptive," and so on. Such lack of terminological consistency makes comprehension of any particular analysis difficult and cross-language comparison nearly impossible.[1] It is appropriate, therefore, to begin with the definition of aspect to be used here: "Aspect signifies the relative duration or punctuality along a time line that may inhere in words or constructions."[2]

To avoid further terminological confusion and to facilitate the formulation of GENERAL statements about the dynamics of aspect, this discussion will be in terms of a single, broad opposition: punctual versus linear. For purposes of this analysis, all traditional aspect oppositions can be subsumed under the opposition punctual–linear, as illustrated in (1).[3]

(1)	Punctual	Linear
	perfective	nonperfective
	completive	noncompletive
	inceptive	noninceptive
	semelfactive	iterative
	nondurative	durative
	nonprogressive	progressive

The issue of whether punctuals should be defined in terms of linears or vice versa will be addressed in Section 4.4.

---

[1] Terminological confusion is of course widely recognized. See Comrie (1976, p. 1), Friedrich (1974, S2–3, S6–9), Klein (1974, p. 76), among many others.

[2] This definition is from Friedrich (1974, S1). It is consistent with, but more meaningful than, that of Jakobson (1957), according to which aspect characterizes "the narrated event itself without involving its participants and without reference to the speech event [p. 4]." Further discussion of Jakobson's definition can be found in Aronson (1976). The definition adopted by Comrie (1976), after Holt, "aspects are different ways of viewing the internal temporal constituency of a situation [p. 3]" is perhaps not in conflict with the definition presented here, but is conceptually less clear.

[3] Use of the term "punctual" to characterize the main aspectual opposition of language is hardly novel. It figures in the work of Delbrück (1897) and Curtius (1846), among others. In a later work on Greek, Curtius distinguishes three "kinds of time": going on (e.g., *learn to know*), momentary (e.g., *perceive*), and completed (e.g., *to have learned*). Then he observes: "The momentary action may be compared to a point, the action going on to a line, and the completed action to a surface [1882, p. 273]."

King (1969), after Poutsma, takes the punctual–durative opposition as central to his discussion of verbs uses in English.

2.2. Real World Facts versus Linguistic Facts

Before the terms punctual and linear can be defined, a second source of confusion prevalent in aspect studies must be operationally resolved. Linguists often confound real world facts about time with grammatical ones about aspect. Garey (1957) has succinctly criticized the

> confusion of a feature of the referent with a feature of the linguistic expression which denotes it (the explosion of a bomb, although of short duration, can be envisaged, like any other event in its duration or as accomplished, etc.) [p. 92]."[4]

Because aspect is a grammatical category, aspectual oppositions must be defined in grammatical terms. One possible approach is to demonstrate that rules of the language under consideration are sensitive to the distinctions being proposed. The clearest cases of this to date involve those rules that govern the combination of elements. As Friedrich observed, "The possibility of co-occurrence between verbal and adverbial subcategories is the *universal* criterion for aspect [1974, S4]."

In this analysis, then, an aspectually punctual verb is NOT defined as one that refers to a punctual event in the real world. A punctual verb, rather, is one coded in the grammar (here: Georgian grammar) for a category of punctuality. It is, of course, necessary to demonstrate that the language has such a category and, furthermore, to provide explicit, nonintuitive criteria for deciding whether a given form is punctual or not.

Indicative of punctual meaning is occurrence in time frames expressing one single point in time (*at 8:13 p.m.*, or *just at that very moment*), which I will call "punctual time frames." Punctual verbs do not occur in time frames that express a period of time (*all day long* or *from 8 a.m. to 10 p.m.*),[5] which will be called "linear time frames."

As an example, consider the Georgian verb *šemcivda* 'I became cold [cited in the Aorist]'. In the sentences of (2), which contain punctual time frames, this verb form is acceptable, but in the sentences of (3), which contain linear time frames, it is not acceptable.

---

[4] Lyons (1968, p. 314) and (1977, p. 709) makes a similar point. The student is also cautioned against such confusion by Comrie (1976, p. 4), who in later discussion (1976, pp. 42–43) seems to obscure the difference himself.

[5] This is a descriptive generalization which may have to be refined in later work, when additional field work enables me to incorporate facts of this analysis with marking principles. Though marked and unmarked punctual verbs occur in punctual time frames, I strongly suspect that only verbs marked for punctuality will fail to occur with linear time frames.

(2) a. *At saatze   šemcivda.*[6]
         10 hour-at me-became-cold
         'I became cold at 10:00.'
     b. *Šemcivda   tu ara,   mze gamovida.*
         me-became-cold just when sun came-out
         Just when I became cold, the sun came out.'

(3) a. **Sami saati šemcivda.*
         three hour me-became-cold
         *'For three hours I became cold.'[7]
     b. **Didixnis   ganmavlobaši šemcivda.*
         long-time-GEN course-in   me-became-cold
         *'For a long time I became cold.'

Šemcivda, we conclude, is punctual.

A linear verb, on the other hand, is coded for a category of linearity. Unlike a punctual verb, a linear CAN occur in linear time frames [as in (4)]; a linear can also occur in SOME punctual time frames [as in (5)].

(4) a. *Mteli dγe viṭire.*
         whole day I-cried
         'I cried all day.'
     b. *Xuti çeliçadi Vano miqvarda.*
         five year   Vano me-loved-he
         'I loved Vano for five years.'

(5)   *Xut saatze mcioda.*
         5   hour-at me-was-cold
         'I was cold at 5:00; At 5:00 I was cold.'

Other punctual time frames, however, are more restrictive, in that they do NOT allow linear verbs. This subset includes the expressions *tu ara* and *rogorc ḳi,* both of which coordinate two clauses and can be glossed 'just at the moment when *x,* then *y*'. Both clauses *x* and *y* must contain punctual verbs [as in (6)]. Linear verbs are not allowed in either clause, as is illustrated by the unacceptable sentences of (7).

---

[6] All examples are from field work in Tbilisi, conducted in 1974–1975. In the transcription, a dot under or over a letter indicates glottalization; in the section where preverbs are discussed, the preverb is separated from the rest of the verb by ''=''.

[7] In some cases the durational adverb in English may be interpreted as modifying the state resulting from the event, as in (3a). To help exclude such readings, I have repositioned the adverbial. This interpretation is not possible in Georgian.

It should be noted that the unacceptability of (3) must be due to something about the particular verb and not to use of the Aorist. Sentence (4a) contains an Aorist in a linear time frame which IS acceptable.

(6) a. *Rogorc ķi dedam saxli   daalaga, priad gaixara.*
         just as   mother house cleaned   very became-happy
         'When mother finished cleaning the house, she became very
         happy.'
     b. *Imas coli mouķvda tu ara, lotoba   daiçqo.*
         him wife died   just as drinking began
         'No sooner did his wife die than he began drinking.'
     c. *Rogorc ķi mamam supra gaaçqo, sţumrebi šemovidnen.*
         just as   father table set   guests   entered
         'Just when father finished setting the table, the guests entered.'

(7) a. **Rogorc ķi saxli   daalaga, uxaroda.*
         just as   house cleaned   was-happy
         ?'Just when he finished cleaning the house, he was happy.'
     b. **Vano miqvarda   tu ara, sxva   kalakši gadavida.*
         vano me-loved-he just as other city-to moved
         ?'Just at the moment when I loved Vano, he moved to another
         city.'
     c. **Rogorc ķi teleponma dareķa, saxlši   viqavi.*
         just as   telephone rang   home-in I-was
         ?'Just when the phone rang, I was at home.'

These expressions coordinate two consecutive points in time, each of
which must be the "unique" moment of the situation it depicts, and not
one of many other possible moments. These time frames will be referred
to as "unique punctual time frames."

In the following discussion, when a Georgian verb form is called "punctual," it does not occur in linear time frames; when a form is called "linear," it does not occur in unique punctual ones. Because *tu ara* and *rogorc ķi,* as indicated, are among the most restrictive time frames, they will
be the only ones used here. Punctuals can be used with them, linears
cannot.

To reiterate, the definition of aspect oppositions in Georgian by means
of time frames or other objective criteria from Georgian is essential. It is
not sufficient to assert that a particular Georgian form is punctual or linear
on the basis of either intuitions about the semantics of the English equivalent or an interpretation of amount of real time expended during a real
world situation which that linguistic form may be used to encode.

2.3. Lexical Information Combined with Morphological Information

Previous analyses of aspect in Georgian, as in many other languages,
have focused on one or very few overt, morphologically marked opposi-

tions, such as perfective–imperfective.[8] Such oppositions are often restricted to some subset of the verbs of the language (e.g., the perfective–imperfective opposition is restricted to nonstatives). Understanding of this ubiquitous category of aspect is seriously skewed when one concentrates on one part of the system to the exclusion of others.

In any language, a particular verb form may have a particular aspect (e.g., punctual) by virtue of a number of different factors. English *find* is punctual by virtue of its lexical meaning; a Greek Aorist is punctual by virtue of its verbal theme; a -*d*- form in Georgian is punctual because of its derivational class; the punctuality of English *burn up* (as opposed to *burn*) or *wrote a letter* (as opposed to *wrote letters*) is due to syntactic or compositional factors. Yet, all of these forms are punctual and somewhere in the grammar we must be able to take account of their aspectual character.[9]

The following analysis unifies some information about Georgian aspect that would traditionally be considered lexical with facts about derivation and inflection. Five sets of aspect pairs will be examined and compared. By treating various levels of aspect oppositions as "pairs of verbs" I mean to be quite neutral about the particular relationship involved in each case. The claim is that the two forms are related and that a major part of the difference between them is aspectual. Whatever mechanism is ultimately adopted to account for differences and similarities of forms discussed, it will have to incorporate the particular facts about aspectual meaning and restrictions of morphemes presented here.

2.4. Summary of Vendler

Because familiarity with the verb classification established by Vendler (1967) will be assumed in the remainder of this chapter, a short summary of it seems appropriate. In an attempt to account for various uses of English verbs, Vendler set up a quadripartite division, based on "time schemata."[10] Those verbs that occur in progressive tenses were said to be "processes going on in time." They are of two types: ACTIVITIES are

---

[8] Čikobava (1950, p. 61), Mačavariani (1974), Šanije (1973, p. 262) and Tschenkéli (1958, p. 80) all define the word "aspect" in terms of the morphological opposition preverb (perfective)–no preverb (imperfective). Broader treatments can be found in Schmidt (1963) and Vogt (1971, pp. 180–195).

[9] This discussion draws heavily on Friedrich (1974, S3–6).

[10] This summary is in Vendler's own words, as indicated by double quotation marks. Both Vendler's particular classification and his classificatory criteria have received much attention, including criticism, in the literature. For elaboration of the linguistic differences between these four types and problems in this division, see Dowty (1972, pp. 19–34). Alternative proposals for verb classifications include those of Kenny (1963), Mourelatos (1978), and others. The present analysis of Georgian utilizes Vendler's schema and terminology

those processes that go on in time "in a homogeneous way; any part of the process is of the same nature as the whole." Examples of activities include *run, push a cart, cry*. For activities, the question "For how long?" is meaningful; "How long did it take?" is somewhat odd:

(8)   a.   *For how long did he push the cart?*
           How long did the baby cry?
      b.   *?How long did it take to push the cart?*

ACCOMPLISHMENTS "also go on in time, but they proceed towards a terminus which is logically necessary to their being what they are." Examples include *run a mile, draw a circle, recover from the measles*. The observations about relevant questions are reversed here: The question "How long did it take?" is meaningful for accomplishments, whereas "for how long?" is odd:

(9)   a.   *How long did he take to recover from the measles?*
      b.   *?For how long did he recover from the measles?*

Note that, although accomplishments have a built-in end point, it is not necessarily always the case that that end point is reached. Some instances of accomplishment verbs carry the implication that the terminus is reached (e.g., *John wrote the letter* implies the letter is finished); other instances, the English progressive form is an example, do not (e.g., *John was writing the letter, when a prowler knocked him out with a crowbar* does not imply letter was ever completed).[11]

Verbs that do not occur in progressive tenses are also divided into two types: ACHIEVEMENTS "occur at a single moment," "can be predicated only for single moments of time," and include *spot the plane, find a husband, reach the mountain top*. They are appropriate with a question "At what time?" but not with "For how long?":

(10) a.   *At what time did you reach the top?*
      b.   *?For how long did you reach the top?*

Finally, there are STATES, which, in contrast to achievements, "last for a period of time." They "can be predicated for shorter or longer periods of time." Examples are *love someone, know the answer, be cold*. A state would be appropriate with the question "For how long?"

(11) *For how long did you love her?*

---

because they are perhaps the most familiar to linguists, but does not in any way depend on the particulars of it. Tests for distinguishing the four verb types of Vendler in Georgian have been presented in Holisky 1978.

[11] Further discussion and formal treatment of this problem can be found in Dowty 1977.

Although Vendler was classifying surface instances of English verbs and his criteria for classification (e.g., occurrence in progressive form) are particular to English, there is something potentially universal about such a schema. For our purposes, it is sufficient to note its direct applicability to the Georgian verbal system. My use of Vendler's four terms will be more extended than his. "Activity" may refer to a surface instance of a verb with activity sense or it may refer to an inherent meaning of a verbal root, whose surface occurrence (depending on the particular derivation involved) may or may not be an activity. The same applies to accomplishment, achievement, and state.

3. ANALYSIS OF ASPECT IN GEORGIAN

The primary data of the Georgian aspect system will be presented here as pairs of related verbs that differ aspectually: one verb is punctual, the other linear. Two major sets of such pairs, described in Sections 3.1 and 3.2, represent highly productive relationships in the language. The three sets of verbs discussed in Sections 3.3, 3.4, and 3.5, constitute minor, more restricted relationships.

3.1. Preverb

The first set of aspect pairs can be characterized morphologically by the presence or absence of a preverb, as indicated in (12).[12]

(12)	Preverb Opposition	
(a) Without preverb	(b) With preverb	(c) Gloss
çers	da=çers	'write something'
açqobs	ga=açqobs	'set (a table)'
kidavs	da=kidavs	'hang (a picture)'
klavs	mo=klavs	'kill someone'
alagebs	da=alagebs	'put (a room) in order'
çmends	ga=çmends	'clean (clothing)'
imaleba	da=imaleba	'hide (intransitive)'
xdeba	mo=xdeba	'happen'
kvdeba	mo=kvdeba	'die'

The forms of (12a) are linear aspect forms, those of (12b) are punctual.

[12] Šanije (1973, p. 262), Tschenkéli (1958, p. 75, pp. 80–83), and Vogt (1971, pp. 183–187) all present a more traditional view of preverbs in Georgian. Verbs listed here are cited in third person singular subject form (with direct object, if any, also in third singular).

(13) a. *Rogorc ḳi mama supras aċqobs, sṭumrebi šemodian.
          just as   father table set   guests   come-in
          ?'Just at the moment father is setting the table, the guests enter.'
      b. Rogorc ḳi mama supras gaaċqobs, šemovlen.
          just as   father table will-set   will-enter
          'Just at the moment when father will finish setting the table,
          they will enter.'

(14) a. *Kabas švils vuċmend tu ara, imas vban.
          dress child I-clean   just as him I-wash
          *'Just at the moment I'm cleaning the dress for the child, I'm
          washing him.'
      b. Kabas švils gavucmend tu ara, imas davban.
          dress child I-will-clean just as him I-will-wash
          'At the moment I finish cleaning the dress for the child, I'll
          wash him.'

There are two additional relevant differences:

1. The verbs in (a) are Present Tense forms, those of (b) are Future
   Tense.[13]
2. All verbs in (12) are accomplishments, but only the forms of (b)
   carry an implication that the action has been or will be completed.
   The verbs of (a) have no implication.

All accomplishment verbs in Georgian that have been examined fit this
pattern: Present tense—no preverb and no implication of completion; Future tense—preverb and implication of completion.

3.2 Doni

The second aspect opposition to be discussed involves pairs of verbs
like those in (15) and (16), with the second member of each pair being
characterized by the suffix -d-. (In Georgian grammatical tradition these
are known as doniani, doni being the name for the Georgian letter d.)[14]

---

[13] "Present Tense" and "Future Tense" are used here as they are in traditional Georgian
grammar, to name paradigmatic sets. A topic for further study is whether reference to future
time is the basic meaning of these particular Futures, or whether this meaning is an implied
one, resulting from accomplishment meaning of verbal root plus marker of completion (preverb).

[14] This analysis of Georgian doni forms is radically different from that in Georgian grammatical tradition. These are elsewhere considered to be passives. See Šanije (1973, pp. 289–
90), Mačavariani (1973, pp. 108–121), Tschenkéli (1958, pp. 280–282), Vogt (1971, pp. 104,
106–107).

Doni Opposition.

(15)	(a) Activity	Gloss for (a)	(b) Doni
	ţiris	'cry'	*a= ţir-d-eba*
	duɣs	'boil'	*a =duɣ-d-eba*
	ķanķalebs	'tremble'	*a= ķanķal-d-eba*
	qebs	'bark'	*a= qep-d-eba*
	qviris	'scream'	*a =qvir-d-eba*
(16)	(a) State		
	mepea	'(be) king'	*ga=mep-d-eba*
	ţķbilia	'(be) sweet'	*ga =ţķbil-d-eba*
	uqvars	'love someone'	*še =uqvar-d-eba*
	sciva	'(be) cold (a person)'	*še =sciv-d-eba*

The forms of (a) are aspectually linear, those of (b) are punctual.

(17) a. **Vano miqvarda tu ara, sxva kalakši gadavida.*
          Vano me-loved just as other city-in moved
          ?'Just at the moment I loved Vano, he moved to another city.'
      b. *Vano šemiqvarda   tu ara, manana šeirto.*
          Vano me-love-begin just as manana married
          'Just as I fell in love with Vano, he married 'Manana.'

(18) a. **Rogorc ķi bavšvi ţiris, deda saxlši   šedis.*
          just as   baby   cries mom house-in enters

Although the forms of (15a) and (16a) are Present Tense forms and those of (15b) and (16b) are Future Tense forms, we would not want to claim they are members of the same paradigmatic set. The verbs of (a) have Future forms which share their linear aspect:

(i)   *Ţiris.*
      'He cries. He is crying.' (Present)
(ii) *I-ţir-ebs.*
      'He will be crying.' (Future)

Some of the verbs of Column (b) have corresponding Present Tense forms:

(iii) *Aduɣ-d-eba.*
      'It begins to boil.' (Future)
(iv) *Duɣ-d-eba.*
      'It is beginning to boil.' (Present)

This is different from the relationship between the verbs of (a) and (b) of (12). The only way to express 'write' in the Present in Georgian is to use *cer* (a linear form), and the only way to express its Future is to use *da =cer* (a punctual) (or, *cer* plus some OTHER preverb, resulting in an altered lexical meaning, but the same aspectual one, i.e., punctual).

?'Just at the moment when the baby is crying, the mother enters the house.'

b.   *Rogorc ḳi bavšvi aṭirdeba, . . .*
     just as   baby   cry-begin
     'Just at the moment the baby begins to cry, . . .'

The forms in (a) are activities (15) or states (16).[15] Their counterparts in (b) are achievements that indicate the initial point of the activity or state. *Aṭirdeba* means 'begin to cry', *aduɣdeba* 'begin to boil', *gamepdeba* 'become king' and so on.

Although it is not the case that ALL states and activities have corresponding doni punctual forms (many, for instance, are ruled out by constraints of semantic contradiction), ONLY states and activities have doni forms. There are no doni's related to achievements or accomplishments.

(19) a.   *Çers.*
           'He writes it.'
      b.   **A =çer-d-eba.*
           'He begins to write it.'

(20) a.   *Ḳvdeba.*
           'He is dying.' (Here -*d*- is part of the root.)
      b.   **A =ḳvd-d-eba.*
           'He begins to die.' (The sequence -*dd*- is not ruled out in Georgian.)

Note that there is nothing semantically anamolous about such combinations of meaning. They can be expressed periphrastically in Georgian, just as in English:

(21) a.   *Çeras daiçqebs.*
           'He begins to write.'
      b.   *Da=çeras daiçqebs.*
           'He begins to write.'

3.3. Ulob

The third aspectual opposition involves a rather restricted number of verb pairs.

(22)	*Ulob* Opposition	
(a)	gloss for (a)	(b) with -*ulob*
ipovnis	'find something'	*ṗo-ulobs*

---

[15] A third type also belongs here: activity verbs of motion and their doni counterparts: *srialebs* 'it slithers'–*še=srial-d-eba* 'it slithers in (= is in by slithering)'. These doni forms occur with a wide range of preverbs which indicate direction.

itxovs	'borrow something'	*txo-ulobs*
išovis	'get something'	*šo-ulobs*
iḳisrebs	'take something on (e.g. a task)'	*ḳisr-ulobs*

(N.B. Loss of -*v*- before labials is predictable.) The forms of (a) are punctual Future Tense forms. They are achievements. The forms of (b) are their respective Present Tense counterparts, with linear aspect.[16]

3.4. *Ia*

A fourth aspect opposition is also restricted to a small number of verbs.

(23)   *Ia* Opposition

(a)	Gloss for (a)	(b) with -*ia*
(*da* =) *çers*	'write something'	(*s*) *çer-ia*
(*da* =) *xaṭavs*	'paint something'	(*h*) *xaṭ-ia*
(*da* =) *abams*	'bind something'	*ab-ia*
(*da* =) *ḳidavs*	'hang something'	(*h*) *ḳid-ia*

The verbs of (a) are accomplishments; with preverbs they are punctual and without preverbs they are linear (see Section 3.1). The verbs of (b) are passives of state, related to the accomplishments, and always linear.[17]

(24) a. *Vanos çerili mi=vçere tu ara, čamovida.*
          Vano letter I-wrote   just as arrived
          'Just when I finished writing a letter to Vano, he arrived.'
      b. **Čemi gvari siaši eçera   tu ara, šemešinda.*
          my   name list-in was-written just as me-afraid-begin
          'Just as my name was written in the list, I became frightened.'
          (*eçera* is past tense form for *çeria*.)

---

[16] For earlier discussion of -*ulob* see Tschenkéli (1958, pp. 318–319) or Vogt (1971, pp. 141–142). The reader should be warned that this particular relationship is much more complex than indicated in Section 3.3. The specific meaning of the -*ulob* forms is poorly understood at this time. Much more detailed investigation, especially additional field work is necessary.

Verb roots that do not take preverbs, but yet have punctual aspect [as the verbs in this set, Column (a)], are vestiges of the aspect structure of Old Georgian, where aspect differences were always coded by verbal roots or inflectional stems and not by preverbs (Šanije, 1973, pp. 266–273; Schmidt, (1963). Preverbs as regular markers for punctual aspect are recent. At the present stage of the language, preverbs in this function are productive only with roots that are accomplishments. Punctual aspect for achievements, on the other hand, for those achievements where an opposition punctual–linear is possible, is expressed in one of three possible ways (see Section 4.2).

[17] See also discussion in Šanije (1973, pp. 312–323). Tschenkéli (1958, pp. 434–445), Vogt (1971, pp. 154–162). Holisky (1978) contains an elaboration of the aspectual properties and syntactic and morphological restrictions of these verbs.

3.5. Preverb[2]

Fifth and finally, there are the following pairs of verbs in Georgian:

(25)	Preverb[2] Opposition	
(a)	Gloss for (a)	(b) with preverb
iṭirebs	'cry'	*ça=iṭirebs*
iqepebs	'bark'	*da=iqepebs*
iqvirebs	'scream'	*da=iqvirebs*
ibɣavlebs	'bleat'	*amo=ibɣav-lebs*

Column (a) lists linear Future Tense forms of activity verbs; the verbs of (b), where a preverb has been added, are punctual counterparts for these linear forms. Verbs of (b) have semelfactive meaning, and can be glossed as "cry out', 'scream out', *etc.*

(26) a. **Rogorc ḳi jaɣlma iqepa, kurdi gaikca.*
     just as   dog   barked thief ran-away
     'Just when the dog barked, the thief ran away.'
  b. *Rogorc ḳi jaɣlma da=iqepa, kurdi gaikca.*
     just as   dog   barked-out thief ran-away
     'Just when the dog barked out, the thief ran away.'

(27) a. **Bavšvi iqvirebs tu ara, gamomeɣvijeba.*
     baby   screams just as me-wake-up
     ?'Just at the moment the baby will be screaming, I will wake up.'
  b. *Bavšvi da=iqvirebs tu ara, gamameɣvijeba.*
     baby   screams-out just as me-wake-up
     'Just at the moment the baby screams out, I will wake up.'

4. CONCLUSIONS

A number of conclusions about the aspect system of Georgian can be drawn from the five aspect patterns just presented.

1. First of all, to describe the verbs of each set, Vendler's quadripartite division was employed. (For example, a doni form was said to relate to an activity or a state, but not to an achievement or an accomplishment.) I know of no other way to precisely and accurately characterize these patterns. It has been shown elsewhere that a classification schema such as Vendler's is relevant in a syntactic description of Georgian (Holisky, 1978). The above examples make it clear that morphological processes of word formation and inflection—however they are stated in a grammar— must be sensitive to such a verb classification.

2. Moreover, the characterization of aspect types must be made with reference to the verbal ROOT of Georgian, and not merely to a particular surface verb form. The doni forms relate to activities and states, as noted, but only to INITIAL or INHERENT ones. No doni forms relate to derived states (e.g., those of Section 3.4). I therefore make the claim that each verb root in Georgian must be marked for aspect; each root will be in one of Vendler's four classes.[18] A verb root may undergo derivational or inflectional processes whose effect may be to alter the initial aspect, and MUST undergo some process in order to be used in a time frame requiring a different aspect (e.g., a linear stative cannot be used in a unique punctual time frame without having undergone some aspect-changing process).[19]

To take a specific example, the root *civ* 'cold' is a stative root; states are aspectually linear. This root may undergo a process which changes it to a punctual achievement: *šesciv-d-eba* 'became cold'. It MUST have undergone some process whose effect is to change aspect in order to be able to occur in a context that demands a punctual (as a unique punctual time frame does). The root *pov* 'find something', on the other hand, is an inherent achievement, aspectually punctual, and may occur in a unique punctual time frame without further ado. It receives a special marking (*-ulob*) when used in aspectually linear contexts.

A summary of some systematic properties of each type of aspectual root in Georgian is given in (28)–(31).

(28)   Accomplishments
  • Present Tense is linear; no preverb and no implication of completion.
  • Future Tense is punctual; preverb and implication of completion.
  • Past consists of two-way opposition:
    Imperfect is linear; no preverb and no implication of completion.
    Aorist is punctual; preverb and implication of completion.
  • Derivations: *-ia* forms with linear aspect (specifically, passive-of-state meaning).

---

[18] An inherent aspect for verb roots was also assumed for Onondaga by Chafe (1970). I do not mean to exclude the possibility that a verb root could be in more than one aspect class.

[19] I have not discussed wider syntactic contexts and their effect on the aspect of the verb root or derived verb form. It is well known, for example, that plural, indefinite, or mass noun objects (or subjects) can completely alter the aspectual properties of the verb phrase (e.g., Dowty 1972, pp. 30–34, 48–59).

In this chapter I have specifically avoided reference to aspectual categories as they relate to tense. An integration of the system developed here with tense categories is, of course, necessary.

(29)   Activities
- Present Tense is linear.
- Future Tense is linear; formed with *i-* . . . *-eb*.
  Some have second Future Tense which is punctual; preverb is
  added to *i-* . . . *-eb* form (specifically, semelfactive meaning).
- Past:
  Most have no opposition: only a linear Imperfect.
  Some have two-way opposition:
    Imperfect, which is linear.
    Aorist, which is ??
    (N.B. Such Aorists are recent; the difference between Aorist and
    Imperfect of these verbs is vague; it is not clear whether Aorist
    here is linear or punctual.)
- Derivations: doni forms with punctual aspect (specifically, incep-
  tive meaning).

(30)   States
- Present Tense is linear.
- Future Tense is linear; formed primarily with *e-* . . . *-eba*.
- Past: no opposition, past is always linear. (Some have Imperfect
  form and others have Aorist form.)
- Derivations: doni forms with punctual aspect (specifically, incep-
  tive meaning).

(31)   Achievements[20]
- Future Tense is punctual.
- Present Tense:
  Some in *-ulob* (linear aspect, often iterative meaning).
  Some have same form as Future.
  Some have Future minus preverb.
  Some have no Present Tense.
- Past: not clear.
- Derivations: no *-ia* forms, no doni forms.
  (It is generally true that a root which is an achievement either al-
  ways occurs with a preverb or never occurs with one.)

3. A curious observation results from comparing the aspect pairs of
Section 3.1 and 3.2. There are two principal markers of punctual aspect:
preverbs and the doni suffix. Their distribution is complementary insofar
as preverbs mark the punctuality of accomplishments (and some achievements), whereas the doni suffix punctualizes activities and states. There is

---

[20] Achievements do not constitute a morphological class in the way the other three aspect
types do. Achievements are lexically determined.

a sense in which their aspectual function is also complementary: Preverbs punctualize toward the end point. In sentences like (13b) and (14b), the particular point that is picked out by the expressions *rogorc ķi* and *tu ara* is the point at which the situation is completed, the END point. The doni marker, on the other hand, picks out the BEGINNING point. In (17b) and (18b), *rogorc ķi* and *tu ara* pick out the beginning of the situation (the state of loving and activity of crying).

4. Finally, there is one important issue which should be mentioned, but which I am not prepared to resolve in this chapter. Can the opposition introduced as punctual–linear be more strictly defined as punctual–non-punctual or linear–nonlinear, or is there a need in Georgian for both oppositions? Related to this is the question of marking.[21] Is the punctual member of the five oppositions discussed the marked or unmarked member? As additional field work would be necessary to adequately answer this question, I can only provide some comments here.

I am certain the answer will not be the same across all five verb pairs presented in the chapter and I do not believe that it can be answered without reference to the inherent aspect type (Section 4.2). Intuitively, considering stative roots, one would expect surface instances that are linear to be unmarked as opposed to surface occurrences that are punctual. So, for stative roots, we would no doubt want to argue of the opposition given in (16), that the doni form is marked for punctuality and the stative form is unmarked. For accomplishments and achievements, however, the answer is less clear.

5. IMPLICATIONS

This analysis of Georgian aspect has integrated information about the lexical properties of verbs, considered inherent, with inflectional and derivational processes, which frequently serve to alter these inherent properties. I have argued that an analysis of aspect in any particular language must take account both of the particular processes and markings of aspectual relevance (preverbs, suffixes, thematic roots, *etc.*), and also of the lexical types to which the marking applies (as well as wider syntactic context, as indicated in Note 19). This approach is necessary, not only in the description of a particular language, but also in order to be able to

---

[21] I refer to a Prague School notion of marking: "The general meaning of a marked category states the presence of a certain . . . property A; the general meaning of the corresponding unmarked category states nothing about the presence of A . . . [Jakobson, 1957, p. 6]."

compare aspect systems of different languages, especially where one relies heavily on lexical and the other on morphological aspect coding.

Such a view of aspect patterning also puts historical change in a new light. A particular aspect marking first appears in a specific function when applied to one particular verb type. For example, take a historical case in which preverbs are added to accomplishments and specify completion of the goal inherent in the meaning of the verb. Later, preverbs come to be used with OTHER verb types as well. Concomitantly, the aspectual meaning of the preverb, although remaining punctual, becomes more general. It is not possible that the preverb could continue to mean attainment of goal inherent in the verb when applied to a state, because there is no inherent goal with a state. A state plus punctual aspect marking, as a preverb in this example, might refer to the inception of the state (as in Russian—see Miller, 1970, p. 491), or possibly, to the termination of the state.[22]

Three relevant questions for historical investigation thus emerge:

1. To verbs of which aspect type is an aspect marking first applied?
2. What is the aspectual effect of the marking? (i.e., Does it linearize or punctualize? If the latter, does it mark inception, completion, *etc.*?)
3. How does the use of the marker diffuse through the verbal system of the language? What concomitant changes in meaning of the marker result?

In conclusion, considering aspectual processes with reference to both the marking of inflectional and derivational systems AND the inherent verbal meanings the marking applies to is relevant to at least three areas of linguistic research: the description of aspect systems of individual languages, the comparison of systems of different languages, and the explanation of the mechanism of historical changes in the structure of aspect systems of languages and language families.

REFERENCES

Aronson, H.I. (1976). Interrelationships between aspect and mood in Bulgarian. In K. E. Naylor and D. Koubourlis (Eds.), *Studies in Slavic Morphology,* Columbus, Ohio: Slavica.

Chafe, W.L. (1970). Semantically based sketch of Onondaga. *Indiana University Publications in Anthropology and Linguistics,* Memoire 25.

Comrie, B. (1976). *Aspect.* Cambridge: Cambridge University Press.

Curtius, G. (1846). *Die Bildung der Tempora und Modi im Griechischen und Lateinischen sprachvergleichend dargestellt.* Berlin: Wilhelm Besser.

[22] Lyons (1977, pp. 712–713) offers an extremely clear statement of this; though not specifically intended about historical processes, it can be so interpreted.

Curtius, G. (1882). *A Grammar of the Greek Language*. New York: Harper & Brothers.

Čikobava, A. (1950). *Kartuli Enis Ganmartebiti Leksiǩoni* [Explanatory Dictionary of the Georgian Language]. Tbilisi: Mecniereba.

Delbrück, B. (1897). *Vergleichende Syntax der Indogermanischen Sprachen* (Pt. 2). Strassburg: Karl J. Trübner.

Dowty, D. (1972). *Studies in the Logic of Verb Aspect and Time Reference in English*. Doctoral Dissertation, University of Texas at Austin.

Dowty, D. (1977). Towards a semantic analysis of verb aspect and the English 'imperfective' progressive. *Linguistics and Philosophy*, **1**, 45–77.

Friedrich, P. (1974). On aspect theory and Homeric aspect. *International Journal of American Linguistics*. (Memoirs 28), **40**, 2, Pt. 2.

Garey, H.B. Verbal aspect in French. *Language*, **33**, 91–110.

Holisky, D.A. (1978). Stative verbs in Georgian, and elsewhere. In B. Comrie (Ed.), *International Review of Slavic Linguistics*, **3**, 139–162.

Holt, J. (1943). Etudes d'aspect. *Acta Jutlandica*, **15**, 2.

Jakobson, R. (1957). Shifters, verbal categories, and the Russian verb. Cambridge, Mass. [Reprinted in R. Jakobson (1971), *Selected Writings*, **2**, The Hague: Mouton. Pp. 130–147.]

Kenny, A. (1963). *Action, Emotion and Will*. London: Routledge & Kegan Paul.

King, H.V. Punctual versus durative as covert categories. *Language Learning*, **19**, 183–190.

Klein, H.G. (1974). *Tempus, Aspekt, Aktionsart*. Tübingen: Niemeyer.

Lyons, J. (1968). *Introduction to Theoretical Linguistics*. Cambridge: Cambridge University Press.

Lyons, J. (1977). *Semantics*. (Vol. 2). Cambridge: Cambridge University Press.

Mačavariani, G. (1973). Vnebitis supiksuri ṭipis genezisis saǩitxi Kartvelur enebši [The question of the genesis of suffixal type passive in the Kartvelian languages]. *Macne* (enisa da liṭeraṭuris seria, I, 108–121).

Mačavariani, G. (1974). Aspeǩetis ǩategoria Kartvelur enebši [Category of aspect in the Kartvelian languages]. *Kartvelur enata sṭrukṭuris siǩitxebi*, **4**, 118–142.

Miller, J. (1970). Stative verbs in Russian. *Foundations of Language*, **6**, 488–504.

Mourelatos, A. (1978). Events, processes, and states. *Linguistics and Philosophy*, **2**, 415–434.

Schmidt, K.H. (1963). Zu den Aspekten im georgischen und in indo-germanischen Sprachen. *Bedi Kartlisa*, XV–XVI, 107–115.

Šanije, A. (1973). *Kartuli enis gramaṭiǩis sapujvlebi* [Fundamentals of Georgian Grammar]. I. Tbilisi: Tbilisi University Press. Chapters 326–343.

Tschenkéli, K. (1958). *Einführung in die Georgische Sprache I*. Zürich: Amirani Verlag.

Vendler, Z. (1967). Verbs and times. In Z. Vendler, *Linguistics in Philosophy*. Ithica: Cornell University Press. Pp. 97–121.

Vogt, H. (1971). *Grammaire de la langue géorgienne*. Oslo: Universitetsforlaget. Pp. 180–195.

A UNIFIED TEMPORAL THEORY
OF TENSE AND ASPECT[1]

MARION R. JOHNSON

1. INTRODUCTION

Many current theories of natural language time reference have been influenced in important ways by Hans Reichenbach's (1947) work on tensed verb forms.[2] Reichenbach analyzed the semantic distinctions among temporally inflected verb forms in terms of relations among three temporal points, which he identified as the "point of speech," the "point of reference," and the "point of the event." This analysis has been influential because, for example, it provides a satisfactory account of the difference

[1] This chapter presents a theory that is an extensive revision of the one originally proposed in my dissertation (Johnson 1977), which was done at The Ohio State University under the direction of Arnold Zwicky and David Dowty. I am indebted to the Canada Council for a travel grant which allowed me to do field work in Nairobi, Kenya in the summer of 1976, and to the government of Kenya for permission to do research. The Institute for African Studies, the Department of Linguistics at the University of Nairobi, and Dr. Kevin Ford provided invaluable practical assistance in the field. I am especially grateful to John Gĩtaũ Mũigai, Shem Kimani Macharia, David Nyĩka Kiromo, and Anthony Kinoru Gachinga, the Kikuyu speakers who worked with me on this project.

[2] Some recent linguistic articles that have dealt with Reichenbach's system are Hofmann 1974, Hornstein 1977, and Smith 1978. These articles approach Reichenbach's work from a different point of view than that taken in this chapter.

145

between a simple past tense form (as in the English *he left*), and a present perfect form (as in *he has left*). For the former, both the point of the event and the point of reference are earlier than the point of speech, whereas for the latter only the point of the event is earlier.

In this chapter, I will make use of Reichenbach's three time points in developing a unified temporal theory of the categories of tense and aspect found in the inflectional systems of natural languages. The theory I will develop provides an explicit definition of the terms "tense" and "aspect" (in relation to their roles in inflectional morphology), and an account of their complementary semantic functions. This theory also gives a unified temporal characterization for each of the major aspect categories, including, in particular, the problematic category of "imperfect aspect." In addition, the theory brings to light a third significant type of temporal category, which will be designated "existential status." The possibility for such a category type is implicit in Reichenbach's system, although the actual existence of such categories has not been previously established. Finally, the theory presented here reveals important features of a systematic relationship between form and meaning in inflectional morphology. The complex nature of this relationship is demonstrated for Kikuyu, a Bantu language in East Africa with an elaborate tense and aspect system, in which the form–meaning relationship is in many ways problematic.

The conception of tense, aspect, and existential status that underlies the theory presented here is that these categories are concerned with the ebb and flow of events through time. Taken together, these categories provide a system for describing the evolutionary condition of any given situation, when considered from certain temporal points of view. Thus, the meaning of each category has two components: (*a*) the relation between the time of a given situation and the time at which it is considered; and (*b*) the ontology of that situation, considered from that point of view. What I mean by the ontology of a situation is the degree to which the situation can be considered as a real part of the course of events in the actual world, as opposed to being part of some projected course of events which has not yet been actualized. In brief, what is involved is this: Any particular point in time may serve as a dividing line in the course of events, between a set of "real" situations, which precede that time, and a set of "projected" situations, which follow it. The situations that precede the selected point of reference are those whose development is already determined, and can therefore be known to a human observer. In contrast, the situations that are to follow the point of reference are merely hypothesized states of affair: It is not possible for a human observer to KNOW (by ordinary means) exactly how they will turn out, although it is possible to form hypotheses of greater or less probability about them. There is thus an intimate relationship between the two components of meaning that I have identified for each temporal category—namely, the ontology of a situation, and the relation between the time of the situation and the time at which it is considered. The time at which it is considered is the most important element (although not the only one) in determining the ontology of a given state of affairs, because this time is the principal dividing line between real and hypothesized states of affair.

A complete theory of tense, aspect, and status, then, must provide a way of representing the determinacy of states of affairs that precede any given point in time, and the relative indeterminacy of states of affairs that follow it, as well as show how each category specifies a temporal point of view concerning some particular state of affairs. This is the long range goal of my theory, although I will not attempt to accomplish all of this in the present chapter. Instead, I will concentrate on developing the temporal component of the theory by providing definitions for the categories of tense, aspect, and status in terms of ordering relations among various discourse-defined times—namely, "speech time," "reference time," and "event time." To accomplish this much, I will work with a linear model of time, and concentrate the more detailed discussion on the categories that are primarily concerned with situations that lie in the actual (rather than the projected) course of events.

The first part of the chapter gives a general semantic characterization of the major categories of tense and aspect, in terms of relations among Reichenbach's three temporal points. The discussion here includes a consideration of these categories in Kikuyu. I also introduce the third type of temporal relation, "existential status," which is also characterized in terms of relations among Reichenbach's three time points. In the second part of the chapter, I turn to a detailed analysis of the Kikuyu temporal paradigm. This analysis is of interest because it illustrates the role of existential status distinctions in a language, and because it demonstrates many important features of the relationship between form and meaning in inflectional morphology.

The approach to the study of tense and aspect that I am proposing in this chapter has been influenced in important ways by the approach to English tense and aspect taken in Bennett and Partee 1972. Bennett and Partee are concerned with a syntactic analysis of sentences, and they adopt a model-theoretic approach to the semantics of time. The main innovative feature of their system is that truth for sentences is defined relative to an interval of time. In this chapter, I will not be concerned with truth definitions for sentences, as my goal is to describe the semantic organization of inflectional paradigms. Nevertheless, a number of ideas on temporal meaning suggested by Bennett and Partee are applicable in the present context as well; in particular, the notion of truth for an interval of time will be translated here into the related notion of an event as occurring at an interval of time. This is further discussed in the next section of the chapter.

2. A UNIFIED THEORY OF TENSE, ASPECT, AND STATUS

2.1. Some Preliminaries on the Nature of Time

As I have already indicated, I consider time to be the semantic domain of tense, aspect, and status distinctions. This domain contains three categories of time which are significant in relation to an act of speaking. First, there is the time at which the act of speaking itself takes place. Second, there is a large set of times at which various events take place, events that might be mentioned in the speech act. Third, there are all the times other than the time of speaking, which can serve as alternative points of reference for the speaker. These alternative points of reference are the times of situations other than the speaker's own which he might want to talk about. Linguistic provision for identifying these other points of reference is important, because it means that a speaker is not constrained to talk only about the actual situation he is in; he can select any other time, and use that time as the one he is principally referring to. These three sets of times, developed from the three times first identified by Reichenbach, we will call speech time (S), event time (E), and reference time (R).

The major proposal of this chapter is that these three times can be used to characterize the three classes of semantic categories found in the temporal inflectional systems of diverse languages. Specifically, the categories of tense, aspect, and status correspond to the three logically possible combinations for paired relations among S, R, and E. The idea is that tense categories relate reference time to speech time, aspect categories relate event time to reference time, and status categories relate event time to speech time. In each case, one of the two times is used to provide a temporal point of view on the situation that exists at the other time. In a tense category, speech time is the point of view from which the situation at reference time is considered; in an aspect category, reference time is the point of view from which the situation at event time is considered; and in a status category, speech time is a second point of view from which the situation at event time is considered. This relation of categories to time points is summarized in Diagram (1):

(1)

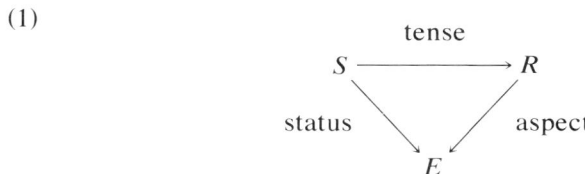

Before considering the implications of this schema, it will be helpful to discuss in greater detail the properties of time, and of the three temporal entities S, R, and E.

In the paper referred to earlier, Bennett and Partee follow a familiar logical tradition in identifying the set of times (T) with the real numbers. Their main reasons for doing this are, first, that it reflects the intuition that time is infinite both ways, and, second, that it reflects the intuition that there is a dense simple ordering of time. For the same reasons, I will also assume an identification of time with the set of real numbers. In addition, I will follow Bennett and Partee in working with the higher order concepts, INTERVAL OF TIME and MOMENT OF TIME, in place of Reichenbach's single notion of a point in time. An interval of time is to be defined in a standard set-theoretic way, as a set of times with no "gaps" between members of the set. (A precise definition will be given in what follows.) A moment of time is defined as a set of times with just one member; thus, a moment is, by definition, a special type of interval. The reason for working with intervals in the analysis is that the time at which an event occurs in the world is typically longer than a single point in time. Although there are a few events that can be viewed as instantaneous (such as realizing the solution to a problem), the great majority of events require some period of time to happen. Obvious examples of this are building the Canadian Pacific Railway, driving from Montreal to Vancouver, or singing "The Maple Leaf Forever." To accommodate this fact, we will assume that event time—which is simply the time at which some event occurs—is an interval of time, rather than a point of time. Each interval of event time either is to be the time of an individual instance of some event of a certain type, or is to contain a sequence of intervals, each of which is the time of a single instance of a certain type of event. An INSTANCE of an event is simply a unit of activity that can be singled out as "an event," in the ordinary language sense of the term. Any member of the set of event times must contain the time of at least one instance of an event of a certain type, although it may contain multiple instances of events of the same type. In the latter case, event time is the time of a repeated or habitual event.

Although event time is an interval, we will restrict the notion of speech time so that its value can only be a moment of time. This restriction is a slight distortion of reality, as speaking itself is an event that takes place over time. However, it contributes greatly to the simplicity of the analysis if we assume that a speech act is instantaneous, and this assumption does not appear to create any significant distortion in the analysis.

Given that S is a moment of time and E is an interval of time, how should we view R, the reference time? In order to allow for the possibility that R is identified with E, we take R also to be an interval of time. However, we have characterized R intuitively as a point of reference that functions for the speaker as an alternative to the time of speaking, in the sense of being the time of some situation other than his own that the speaker might want to describe. Hence, it seems reasonable to view R as a moment of time whenever the semantics of an utterance does not explicitly require us to do otherwise. In a number of examples, therefore, the reader will find both R and S represented as moments of time.

With the foregoing in mind, we now introduce set-theoretic definitions for the temporal entities S, R, and E. Note that in defining E and R [in (5)], we restrict them to NONEMPTY intervals of time. The reason for this is obvious: It would be bizarre to think of an event as occurring at an empty set of times, or of a speaker referring to an empty set of times. The definitions are, then, as follows:

(2)   Let T be a set of times, and $\leqslant$ a dense, linear ordering of T. If t, t' are members of T, then $t < t'$ abbreviates $t \leqslant t'$ and $t \neq t'$.

(3) I is an INTERVAL OF TIME if and only if $I \subseteq T$, and for all t_0, t_1, t_2 in T, if t_0, t_2 are in I and $t_0 \leqslant t_1 \leqslant t_2$, then t_1 is in I. $[I]$ stands for the set of intervals of time.

(4) m is a MOMENT OF TIME if and only if for some t in T, $m = \{t\}$.

(5)   Let E and R be nonempty intervals of time, distinguished as "event time" and "reference time," respectively, and let S be a moment of time, distinguished as the "moment of speaking."

In addition to (2)–(5), we need to define a relation of strict precedence for intervals of time; this relation is to be used later in defining various tense, aspect, and status categories. The definition is as follows:

(6)   If I, I' are members of $[I]$, then I ($<$) I$'$ (to be read: I is earlier than I') abbreviates: for all t in I and all t' in I', $t < t'$.

What this definition says is that the formula I ($<$) I' is true if and only if EVERY time in I is earlier than EVERY time in I'.

In what follows, we will use diagrams to illustrate various category analyses, with a horizontal line representing the set of times, and parentheses enclosing the limits of an interval of time.[3] For example:

(7)

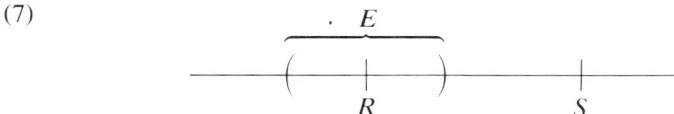

E is shown as an interval of time, R and S as moments of time.

2.2 Tense, Aspect, and Status Categories Defined

As I indicated earlier, the three types of temporal categories are to be analyzed in terms of the schema illustrated in (1):

(1)

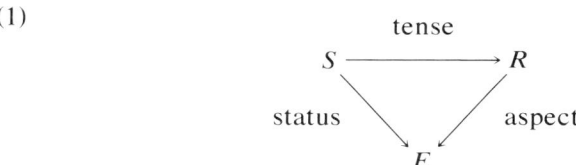

What this diagram represents is that a tense category uses speech time to provide a temporal perspective on the situation at reference time; an aspect category uses reference time to provide a temporal perspective on the situation at event time; and a status category uses speech time to give a second temporal perspective on the situation at event time. I will begin the discussion with a consideration of the major tense categories.

2.2.1. TENSE

The function of a tense category is to locate the position of the speaker's reference time, by relating it to the position of the time of speaking. The three primary possibilities for this relationship correspond to the categories past, present and future tense in the following manner:

(8)   Past $R\ (<)\ S$
               Present $R\ =\ S$
               Future $S\ (<)\ R$

Kikuyu presents a considerably larger and more interesting set of possibilities for identifying the relation between R and S. This language has

---

[3] This use of parentheses should not be confused with their use to indicate open intervals. An open interval from t_0 to t_1—written (t_0, t_1)—is defined as: $\{t: t_0 < t < t_1\}$. The difference between open and closed intervals does not affect any of the analyses given here.

seven tenses, which include, in addition to present tense, three past tense categories and three future categories. In this chapter, I will attempt to characterize only the past tenses, which are known in traditional terminology (cf. Barlow 1960) as "immediate," "near," and "remote" past tense. These three tenses divide the past (of a moment of speaking) into three subperiods, and each tense locates R in one of these subperiods (the details are given in Section 3). I shall omit discussion of the future tenses because these tenses cannot be adequately described without introducing a theory of the ontology of projected events at different points in time. As I already indicated, such a theory is beyond the intended scope of this chapter.

2.2.2. ASPECT

The linguistic term VERB ASPECT has a long and complex history, having been applied to a broad range of semantic problems and grammatical constructions. I propose to use this term with the following semantically based definition: Verb aspect involves reference to one of the temporally distinct phases in the evolution of an event through time. The key point here is that an event is said to evolve through a series of temporal "phases." One of these temporal phases is the actual time of the event itself, inclusive of its end-point. Thus, for example, the time of an event of building a house includes the moment at which the house may be said to be finished. Distinct from this is the "developmental phase," which is the period of time PRIOR to the end of the event; this phase includes, in the above example, those times at which various processes associated with house-building are taking place. And, in addition to these two phases, there is the "result phase," which FOLLOWS the end of the event and which includes the times at which the house exists. The aspect of a verb which describes an event of house-building, then, is whatever determines whether the verb refers to the time of the whole event itself, or to its coming about, or to the subsequent state.

This definition of verb aspect may be usefully contrasted with that given in Comrie 1976. The latter definition proposes that "aspects are different ways of viewing the internal temporal constituency of a situation [p. 3]." The essential difference between this definition and my own is that, according to Comrie, aspect involves only times that are INTERNAL to an event. In contrast to this, my definition involves the idea of temporally distinct PHASES of an event, which are to be understood broadly as encompassing the whole sequence of an event's evolution through time. That is, the phases of an event begin with the earliest time that the event may be taken to be a concrete reality in the projected course of events, and lasts until the latest time that the event continues to affect the shape of later events. Consequently, the phases of an event include times that are strictly earlier or later than the time of the event itself. The significance of this point will become apparent as the analysis of the individual aspect categories develops.

The aspect of a verb may be realized in one of two ways grammatically, either by the aspect CLASS or the aspect FORM of a verb. The aspect class of a verb is the lexical classification of the verb, which determines which part of a complex event is the basic denotation of a verb stem. For example, with an inchoative event such as coming to know something, a verb stem may refer either to the change of state (as in English *realize*), or to the resulting state (as in English *know*). Temporal analyses of categorizations of this type have been proposed by a number of people (e.g., Vendler, 1967; Dowty, 1972, 1977; Taylor, 1977; and Nordenfelt, 1977). The aspect class of a verb may be modified by the aspect form of the verb. As aspect form—such as English *run, be running* or *have run*—is any form of a verb whose temporal meaning (in relation to some event named by the verb) contrasts systematically with the temporal meanings of other forms of the verb. For example, if the basic form of a verb stem refers to some change of state, and a modified form refers to the enduring state that follows the change, then both the basic and the modified form qualify as aspect forms of the verb. Distinctions of this sort are the concern of the present discussion, and so the term verb aspect will be used here in the particular sense of aspect form. What I am proposing concerning the semantics of these forms is that they specify the relation between reference time and event time in an utterance. The reference time may be the same as event time, or it may fall within some temporal phase of the event defined relative to the time of the event itself. In this way, the aspect forms of a verb provide a way for a speaker to make reference to the separate phases of the event named by a verb.

Three principal categories of verb aspect form have been identified in various languages. These three categories—which I will refer to as "completive," "imperfect," and "perfect" aspect—have been previously discussed on a broad comparative basis in Comrie 1976.[4] All three are separately marked in Kikuyu, and my analysis of them was based originally on the facts of this language. However, the analysis is not intended to be specific to Kikuyu, as a major part of the motivation for it is a consideration of the logical possibilities provided by the system. That is, in relation to the time of an event, it is possible to distinguish three temporal phases which are significant in terms of the evolution of the event through time:

---

[4] My terminology here is close to Comrie's usage. However, I use "imperfect" where he uses "imperfective," and the term "completive" in place of what Comrie (following the Slavicist tradition) calls "perfective aspect." I have made the latter change in terminology in order to avoid confusion between this category and the semantically distinct category known as "perfect aspect."

(*a*) the actual time of the whole event itself, including its completion; (*b*) the range of times leading up to the completion of the event, during which various developments take place which bring the event into being; and (*c*) the range of times that follow the end of the event, and contain its results. The three aspect form categories each allow for reference to one of these phases: completive aspect to the time of the whole event itself; imperfect aspect to times in the developmental phase which are prior to the end of the event; and perfect aspect to times later than the event, which are in the result phase. This is illustrated in Diagram (9), where brackets enclose the interval of time identified as *E*:

(9) $R = E$ for completive aspect

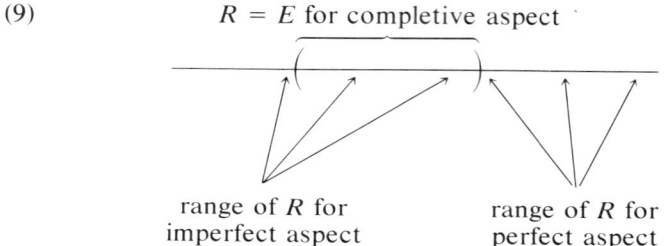

              range of *R* for   range of *R* for
             imperfect aspect   perfect aspect

This conception of aspect leads to the following general definitions for each category:

(10)   Completive: $R = E$
                Imperfect: For some t in E, R $(<)$ $\{t\}$
                Perfect: E $(<)$ R

The definition of imperfect aspect requires that some PORTION of E be later than R, whereas the definition of the perfect requires that all of E be earlier than R. Examples of each of the three categories are given in (11)–(13) for the near past (NP) tense of Kikuyu:[5]

---

[5] Kikuyu forms are cited in the standard orthography. The one peculiarity of this system is the use of the orthographs ī and ū for phonetic [e] and [o], respectively. (The Kikuyu orthographs e and o stand for phonetic [ɛ] and [ɔ], respectively.)

The morphological details of aspect marking in Kikuyu are quite complicated. For the sake of clarity and typographical convenience, I have rendered the morphological breakdown of forms slightly inaccurately in this chapter. In a careful analysis, the aspect markers would not be given as the "suffixes" *-ire, -aga,* and *-ite* (~ *-ete*), but the morphemes *-ir-, -ag-,* and *-īt-* (~ *-et-*). The latter group of markers are in some instances clearly infixed into the verb stem, although in other cases they seem to be analyzable as suffixes rather than infixes. Two of the aspect markers, *-ir-* and *-īt-*, trigger a morphophonemic change (a → e) in the final vowel of a verb stem. It is the problematic status of this final vowel as a suffix or an intrinsic part of a verb root that makes the morphology of the aspect markers ambiguous. As the semantics of aspect does not in any way depend upon the precise shape of its morphological realization, I have taken the liberty of simplifying the morphological breakdown of the relevant Kikuyu forms.

(11)   Completive: *a-ra-ak-ire*   *nyūmba*
                     he-NP-build-Comp house
                     'he built a house (in the near past)'

(12)   Imperfect: *a-ra-ak-aga*   *nyūmba*
                     he-NP-build-Imperf house
                     'he was building a house (in the near past)' (refer-
                     ence to a time prior to the completion of the house)

(13)   Perfect: *a-ra-ak-īte*   *nyūmba*
                     he-NP-build-Perf   house
                     'he had built a house (in the near past)' (reference
                     to a time in the near past after the house was com-
                     pleted)

The definition I have given in (10) for imperfect aspect requires some
additional comment. There are many languages in which the imperfect is
used to express iterated/habitual action, as illustrated for Kikuyu in (14):[6]

(14)   *nī a-ra-hanyūk-aga*
        he-NP-run-Imperf
        'he repeatedly/habitually ran (in the near past)'

I believe that this interpretation of the imperfect is a case of semantic
vagueness rather than ambiguity, in the sense that the imperfect simply
fails to specify whether the event involves a single instance or multiple
instances; hence, the imperfect leaves open the possibility of interpreting
the event either way. It seems to me that all of the aspects are essentially
vague in this respect. However, it is very often the imperfect that is chosen to express iterated and/or habitual action. I believe that this is a natural choice for the following reason. The imperfect involves reference to an
event that goes on beyond the speaker's point of reference. It is a characteristic property of iterated or habitual action that, once initiated, it can
continue into the future for indefinitely long periods of time. Because the
imperfect involves times prior to the end of an event, it can readily be
used to implicate the indefinite continuation of a series of related events.
In addition, because the imperfect involves reference to times internal to
an event, it is the natural choice for describing a situation in terms of some
repeated or habitual act which begins before the reference time, and continues after it. That is, the imperfect allows for reference to a situation
during which some habit may be thought of as in existence, although the

---

[6] In this example, *nī* is required in order to ensure that the sentence is an assertion. Without *nī*, it would only be used as a question. See Myers (1971) for some comment on this
particle.

time of the situation does not encompass the whole time of the habitual action.

Another significant feature of the meaning I have assigned to imperfect aspect is the possibility of interpreting it as a description of an event that has not yet begun at the speaker's reference time. This interpretation arises from the possibility, allowed for in the definition of imperfect aspect, that reference time is earlier than ALL of event time. This sense of the imperfect is illustrated for Kikuyu in (15):

(15)   *nĩ a-ra-hanyũk-aga*
         he-NP-run-Imperf
         'he was just about to run (in the near past)'

There is a similar use of the progressive form in English. For example, I can truthfully say *I am building a house* as soon as I have formed the intention to do so, even if I have not yet undertaken any specific planning or building activity. I believe that the possibility for this use of the imperfect is intrinsic to its meaning, for two reasons. First, this feature of the imperfect is shared by a number of unrelated languages. Second, the imperfect always involves the idea of an event that continues beyond the speaker's point of reference, into a period of time in which the course of events is only partially determined from the perspective of that reference point. In other words, the imperfect always involves mentioning an event whose full realization in actual time, when considered from the position of the reference time, is only a highly probable development, but cannot be called an absolute certainty. When reference time precedes all of event time, we simply have the special case in which the part of the event which exists only in the indeterminate future of R is in fact the whole event. Hence, what I have earlier described as the "developmental phase" of an event, which constitutes the temporal range of R for an imperfect form, begins with the earliest time that the event may be regarded as virtually certain to occur, and ends with the end of the event. These considerations suggest that the temporal characterization given thus far for imperfect aspect is too weak, and needs to be strengthened with a further condition, such as the one incorporated into the following revised definition:

(16)   Imperfect: For some t in E, R $(<)$ $\{t\}$, and the event at E is a
                      (virtual) certainty from the perspective of R.

I will leave for another time the task of making this feature of the meaning of imperfect aspect more precise. Incidentally, it should be obvious that a parallel condition is not necessary for completive or perfect aspect, because the whole event has already come into existence by any of the times to which these aspects can refer.

The discussion moves on now to the possible relations between event time (E) and speech time (S), as defined by the existential status categories.

2.2.3 EXISTENTIAL STATUS

Although it is not difficult to grasp in an intuitive way the functions of tense and aspect categories when interpreted in terms of E, R, and S, it is perhaps more puzzling to consider the possible function of an existential status category. What is the significance of the relation between event time and speech time? The answer is that the position of an event vis-à-vis the time at which the event is talked about determines the status of the event as a historical fact. An event qualifies as a historical fact once it has undergone the full sequence of its development in real time. If some or all of the event occurs only in a hypothetical future time, then the whole event is not yet a historical fact. This status distinction between "historical" and "nonhistorical" facts cuts across the more familiar categories of past, present, and future, because of the peculiar relation of present time to the existential status of an event. That is, whereas the past is clearly historical and the future nonhistorical, the present must be viewed as "semi"-historical—certain events concurrent with the present situation have evolved to the status of historical facts, others remain only partially realized. An event is fully realized in the present if it has already undergone every stage of its development prior to the time of speaking; whatever portion of the event continues to be realized is mere repetition within an established pattern. However, if some portion of the event has not as yet been realized at any time that is prior to S, then the event itself is not yet a member of the category of historical fact.

The role of an existential status category in temporal semantics was originally suggested to me by Benjamin Whorf's (1950) description of the "manifest/manifesting" distinction in Hopi. Whorf appears to be dealing with the same variable as I have discovered in Kikuyu (or a related one), when he says the following concerning Hopi:

"The objective or MANIFESTED comprises all that is or has been accessible to the senses; the historical physical universe, in fact, with no attempt to distinguish between present and past, but excluding everything we call future. The subjective or MANIFEST-ING comprises all that we call future. . . . This realm of the subjective or of the process of manifestation . . . includes also—on its border but still pertaining to its own realm —an aspect of existence that we include in our present time. It is that which is beginning to be done, like going to sleep or starting to write, but is not yet in full operation [quoted from Whorf, 1956; pp. 59–60]."

In order to understand this unfamiliar kind of temporal category, we need to see how it functions in some natural language that makes explicit provision for it. Consequently, in the next section of the chapter, I will illustrate the role of an existential status distinction between "manifest action" and "imminent action" in the Kikuyu verb paradigm. (Although the term "manifesting" is more precise than "imminent" for the converse of "manifest," the latter term seems less likely to be confused with "manifest.")

3. A CASE STUDY: KIKUYU

3.1. The Organization of the Paradigm

The most striking feature of the Kikuyu verb paradigm is that the different tenses do not all share the same number of aspect distinctions. The future tense forms in the basic inflectional paradigm do not allow for any aspect distinctions at all. Each of the past tenses has a three-way contrast of perfect, imperfect, and completive aspect, as illustrated in the previous discussion. The present tense, however, makes a further distinction between a "short-perfect" and a "long-perfect" meaning, as illustrated in (17)–(18):

(17)   Short-perfect: *a-a-hanyūka*
                          he-Perf$_S$-run
                          'he has **just** run'

(18)   Long-perfect: *a-hanyūk-īte*
                          he-run-Perf
                          'he has run (**some time ago**)'

Similarly, there is a present tense distinction between a "short-imperfect" and a "long-imperfect" meaning, as shown in (19)–(20):

(19)   Short-imperfect: *a-ra-hanyūka*
                            he-Imperf$_S$-run
                            'he is running right now (but he hasn't been running for long)

(20)   Long-imperfect: *a-hanyūk-aga*
                           he-run-Imperf
                           'he habitually runs' (i.e., 'he has been running repeatedly for a long time')

No similar contrast exists for completive aspect, as there is only a form that is morphologically equivalent to the "long" forms in the other two aspects, and which, as we will see shortly, has its own semantic peculiarities.

Another curious feature of the Kikuyu system is the morphological parallellism between the present long-perfect and the three past perfect forms, which does not seem to correspond to a semantic parallellism. This is shown by the contrast between (21) and (22)–(24):

(21) Present, long-perfect: *a-hanyūk-īte*
                                        he-run-Perf
                                        'he has run **(some time ago)**'

(22) Immediate past (IP), perfect: *e-kū-hanyūk-īte**
                                        he-IP-run-Perf
                                        '(in the immediate past) he had run'
                                        *a → e/__-kū-

(23) Near past (NP), perfect: *a-ra-hanyūk-īte*
                                        he-NP-run-Perf
                                        '(in the near past) he had run'

(24) Remote past (RP), perfect: *a-a-hanyūk-īte*
                                        he-RP-run-Perf
                                        '(in the remote past) he had run'

On the basis of comparison with the past tense forms, we would expect the present tense form (with "zero" in the tense slot before the verb) to mean simply 'he has run.' But the presence of the feature present tense is the occasion for a shift in the meaning of the form to the narrower category of "long"-perfect aspect, which implies that the running occurred some time ago. There is an analogous puzzle with the imperfect forms, as illustrated by the data in (25)–(26):

(25) Present, long-imperfect: *a-hanyūk-aga*
                                        he-run-Imperf
                                        'he habitually runs'

(26) Immediate past, imperfect: *e-kū-hanyūk-aga*
                                        he-IP-run-Imperf
                                        'he was running (in the immediate past)'

In this case, the present tense form is restricted to a habitual action interpretation, whereas the past tense forms are not. (Recall that "habitual action" is just one of several possible interpretations for a Kikuyu imperfect form.)

An even more striking case of seeming asymmetry in the meanings of morphologically parallel forms involves the zero-tense completive form, which is

(27)   Zero-tense, completive: *a-hanyūk-ire*
                                   he-run-Comp/IP(?)
                                   'he ran (in the immediate past)'

It would appear from the meaning of this form that *-ire* is a mixed tense–
aspect marker, with the meaning "$R = E$, and R is in the immediate past
of S." However, comparison of the zero-tense, completive form with the
parallel near past and remote past forms:

(28)   Near past, completive: *a-ra-hanyūk-ire*
                                    he-NP-run-Comp
                                    'he ran (in the near past)'

(29)   Remote past, completive: *a-a-hanyūk-ire*
                                    he-RP-run-Comp
                                    'he ran (in the remote past)'

suggests rather than *-ire* is strictly an aspect marker (like *-aga* and *-īte*),
with the meaning of completive aspect. There is yet another curious feature of the zero-tense, completive form. Comparison of this form with the
other zero-tense forms (the long-perfect, and long-imperfect) would suggest that its meaning ought to be PRESENT tense, as that is how the other
forms are interpreted when tense is not explicitly marked. How, then, do
we account for the immediate past tense meaning of this form?

The explanation for all of these asymmetries lies in the existential status
categorization that is built into the structure of the Kikuyu paradigm. To
see this, we need to consider the organization of the overall inflectional
system. The forms in this system fall into two formal groups—those
marked only with a prefix expressing a combination of tense and aspect,
and those that are separately marked with a tense prefix (which may be
"zero") and as aspect suffix. Schematically:

(30)   a. Subject - Tense+Aspect - Stem
        b. Subject - (Tense) - Stem - Aspect

The members of Group (a) are shown in Table 9.1. The important thing
to notice about these forms is the time span of the events they describe.
These events fall within a continuous period of time, which stretches from
the indefinitely remote future to the set of times JUST prior to the moment
of speaking. Note how both the short-perfect and the short-imperfect
forms in this subparadigm fulfill this condition: The short-perfect means
that the action of the verb took place just prior to speech time; the short-
imperfect form includes in its meaning the idea that, if the action has already begun, it began just prior to S. The latter form involves neverthe-

TABLE 9.1 SUBPARADIGM (A): IMMINENT ACTION

	Completive	Imperfect	Perfect
Present	————	*a-ra-hanyūka* 'he is running (right now)'[a] (but he hasn't been running for long) Short-imperfect	*a-a-hanyūka* 'he has just run' Short-perfect
Immediate future	*e-kū-hanyūka* 'he will run (today, within a few hours)'	————	————
Near future (Indefinite future)	*a-rī-hanyūka* 'he will run (soon)' (speaker usually has no definite time in mind)	————	————
Remote future	*a-ka-hanyūka* 'he will run (tomorrow or later)'	————	————

[a] Glosses indicate typical time interpretations for the tenses.

less essentially the same imperfect category found in the past imperfect forms of Group (b), as it can express habitual action (provided it did not begin more than just prior to S), as shown by the following example:

(31)   *nī a-ra-rīkia   nyūmba*
        he-Imperf$_S$-finish house
        '(these days) he finishes a house'
        (implies that at times which are considerably before S, he did not do so)

Sentence (31) describes a recently formed habit, which is implicitly contrasted with the state of affairs that existed at times considerably earlier. The form involves, therefore, ordinary imperfect aspect, but with the additional restriction in the meaning of the form that the action of the verb is no earlier than just prior to the time of speaking.

The members of the Kikuyu verb paradigm that are inflected according to Pattern (30b) are shown in Table 9.2. Semantically, these Group (b) forms are the complement of the Group (a) ones in Table 9.1: They describe events falling within the range of times from the indefinitely remote past, up to times considerably before the time of speaking. Note, however, that the event described may CONTINUE up to the time of speaking, so long as it is not one that ORIGINATED just prior to that time. This fact is illustrated by the long-perfect and long-imperfect forms. The long-perfect form means that the time of the event itself is considerably prior to the time of speaking (which in this case is identified with the reference time).

TABLE 9.2 Subparadigm (b): Manifest Action

	Completive (-ire)	Imperfect (-aga)	Perfect (-īte)
"Zero" tense	a-hanyūk-ire 'he ran (earlier today)'[a]	a-hanyūk-aga 'he is habitually running'	a-hanyūk-īte 'he has run (some time ago)'
Immediate past (-kū-)[b]	——— (No form exists; see text for comment)	Long-imperfect e-kū-hanyūk-aga 'he was running (earlier today)'	Long-perfect e-kū-hanyūk-īte 'he had run (earlier today)'
Near past (-ra-)	a-ra-hanyūk-ire 'he ran (yesterday)'	a-ra-hanyūk-aga 'he was running (yesterday)'	a-ra-hanyūk-īte 'he had run (yesterday)'
Remote past (-a-)	a-a-hanyūk-ire 'he ran (before yesterday)'	a-a-hanyūk-aga 'he was running (before yesterday)'	a-a-hanyūk-īte 'he had run (before yesterday)'

[a] Glosses indicate typical time interpretations for the tenses.

[b] -kū- changes a preceding a to e.

The long-imperfect means that the event involves a long-established, habitual action, hence that it must have begun considerably prior to the time of speaking.

In summary, then, the Group (a) forms involve event times ranging from the indefinitely remote future to times just before S, whereas Group (b) forms involve event times from the indefinitely remote past to considerably before S. The significance of this difference can be understood if we think of the latter period as the "historical past," that is, that period of time which contains events that have fully evolved, so that there is no indeterminacy left in their realization. In other words, the Group (b) forms —which express the existential status category of "manifest action"—all describe events that have fully developed in history because at least their initial occurrence is considerably prior to the time of speaking. This considerable time gap ensures that their development has stabilized, rendering them to a complete degree "manifest events." Note that this does not necessarily mean that every part of the event is over with at the moment of speaking. What it does involve is the idea that any portion of the event that continues into the present—such as the maintenance of a habit or the continuance of a stable result state—no longer shows a changing course of development. In contrast to this, the Group (a) forms—which express the existential status category "imminent action"—describe events that are still manifesting themselves, because they have not yet passed sufficiently far beyond the moment of speaking so that they (with their results) have entered the world of historical fact.

In the next section of this chapter, I will propose an explicit temporal characterization for the two status categories, and then show how this temporal interpretation correctly predicts the meanings of all of the "zero"-tense forms in the manifest subparadigm.

3.2. A Temporal Interpretation of the Manifest–Imminent Distinction

In the present tense, the "imminent" short-perfect and "manifest" long-perfect forms differ as to how much time has elapsed between the time of an event and the time of speaking (which happens to coincide with reference time in the present tense). This difference is shown diagrammatically in (32). The broken line represents some (vague) boundary between two categories of times, those which are "just prior to speech time (S)" (on the right of the line), and those which are "considerably prior to S," and therefore in the historical past (on the left). (Typically, events just prior to S are interpreted in the Kikuyu system as those falling within the last few hours, but this depends in part on what is being talked about.)

(32)

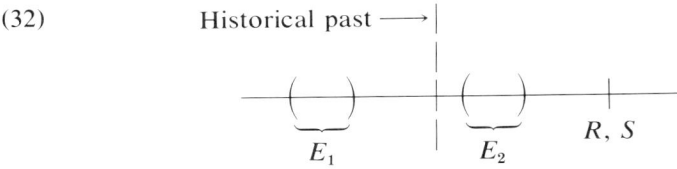

The position of E_1 in the diagram would dictate the use of the manifest action form, that is, the long-perfect, whereas the position of E_2 would indicate the use of the imminent action form, that is, the short-perfect.

A parallel but somewhat more complex contrast exists between the (present tense) short-imperfect from the imminent subparadigm, and the (zero-tense) long-imperfect form from the manifest subparadigm. Because, for any imperfect form, event time must continue beyond reference time, and because for these forms reference time is the same as speech time, the only possible difference in event time is that, for the (manifest) long-imperfect, a significant portion of event time falls within the historical past, whereas none of it does for the (imminent) short-imperfect. In other words, these two forms differ as to the implied time lapse between the beginning of event time and the moment of speaking. The situation typically described by the long-imperfect form is illustrated in Diagram (33).

(33)   Historical past $\longrightarrow$

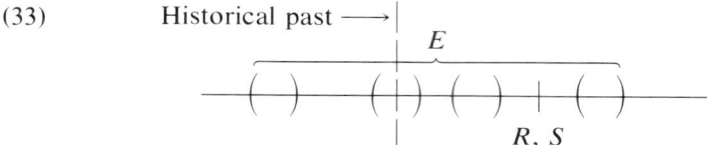

In this case, I have represented the interval E as divisible into a series of subintervals, each of which contains an instance of the event. Earlier in the chapter, I stated that the imperfect is vague as to whether or not event time is divisible in this way; in the present example, however, the length of time involved in the event makes this the most plausible interpretation of the internal structure of event time.

The diagrammatic representations I have given for the long-perfect and the long-imperfect indicate that what these two manifest status forms have in common is that at least one instance of the event lies within the period of time that is more than just prior to S—that is, within the historical past. In contrast, the two imminent forms, the short-perfect and short-imperfect, share the semantic feature that no instance of the event is more than just prior to S. To see this, compare the diagrammatic representation of the short-perfect, given in (32), with the following representation of the short-imperfect:

(34)   Historical past $\longrightarrow$

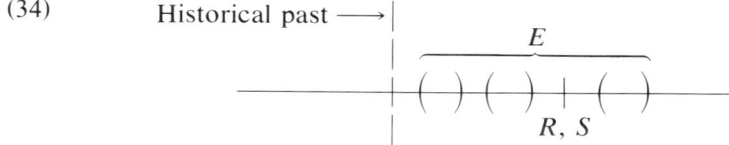

In diagramming the situation described by the short-imperfect, I have again chosen to represent event time as composed of a series of individual instances of some event. The possibility of dividing E in this way is not, of course, essential to the meaning of the short-imperfect (although it is consistent with that meaning). I have represented the short-imperfect in this way in order to emphasize the crucial difference in meaning between the short-imperfect and the long-imperfect: namely, the fact that, for the short-imperfect, the initial instance of the event has not yet moved into the historical past, so that the development of the event still has imminent status.

We can now give an intuitive temporal characterization of the status category "manifest action," as in (35):

(35)   A verb form describes a MANIFEST ACTION if and only if at least one instance of the event described is in the historical past.

As we have seen, the category of manifest action is not explicitly marked by any morpheme in the Kikuyu system. The best approach seems to be to consider it as a condition on the possible meaning of a form within the manifest subparadigm. This condition applies vacuously in the case of a past tense form, but plays an active role in determining the meanings of the zero-tense forms. This will be shown in detail in what follows.

In order to give a set-theoretic definition of the category "manifest action," we need to introduce first a set-theoretic definition of the subsidiary notion, "historical past." To accomplish this, we now introduce a function P_H, whose role is to designate the historical past time period; this period is to include any time sufficiently far removed from the time of speaking that events occurring at that time may be considered to be "manifest," that is, to have revealed the full sequence of their development. Because what constitutes the historical past depends on the moment of speaking, we let P_H be a function whose domain is the set of moments of time, and for all moments m in the set, the value of P_H for that moment—or, $P_H(m)$—is an interval of time. The possible values for $P_H(m)$ are to be constrained by two conditions. First, the historical past must extend infinitely far back into the past; and, second, it must end considerably prior to the time of speaking. These conditions on P_H are given in (36):

(36)   Let P_H be a function whose domain is the set of moments of time, and for all moments m,
   a. $P_H(m)$ is a member of $[I]$ (the set of intervals);
   b. there is no moment m' such that $m' (<) P_H(m)$; and
   c. there is some I in $[I]$ such that $P_H(m) (<) I (<) m$.

Condition (b) says that no moment of time is earlier than all of the historical past; hence, $P_H(m)$ extends infinitely far back. Condition (c) says that some interval of time intervenes between the historical past and the moment at which it is evaluated; hence, there is always a gap between $P_H(m)$ and the moment of speaking.[7] When these conditions are met, we have a situation that may be diagrammed as follows:

(37)   Historical past |

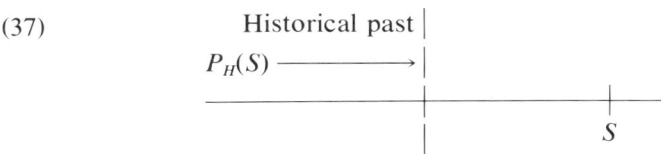

---

[7] The actual size of the gap will depend on contextual factors which I have not attempted as yet to include in the analysis (cf. some comments in the Section 3.3 on a parallel problem with the past tenses).

We can now define the status category "manifest action." The temporal specification common to all manifest action forms is that at least one instance of the event is within the historical past. Hence, a verb form describes a manifest action if and only if the following semantic condition holds:

(38)   Manifest action: For some $E' \subseteq E, E' \subseteq P_H(S)$, where E and E' are the times of events of the same type.

The status category "imminent action" is simply the converse of manifest action. That is, a verb form describes an imminent action if and only if the following condition holds:

(39)   Imminent action: There is no $E' \subseteq E$ such that $E' \subseteq P_H(S)$, where E and E' are the times of events of the same type.

Thus, a verb form is included in the manifest action category if there is at least one instance of the event it describes that is in the historical past; the form is in the imminent action category if this condition fails. Consequently, any imminent action form describes an event that occurs either later than the time of speaking or within the gap between the historical past and S. Note that this characterization of imminent action correctly predicts that there can only be a short-perfect form and a short-imperfect form for present tense within the imminent action subparadigm. The reason is that, in the case of the perfect, a result phase of considerable length would stretch back into the historical past, and, in the case of the imperfect, a developmental phase of considerable length would do likewise.

Before considering further how the definition of manifest action predicts the meanings of the zero-tense forms, we will briefly describe the meanings of the Kikuyu past tenses.

3.3. Past Tense and the Zero-Tense Forms

Within the manifest action subparadigm, Kikuyu distinguishes three past tense categories, namely, "immediate," "near," and "remote" past tense. The most usual time reference for these three tenses is "a previous period on the same day (ending a few hours earlier)," "yesterday," and "before yesterday," respectively. These time references can be determined from co-occurrence restrictions with time adverbs. For example:

(40)   Immediate past: *e-kū-hanyūk-īte rūcinī*
                            he-IP-run-Perf morning
                            'he had run this morning' (speaking in the afternoon)

(41)   Near past: *a-ra-hanyūk-īte ira*
                             he-NP-run-Perf yesterday
                             'he had run yesterday'

(42)   Remote past: *a-a-hanyūk-īte iyo*
                             he-RP-run-Perf day-before-yesterday
                             'he had run the day before yesterday'

However, the boundaries of the past tenses are not so clear-cut as these
initial examples suggest. If, for example, habitual instances of running are
at issue, rather than an individual instance which takes a relatively short
period of time, then the near past tense denotes an interval of time END-
ING yesterday, whereas the remote past designates an interval ending two
or more days ago. For example (only the relevant interpretation of imperfect aspect is given in the glosses):

(43)   Near past: *a-ra-hanyūk-aga*
                             he-NP-run-Imperf
                             'he used to run (until very recently)'

(44)   Remote past: *a-a-hanyūk-aga*
                             he-RP-run-Imperf
                             'he used to run (but this habit ended some time
                             ago; at least prior to yesterday)'

What Examples (43) and (44) indicate is that the past tenses do not necessarily involve disjoint time periods, but may refer instead to overlapping intervals, ending relatively near to or far from the time of speaking.
Moreover, there is evidence that HOW near or far from the moment of
speaking the position of each past time interval is depends on a variety of
contextual factors, including such considerations as speaker, topic, and
relevant time unit. Unfortunately, there is little information currently
available on this interesting aspect of the Kikuyu tenses. As my own field
work was concerned with determining the overall shape of the system, I
was not able to investigate this topic in any detail. The standard grammar
of Kikuyu (Barlow 1960) is fairly noncommittal on the time reference of
the tenses, although it does say that the near past can be used either to
refer to yesterday or, more generally, "in reference to an event which is
relatively recent, although it took place prior to yesterday [p. 62]." More
information is available on this topic in the grammar of Luyia, a Bantu
language closely related to Kikuyu. The Luyia grammar, (Appleby 1961)
has the following to say:

   There is no general past tense; any one of the past tenses indicates roughly how long
   past you are referring to. This indication is sometimes relative rather than absolute; e.g.
   the Near Past tense indicates the near past period of time, usually within the preceding

24 hours or so; but in speaking of years, it would be used of last year; in speaking of
generations, it would be used of the last generation; of wars, of the last war; and so on.
[p. 40].

Clearly, there are significant pragmatic factors that must be taken into account in interpreting the Kikuyu (and other Bantu) tenses. However, as I
do not have the data that would allow these principles to be built into the
analysis of tenses given here, we will concentrate on those features of the
meanings of each tense that depend only on the moment of speaking.

The primary role of the Kikuyu past tenses, then, is to provide a partition of the historical past into three overlapping subperiods, designated
"immediate," "near," and "remote" past. This partition of past time
may be represented diagrammatically as in (45) (note that the immediate
past coincides with the historical past on this interpretation):[8]

(45)

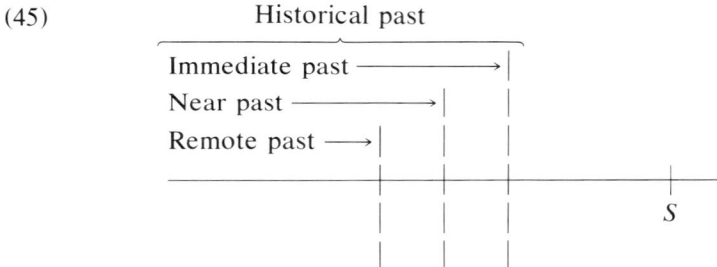

The information represented in this diagram is that each past time category extends indefinitely far back into the past, but ENDS at a point in time
relatively near to, or far from, the present moment. Additionally, the diagram shows that the three past intervals exhaustively cover the time span
of the historical past.

As we did previously in defining the status category "manifest action,"
we now proceed to define the three past tenses in two steps; first, we introduce a set of functions whose role is to designate the three past time
periods, and then we define the tense categories themselves in terms of
these periods. To accomplish the first step, let P_I, P_N and P_R be functions
whose domain is the set of moments of time, and for all moments m,
$P_I(m)$, $P_N(m)$, and $P_R(m)$ are continuous stretches of time. Thus, $P_I(m)$,
$P_N(m)$, and $P_R(m)$ may be understood as designating the "immediate

---

[8] A more refined analysis might not allow the immediate or near past to extend infinitely
far back, as speakers seem to have a preference for using only the remote past when the
event extends indefinitely far back into the past. I have not investigated this aspect of the
tense system carefully enough as yet to decide the issue.

past," "near past," and "remote past" intervals, respectively. The following conditions define the relative positions of these three intervals:

(46) Let P_I, P_N, and P_R be functions whose domain is the set of moments of time, and for all moments m
   a. $P_I(m)$, $P_N(m)$, $P_R(m)$ are continuous stretches of time;
   b. $P_I(m) = P_H(m)$, $P_N(m) \subset P_I(m)$, $P_R(m) \subset P_N(m)$; and
   c. there is no moment m' such that m' ($<$) $P_N(m)$ or m' ($<$) $P_R(m)$.

Condition (b) identifies the immediate past with the historical past; in addition, it defines the near past as a PROPER subset of the immediate past, and the remote past as a PROPER subset of the near past. Condition (c) specifies that each of the past time intervals extends infinitely far back into the past. It follows from this condition, in conjunction with Condition (b), that some part of the near past is later than all of the remote past, while some of the immediate past is later than all of the near past. This is the situation that was illustrated in the preceding diagram.

We now define each tense category as follows. Recall that tense expresses a relation between reference time (R) and speech time (S). In the Kikuyu system, each past tense category indicates which subpart of the historical past the reference time is included in. Thus, we may define the categories as follows:

(47)   Immediate past tense: $R \subseteq P_I(S)$ and $R \nsubseteq P_N(S)$

(48)   Near past tense: $R \subseteq P_N(S)$ and $R \nsubseteq P_R(S)$

(49)   Remote past tense: $R \subseteq P_R(S)$

Note that the definition of "immediate past tense" requires that the reference time of a sentence in that tense fall within the immediate past interval, but NOT wholly within the near past interval, that is, R must lie in part, and may lie entirely, within that portion of the immediate past interval that does not overlap with the near past. Similarly, for the near past to be used correctly, the reference time must be at least in part, and possibly wholly within the near past, but not wholly within the remote past. Thus, for example, the position of the reference time R in the following diagram would dictate the use of near past tense, whereas the position of R' would allow only remote past tense:

(50)

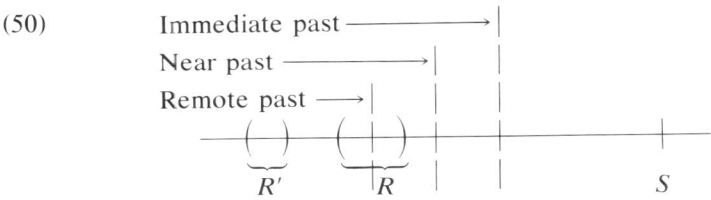

We are now in a position to account for the meanings of the three zero-tense forms of the manifest subparadigm. Given the large number of languages for which the unmarked tense form is the present tense form, we would anticipate a principle for the interpretation of an unmarked form such as the following: "When not otherwise specified, $R = S$." The Kikuyu system, however, shows that this principle is inadequate to cover all of the cases, as, although two of the Kikuyu zero-forms have a present tense meaning, the third has an immediate past tense meaning. A more general interpretive principle which would cover the Kikuyu system is the following:

(51)   When not otherwise specified, R takes on the available value in the system which is closest to S and still consistent with the meaning of the form.

This principle predicts the meaning of a manifest, zero-tense completive form [e.g., *a-hanyūk-ire* 'he ran (in the immediate past)'] in the following manner. The completive marker itself (*-ire*) contributes the meaning $R = E$. The semantic condition on manifest action forms specifies that some subinterval of E, which contains the time of an event of the same type as the event at E, is within the historical past. It follows that at least part of R is in the historical past. Hence, a present tense meaning for the form is ruled out, because it is inconsistent with the conditions already set for the value of R. The other possible values in the system are the three past tenses. As the value, "immediate past tense," is the one which allows R to be closest to S, the form is understood with an immediate past tense meaning.

It is worth pointing out that the interpretive principle described makes a somewhat weaker contribution to the meaning of a form than an explicit morphological marker. This is evident from a remark made by one of my informants. He agreed with the other informants that the unmarked completive form implies a time somewhat earlier on the same day. However, he commented that the emphasis of this particular form is on establishing that the action is already accomplished, rather than specifying a particular time interval within which the action occurred. Establishing that the action named is within the historical past is, of course, precisely all that is required in the explicit semantics of this form under my analysis.

Some comment is also appropriate here on the absence, in the Kikuyu system, of a form that combines the immediate past prefix *kū-* with the completive suffix *-ire* (cf. Table 9.2), even though it is obvious what such a form ought to mean (namely, "he V*ed* in the immediate past"). When I suggested such a combination, the informants reacted with surprise (and a certain amount of politely guarded amusement), but they did not venture a translation. It seems obvious that the absence of this form is related to the fact that it would be completely synonymous with the normal meaning of the unmarked completive form, but I am not sure what the status of this observation is as an explanation of the facts. I suspect that the introduction of the category "immediate past tense" is a relatively recent innovation in the Kikuyu system, so perhaps the *kū-* completive form has never been coined because no one has felt the need for it as yet. However, I would not want to rule out the possibility that such a form might eventually emerge in the system. This is a question that can only be resolved through time, and comparison with parallel cases of paradigmatic synonymy in other languages.

Turning finally to the long-perfect and long-imperfect forms of the manifest subparadigm, a present tense meaning for these forms is predicted by the interpretive principle, because assigning R the value of S is consistent with the meanings of these forms, as determined by their explicit morphology. The semantic asymmetry between these two forms and the parallel past tense forms is explained as follows. Consider first the long-perfect form, with zero-tense marking and the perfect suffix *-ite* (e.g., *a-hanyūk-īte* (he-run-Perf) 'he has run some time ago'). The meaning of this form arises from (*a*) the meanings of the constituent morphemes; (*b*) the semantic condition on manifest action forms; and (*c*) the interpretive principle governing unmarked tense forms. These three jointly determine the temporal specification: (*a*) that event time is earlier than reference time; (*b*) that one instance of the event described is in the historical past; and (*c*) that reference time is the same as speech time. More formally, the temporal specification is:

(52)   a. $E (<) R$,
      b. for some $E' \subseteq E$, $E' \subseteq P_H(S)$, where E and E' are the times of events of the same type, and
      c. $R = S$.

(Note that these conditions are satisfied if we simply assume that $E' = E$. For easier exposition, therefore, we will make this assumption.) Because event time is in the historical past, and reference time is identified with the moment of speaking, E must be considerably prior to R. In contrast, for any of the past tense forms, because R itself falls within the historical past, it is possible for E to be only just prior to R. That is, the semantic condition imposed by the manifest action category does not affect the relation of E and R, once both E and R are located within the historical past. This explains the fact that a manifest perfect form takes on a more general meaning when in the past tense than when in the present tense.

The analysis provides a parallel explanation for the generalization in meaning of a manifest imperfect form (marked with -*aga*) in the move from present to past tense. The long-imperfect form (with zero tense marking and the suffix -*aga* — e.g., *a-hanyūk-aga* 'he habitually runs') has the temporal specification: (*a*) part of event time is later than reference time; (*b*) one instance of event time is in the historical past; and (*c*) reference time is identified with speech time. More formally:

(53) a. For some t in E, R ($<$) $\{t\}$,
      b. for some $E' \subseteq E$, $E' \subseteq P_H(S)$, where E and E' are the times of events of the same type, and
      c. $R = S$.

The situation thus described can be diagrammed as follows:

(54)

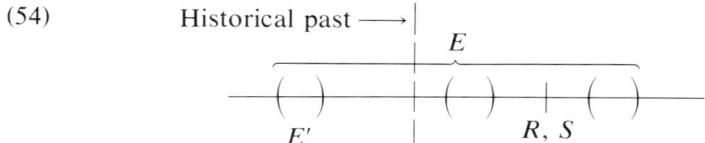

Thus, the information provided by a long-imperfect form is that event time includes more than one instance of the event and that these instances occur over a relatively extended period of time. This information makes the habitual action interpretation of the imperfect the only plausible one in the case of a zero-tense form. However, if a manifest imperfect form is marked for some past tense, then interpretations other than habitual action are equally viable. The reason is that a past tense form assigns R a value within the historical past; consequently, the condition on the relation between E and S which is imposed by the status category manifest action is readily fulfilled in a past tense form without affecting the relation between R and E. To see this, consider Diagram (55), which illustrates one way in which the temporal specification for a near past imperfect form can be fulfilled:

(55)

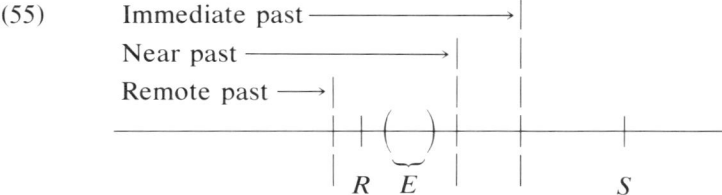

This is the situation that corresponds, for example, to the interpretation 'he was just about to run' for the near past, imperfect form *a-ra-hanyūk-aga* (he-NP-run-Imperf). What is required for any near past, manifest

TABLE 9.3. SUMMARY OF THE KIKUYU CATEGORIES (EXCLUSIVE OF FUTURE TENSES)

Category	Meaning	Comment
A. Status		
Manifest action	For some $E' \subseteq E$, $E' \subseteq P_H(S)$ where E and E' are the times of events of the same type.	At least one complete instance of the event is in the historical past
Imminent action	There is no $E' \subseteq E$ such that $E' \subseteq P_H(S)$, where E and E' are as above.	No complete instance of the event is in the historical past.
B. Aspect		
Completive	$R = E$	Reference time coincides with event time.
Imperfect	For some t in E, $R\ (<)\ \{t\}$, and the event at E is a (virtual) certainty from the perspective of R.	Reference time is prior to the end of event time.
Perfect	$E\ (<)\ R$	Reference time is later than event time.
C. Tense		
Present	$R = S$	Reference time coincides with speech time.
Immediate past	$R \subseteq P_I(S)$ and $R \not\subseteq P_N(S)$	Reference time is within the immediate past.
Near past	$R \subseteq P_N(S)$ and $R \not\subseteq P_R(S)$	Reference time is within the near past.
Remote past	$R \subseteq P_R(S)$	Reference time is within the remote past.

form is that R be in the near past, and E in the historical past (in part at least). As illustrated in Diagram (55), these conditions can both be fulfilled, while still allowing R to be earlier than E.

This completes the discussion of the semantic categories of the Kikuyu system (ignoring the future tenses). Table 9.3 provides a summary of the semantic analyses that have been proposed for the various categories.

4. CONCLUSION

In conclusion, I would like to briefly summarize the important points that have been made in this chapter. The purpose of this chapter has been to analyze the temporal relations that are expressed by the inflectional systems of natural languages. The point of departure for this analysis was the work of Hans Reichenbach, who has proposed that three distinct temporal entities—namely, speech time (S), reference time (R), and event time (E)—are involved in the temporal specification of all sentences. In the course of the discussion, it was argued that the morphological categories of tense, aspect, and existential status can be defined set-theoretically in terms of relations among S, R, and E. It was shown that TENSE categories can be analyzed as expressing relations between S and R, ASPECT categories as expressing relations between R and E, and STATUS categories as expressing relations between S and E. Moreover, it was shown that each of these temporal relations corresponds to a specific semantic function in the grammar of a natural language. In addition, it has been shown that this approach leads to an understanding of the underlying unity of the category "imperfect aspect," and of the functional relation of this category to the other aspect form categories.

In the latter part of the chapter, the theory was applied in detail to the specific case of Kikuyu, a Bantu language with a temporal reference system rich enough to illustrate all three classes of temporal relations. The point was made that the structural duality of the Kikuyu verb paradigm reflected an underlying distinction between the categories of "manifest action" and "imminent action." Recognition of this category distinction, and a correct temporal interpretation of it, led to a coherent semantic interpretation of all forms in the Kikuyu paradigm. In addition, the analysis demonstrated that there is a systematic relationship between form and meaning in the Kikuyu verb paradigm. Specifically, the meaning of any member of the verb paradigm depends on three properties of its form: (*a*) the meanings of the constituent morphemes; (*b*) semantic conditions imposed on certain structurally defined subgroups of the paradigm; and (*c*) an interpretive principle governing the meaning of the unmarked member of a tense paradigm. Finally, it was demonstrated that each STRUCTURAL class of morphemes in the Kikuyu system is also a SEMANTIC class. Specifically, it was shown that the suffixes are aspect markers, the prefixes co-occurring with a suffix are tense markers, and the prefixes occurring independently of the suffixes are mixed tense and aspect markers (within the domain of "imminent action"). Naturally, it does not follow from such a result in one language that there is a correlation between form classes and meaning classes in all languages. Nevertheless, the fact that this result has been achieved somewhat unexpectedly in Kikuyu suggests that this is a hypothesis well worth investigating.

In closing, I would like to emphasize the importance of considering paradigmatic relationships in the study of temporal relations, and in particular, of taking account of the way that verbal paradigms organize their semantic domain. This approach to the problems of tense, aspect, and status is important, because the meaning of a temporally inflected verb form depends on the functional relations of one form to contrasting forms in the same paradigm. Moreover, there is a tendency within verb paradigms, when considered on a cross-linguistic basis, to exploit all of the logical possibilities for semantic contrasts inherent within their semantic domain. By approaching the semantics of time on a paradigmatic basis, we are able to anticipate, and consequently to uncover, the role of more unusual semantic contrasts, such as the manifest–imminent distinction in Kikuyu. In addition, a study of verb paradigms brings to light the systematic relationship between form and meaning in inflectional morphology, which differs in interesting ways from the form–meaning relationship that characterizes syntax. An adequate linguistic theory of tense and aspect, therefore, will have to encompass a complementary study of both the morphology and the syntax of temporal expressions in natural languages.

REFERENCES

Appleby, L.L. (1961). *A First Luyia Grammar* (revised edition). Nairobi: The East African Literature Bureau.

Barlow, A.R. (1960). *Studies in Kikuyu Grammar and Idiom.* Edinburgh: Blackwood [Revision of A.R. Barlow *Tentative Studies in Kikuyu Grammar and Idiom,* Edinburgh: Church of Scotland (1914).]

Bennett, M., and Partee, B. (1972). *Toward the logic of tense and aspect in English.* System Development Corporation, Santa Monica, Calif. (Available through Indiana University Linguistics Club.)

Comrie, B. (1976). *Aspect.* Cambridge: Cambridge University Press.

Dowty, D.R. (1972). *Studies in the Logic of Verb Aspect and Time Reference in English.* Doctoral dissertation, University of Texas at Austin.

Dowty, D.R. (1977). Toward a semantic analysis of verb aspect and the English 'imperfective' progressive. *Linguistics and Philosophy* 1, 45–77.

Hofmann, T.R. (1974). Expression of time relations in English. Unpublished manuscript, University of Ottawa.

Hornstein, N. (1977). Towards a theory of tense. *Linguistic Inquiry,* 8, 521–557.

Johnson, M.R. (1977). *A Semantic Analysis of Kikuyu Tense and Aspect.* Unpublished doctoral dissertation, Ohio State University.

Myers, A. (1971). Assertion and presupposition in Kikuyu. In C.-W. Kim and H. Stahlke (Eds.), *Papers in African Linguistics.* Edmonton: Linguistic Research. Pp. 135–140.

Nordenfelt, L. (1977). *Events, Actions, and Ordinary Language.* Lund, Sweden: Bokförlaget Doxa.

Reichenbach, H. (1947). *Elements of Symbolic Logic.* New York: Macmillan.

Smith, C. (1978). The syntax and interpretation of temporal expressions in English. *Linguistics and Philosophy* 2, 43–100.

Taylor, B. (1977). Tense and continuity. *Linguistics and Philosophy,* 1, 199–220.

Vendler, Z. (1967). *Linguistics in Philosophy.* Ithaca: Cornell University Press.

Whorf, B.L. (1950). An American Indian model of the universe. *International Journal of American Linguistics,* 16, 67–72. [Reprinted in B.L. Whorf (1956), *Language, Thought and Reality,* Cambridge: MIT Press.]

ASPECT, MARKEDNESS, AND t_0

HENRY KUĆERA

1. INTRODUCTION

In this chapter, I will consider certain contrastive aspectual phenomena of Czech and English, focusing, first of all, on some previous claims that have been made with regard to the two systems and, subsequently, proposing a reanalysis of my own to account more adequately for the observed facts.

Among the Slavic languages, Czech has perhaps the most complex aspectual system. Aside from the basic imperfective versus perfective distinction and an intricate subcategorization of determinate and indeterminate verbs of motion (the outlines of which I presented in Kučera 1976), Czech also has a large class of verbs which are commonly referred to in the literature as ITERATIVES (usually called *násobená slovesa* by Czech linguists). Although Russian, for example, also has a small number of iterative verbs, this aspectual class is unproductive in Russian and actually quite marginal in standard usage. In contrast to this, Czech iteratives, which are derived from simple imperfectives by the infix *-va-*, are common in all styles of speech; the productivity of the iterative derivational process is evidenced by the fact that even recent loan words can have derived iteratives. Some examples of the corresponding pairs of sim-

177

Syntax and Semantics, Volume 14
Tense and Aspect

ple imperfectives and iteratives are given in (1):

(1)   Imperfective   Iterative
         psát   psávat   'to write'
         hrát   hrávat   'to play'
         přát   přávat   'to wish'
         mít   mívat   'to have'
         telefonovat   telefonovávat   'to telephone'

It should be noted that, in addition to the type of iteratives given in (1), Czech also has a set of expanded iterative verbs, formed from imperfectives by the infix *-váva-*. These are usually considered to be emphatic variants of regular iteratives. Most of them unquestionably have a definite connotation of a more sporadic action or state: Whereas *mívat* normally means 'to have occasionally', the expanded iterative *mívávat* can be best translated as 'to have once in a great while'. In this chapter, I shall not treat the semantics of these expanded iteratives nor will I address the problem of some other verbs which are sometimes included by Czech linguists in the iterative class on purely semantic grounds, be it such imperfectives as *stýkat se* 'to meet with, to keep company with' or the perfective distributives of the type *pozavírat* (*okna*) 'to close (the windows one by one)'. In the rest of the chapter, I shall use the term iteratives solely for the large class of verbs derived by the infix *-va-* as exemplified in the examples in (1).

2. MARKEDNESS ANALYSIS

Much of the more recent analysis of Slavic aspectual systems, including the Czech one, clearly shows the influence of European structuralism, particularly of the morphological markedness theory of the Prague Linguistic Circle. Having evolved as an extension of the markedness analysis in phonology (as presented, in a systematic way, in Trubetzkoy 1939), the theory of binary morphological oppositions was originally formulated by Jakobson (1932) with regard to the Russian verb system. Although the grammatical and semantic analysis within this framework also posits a marked and an unmarked member of the opposition, the relation is, strictly speaking, not a privative one in the sense of Trubetzkoy, but rather a hierarchical one. (The morphological opposition has been also called "subordinate" by Janakiev, as cited in Chvany 1975.) Essentially, the marked form of the morphological opposition is said to designate, aside from its lexical meaning, some additional property (or "distinctive feature"), whereas the unmarked form is either noncommittal as to the presence or absence of this property (in its general meaning) or may, in specific contexts, designate the absence of the "distinctive feature" (in the nuclear meaning of the unmarked form: cf. Jakobson 1957). Schematically, the relationship between the marked and unmarked grammatical forms thus appears to be basically as follows:

MARKED = LM (lexical meaning) + α ("distinctive feature")

UNMARKED = LM (no indication of α or, in certain contexts, $-\alpha$)

The morphological markedness theory—which, presumably, is a language universal—thus requires of the linguistic analyst the identification of the distinctive feature α. Because grammatical forms may have somewhat different meanings in various contexts, structural analysts find it frequently necessary to speak of primary and secondary functions of the marked forms. It would seem, nevertheless, that the common denominator of the meanings of the marked forms clearly needs to be identified if the markedness analysis is to offer a significant semantic insight into the structure of natural languages.

3. IMPERFECTIVES AND ITERATIVES

In the structuralist analysis of the Czech opposition of simple imperfectives versus iteratives, the former are generally considered unmarked and the latter marked. The basic distinctive property of iteratives is usually said to be the repetition, recurrence or successiveness of the designated action or state. (The term *sukcesívnost* 'successiveness' is due to Poldauf 1966.) Although iteratives, in many instances, do indeed denote repetition, recurrence or, more generally, successiveness, this is by no means always the case. Consider the examples in (2), where all iteratives are in boldface. (In all the examples given in this chapter, the English translations are intended to be close paraphrases of the Czech sentences and, consequently, some of them may not be grammatical.)

(2) a. *Stával tam voják.*
        'A soldier used to stand there.'
    b. *Stával tam dům.*
        'A house used to stand there.'
    c. *Mívala ho ráda.*
        'She used to like him.'
    d. *Znával jsem ho dobře.*
        'I used to know him well.'

Although (2a) can clearly be interpreted as designating repetition, (2b)–(2d) have no such iterative meaning at all. What these last three sentences do designate is a state asserted to exist over an extended duration in the DISTANT past, with the implicature that the proposition is no longer true at the present time.

About 15 years ago, the Czech linguist František Kopečný proposed a different analysis of Czech iteratives which, although not originally intended to address such problems as I pointed out in (2), might conceivably avoid these complications (cf. Kopečný 1962). Kopečný's analysis created a great deal of debate in Slavic linguistic journals and has remained controversial up to the present day. The essential observation that Kopečný made was that Czech iteratives with present tense morphological endings can never denote an action simultaneous with the speech event, that is, one taking place at t_0. The sentences given in (3), and all sentences like these, are clearly ungrammatical:

(3)   a.   *Zrovna ted' mi **psává** dopis.
           'Right now he writes me a letter.'
      b.   *Právě ted' **hrává** na klavir.
           Right now he plays the piano.'

Kopečný, who is also an adherent of the morphological markedness theory, considered the distinctive feature of the Czech iteratives to be that of NONACTUALITY (the Czech term being neaktuálnost). Although this characterization may be somewhat unfortunate in its English translation, one need only recall the meaning of the French actuel or the German aktual ('present, current')—or for that matter a secondary meaning of the English adjective actual—to see that the term is intended to denote the inability of an iterative verb to express an action simultaneous with t_0. In fact (as Kopečný was also aware), a similar constraint applies to all other tenses of iterative verbs as well. Their usage is ungrammatical in any sentence in which the predication is supposed to be taking place at a specific point in time, as is the case in (4):

(4)   a.   *Když jsem vešel do pokoje, Petr **hrával** na klavir.
           'When I entered the room, Peter used to play the piano.'
      b.   *Budu vás **čekávat** zítra v sedm hodin večer.
           'I will wait for you tomorrow at seven in the evening.'

Kopečný, who was rather intrigued by the supposed universality of the markedness theory, supported his solution for Czech by pointing out that, in languages that have the opposition of progressive versus nonprogressive (such as English or Spanish, among others), the situation is, in a sense, a mirror image of the Czech system as far as markedness is concerned. So, in his view, the English present progressive, for example, is to be considered marked for ACTUALITY, that is, analyzed as a form that inherently signals an action simultaneous with t_0. The English nonprogressive present is then the unmarked member of the opposition and thus presumably may, but need not, signal an action taking place at t_0. As already pointed out, Czech, in contrast to English, has grammatical forms marked for nonactuality, namely the class of iterative verbs. There is no marking for actuality in Czech or, for that matter, anywhere in Slavic; Slavic languages have no progressive forms and the simple imperfectives are thus to be considered as the unmarked members of the system.

4. COUNTEREXAMPLES TO THE MARKEDNESS ANALYSIS

4.1. Czech Iteratives

The contrastive Czech–English analysis looks neat and elegant. Unfortunately, it has the rather fatal flaw of being easily falsified by numerous counterexamples. I shall try to offer some reasons why I consider the analysis untenable for English in Section 4.2 of the chapter. First, however, let me untangle the problem of the Czech iteratives.

The question that arises immediately, of course, is what the morphological present tense of Czech iteratives designates if it cannot denote an action at t_0; given the semantic constraint, one might even ask why iteratives have present tense forms at all. The answer to these questions is not difficult to find; consider the example in (5):

(5)   *Maminka sedává na pavlači.*
       'Mother sits (is in the habit of sitting) on the porch.'

Obviously, the proposition asserted in (5) has a truth value at t_0. But what is asserted is NOT an activity at t_0, but rather a STATE, in the sense of these terms as defined by Vendler (1967). In Vendler's analysis, habits (in a broader sense including occupations, dispositions, abilities, and so forth) are states. Vendler illustrates this fact by the difference between the two questions *Are you smoking?* and *Do you smoke?* The first one asks about an activity, the second, about a state. It seems clear to me that the principal characteristic of Czech iteratives is that they represent states, not activities. As Vendler points out, states may arise not only from habitual activities but also from habitual accomplishments (e.g., *He writes books*) or achievements (e.g., *He catches dogs*). All this, too, is also the case in Czech iteratives, but I will leave this further semantic differentiation aside in this chapter, as it would require an additional lengthy argument, involving the entire nature of the complex perfective versus imperfective distinction.

The simple claim that Czech iteratives denote states is not, however, a sufficient explanation of all the essential properties of these verbs. The states that Czech iteratives designate are, in the analysis I am proposing here, of a special kind: They are essentially QUANTIFIED STATES. My claim is that this quantification may manifest itself in various ways. It may, of course, apply to the predicate verb itself, in which case the sentence designates a proper habit, that is, a state that arises from repeated or recurrent activity, accomplishment, or achievement. But the quantification may also extend over the scope of a temporal adverbial in the sentence, or the subject of the sentence, or—more rarely—even the object of the verb. Consider the following examples:

(6)   a. *Petr mi psával.*
         'Peter used to write to me.'
      b. *V sobotu Pavel sedává v hospodě.*
         'On Saturday, Paul (usually) sits in the pub.' (i.e., on most Saturdays)
      c. *Němci mluvívají spatně česky.*
         'Germans tend to speak Czech badly.' (i.e., of those Germans who speak Czech, the majority speak it badly)
      d. *Rušti generálové umírávají v mladém věku.*
         'Russian generals tend to die young.' (most but not all generals)
      e. *Čapek v těch letech psával romány.*
         'Čapek wrote (mostly) novels in those years.' (possibly in addition to other things)

Although (6a) could be fitted into the conventional semantic analysis of iteratives as designating repetition, the rest of the sentences in (6) cannot. The natural reading of (6b) is clearly one that quantifies the temporal adverbial: The sentence says that Paul sits in the pub on most Saturdays, not that he sits there several times on every Saturday. In the next two sentences, it is the plural subject that is quantified. This is particularly clear in (6d), where the quantification obviously must be over the noun phrase *rušti generálové* 'Russian generals' as the semantic properties of the verb *umírávají* 'die' clearly prevent any iterative reading of the sentence. The last example is admittedly somewhat controversial. Some Czech speakers may well be uncertain whether there is any implicature in (6e) that, in addition to novels, Čapek produced works in other genres of writing during the specified period. But, because object quantification is not crucial to my argument about the nature of Czech iteratives, such disagreement is of no great import.

The analysis of iteratives as quantified states also explains, in a natural way, the impossibility of the co-occurrence of an iterative verb with a time adverbial or other temporal expression that denotes a point in time, be it t_0 or a specific point in the past or in the future. Because a quantified state must extend over an interval of time of sufficient length to accommodate the notion of habituality (in the broad sense of habit cited earlier), it is by definition incompatible with any specification of temporal scope that consists only of a moment. The analysis that I propose thus also predicts that sentences such as those that were given in (3) and (4) must all be ungrammatical.

The examples that still need to be considered are Sentences (2b)–(2d). Although the verbs in these examples clearly designate past states, the quantification, characteristic of other iterative expressions, is not obvious in these sentences. Recall, however, that what we have here is not simply a long-duration state localized in the past but rather one localized in the DISTANT past. Any attempt to contradict the distant-past denotation in such ''iterative'' constructions results in considerable semantic anomaly:

(7) a.   *V mládí jsem ji **míval** rád.*
            'In my youth I used to like her.'
     b. ?* *Až do včerejška jsem ji **míval** rád.*
            'Until yesterday, I used to like her.'
     c.   *Až do včerejška jsem ji měl rád.*
            'Until yesterday, I liked her.'

Sentence (7a) is quite natural, implying that my youth belongs to the distant past. Sentence (7b), on the other hand, is extremely dubious because the adverbial *do včerejška* 'until yesterday' contradicts the distant-past meaning of the verb phrase *míval rád* 'used to like'. The same adverbial is quite proper in (7c), however, because in this sentence the verb phrase is no longer an iterative one but rather the simple imperfective *měl rád* 'liked'.

The obligatory (but subjectively conceived) remoteness from t_0 in sentences such as those given in (2) and (7) thus points to the possibility of dividing the past continuum in Czech into two distinct segments: distant past and recent past. This type of distinction is by no means unknown in natural languages. In Kikuyu, for example, distinct tense forms exist not only for remote past and near past but also for remote future and near future (cf. Johnson 1977). When no quantification, in the sense discussed earlier, is possible, Czech iteratives thus signal the digitalization of the past continuum: The state is asserted to be true in some distant past, with the clear inference that there exists a nonempty interval between this distant past and t_0 for which the state is not asserted to be true. Although it seems to me that there is a distinct connection between quantification and such a digitalization of the past continuum, I cannot present as yet an entirely satisfactory explanation of why the same verbal forms may assume both functions.

In a relatively brief discussion such as this, it is not possible to consider in detail whether the quantified state analysis of iteratives which I presented could be made compatible with some modified version of the Prague School's morphological markedness theory. But it would certainly appear that the very need for introducing the opposition of states versus activities into the analysis of a systematic aspectual distinction makes a hierarchical relation, on which the markedness theory is based, a rather unnatural framework within which to explain these linguistic facts.

4.2. The English Progressive

Turning to English, let us first consider the claim that the progressive versus nonprogressive opposition represents a morphological markedness relation, with the progressive marked for actuality and the nonprogressive unmarked. The appropriateness of such an analysis depends on the validity of two assumptions: (a) that the progressive–nonprogressive relation is indeed the hierarchical one which the markedness theory requires; and (b) that the progressive inherently designates actuality. As I shall demonstrate presently, both of these assumptions are false.

Most analyses of the English progressive focus on the activity function of these forms. One can certainly argue that, in this sense, the present progressive does indeed designate what Slavic linguists have been calling "actuality." In isolation, the sentence *Paul is playing tennis* implies an activity at t_0, whereas *Paul plays tennis* does not. But evidence such as this is insufficient to substantiate the markedness analysis. In fact, the necessary interpretation of the form *plays* in the latter sentence as NOT designating actuality already points to a major problem. As I argued at greater length in a previous paper (Kučera 1979), the markedness theory requires that the unmarked form—in this case the nonprogressive present—may be properly used not only in its "nuclear" meaning (i.e., as nonactual) but also in the general meaning (i.e., with no information as to actuality). This would then presumably predict that the nonprogressive present could co-occur with such adverbials as *at this moment, right now, etc.*, that denote t_0. But this is clearly not the case with so-called nonstative verbs which are precisely the ones that exhibit the systematic opposition of progressive versus nonprogressive:

(8) a.   *Peter is reading today's newspaper right now.*
     b. * *Peter reads today's newspaper right now.*

    c.   *At this moment it is raining outside.*
    d. * *At this moment it rains outside.*

The ill-formed (8b) and (8d) show that the nonprogressive present of *read* and *rain* does not have the general meaning, posited for an unmarked category by Jakobson, but rather seems to be limited to the designation of nonactuality. Instead of the proper markedness relation, we thus have here, at best, only the nuclear meaning of the allegedly unmarked form (i.e., only the $+\alpha$ versus $-\alpha$ opposition). I will show presently that even this "partial" markedness relation does not hold in English. Before doing so, however, let me dispose of yet another argument that has been presented in support of the markedness analysis of the English opposition.

    Kopečný (1948), in an attempt to substantiate his claim about English, argues that the sentence *He plays well* "can be said about an actual acting [sic] performance on the background of its general validity [p. 153]." In fact, of course, the form *plays* can refer only to the general ability of the player, whether or not it is pragmatically substantiated by his current performance. *Peter plays well* designates a state (i.e., the proposition that Peter is a good player), not an activity (which, of course, would have to be expressed by the progressive). Were such a sentence to contain an adverbial that requires an activity reading of the predication, the result would be ungrammatical: **Peter plays well in this period* is surely a bad sentence.

    Although the semantic analysis of the English nonprogressive present is not without complications, it seems reasonable to say that the basic meaning of this form is the designation of a state without any temporal limitations. It is for this reason that the nonprogressive present often designates atemporality, that is, a proposition which, within the limits of human experience, is either truly timeless (*The earth revolves around the sun*) or one which is viewed as having no definite temporal boundaries (*Jimmy speaks with a Southern accent*). It is significant, in this regard, that in the case of stative verbs—which are supposed not to have progressive forms (cf. Lakoff 1966)—the progressive does indeed occur whenever the proposition is intended to express an activity: *I am appreciating her kindness more and more every day*.

    Even in its special functions, the present nonprogressive cannot be viewed, in my opinion, as denoting activities. In these usages, the nonprogressive forms either have a general validity, as in stage directions (*Hedda enters from the left*), ritual instructions (*The candidates remain seated*), etc., or are used to describe or report events (not ongoing activities), as in newspaper headlines (*Lance resigns*), play-by-play accounts (*Smith passes to Jones*), demonstrations (*Now we take the rabbit out of the hat*), etc. (For a concise discussion of these usages, see, for example,

Twaddell 1963.) The final consideration that makes the markedness analysis of the progressive versus nonprogressive opposition untenable is the fact that the present progressive need not designate actuality either. Even leaving aside such cases as the "programmed future" function of these forms (*Peter is leaving tomorrow*), the present progressive can quite normally express a predication that is not taking place at t_0. The sentence *Harry is playing a lot of tennis this summer,* in order to be true, surely does not require Harry's presence on the tennis court at t_0. Notice, moreover, that it is quite easy and entirely natural to cancel the actuality of the present progressive forms:

(9) a. *Charles is giving a lecture every day this week, except today.*
   b. *I am fixing the roof this summer but I haven't been able to do a bit of work on it for the past 2 weeks.*
   c. *Nastase is winning a lot this year but he just lost in three straight sets to Borg 5 minutes ago.*

All the sentences in (9) contain an explicit denial that the activity to which the progressive could refer is taking place at t_0; nevertheless, no contradiction results. This does not mean, of course, that the propositions in (9) do not have a truth-value at t_0. Similarly to the Czech iteratives discussed earlier, the present progressive in these sentences designates states. There is a major difference, however, between the Czech and the English situations: Whereas the Czech iteratives normally denote habits (which, by necessity, are indefinite–duration states), the English progressive in the preceding examples designates limited-duration states. Notice, for example, that the sentence *Charles is giving a lecture every day this week* is prefectly well-formed, even in isolation. In contrast to this, the same sentence without the time adverbial, that is, **Charles is giving a lecture every day,* is not acceptable (unless, of course, the context is sufficient to specify that the proposition is of limited duration).

The fact that the English progressive can designate activities (and actuality) as well as limited-duration states suggests that the analysis of these forms given by Twaddell (1963), Joos (1964), and Leech (1970), among others, is at least on the right track. These linguists essentially agree that one of the basic functions of the progressive is the designation of limited duration. Without a systematic distinction between activities and states, however, such an analysis also runs into problems. Leech, for example, is forced to admit that the limited-duration connotation is canceled in sentences that denote a "ceaseless persistence of the process", for example, *Death is getting nearer every day; He is always making fun of me.* This is not a happy state of affairs as limited duration and ceaseless persistence are clearly antonymous. Woisetschlaeger (1977), in arguing against

Leech, has seized upon this contradiction, claiming that Leech's analysis "makes it hard to understand how the meaning of the progressive form could be learnable [p. 47]." Woisetschlaeger considers an account that assigns two contradictory meanings to a single grammatical form within a single semantic domain to be the worst possible way to design the syntax and semantics of a verbal category.

Woisetschlaeger has proposed, among other things, two different syntactic structures for the *be + -ing* forms, one with an aspectual (main verb) *be* and one with an epistemic (auxiliary verb) *be*. Although I have serious reservations about this model, Woisetschlaeger's arguments are much too complex to allow me to discuss them fairly in this brief chapter. But whatever the merits of Woisetschlaeger's analysis might be, his elaborate schema does not really solve Leech's problem either, because it, too, fails to take into account that the progressive may designate limited-duration states. The real nature of the problem can perhaps be seen in the following examples:

(10) a. *Bill is always arguing.*
      b. **Bill is always arguing well.*
      c. *Bill always argues well.*
      d. **I am always teaching only one hour on Friday.*
      e. *I always teach only one hour on Friday.*

The progressive in (10a) is entirely appropriate because a continuous activity is being asserted. The fact that the activity is really objectively not continuous in a strict sense, but that the assertion of continuousness represents a deliberate exaggeration on the part of the speaker, is precisely the reason why such sentences as (10a) have the "emotional coloring" that was already noticed by Jespersen (1931). On the other hand, the progressive is not felicitous in (10b) and (10d), because these predications are naturally interpreted not as continuous activities but rather as states without durational limitation. It is this fact that requires the nonprogressive in such instances, as (10c) and (10e) illustrate.

Before concluding, let me offer an additional piece of evidence for the analysis that I have proposed. Consider the following examples:

(11) a. *Dad smokes a lot right now.*
      b. **Dad talks on the phone right now.*
      c. **Dad answers today's mail right now.*

The first sentence is quite acceptable; the adverbial *right now* must, of course, be interpreted here as designating an interval, not a point in time. Why then is this interpretation not feasible in (11b)? Clearly, smoking a lot can be quite naturally viewed as a state, in Vendler's sense. Simple talking on the phone, on the other hand, is a very poor candidate for a state. Notice that an appropriate manner adverbial that forces the interpretation of (11b) as a state, makes this sentence much more respectable: *Dad talks on the phone a lot right now.* But the only reading—a very belabored one—that could make the original (11b) acceptable would be a context that would ascribe to Dad the habit of talking on the phone these days, an interpretation which, of course, would again assume that the phone–talking activity is one of Dad's present characteristics, that is, a state. Sentence (11c), on the other hand, is even beyond such a salvation, as the uniqueness of the object (*today's mail*) allows only an activity reading of the sentence and would thus admit only the progressive *is answering.*

5. CONCLUSIONS

This chapter cannot pretend to solve all the problems of even the limited subset of aspectual phenomena in Czech and English on which I focused. I hope, however, that I have been at least able to put to rest the notion that the contrastive Czech–English facts can be insightfully explained within the framework of "mirror image" markedness relations. There seems little doubt that the facts discussed in this chapter require us to make the basic distinction between activities and states. The Czech iteratives fall exclusively into the state category. The English nonprogressive present has basically a state function, although it can, in special usage, denote reported events. Moreover, the English progressive, although generally used to denoted activities, is commonly used for limited-duration states as well.

REFERENCES

Chvany, C.V. (1975). *On the Syntax of BE-Sentences in Russian.* Cambridge, Mass.: Slavica Publishers.
Jakobson, R. (1932). Zur Struktur des russischen Verbums. Charisteria Gvilelmo Mathesio. [Reprinted in R. Jakobson (1971), *Selected Writings 2,* The Hague: Mouton.]
Jakobson, R. (1957). *Shifters, verbal categories, and the Russian verb.* Cambridge, Mass.: Russian Language Project, Harvard University. [Reprinted in R. Jakobson (1971), *Selected Writings 2,* The Hague: Mouton.]
Jespersen, O. (1931) *A Modern English Grammar on Historical Principles.* London: George Allen and Unwin.
Johnson, M. (1977). *An interval-based theory of tense and aspect.* Unpublished manuscript, Ohio State University.
Joos, M. (1964). *The English Verb.* Madison: University of Wisconsin Press.
Kopečný, F. (1948). Dva příspěvky k vidu a času v češtině, *Slovo a slovesnost,* **10,** 151–158.

Kopečný, F. (1962). *Slovesný vid v češtině*. Prague: Nakladatelství československé akademie věd.

Kučera, H. (1976). *Markedness in Motion*. Manuscript, Brown University. [Also in C. Chvany and R. Brecht. (Eds.), (1980). *Morphosyntax in Slavic*, Columbus, Ohio: Slavica Publishers.]

Kučera, H. (1979). Some aspects of aspect in Czech and English. *Folia Slavica, 2*, 196–210.

Lakoff, G. (1966). Stative adjectives and verbs in English. *Mathematical Linguistics and Automatic Translation* 17. Cambridge, Mass.: Computation Laboratory, Harvard University.

Leech, G.N. (1970). *Towards a Semantic Description of English*. Bloomington and London: Indiana University Press.

Poldauf, I. (1966). Neaktuálnost jako gramatická kategorie českého slovesa? *Slovo a slovesnost, 27*, 23–28.

Trubetzkoy, N. (1939). *Grundzüge der Phonologie*. Prague: Cercle linguistique de Prague.

Twaddell, W. F. (1963). *The English Verb Auxiliaries*. Providence: Brown University Press.

Vendler, Z. (1967). *Linguistics in Philosophy*. Ithaca: Cornell University Press.

Woisetschlaeger. E.F. (1977). *A Semantic Theory of the English Auxiliary System*. (Distributed by the Indiana University Linguistics Club.)

EVENTS, PROCESSES, AND STATES[1]

ALEXANDER P. D. MOURELATOS

1. INTRODUCTION

In 1957, in an article published in the *Philosophical Review,* Zeno Vendler presented a fourfold distinction of verb types: activities, accomplishments, achievements, and states.[2] The Vendler scheme was intended as a refinement and systematization of a host of related distinctions that had been drawn in an informal and ad hoc manner by Ryle and others— for example, "dispositions" versus "occurrences," "achievements versus "tasks." The scheme can be grasped intuitively by reflecting on some of the examples Vendler cites under each category:

ACTIVITIES	ACCOMPLISHMENTS
run (around, all over)	*run a mile*
walk (and walk)	*paint a picture*
swim (along, past)	*grow up*
push (a cart)	*recover from illness*

[1] This chapter was originally published in *Linguistics and Philosophy,* **2** (1978), 415–434. It is reprinted here, with a few changes, by permission of D. Reidel Publishing Company.

[2] This article, "Verbs and Times," was later incorporated with revisions as Chapter 4 in *Linguistics in Philosophy* (pp. 97–121). References here will be to the latter (1967) version.

ISBN 0-12-613514-2

Syntax and Semantics, Volume 14
Tense and Aspect

ACHIEVEMENTS	STATES
recognize	*desire*
find	*want*
win (*the race*)	*love*
start/stop/resume	*hate*
be born/die	*dominate*

ACHIEVEMENTS capture either the inception or the climax of an act; they can be dated, or they can be indefinitely placed within a temporal stretch, but they cannot in themselves occur OVER or THROUGHOUT a temporal stretch. (They do, however, "take" time, in a sense that will shortly be explicated.) In contrast, ACCOMPLISHMENTS have duration intrinsically. So in the case of accomplishments we can properly say "*X V*-ed" with reference to the whole of that time segment, not just with reference to a single moment—for example, *Jones wrote the letter over the lunch break*. Moreover, accomplishments are not "homogeneous." To quote Vendler (1967), "in case I wrote a letter in an hour, I did not write it, say, in the first quarter of that hour [p. 101]."

It is an essential feature of ACTIVITIES that they ARE homogeneous. If Jones is (or was or will be or has been or had been) running for half an hour, then it must be true that he is (or was, *etc.*) running for every time stretch within that period. Vendler comments: "any part of the process is of the same nature as the whole [p. 101]." Moreover, at each moment it is correct to say both *Jones is running* and *Jones has run*. Most saliently, the time stretch of activities is inherently indefinite; they involve no culmination or anticipated result.

Finally, STATES, which may endure or persist over stretches of time, differ from accomplishments and activities in that they "cannot be qualified as actions at all [p. 106]." Verbs expressing states do not have progressive forms: we cannot say—at any rate not in good English—*I am knowing* or *I am loving*. A state, as the name implies, involves no dynamics. Though it may arise, or be acquired, as a result of change, and though it may provide the potential of change, the state itself does not constitute a change.[3]

A similar distinction, but with three rather than four types, was later developed, independently, by Anthony Kenny and published in his 1963 book *Action, Emotion and Will*. Kenny's three categories are activities, performances, and states. The main difference from Vendler is that achievements and accomplishments are not recognized as separate

---

[3] Vendler speaks very suggestively of states as "that puzzling category in which the role of verb melts into that of predicate, and actions fade into qualities and relations [p. 109]."

types.[4] In Kenny's scheme, *discover, find,* and *convince,* which clearly are achievements in Vendler's scheme, count as performances, along with such clear Vendler-scheme accomplishments as *grow up* and *build a house* (p. 175). It is not unreasonable to integrate the two schemes by regarding Vendler accomplishments and achievements as two subspecies of the more encompassing species of Kenny performances. This integration, however, cannot be brought off without correcting one of the criteria of the typology posited by Vendler and, correspondingly, making a different correction on one of the criteria posited by Kenny.

Vendler argued (pp. 100, 102) that accomplishments together with activities form one "genus," and achievements together with states, another, because—as he thought—achievement verbs are like state verbs in not admitting the progressive. This distinction in terms of two genera fails because the grammatical criterion on which it is based fails. One can easily cite or compose well-formed sentences in which any of the verbs in the achievements list given earlier appear in the progressive, for example, *He is winning the race.* In Kenny's scheme what stands in the way of integration is Kenny's adoption of "finish/not finish V-ing" as one of the criteria for performances (p. 177). The criterion, clearly, works only for accomplishments; it does not work for achievements, and, in fact, rules out five of Kenny's own examples of performances—the three cited earlier as qualifying as Vendler achievements, plus *kill* and *decide whether.* What argues strongly for the integration of accomplishments and achievements is that both are actions that involve a product, upshot, or outcome. Moreover, there cannot be an accomplishment without a closely related end-point achievement—one cannot say *I wrote (shall write) the letter* if he cannot say *I finished (shall finish) the letter.* Significantly, both accomplishments and achievements "take" time, indeed definite time—that is, they are

---

[4] Kenny points out the affinity of his own scheme with one introduced by Aristotle in *Metaph.* Θ. 1048b18–36, the famous distinction between *kinēseis* (performances) and *energeiai* (activities or states). In the linguistic literature, precursors of the Kenny–Vendler typology appear already in the nineteenth century; see Otto Jespersen (1924, pp. 272–273). Jespersen's own distinction is two-fold, "conclusive" versus "non-conclusive" (p. 273). In 1957, the year Vendler's original article appeared, a linguist, Howard Garey, presented a classification scheme for verbs under the rubrics "telic," which express "action tending towards a goal" (cf. Kenny performances), and "atelic," which express actions that "are realized as soon as they begin" (Kenny–Vendler activities). In spite of the strikingly Aristotelian terminology, Garey took no note of Book Θ of the *Metaphysics.* In Rescher and Urquhart (1971, p. 160), "processes or activities" are subdivided into "homogeneous," "majorative," "occasional," and "wholistic." The first three correspond to Kenny–Vendler activities, the fourth to Vendler's accomplishments. Bennet and Partee (1972, pp. 16–19) propose the categories "stative," "subinterval" (activities), and "nonstative, nonsubinterval" (performances).

both admissible into contexts of the form, "It took him N Ts to V," where N is a count expression and T is a unit of time. (It is tempting to say further that both accomplishments and achievements also admit adverbials of the form "in N of T." It appears, however, that for many achievements this type of adverbial is indistinguishable in its entailments from "after N of T." Thus *We shall start in two minutes* is indistinguishable from *We shall start after two minutes*. By contrast, *I shall run a mile in five minutes* means something quite different than *I shall run a mile after five minutes*.)

The distinctions worked out by Vendler and Kenny are conceptual tools of great usefulness in the philosophy of action, the philosophy of mind, in ontology generally, as well as in linguistics, and even in the history of philosophy—notably the study of Aristotle. But just because they are so very useful it is important for us to realize that they could, and indeed should, be conceived more broadly—in a wider linguistic context, and in a wider ontological context.

2. VERB ASPECT

A significant advance in Kenny's (1963) analysis is that it introduced a table of "tense-implications" and nine supplementary linguistic criteria —involving permissible adverbial phrases, paraphrase possibilities, and transformations of mood or voice—for the purpose of grouping verbs under the three types (pp. 174–179, 182–186). This very advance, however, points up a crucial limitation, one that equally as much limits the purview of Vendler's analysis.[5] At the time they published their respective schemes, neither Vendler nor Kenny realized that the distinctions they sought to articulate had long been studied by linguists under the heading of "verb aspect."[6] This linguistic phenomenon, a common heritage of Indo-European languages but also pervasively important in many languages outside the Indo-European family, was first correctly understood by the grammarians of Slavic languages. In Russian, for example, verbs articulate themselves in what are known as "imperfective versus perfective aspectual pairs." Thus, corresponding to the two English verbs *treat* and *cure*, Russian has a single verb in two aspectual forms—*lečit'*, imperfective, conveying the activity sense of *treat*, and *vylečit'*, perfec-

---

[5] And, needless to say, the work of Ryle, and that of others who drew informal ad hoc distinctions, in the spirit of Oxford post-World War II analysis.

[6] There is now a comprehensive, introductory treatment of this topic, Comrie (1976). Linguists had no difficulty recognizing that the work of Vendler and Kenny was an attempt to deal with aspect distinctions in English; see Dowty (1972, Chapter 2, especially pp. 27–30), Verkuyl (1971, pp. 5, 8n., 93, 157n.); Comrie (1976, pp. 41–51).

tive, carrying the achievement sense of *cure*. Correlatively, whereas the same English verb form, for example, *sang*, can have the sense of activity in one context, the sense of accomplishment in another, Russian requires that the two senses be shown as distinct through use of the aspectual marker: thus *pel* for the activity context (*He sang for hours*), but *spel* for the accomplishment context (*He sang the International*). Greek, too, both Ancient and Modern, shows aspectual distinctions sharply. In Plato's *Ion* 530A, Socrates asks: "ἠγωνίζου [imperfective preterite] τι ἡμῖν; καὶ πῶς τι ἠγωνίσω [same verb, perfective preterite]" 'And did you compete [activity]? And how did you succeed [achievement]?'[7]

Aspectual distinctions, without being so overtly and perspicuously marked as they are in the Slavic languages or in Greek, are also found in English.[8] Here is an especially suggestive example, from actual television script: "I can't wait to see what he's been doing [activity, imperfective] when he's done it [accomplishment, perfective]."[9] Standard examples are *John was reading* (activity, imperfective) *when I entered* (achievement, perfective), and the contrast between *I saw the accused stab* (accomplishment, perfective) *the victim* and *I saw the accused stabbing* (activity, imperfective) *the victim*.

The terminology of "perfective" versus "imperfective" is not yet standard in English, though it appears to be gaining currency.[10] It is adequate for our purposes here, but we must guard against confusing perfective ASPECT with the perfect TENSES (present perfect, pluperfect). The function of the latter is not to provide a categorization of the type of action, in the way suggested by the preceding examples; it is rather to encode the "phase" of time reference, specifically, to mark a certain action, occurrence, or situation[11] as temporally prior and relevant to a given reference point.[12] The simple perfect in English is often, but not always, perfective. (*He has arrived* and *He has been to Australia,* are both perfective, whereas *He has lived here all his life* is imperfective.)

[7] For Russian, see Unbegaun (1957, pp. 206–209), Ward (1965); for Ancient Greek, see Schwyzer (1950, pp. 248–269); and for Modern Greek, see Householder, Kazazis, and Koutsoudas (1964, pp. 104–105).

[8] See Allen (1966, Chapter 8), Hirtle (1967); Joos (1968, Chapter 5), Verkuyl (1971), Dowty (1972), Scheffer (1975), Comrie (1976, pp. 16–40, 124–125).

[9] Broadcast by KRO, April 17, 1972; quoted from Scheffer (1975, p. 42).

[10] It is employed by Hirtle (1967), by Dowty (1972), in part by Scheffer (1975), and by Comrie (1976).

[11] For the meaning I attach to "situation," see Section 3.

[12] See Reichenbach (1947, pp. 288–298), Comrie (1976, pp. 12, 52–64). For "phase" as the appropriate concept to subsume the distinctive functions of perfect forms, see Joos (1968, pp. 138–146), Cattell (1969, pp. 120–123). It is unfortunate that Comrie adhered to a traditional (and misleading) classification of the perfect as an aspect.

The relevance of verb aspect to the questions of verb typology that were studied by Vendler and Kenny must now be obvious. Many of the distinctions will be misdescribed if it is thought that they arise mainly from the semantics of individual verbs, when in fact they involve fundamental linguistic categories reflected partly at the lexical level and partly —in the case of Indo-European languages, pervasively—at the morphological and syntactic level.[13] Here are three cases in point of how the failure to diagnose distinctions as ones of aspect either raises problems for the accounts offered by Vendler and Kenny or has the effect of leaving the accounts misleadingly incomplete.

2.1. Semantic Multivalence of State Verbs

Vendler, (1967, pp. 111–112) classifies *know* as a state, but then has no way to explain how in *And then suddenly I knew!* it can have the "insight sense," which is the sense of an achievement. Kenny does not discuss divergent uses for his examples of state verbs. But it is not difficult to imagine cases where a Kenny state verb, for example *understand,* would be more appropriately classified as a Kenny performance; for example, *Once Lisa understood (grasped) what Henry's intentions were, she lost all interest in him* or *Please understand (get the point) that I am only trying to help you!* There is, of course, no aberrance of English idiom in either case. The special affinity of *know* or of *understand* for state contexts is beyond doubt; but, given the possibilities of semantic transposition provided by the aspectual system, these two verbs, or others that are semantically similar, can function quite aptly in a performance context—or, for that matter, in an activity context: *I'm understanding more about quantum mechanics as each day goes by* (cf. Comrie, 1976, pp. 36ff.). This sort of semantic multivalence constitutes enough of a pattern to make it quite wrong for us to talk in terms of exceptional or catachrestic uses of certain verbs.[14] Accordingly, some linquists, when they operate in the territory of phenomena explored by Vendler and Kenny, speak not of types of verbs but of types or categories of verb predication.[15]

---

[13] See Comrie (1976, pp. 6–11). Without taking note of the linguistic literature specifically on the topic of verb aspect, Timothy C. Potts, in a symposium discussion of Kenny's work was first to point out that in Kenny's table of "tense implications" temporal tense distinctions (present versus past) in fact play no role, the crucial contrasts being between the two underlying "operators," "continuous" versus "perfective" (Potts, 1975).

[14] This multivalence is, in fact, the rule rather than the exception. See Joos (1968, pp. 114– 17), Hirtle (1967, pp. 69–84), Scheffer (1975, pp. 61–75).

[15] The approach is sometimes promoted as a corrective to Garey's (1957) misplaced emphasis on verb types: See Allen (1966, p. 198), Leech (1969, p. 135).

2.2. Performance–Activity Transpositions

My second point I draw from Vendler's account alone. It will have been noticed that in his scheme *run* forms an activity predication in some contexts, a performance predication in others. He discusses the distinction as follows:

> But even if it is true that a runner *has run* a mile in four minutes, it cannot be true that he *has run* a mile in any period which is a real part of that time, although it remains true that he WAS RUNNING, or that he WAS engaged in RUNNING a mile, during any substretch of these four minutes [p. 101; my italics and small capitals].

In the phrases marked here in italics the verb is in an accomplishment predication, as marked by the adverbial *in four minutes,* which is one of Vendler's tests for accomplishments. In the phrases marked by small capitals, the verb is in activity predication, as marked by the adverbial phrase *during any substretch . . . ,* which expresses the homogeneity condition, the prime test for activities. It might seem at first blush that the distinction hinges on the presence of a verb object in the one case and its absence or suppression in the other. (As Vendler's punctuation indicates, what corresponds to the objectless phrase "was running" is the whole phrase "was engaged in running a mile," which is what I mean in saying that the object is here suppressed.) But this difference in fact plays no role. Vendler's point would hold even had he written simply: ". . . it remains true that he WAS RUNNING a mile during any substretch. . . ." The generic activity of running can be further differentiated into a species (one among indefinitely many) of running-a-mile without losing its character as an activity. In other words, regardless as to whether a mile is or fails to be run, any substretch of running-a-mile activity divides homogeneously into substretches of the same. There is, after all, a qualitative distinction between the activity of running a mile and the activity of running the hundred-meter dash or the marathon.

We need not assume, of course, that the distinction the two contexts make clear must also be marked in the verb itself or in the verb's arguments (subject, object). In the example at hand, however, the distinction is marked, morphologically: by the use of simple forms in the phrases printed in italics (perfective aspect) and use of progressive forms (imperfective aspect) in the phrases printed in small capitals.[16]

---

[16] It is instructive to consider how the distinction would show in Indo-European languages that are even more strongly marked for aspect than English is. In the case of the runner, in Greek the forms in italics would appear in perfective [aorist] aspect as *edramen*; the forms in small capitals would even require a different verb root, *etrechen,* which is the imperfective suppletive of *edramen.* In Russian the forms would be the perfective *pobežal* and the imperfective *bežal,* respectively.

2.3 Aspect in Inferences with Tenses

My third case in point involves a passage in Kenny (1963, p. 174). To show the logical importance of his scheme of verb types he makes this observation:

> It is sometimes said by logicians that if a proposition is true now, then the correspond-ing past-tensed proposition will be true in the future; e.g., if "Mr. McMillan is Prime Minister" is true now, then Mr. McMillan was Prime Minister will be true in the future. This rule as it stands does not apply to performance-verbs. A man may be walking to the Rose and Crown, and yet never walk there, perhaps because he is run over on the way.

The observation is valid enough. Yet the right thing to do with the logi-cians' rule is not list types of verbs for which it does not hold, but to ad-here more carefully to the rule's terms. The crucial words are "corre-sponding past-tensed." What the unnamed logicians had obviously taken for granted was that the aspect of the verb is to remain unaltered in the transposition from present to past tense.[17] In Kenny's example of the walk to the Rose and Crown, the first occurrence of the verb is in imper-fective, the second in perfective aspect.[18] The contrast is easily missed because English -*ing* is not only part of the marker of the imperfective aspect but often simply a neutral participial or gerundial ending. In the example at hand, to keep parity of aspect we have two options:

1. Perfective aspect throughout: If it is true now that he has this very moment walked to the Rose and Crown, it will be true in the future that he did walk, or had walked, to the Rose and Crown.[19]

---

[17] Kenny (1963, p. 174) comes close to seeing this ("we might say that the past tense which corresponds to 'is knitting' is 'was knitting' rather than 'knitted' ") but abandons the approach in the belief that it leads to a differently formulated but equivalent exception to the logicians' rule (cf. Note 19).

[18] In Ancient Greek a counterpart to Kenny's sentence would be Ἔξεστι αὐτὸν βαίνειν (imperfective, present-stem infinitive ἀλλὰ μὴ βῆναι (perfective, aorist-stem infinitive). In Russian one would say something of the order: He may *idti* (imperfective infinitive) but not *doiti* (perfective infinitive, derived from *idti* by addition of the perfectivizing prefix *do-*).

[19] The reader might protest that in (1) the action is viewed as already having taken place, and that the antecedent fails to qualify as a present tense proposition. Now the misconcep-tion that the English present perfect is intrinsically a "past" tense has often been exposed. To draw only on authors previously cited in this chapter, see Reichenbach (1947, pp. 289–290, 295), Joos (1968, p. 144), Leech (1969, pp. 152–158), Potts (1965, pp. 71, 77), Comrie (1976, pp. 52ff., 106–108). In any event, a variant of (1) with the simple present in the ante-cedent and the simple past in the consequent is also possible if *walks* is construed as in "re-portive" use (cf. *And there you have it, Ladies and Gentlemen, he walks to the Rose and Crown,* spoken by an on-the-scene radio or television reporter, seconds after the subject has crossed the pub's threshold). On this perfective use of the simple present, see Leech (1969, p. 139); cf. Scheffer (1975, p. 77). This is the only nonfrequentative use of the simple pres-ent, and (*pace* Kenny 1963, p. 174) what corresponds to it for all verbs is the simple past.

2. Imperfective aspect throughout: If it is true now that he is walking, or has been walking, to the Rose and Crown, it will be true in the future that he was walking, or had been walking, to the Rose and Crown.

2.4 Six Determinants of Verb Predication

The critique offered in my three cases in point might lead to certain mis-understandings, which I hasten to forestall. The function of aspect is not limited to providing assignment to one or another of the categories activ-ity–performance (accomplishment/achievement)–state. One of the major functions that lies outside the Kenny–Vendler typology is the encoding of patterns of frequency or habituation. This is characteristically true of the imperfective aspect: Consider French *j' écrivais* (imperfective) *souvent* 'I wrote frequently'; or Russian *ja begal* (imperfective) 'I used to run.' A wide variety of other points of information, also unrelated to the Kenny–Vendler typology, may be encoded through aspect—for example, en-deavor, serialization, spatial distribution, temporary or contingent state. Moreover, even in those cases where the predication is classifiable under one or another of the Kenny–Vendler categories, the verb's aspectual marking does not by itself specify the relevant category. In all cases a total of six factors are involved: (*a*) the verb's inherent meaning; (*b*) the nature of the verb's arguments, that is, of the subject and of the object(s), if any; (*c*) adverbials, if any; (*d*) aspect; (*e*) tense as phase (e.g., the per-fect); (*f*) tense as time reference to past, present, or future. An account of how these factors interact with one another to determine the resulting verb predication lies outside the scope of this chapter. On the basis merely of the list just cited, my critique so far of the Kenny–Vendler ap-proach can be put as follows. Kenny and Vendler sought to classify verb types by noticing selections and restrictions that factors (*b*), (*c*), and (*e*) together with (*f*) exercise on candidate verbs. What they did not notice is the heavy role played by factor (*d*). They also did not realize that factors (*b*) through (*f*) work selections and restrictions on one another as well as on the candidate verbs.

3. THE ONTOLOGICAL TRICHOTOMY

Even without expanding our horizon so as to take in the linguistic phe-nomenon of verb aspect, it is not difficult to realize that there are verbs and verb uses that are classifiable neither as activities nor as perform-ances, but that may not be classifiable as states either. This is a second respect in which the Kenny–Vendler typology is too narrowly conceived. Philosophical interest in distinctions between verbs arose from discussions in the philosophy of mind and the philosophy of action. Yet the trichotomy activity–performance–state obviously falls under an ontological trichotomy of wider scope, namely, process–event–state. Vendler and Kenny were doubtless aware of this wider ontological context, but they failed to appreciate how its existence renders their respective typologies incomplete.[20]

In Vendler's account the incompleteness shows up in a counterintuitive analysis of *see*. He observes, first, in agreement with Ryle, that there is "no question that seeing can be an achievement," and speaks of a " 'spotting' sense of seeing" (p. 113). He then recognizes that in *I saw him run (cross the street)*, seeing cannot be an achievement, for it "must have a sense that admits a period of time" (p. 115). He then reasons that, as it cannot be an activity, nor an accomplishment—not a "process," as he puts it—the *saw* of *I saw him run* must refer to a state. This diagnosis hardly accords with our intuitions. There is no difficulty in paraphrasing *He was running* as *He was engaged in the activity of running*. But would we really be tempted to paraphrase *I saw him run* as *I was in a state of visual awareness of him running*? Besides, we could easily supply a context for *I saw him run* that would make it appropriate for this sentence to be an answer to the question *What happened next?*—a question that could not envisage a state predication as one of its possible answers. It is certainly significant that, in languages with a sharp perfective–imperfective distinction in the past tense (French, Greek, Russian), a perfective form in the main verb would be required to translate the sentences *I saw him run* and *I saw him cross the street*. So the force of *I saw* in these two sentences is not to convey the state of the subject but to record A SIGHTING or A SEEING, however protracted, as an occurrence, as an individuated something that took place. The correct category for the *saw* of Vendler's sentence is EVENT. The notion of "event" I have invoked here will become precise in the concluding section of this chapter. Meanwhile, relying still on intuitions, I should point out that event is the right classification for the focal referent not only of sentences similar to *I saw him*

---

[20] Vendler (1967, p. 108) takes note of a distinction in the physical realm between states and what we might noncommittally call "changes": *to be hard* or *to be yellow* versus *to harden* or *to yellow*. He even employs the term "process" with reference to the latter two; yet he quickly glosses the term as "activity or accomplishment." At one point he expresses hopeful confidence that "all verbs can be analyzed in terms of these four schemata [p. 107]." Kenny (1963) in spite of the subject matter limitation implied by the title and theme of his book, does not limit his survey to states that are properly of agents but includes such physical or neutral states as *exist, be able, be blue, be taller than* (p. 175).

run, that could not be classed as referring to performances, but also of all sentences referring to performances. Event is simply the topic-neutral category. If there is a performance *A*, there is also an event *A*, but not vice versa. Performances are those events that are instances of human (or personal, or quasi-personal) agency.

Tracing this line of thought further, it appears that purely natural events can be differentiated into: (*a*) topic-neutral DEVELOPMENTS, the counterpart of Vendler's accomplishments; and (*b*) topic-neutral PUNCTUAL OCCURRENCES (i.e., various starts, resumptions, split-second events, stoppings, and climaxes), the counterpart of Vendler's achievements. The topic-neutral counterpart of state needs no separate name; it is quite obviously STATE in the widest and quite familiar sense, the one employed by physicists or physiologists when they speak of "the solid state," or of a "metabolic state." PROCESS, a term ready to hand, is the topic-neutral counterpart of activity. (We need, however, to be on guard against possible confusion, as some authors, especially philosophers in the context of discussion of mind–body identity, have used "process" as the counterpart of "accomplishment.") If we now adopt an intermediate generic term, OCCURRENCES will be the topic-neutral counterpart of actions; and if we may coin a term for the encompassing genus, SITUATIONS will comprise occurrences and states. The generalized trichotomy appears embedded in a scheme of nested binary contrasts:

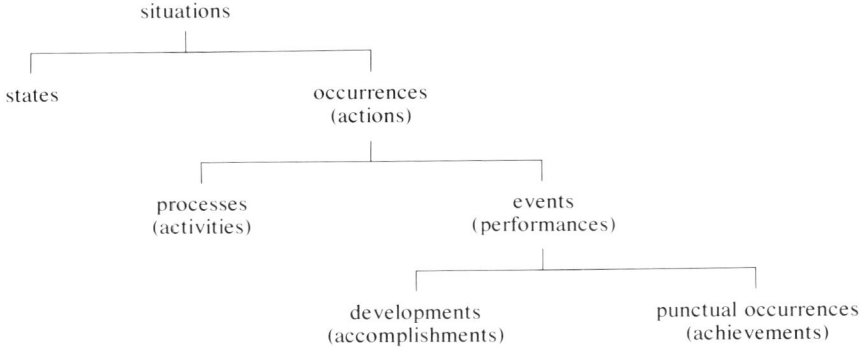

Here are examples of verb predications that refer to purely physical situations:

STATE: *The air smells of jasmine.*
PROCESS: *It's snowing.*
DEVELOPMENT: *The sun went down.*
PUNCTUAL OCCURRENCE: *The cable snapped. He blinked. The pebble hit the water.*

Of special interest are, of course, sensory occurrences. Intimately related to the realm of agency, they do not in themselves constitute actions. But, just as there can be visual or auditory states (e.g., *I see dimly; I hear you well*), so there can be visual or auditory processes (*I'm seeing a bright light; I'm hearing buzzing sounds*), visual or auditory developments (Vendler's example, *I saw him cross the street; I heard him sing a serenade*) and visual or auditory punctual occurrences (*I caught a glimpse of him as he was crossing the threshold,* cf. Vendler's "'spotting' sense of seeing"; *I heard him cough*).[21]

The existence of this wider ontological context is implicitly recognized in the literature of linguistics, where distinctions have been couched in the topic-neutral terms of "process versus state (or 'status' or 'stative') predication,"[22] or of "event versus state predication."[23] What has not been brought out clearly by linguists is that these distinction pairs, together with a third one—process versus event predication[24]—constitute the sort of system I have outlined and diagrammed here. In this respect, in spite of limitations I have discussed, the Kenny–Vendler typology is especially valuable; for it certainly envisages a single scheme rather than a set of ad hoc distinctions.[25]

4. ASPECT AND THE MASS–COUNT DISTINCTION

Even wider theoretical vistas have opened up in recent years as linguists search out the logical or formal-semantic sources of verb types and

---

[21] See Comrie (1976, p. 35). A certain curious disparity between sensory and other natural developments was pointed out to me by Zeno Vendler in the form of a rejoinder to my critique of his diagnosis of *I saw him run*. We can say, Vendler pointed out, *The sun went down in ten minutes* (also *quickly, slowly, etc.*). But we find it strained to say *I saw him in three seconds cross the street*, though we can say *I saw him cross the street in three seconds*. Now it should be noticed that we could, in a suitable context, say *My seeing him cross the street took (all of) three seconds*. Similarly, though we cannot say *I heard Beethoven's Ninth in one-and-a-half hours*, we could say *It took me an hour and a half to hear Beethoven's Fifth* (cf. Vendler's *He saw* Carmen *last night*, pp. 120–121). What makes the "in *N* of *T*" adverbial inadmissible in all these cases is the implication that seeing or hearing, which are PASSIVE developments that necessarily must reflect the duration of the object occurrence they capture, could somehow be sped up or slowed down. For the same reason it is odd to use "in *N* of *T*" with reference to what would clearly qualify as cases of passive accomplishment (e.g., *I videotaped* Carmen *off the TV in three hours, I tape-recorded Beethoven's Ninth off the FM radio in one and a half hours*).

[22] Joos (1968, pp. 116–117). But Joos's "process" is a generic term, corresponding to my "occurrence."

[23] Leech (1969, pp. 134–137). The vocabulary of events–processes–states is also employed by Comrie (1976, pp. 13, 48–51, and passim).

[24] This distinction roughly corresponds to Garey's "atelic" versus "telic" and Allen's "unbounded" versus "bounded" (see Notes 4, 8).

[25] This is also a virtue of the approach by Bennett and Partee.

verb aspect. Of several approaches taken,[26] I turn here to one that seems particularly attractive for the reason that it treats aspectual phenomena as manifestations of the play of categories so fundamental as to span the distinction between verbs and nouns. It has been suggested by several authors that a distinction between count terms (which include, but are not limited to, what philosophers call "sortal terms" or terms that "divide their reference") and mass terms is in some way involved in determining the category of the verb predication.[27] Let me first briefly review the count versus mass distinction as it obtains in its familiar environment, the nominal system.[28]

Nouns such as *squirrel, equation,* and *snowflake* are count terms. Such terms have plural forms that involve no switch of meaning from the singular form; they take cardinal numerals, as well as the indefinite article; they can be governed by the phrase that is the informal equivalent of the existential quantifier, *there is at least one;* they can be used with the adjectives *many, several, few, each,* and *every.* Nouns such as *wine, snow,* and *hunger* are mass terms. They generally do not have plural forms, or if they do there is a meaning shift—wines are TYPES of wine. None of the other adjectives cited as admissible with count terms are admissible with mass terms—except, again, with meaning shifts. Adjectives that go naturally with mass terms are *much, little, too much, too little, enough,* and the like. There are also ambiguous terms, such as *lamb (Mary was given a lamb* versus *Mary had lamb for dinner)* or *noise (There's too much noise in the hall* versus *I heard a noise).* Moreover, there are terms that have the syntax of mass terms even though the ultimate referents are discrete objects that would in themselves be referred to through the use of count terms. An example would be *furniture:* we can say *much furniture, little furniture;* we cannot say *three furnitures* or *many furnitures;* yet the entities referred to are tables, chairs, and the like, entities that have a definite number.[29]

---

[26] See Comrie (1976, pp. 129–133). A number of studies, including Bennett and Partee (1972), favor an approach that utilizes concepts of tense logic and Montague grammar in their analysis of aspect.

[27] These authors include Allen (1966, pp. 192–204), Verkuyl (1971, pp. 54–61), Dowty (1972, pp. 29ff., 48ff.), Leech (1969, pp. 125–126, 134–137), Bolinger (1975, p. 147, cf. Table 6-2, pp. 152–153), Gabbay and Moravcsik (1973, p. 523), Taylor (1977, pp. 199–220, especially p. 210 ff.).

[28] See Jespersen (1924, pp. 188–201), Strawson (1959, pp. 168–172, 202–209), Quine (1960, pp. 90–95), Wallace (1965), Chappell (1970–1971).

[29] There are also two further complications. Many count terms also qualify as sortals, that is, as terms that provide a PRINCIPLE or CRITERION of count, identification, and reidentification, whereas some, such as *thing, red thing,* or *quality,* fail to do so. Correspondingly, many mass terms qualify as "stuff" terms (see Chappell [1970–1971, pp. 72–73]), whereas some, such as *hunger* or *wisdom,* do not.

In exploring analogues of these distinctions in the realm of verbs, linguists have focused mainly on the object of the verb, as it often seems that the object lends its character to the predication as a whole. Thus in *He played a Mozart sonata,* where the object is a count term, we have an event predication, more precisely an accomplishment; but in *He played a little Mozart,* where the object is a mass phrase, we have a process predication, in particular an activity.[30]

This is right so far as it goes. But there is an even more fundamental sense in which the predication can be said to have the feature count or the feature mass. Corresponding to an event predication there is a nominalization equivalent in which the original verb appears as a gerund or deverbative noun (suffixes typically *-ion, -ment, -al, -ure*) that governs an existential construction of the verb *to be.* If the number of occurrences is specified by an adverb in the original version, the number appears as a cardinal numeral modifying the gerund in the nominalized version. If the number is not specified, the existential construction has the characteristic import of the existential quantifier, "There is *at least* one. . . ."[31] Here are examples of the two transcriptions.

1. *Vesuvius erupted three times.* ↔ *There were three eruptions of Vesuvius.*
2. *Mary capsized the boat.* ↔ *There was a capsizing of the boat by Mary.*

The event predication has the count feature in either of the two senses made clear by these transcriptions: Either the occurrences are explicitly counted, or, if they are not, the occurrences are nevertheless implicitly under the governance of terms that presuppose that the occurrences are countable (*a* or *at least one*). To remind us of this feature, let me refer to the existential constructions in the two transcriptions as "count-quantified."

It appears that count-quantified transcriptions are possible and fairly idiomatic in the case of every predication that would otherwise—by Kenny–Vendler and related criteria—qualify as an event predication. Now, if we should find that nominalization transcriptions work quite differently in the case of process predication or state predication, we would perhaps have a simple and abstract criterion for drawing distinctions of predication category. Before we can proceed to this, however, we need to become clear about certain subsidiary distinctions, failure to observe

---

[30] See also Leech (1969, p. 137), on the phenomenon of "semantic concord."

[31] My formulation here is inspired by the work of Davidson (1967, pp. 81–95; 1969, pp. 216–234). Davidson's transcriptions constitute a certain program for semantics and metaphysics. My own argument here is not dependent on that program.

which would tend to muddy the application of the criterion we envisage.

Adverbials such as *twice* or *five times*, which might be called CARDINAL COUNT ADVERBIALS, are to be distinguished from adverbials such as *twice a year, five times a week, often, seldom,* or *always*, which are called FRE-QUENCY ADVERBIALS.[32] Of course, if *three times* is shown in context to be elliptical for *three times in a recurrent period* (e.g., week, year, month), it functions as a frequency, not as a cardinal count, adverbial. Moreover, certain adverbials are ambiguous: *many times* may be an indefinite cardinal count, or it may be a measure of frequency.

Another important distinction is between the OCCASION of a situation and the SITUATION itself.[33] The distinction can be illustrated with examples of the four types of situations discussed in the preceding section—the occasion phrase is indicated by the use of boldface:

1. *Tom loved Mary* (state) **when he was a teenager.**
2. *He swam* (activity) **on Thanksgiving.**
3. *He crossed the street* (accomplishment) **upon seeing her.**
4. *He reached the summit* (achievement) **on three different expeditions.**

In speaking of an event, we could use a cardinal count adverbial with reference either to the event itself (events themselves) or to the occasion(s). Thus we may count the moments or intervals of time in association with which the event occurs (events occur); or we may count, for example, the eruptions, or capsizings, or crossings of the street, or arrivals to the summit. It is, of course, theoretically possible to establish a mathematically tight correspondence between occasion(s) and event(s): Thus, corresponding to a single punctual occurrence (achievement) there is a single point in time, and, corresponding to a development, a certain interval the start and end of which coincide, respectively, with the start and end of the development. But adverbials that count associated occasions never—so far as I can tell—envisage this sort of exact fit between occasion and event. Typically the occasion is a wider frame, specified more or less arbitrarily, by reference to accompanying circumstances—as is the case with the occasion phrases used in (1)–(4). This standard looseness of fit has the effect of allowing double readings for many sentences. Thus *He knocked on the door three times* may mean that there was one knock on the door on three different occasions, or it may mean that there were three knocks on one single occasion (the example is from Leech, 1969, p. 125). What is noteworthy about such cases of double reading is that, even if the cardinal count adverbial is assigned to the occasion, another cardinal count adver-

---

[32] See Leech (1969, pp. 123–129), Bennett and Partee (1972, pp. 26–34), Palmer and Blandford (1969, p. 238).

[33] See Leech (1969, pp. 125–126)—the distinction drawn with reference to events only.

bial, namely, *once,* is implied as assigned directly to the event. It will shortly emerge that it is only in the case of event predication that cardinal count adverbials can be used with reference to the situation (i.e., to the event itself) as distinct (explicitly or implicitly) from the occasion.

Let us now attempt to apply the nominalization transcription in the cases of process predication and of state predication. Consider first two examples of process (activity) predication—one example with the predication category marked primarily through lexical means, and one with it marked through imperfective aspect (progressive):

> *John pushed the cart for hours.*
> *Jones was painting the Nativity.*

The transcriptions are, respectively,

> *For hours there was pushing of the cart by John.*
> *There was painting of the Nativity by Jones.*

What strikes one immediately is the absence of the indefinite article. The pushing and the painting in these contexts do not have the terminus or closure that would allow us to speak of *a* pushing or *a* painting—we are not told that the cart was pushed some place, or that the Nativity did get painted. The parallel with simple nouns for these transcriptions is not in sentences of the form *There is at least one K;* rather, it is in sentences of the same form as *There is snow on the roof,* or *There is gold in this mountain.*[34] And just as we can amplify or supplement the latter two examples with expressions such as *little, much, enough,* and the like, we can use these same expressions to amplify or supplement the nominalization transcriptions of our two examples of process predication.

The last observation already suggests that cardinal numerals are not admissible in nominalization transcriptions of process predications. If there cannot be *a painting* or *a pushing,* in the sense required by the context of our examples, there could not be two, three, or more. I shall accordingly refer to these transcriptions as "mass-quantified." We should expect as a corollary that cardinal count adverbials are generally not admissible with

---

[34] Davidson does not appear to have noticed the infelicity of his formula, "There exists a *V*-ing event," in the case of processes or activities. It was, however, indirectly noticed by Lemmon (1967, pp. 101–102). Lemmon pointed out that *Jones was slowly buttering the toast* differs in its entailments from *Jones slowly buttered the toast* in ways that Davidson's analysis fails to capture. At any rate, it is significant that of all the examples Davidson uses in his articles none are cases of process predication. Even the one possible exception, *Sebastian strolled through the streets of Bologna at 2:00* A.M. (1969, pp. 218–219), is glossed by Davidson as an accomplishment—"Sebastian took *a* stroll" (1969, p. 219; my italics).

process predications (in their normal, nontranscribed form), and that, in the exceptional cases where they are admitted, the reference is not to the situation itself. Certainly we get nonsense if we attach a cardinal count adverbial to our first example: *He pushed the cart twice for hours.* Even more striking is what happens if the example sentence is simply *He pushed the cart.* This sentence could, doubtless, without any other adverbial, have the import of a process predication in a suitable context. Adding, however, the cardinal count adverbial *three times* suffices to transform this prima facie process predication into an event predication. Thus *He pushed the cart three times* has to be construed as elliptical for some performance predication—as the context might implicitly specify— for example, *He pushed the cart three times* **out of his way,** or *He pushed the cart* **over the hill** *three times,* or *He* **started** *pushing the cart three times.* In any of these cases there were, in the relevant sense, three completed pushings of the cart. Similarly with the example used in making the distinction between situation and occasion: *He swam* **three times** *on Thanksgiving* cannot fail to have the implication that he took three swims, that three swims were completed—regardless as to whether the context does or does not indicate the actual distance covered in each of these swims.

Consider now the example in which the predication category is marked solely through imperfective aspect: *Jones was painting the Nativity twice* is, on the face of it, odd and badly in need of interpretation. Assuming that Jones has already painted the Nativity once, the use of the progressive precludes that we can speak of more than one (completed act of) painting. So, if the sentence has any meaning, the adverbial phrase ranges over two occasions of painting, not over two paintings. Thus the meaning may be "He was **again** (or **for the second time**) painting the Nativity." On this interpretation there may not have been even one painting of the Nativity by Jones: There may simply have been two occasions on each of which it was true that *Jones was painting the Nativity.* Doubtless other, more ingenious, interpretations are possible—for example, that Jones was an actor and the two paintings were staged events being viewed prospectively in the past, or that by some rigging device Jones was producing simultaneously two copies of the Nativity. But I trust it is clear that the upshot of these interpretations will be either that *twice* ranges over occasions, or that the use of the progressive was nonaspectual, or that the duality is one of associated objects, not of occurrences. Curiously, it does not appear to have been noticed in the literature that nonartificial, idiomatic uses of the form "*S* is (was, will be, has been, etc.) *V*-ing *N* times" are extremely rare. Examples that come to mind are the auctioneer's

Going once, going twice, or the strain from the Santa Claus song, *He's making a list, he's checking it twice.*[35] Clearly, in neither of these cases do the cardinal count adverbials count the occurrences represented by the verb. In the auctioneer's case what is counted is the auctioneer's calls, not the "goings"; in the Santa Claus case, the meaning is "he's double-checking," or "he's checking for the second time" (an ordinal count of the occasions).

How do the nominalization transcriptions work in the case of state predication? Count-quantified transcriptions do not seem to work at all. We cannot transform *John hates liars* into **There is a hating by John of liars;* nor can we transform *Helen dominates her husband* into **There is a dominating by Helen of her husband.* Correspondingly, cardinal count adverbials do not occur in contexts of state predication—unless they refer purely to the occasions of the state rather than the state itself. *John hated liars three times in his life* is acceptable provided it is stages or junctures of John's life that are being counted. Moreover, if an occasion phrase is already supplied, the use of a cardinal count adverbial in collocation with a prima facie state predication has the effect of transforming the latter into an event predication. Thus *John loved her last summer* is most naturally construed as synonymous with *John was in love with her last summer.* But *John loved her three times last summer* must mean either that John fell in love with her three times last summer or that John made love to her three times last summer.

Mass-quantified transcriptions are, however, possible for state predications. To be more precise, state predications admit of such transcriptions typically through use not of the gerund but of specially associated deverbative nouns. Thus we can say *There is hate by John of liars, There is dominance of her husband by Helen, There is love of her by John.* This avoidance of the gerund forms in the transcription of state predications gives us another intuitive handle on the distinction between states and processes. In syntactical terms, however, the transcription does not differentiate between process and state predications. Both are mass-quantified, both accept expressions such as *much, little, enough.* This is not a disappointing result, as there is a well-known tendency of states to meld with processes and vice versa—*I doubt the truth of this assertion* could mean "I question the truth of this assertion," and vice versa. This is reflected in the affinity of state predication for the imperfective aspect in the case of languages like Greek or Russian that have a sharply marked perfective–imperfective distinction.

---

[35] I am indebted to Steve Strange for this example.

What the device of nominalization transcription enables us to determine is that all and only event predications are equivalent to count-quantified existential constructions. As a corollary, all and only event predications include, or can admit, or imply cardinal count adverbials that refer to the situation itself, as distinct from associated occasions. Thus, in *He crossed himself three times,* the cardinal count adverbial is included; in *He crossed himself,* the adverbial *three times* is admissible; in *Vesuvius erupted,* the adverbial *at least once* is implied; in the ambiguous *He knocked on the door three times,* either the adverb *once* or the adverbial *three times* is implied as referring to a knock or knocks, as distinct from the associated occasions or occasion of knocking.

A strong tie between event predication and cardinal count adverbials shows up in Greek—both Ancient and Modern.[36] Perfective forms (in Ancient Greek aorist forms, in Modern Greek the entire perfective system, which includes aorist, perfective future, and perfect) are employed almost exclusively[37] to express event predication. Even though the converse is not true—not all event predications are expressed in Greek through perfective forms—it is nevertheless true that cardinal count adverbials are used preponderately with perfective forms.[38]

If count-quantified transcriptions, or the co-occurrence of cardinal count adverbials that refer not merely to the associated occasion, provide a simple criterion of event predication, we could correspondingly say, in ontological terms, that events are those situations that can be directly or intrinsically counted. But there is reason to think that in ontology we could go further. For it would seem that events are not merely countable but also fall under SORTS[39] that provide a PRINCIPLE of count: The questions *How many capsizings of the boat were there yesterday?* and *How many times did the boat capsize?* envisage determinate answers. Events thus occupy relatively to other situations a position analogous to the one objects or things or substances occupy relatively to stuffs and properties or qualities. This analogy was already noticed by Allen[40] and has most recently been explored by Barry Taylor.[41] A substance is not homogeneous

---

[36] For Ancient Greek, see Armstrong (this volume).

[37] The only exception being the so-called "gnomic aorist" of Ancient Greek, which, however, involves a quite special and isolated semantic effect.

[38] This is the truth, I believe, that underlies the half-truth of traditional Greek grammar, that the aorist is "punctual"—a doctrine that ignores uses of the aorist with reference to developments (accomplishments) as distinct from punctual occurrences (achievements).

[39] See Note 29.

[40] See Notes 8, 27.

[41] See Note 27.

—or, to use the more precise term used by the ancients, homoeomerous, "like-parted." A clock is not made up of clocks. Correspondingly an event E is not made up of E-events: the capsizing of a boat is not made up of boat-capsizings. Stuffs are homoeomerous: If X is gold, then all parts of X are gold. Processes are homoeomerous in the corresponding sense explicated at the opening of this chapter à propos of Vendler's activities. Moreover, just as we can collect and thus individuate stuffs into such extrinsic containers as bottles or lumps or measures, we can correspondingly collect and individuate activities into stretches, phases, stages, and the like. The two systems converge in their third component: In the case of states, as Vendler (1967) so aptly put it, "the role of verb melts into that of predicate, and actions fade into qualities and relations [p. 109]."

There are—notoriously—complications. Few, if any, stuffs are homoeomerous through and through. With many the homoeomery breaks down even before we reach fine grain—for example, fruit cake. What is remarkable for our purposes is that these complications have counterparts in the domain of situations. If snowing or pushing a cart are paradigms of homoeomerous process, thundering, giggling, or talking may count as paradigms of anhomoeomerous process (Taylor, 1977, p. 212). Moreover, again in linguistic terms, even some of the complications involving mass WORDS are reflected in the language of situations. Thus the duality of *many lambs* versus *much lamb* has its counterpart in the option we have to say: *There were many killings, there were many deaths;* or, with greater pathos, *There was much killing, there was much dying.*

More analogues of complications—even analogues of complications involved in *furniture,* the hybrid mass word mentioned earlier in this section—spring to our notice if we look fully into the role of verb aspect (see Dressler, 1968, pp. 56–95). By way of suggesting the richness and relevance of this body of evidence, let me simply point out that, whereas English has no simple verb predications that correspond to the count-quantified and mass-quantified transcriptions given at the end of the preceding paragraph, Greek does have the equivalent non-nominalized verb predications, namely, ἀπέκτανον, ἀπέθανον (perfective aspect) versus ἀπέκτεινον, ἀπέθνησκον (imperfective aspect, cf. Xenophon *Hellenica* 4.3.19).

ACKNOWLEDGMENTS

For valuable comments, helpful discussion, and corrections, I am indebted to R. David Armstrong, Bernard D. Katz, Anthony Kenny, J. M. E. Moravcsik, Francis J. Pelletier, Tom Robinson, Carlota Smith, J. T. J. Srzednicki and Frank Vlach. I also and specially thank Zeno Vendler for his searching critique of my presentation to the American Philosophical Association's (Pacific Division) meeting in Portland, March 1977. Discussions in early 1978 with Hans Kamp, Dee Ann Holisky, and with members of the Philosophy Department of the University of Wisconsin, Madison, have motivated several improvements over the penultimate version.

REFERENCES

Allen, R.L. (1966). *The Verb System of Present-Day American English*. The Hague: Mouton.

Bennett, M., and Partee, B. (1972). *Toward the logic of tense and aspect*. System Development Corporation, Santa Monica, Calif. (Available from the Indiana University Linguistics Club.)

Bolinger, D. (1975). *Aspects of Language*. New York: Harcourt and Brace.

Cattell, N.R. (1969). *The New English Grammar: A Descriptive Introduction*. Cambridge, Mass.: Harvard University Press.

Chappell, V.C. (1970–1971). Stuff and things. *Proceedings of the Aristotelian Society*, **71**, 61–76.

Comrie, B. (1976). *Aspect*. Cambridge: Cambridge University Press.

Davidson, D. (1967). The logical form of action sentences. In N. Rescher (Ed.), *The Logic of Decision and Action*. Pittsburgh: University of Pittsburgh Press. Pp. 81–95.

Davidson, D. (1969). The individuation of events. In N. Rescher (Ed.), *Essays in Honor of Carl G. Hempel*. Dordrecht: Reidel. Pp. 216–234.

Dowty, D. (1972). Studies in the logic of verb aspect and time reference in English. Doctoral dissertation, University of Texas at Austin (published in *Studies in Linguistics*, No. 1, Department of Linguistics, University of Texas at Austin).

Dressler, W. (1968). *Studien zur Verbalen Pluralität*. Oesterreichische Akademie der Wissenschaften, philosophisch-historische Klasse, Sitzungsberichte, Band 259, Abhandlung 1.

Gabbay, D., and Moravcsik, J.M.E. (1973). Sameness and individuation. *The Journal of Philosophy*, **70**, 513–524.

Garey, H. (1957). Verbal aspect in French. *Language*, **33**, 91–110.

Hirtle, W.H. (1967). *The Simple and Progressive Forms*. Cahiers de psychomecanique de langage, 8. Québec: Les Presses de l'université Laval.

Householder, F., Kazazis, K., and Koutsoudas, A. (1964). *Reference Grammar of Literary Dhimotiki*. The Hague: Mouton.

Jespersen, O. (1924). *The Philosophy of Grammar*. London: Allen and Unwin.

Joos, M. (1968). *The English Verb*. Madison: University of Wisconsin Press.

Kenny, A. (1963). *Action, Emotion and Will*. New York: Humanities Press.

Leech, G.N. (1969). *Towards a Semantic Description of English*. Bloomington: Indiana University Press.

Lemmon, E.J. (1967). Comments on D. Davidson's 'The Logical Form of Action Sentences.' In N. Rescher (Ed.), *The Logic of Decision and Action*. Pittsburgh: University of Pittsburgh Press. Pp. 96–103.

Palmer, H.E., and Blandford, F.G. (1969). *A Grammar of Spoken English* (3rd ed.). Cambridge: Cambridge University Press.

Potts, T. (1965). States, activities, and performances. In *Proceedings of the Aristotelian Society*, suppl. vol. 39, 65–84.

Quine, W.V.O. (1960). *Word and Object*. Cambridge, Mass.: Harvard University Press.

Reichenbach, H. (1947). *Elements of Symbolic Logic*, New York: Macmillan.

Rescher, N., and Urquhart, A. (1971). *Temporal Logic*. New York: Springer-Verlag.

Scheffer, J. (1975). *The Progressive in English*. Amsterdam: North-Holland.

Schwyzer, E. (1950). *Griechische Gramatik, vol. 2, Syntax und syntaktische Stilistik*, ed. A. Debrunner. Munich: C. H. Beck'sche Verlags-buchhandlung.

Strawson, P.F. (1959). *Individuals*. London: Methuen.

Taylor, B. (1977). Tense and continuity. *Linguistics and Philosophy*, **1**, 199–220.

Unbegaun, B.O. (1957). *Russian Grammar*. Oxford: Oxford University Press.

Vendler, Z. (1967). *Linguistics in Philosophy*. Ithaca: Cornell University Press.

Verkuyl, H.J. (1971). *On the Compositional Nature of the Aspects*. Dordrecht: Reidel.

Wallace, J.R. (1965). Sortal predicates and quantification. *The Journal of Philosophy*. **62**, 8–13.

Ward, D. (1965). *The Russian Language Today: System and Anomaly*. Chicago: University of Chicago Press.

SEMANTIC AND SYNTACTIC CONSTRAINTS ON TEMPORAL INTERPRETATION

CARLOTA S. SMITH

1. INTRODUCTION

This chapter discusses some constraints on temporal reference in English. A central fact about temporal reference is that it involves orientation, or anchoring, to a reference point.[1] Many temporal forms are uninterpretable if one does not know how they are anchored—for instance, *yesterday, in 3 hours*. The very basic and general notions of past, present, and future are meaningful only in terms of a particular orientation or anchor; in independent sentences, this anchor is usually Speech Time (*ST*), the moment of utterance.

There are situations, however, where temporal reference has an anchor other than Speech Time. I will be concerned with two aspects of such situations. First, temporal forms differ according to whether and how they may anchor to times other than *ST*; I will explore these differences and propose a classification of temporal forms. Second, I discuss cases of temporal dependency in which one temporal reference is dependent on

---

[1] For simplicity, I shall refer throughout to reference points or reference time. However, both points and intervals can be accommodated in this analysis and neither is to be taken as primary.

213

Syntax and Semantics, Volume 14
Tense and Aspect

another for interpretation. In such cases, the dependent temporal reference is anchored to the other. The discussion will focus on sentences containing two temporal references, where one occurs in an embedded sentence. I will look at the way temporal dependencies are affected by particular temporal forms and by the syntactic structures in which they appear.

Dependency between temporal references can be considered a type of anaphora; One expression is dependent on information in another expression, as in pronominal anaphora. I will compare semantic and syntactic constraints on pronominal and temporal anaphora. Although the two are affected differently by syntactic structure, they have the same general constraint at the semantic level.

The approach to temporal reference that I will take is based on an interpretive analysis. Temporal forms in surface structure are related by interpretive rules to temporal semantic representations; the analysis is presented in detail in Smith 1978. The organization of the chapter is as follows: Section 2, outlines an analysis of temporal reference; Section 3, discusses the anchoring possibilities of temporal forms; Section 4, the principles of temporal dependency in English; and Section 5, temporal anaphora and the effect of surface structure variation.

2. TEMPORAL REFERENCE IN ENGLISH

Temporal reference must be accounted for by a system of some kind, because the values of temporal expressions are not fixed. For instance, as Jespersen and many others have noted, Present tense may indicate past, present, or future time, depending on the sentence in which it occurs. Time adverbials have flexible values as well. To account for the possibilities of temporal reference, I have proposed a system of interpretive rules that relate sentences of English to semantic interpretation; the semantics is based on the temporal analysis of Hans Reichenbach (1947). This chapter is a study of some conditions that affect temporal interpretation and, therefore, of the conditions required for interpretive rules.

Reichenbach argues convincingly that three times are needed to account for temporal reference in languages such as English, because sentences may refer to three different times. According to Reichenbach, sentences are oriented to Speech Time (*ST*), and may indicate a reference time that is simultaneous with or sequential to *ST*. Reference Time (*RT*) corresponds to past, present, and future. A third time, Event Time (*ET*), is needed to account for some cases; *ET* may be simultaneous with or sequential to *RT*. Reichenbach's example of a sentence requiring the notion of *ET* is a sentence like (1), which contains the perfect:

(1)   *Roger had already graduated last week.*

The time of Roger's graduation precedes last week, which precedes ST. Sentences like (2) can also be fruitfully analyzed as involving one *RT* and three times; I discuss such cases in Section 3.

(2)   *John said at midnight that Sue was leaving in 3 hours.*

Independent sentences such as (1) and (2) are oriented to *ST*; but not all sentences are so oriented. In narratives, a time of narration can be established and the sentences of the narrative all understood as oriented to that time. There are at least two other places in English where sentences are oriented to a time other than *ST*. They are exemplified by (3) and (4), and by the complement of (2).

(3)   *Laurie called earlier.*

(4)   *Michael was better now.*

Neither (3) nor (4) can be fully interpreted in isolation, although both are entirely grammatical. They require a specification of the time to which they are oriented, or anchored. The complement of (2) requires the temporal information of the matrix in order to receive a full interpretation.

To deal with all of these interpretations in a unified manner, I propose an extension of Reichenbach's system. I shall say that temporal reference involves three times, ORIENTATION TIME, REFERENCE TIME, and EVENT TIME; for independent sentences, Orientation Time in English is Speech Time. A system with these three times can elegantly handle temporal reference in simple and complex cases. If only one time is indicated in a sentence, the three times are simultaneous for that sentence; if two times are indicated, one follows another; if three times are indicated, they are all in sequence.

Temporal reference is an area where the syntax and semantics of English are quite different. Semantically, three times are involved in the temporal interpretation of sentences. The main linguistic forms with temporal values are tense and time adverbial; of these, only tense is obligatory in an English sentence. Time adverbials occur optionally, one per sentence, and may be of unbounded complexity. (The question of how many time adverbs occur in a sentence is not uncontroversial. For a detailed defense of the position taken here, see Smith 1978.) The basic structure of a time adverbial is [preposition + { $\substack{\text{sentence} \\ \text{noun phrase}}$ }]. In my analysis, both a tense and a time adverbial are necessary for complete temporal interpretation of a sentence.

I shall say that the basic unit for temporal reference in English is a composite consisting of a tense and a time adverbial. The combination of tense and time adverb specifies Reference Time, as described in what follows; the preposition that introduces the time adverb gives the relation between Reference Time and Event Time. Consider as an example the interpretation of (5):

(5)   *Roger called before noon.*

In this sentence the combination of past tense and *noon* specifies a past RT; *before* indicates that ET precedes RT. There is no explicit reference to ST, but the value of RT includes the relation of RT to ST; thus, in the case of (5), RT is Past and therefore anterior to ST.

Fundamental to the system of interpretive rules is the assignment of relational values to all temporal forms. The values are ANTERIORITY ($\leftarrow$), SIMULTANEITY ($=$), and POSTERIORITY ($\rightarrow$). Expressions are assigned the relational value that corresponds to their semantic interpretation; thus *before* has the value $\leftarrow$, *after* has the value $\rightarrow$, *etc.* Combinations of tense and adverb are interpreted according to their relational values. Compatible combinations establish time reference and incompatible combinations do not [see (7) and (8) for examples].

The tenses are assigned values according to the traditional interpretation, Past tense $\leftarrow$ and Present tense $=$. Prepositions, time adverbs, and auxiliary *have* have their normal semantic interpretation, as indicated in (6):

(6)   Relational Values of Temporal Forms in English

	ANTERIORITY	SIMULTANEITY	POSTERIORITY
Tense	past	present	
Adverbs	*yesterday, etc.*	*right now, etc.*	*tomorrow, etc.*
Prepositions	*before, etc.*	*at, on, $\emptyset$, etc.*	*after, etc.*
	have (aux)[2]		
RT	Past	Present	Future

The combinations of tense and time adverbial are given in (7); there are six combinations. Note that some establish RT and some do not. Examples of the combinations are offered in (8).

(7)   TENSE   ADVERB   RT
    a. *Present*   Present   Present
    b. *Present*   Future   Future[3]

---

[2] In this analysis, auxiliary *have* is treated semantically as an adverbial-type element that indicates anteriority. The treatment is presented in Smith 1976.

[3] This analysis of the future involves tense and adverb only. Modals such as *will* and *may*

	c.	*Present*	Past	Past[4]
	d.	*Past*	Present	—
	e.	*Past*	Future	—
	f.	*Past*	Past	Past

(8) a. *Mary is swimming now.*

   b. *Mary is swimming* $\begin{Bmatrix} tomorrow^5 \\ on\ Tuesday \end{Bmatrix}$.

   c. *Last week, Mary is swimming in the lagoon when* . . .
   d. *John understood the situation now.*
   e. *John was leaving in 3 days.*

   f. *John played soccer* $\begin{Bmatrix} yesterday \\ on\ Tuesday \end{Bmatrix}$.

Note that all the combinations occur grammatically in English, so that there is no need to restrict generative rules as has sometimes been proposed.

In summary, combinations of tense and time adverbial form temporal expressions (TEs), and TEs make temporal reference. If a TE establishes RT, it is oriented to ST in independent sentences. Certain combinations of tense and time adverbial do not establish RT: Either the tense and adverb combination is incompatible in terms of relational values, or the adverb is Dependent (see Section 3.3).

Non-RT combinations can be fully interpreted with temporal information from another sentence. The sentences are then semantically related, whether or not they are syntactically dependent. As I have noted elsewhere, the same dependencies hold regardless of whether sentences are syntactically dependent or independent.

There are, of course, many sentences that do not have a time adverbial. Such sentences are vague, or incomplete, from the point of view of temporal interpretation. They are interpreted with information from context, linguistic and other, or by general heuristic strategies. Sentences without time adverbials are discussed in Smith (1977a, 1977b); they will not be considered in this chapter.

---

are not limited to future temporal reference and are therefore not taken as indicating future. For a defense of this approach see Smith (1976, 1978).

[4] This combination exemplifies the Historical Present. It has some special properties, but appears to establish RT. The adverb normally occurs to the left in sentences of this type. The Historical Present cannot be embedded. This follows from the constraints on interpretation of embedded present tense brought out in Section 4.

[5] Aspect is not treated in this study. It is varied where appropriate to focus on a given interpretation.

3. THE ANCHORING OF TEMPORAL EXPRESSIONS

Whether or not they establish RT, TEs differ in anchoring possibilities. Some TEs can be interpreted only as anchored to ST; some are flexible, and may anchor to ST or to another time; some do not anchor to ST, but require an explicit anchor time. The determining factor is the type of time adverb that appears in a TE.

Time adverbs are crucial to temporal reference. Together with tense, they establish the relational value of RT, and they specify RT; they give the relation between ET and RT; under certain circumstance, they specify ET (see the following section for discussion of this last point). They also determine the interpretation of a temporal expression, as anchored to ST or to another time.

Time adverbs may be distinguished by the type and flexibility of their anchoring possibilities. Adverbs such as *yesterday* and *tomorrow* are always understood as anchored to ST. Adverbs such as *on Tuesday* and *at noon* may, but need not, be anchored to ST. Adverbs such as *previously* and *afterward* never anchor to an implicit ST; their anchors must occur on the surface. From this point of view there are three classes of adverbs, roughly as follows (this is not intended to be an exhaustive list):

(9)   Classification of Adverbs According to Anchoring Possibilities

	DEICTIC	CLOCK–CALENDAR (CC)	DEPENDENT
Past ($\leftarrow$)	*yesterday*	*Tuesday*	*beforehand*
	last ——	*midnight*	*previously*
	—— *ago*	S[6]	
Present ($=$)	*right now*		*the same time*
	this moment		*simultaneously*
Future ($\rightarrow$)	*tomorrow*	*Tuesday*	*afterward*
	next ——	*midnight*	*subsequently*
	in ——	S	

I discuss each type of adverb briefly.

3.1. Deictics

These adverbs are generally interpreted as anchored to ST, as the following examples indicate:

(10)   *Sam played last week.*

---

[6] Embedded adverbial sentences such as *John left before Mary called the doctor* and *Sam wrote to the newspaper while his confederate was away* have the relational value of CC adverbs.

(11)   *Dave is arriving in three days.*

(12)   *Sue told me that Mary arrived yesterday.*

For some speakers, a Deictic can sometimes anchor to a time other than *ST*. For such speakers, a sentence such as (13) has two interpretations:

(13)   *Sam said last Tuesday that Vera left three days ago.*

Either Vera left 3 days from *ST*, or 3 days from last Tuesday. Deictics vary in flexibility, that is, in their ability to anchor to a time other than *ST*. The most flexible deictic adverbs are *ago* and *in*; they are particularly susceptible to reanchoring when they appear with verbs of communication of consciousness.

Deictic adverbs have the relational values of Past, Present, or Future and in combination with a tense of compatible value they establish *RT*. If the tense does not have a compatible and informative relational value, the result is a TE that does not establish *RT*; see (7) and (8) for examples.

3.2 Clock–Calendar (CC)

These adverbs are interpreted as anchored to *ST*, in the simplest case, as exemplified by (14). They are flexible, however—they can also anchor to another time, as (15) illustrates.

(14)   *Harry won the race on Sunday.*

(15)   *At midnight, Brenda realized that Paul (had) called three hours ago.*[7]

The main interpretation of (15) is that the embedded adverb, *three hours ago,* is anchored to *midnight*. It also has an interpretation in which both adverbs are anchored to *ST*. In this reading Paul's call was three hours earlier than *ST* rather than three hours before midnight. This second reading is acceptable to speakers for whom *have* is optional in sentences such as (15).

Clock–Calendar adverbs also allow a vague interpretation, where the anchor *(RT)* is unknown and full interpretation is not possible. Sentence (14) has such an interpretation: In this reading, Harry won on Sunday prior to some other time, here unspecified; one knows only that the other time is prior to *ST*. Such interpretations are frequent in informal speech, where there is much shared (and therefore unspecified) knowledge; they also occur in more formal narratives, where a reference time other than

---

[7] For some speakers, *have* is optional in sentences of this type.

ST holds for all or most of the narrative. The complement of (15) also has this vague interpretation.

Clock–Calendar adverbs have the dual relational values of anteriority and posteriority. In combination with different tenses, they can establish *RT* or fail to do so. Aspect is varied in the following examples to facilitate the intended readings:

(16)	*Mary left on Tuesday.*	tense ← adv ←	Past *RT*
(17)	*Mary was leaving on Tuesday.*	a. tense ← adv ←	Past *RT*
		b. tense ← adv →	No *RT*

3.3. Dependents

These adverbs have fixed relational values. Unlike the other adverbs, they never anchor to *ST*. They never occur in such a way as to establish *RT*, regardless of the tense with which they occur. Dependent adverbs require the existence of an explicit anchor time to be completely interpreted. Their anchoring properties are thus considerably different from those of the CC and Deictic adverbs discussed earlier. The following examples illustrate the properties of Dependent adverbs.

(18)   *Mary stomped out afterwards.*

(19)   *John left at noon; Mary stomped out afterwards.*

(20)   *We are going to the theater at 7:30 and Mary is coming afterwards.*

(21)   *Mary called earlier.*

(22)   *John told me at 9:00 that Mary had called earlier.*

Dependent adverbs also allow the vague interpretation that was pointed out previously in connection with CC adverbs. Thus a sentence like (18) or (21) can be taken as semantically incomplete, to be understood with reference to a time that is not *ST* and that is not explicitly given in the sentence.

The preceding discussion brings out the important fact that temporal reference may be ambiguous in two ways. First, a time adverbial may be interpreted as anchored either to *ST* or to a time established in another sentence, as in Sentence (13). Second, a time adverbial may be interpreted as anchored to *ST* or to an unspecified *RT*, as in (14). The second interpretation is the vague one noted in connection with CC and Dependent adverbs. Vagueness differs from ambiguity; in the case of vagueness, too little information is given to allow interpretation; in the case of ambiguity, more than one interpretation can be made. Temporal reference may be vague either because the *RT* of a dependent TE is unspecified, as in (14), or because a sentence contains tense but no time adverbial.

4. TEMPORAL DEPENDENCIES IN COMPLEX SENTENCES

This section deals with the intepretation of temporal expressions in sentences with embeddings, that is, sentences that have two TEs. Under certain conditions, one TE may be semantically dependent on the other, and I outline here principles of interpretation that account for the dependencies that occur in English. I focus on sentences that are both semantically and syntactically related but, as noted earlier, the analysis extends to sentences that are syntactically independent.

There are two main types of temporal dependency between sentences of English. In one type, which I shall call SHARING, a time in S_1 functions as *RT* for S_2. In the other type, called ORIENTATION, a time in S_1 functions as *OT* for S_2. Sentences (23) and (24) exemplify the two possibilities:

(23) *They said last Wednesday that the minister was resigning in three days.*

(24) *The minister will announce at midnight that he burned the documents an hour ago.*

The two principles account for the wide range of relations that are found between temporally dependent sentences. I discuss each principle, together with relevant examples, in this section.

4.1 Sharing

In the Sharing relation, the adverb of S_1 is part of the interpretation of two TEs. The TEs must have the same tense for the Sharing relation to obtain; if it does, the adverb of S_1 specifies *RT* for both S_1 and S_2, and the adverb of S_2 specifies *ET* for S_2. Consider for example the interpretation of (23). The matrix establishes *RT* and the complement does not (because the relational values of Past tense and Future adverb do not combine to establish *RT*). The complement is fully interpretable in this sentence: It specifies a time computed from the RT of the matrix.[8] I shall say that the adverb of S_2 specifies ET; its relational value gives the relation of ET to RT. In (25), another example of Sharing, the complement adverb has the relational value of ←.

(25)   *They said last Wednesday that White had resigned 3 days ago.*

As this analysis predicts, the ET specified in the complement is taken as anterior to RT.

The need for a Sharing principle in English is particularly clear in such examples as these, where the lower sentence does not have an RT. Note that the Sharing relation explains the fact that the adverb of the lower sentence specifies ET. As RT is established for the lower sentence with the adverb of the matrix sentence, this allows the lower adverb to specify ET. In fact, it is a characteristic of English that an ET other than RT is specified only by sentences that have RT specified otherwise.[9]

The Sharing relation accounts for the interpretation of a number of interesting cases. Among them are sentences that have traditionally been characterized as instances of "sequence of tense." Such sentences differ in interpretation, however, and the notion of sequence of tense cannot account for the difference. Compare, for instance, Sentences (26) and (27).

(26)   *Bill said on Tuesday that Mary was sick.*

(27)   *Bill will say tomorrow that Mary leaves in a week.*

Matrix and complement sentence have the same tense in both examples. In (26) the two are taken to be simultaneous (if we exclude the vague reading), whereas in (27) they are not simultaneous. When considered in terms of the Sharing interpretation, the difference is clearly accounted for: In (26), matrix and complement have the same temporal specification and are therefore simultaneous; but in (27) the situation is different. In (27), matrix and complement share the matrix adverb but the complement specifies an ET that follows RT.

Consider, next, Sentences (28) and (29). In both, the complement has a different tense from the matrix, and is attributed to the speaker:

(28)   *Bill said that Mary is sick.*

(29)   *The Egyptians knew that the earth is round.*

---

[8] Careful study shows that it is ET of S_1 that functions as RT for S_2, as discussed in Smith 1978. For simplicity I have constructed examples where $ET = RT$ in S_1, so that it is correct to say that RT of S_1 functions as RT for S_2.

[9] Habitual sentences are an exception; here, the frequency adverb is treated as specifying ET (see Smith, 1978).

What is needed in the analysis of these sentences is a way of relating the lower TE to ST. I have proposed that a higher performative sentence, in which $ST = RT$ and $RT = ET$, can account for them very naturally.[10] The interpretive rules would relate an embedded Present tense to the present tense of the performative sentence by the Sharing principle. However, I shall propose a more satisfactory approach to such sentences at the end of this section.

The sharing relation can explain the interpretation of sentences in which the complement is temporally incomplete but cannot be associated with the matrix sentence. Information from neighboring sentences is necessary for a full interpretation of such sentences. Sentences (30) and (31) can serve to exemplify this point:

(30)   *The narrator says that the heroine was mollified now.*

(31)   *Bill will admit that Mary had been spirited away.*

To interpret sentences like these, a Sharing relation must be established between their complements and a syntactically independent sentence with the same tense.

Sharing applies within and across sentence boundaries; recall that this relation requires that both TEs involved have the same tense.

4.2. Orientation

The second type of dependency, Orientation, is crucial for explaining one interpretation of sentences like (24), repeated here:

(24)   *The minister will announce at midnight that he burned the documents an hour ago.*

In the interpretation I will explicate, the TE of the complement indicates a time that is anterior to the matrix time, but that is not (necessarily) anterior to ST. This is not the usual interpretation of [Past tense + Past adverb], of course.

In the Orientation relation, a time in S_1 functions as OT for S_2. This means that, if one sentence is oriented to another, its RT is interpreted in relation to the other TE rather than to Speech Time. Thus in (24) the Past RT in S_2 has the relational value of anteriority, as usual; the sentence containing this RT is dependent on the matrix and the Past RT oriented to the matrix time. Because the matrix RT is Future, the RT of S_2 is interpreted as anterior to the Future RT. Examples like this show that dependent sentence may have an OT that is different from ST. When two sentences have

[10] See Smith (1978).

different tenses, they can be semantically related by Orientation only if they are syntactically related to each other.

The Orientation relation can also be stated for sentences such as (32), where matrix and complement have the same tense, and the complement has an *RT* combination of tense and adverb.

(32)   *Bill told me last Tuesday that Carol arrived on Friday.*

There is an interpretation of (32) in which the complement Past *RT* is oriented to the time of the matrix. In this interpretation, the Friday of Carol's arrival is anterior to last Tuesday. Here, the Past *RT* has the relational value of anteriority as usual but the *OT* is the time of the matrix rather than *ST*.

Both Sharing and Orientation principles can explicate sentences like (32), in which both TEs have the same tense and both establish *RT*. The interpretations are the same, although arrived by different routes. By the Sharing principle, the complement and matrix share *RT*, and the complement specifies *ET* that is anterior to *RT*. By the Orientation principle, the complement Past *RT* is oriented to the matrix and anterior to it; $ET = RT$ in the complement. The two interpretations are given schematically in (33):

(33)   a. *Sharing*
           S_1: Past + Past adv: Past *RT* S_2: Past + Adv_1: *RT*
               prep = $\emptyset$ $ET = RT$ rel value Adv_2: $ET \leftarrow RT$
                                                           ET: Adv_2

        b. *Orientation*
           S_1 as in (a) S_2: $RT \leftarrow RT_1$
                                  tense + adv: *RT*
                                  prep = $\emptyset$ $ET = RT$

Thus sentences such as (32) can be analyzed with either principle of dependency. If the complement has no adverb, it is taken as either simultaneous with the matrix or vague.

There is another set of cases, however, for which the Orientation relation is essential. These are the cases of vagueness due, not to the absence of an adverb, but to an interpretation that interprets an adverb as anchored to an *RT* specified elsewhere or unspecified. Sentence (34) exemplifies this type of vagueness.

(34)   *They said last night that Gertrude resigned on Sunday.*

On one interpretation, *on Sunday* is anchored to *ST*; on another, it is anchored to *RT* in S_1. But there is also a third interpretation, in which *on Sunday* is anchored to a time not specified in the sentence. And although this RT is unknown, one does know something about its relation to the matrix RT—the unknown RT is anterior to the other. This explains the fact that one knows that *Sunday* precedes *last night,* without knowing anything else about *Sunday.*

This vague interpretation can be captured by the Orientation principle. In (34) S_2 is oriented to S_1 rather than to ST: Its RT is therefore oriented to that of S_1. But in the vague interpretation the tense and adverb of S_2 do not establish RT. Instead, RT is specified by another sentence and the adverb of S_2 specifies ET. The other sentence has the Sharing relation with S_2. For instance, the following sequence exemplifies a case where a neighboring sentence provides information that specifies RT_2:

(35)   *Jimmy and Ross told us all about the events of 2 weeks ago. They said last night that Gertrude resigned on Sunday.*

The example indicates that the Orientation relation holds for sentences that are syntactically independent, if they have the same tense.

It is important to note that the Orientation principle must be prevented from applying where two TEs have different tenses and the lower tense is Present. If it were to apply to such sentences, it would incorrectly predict that the matrix and complement are simultaneous. To see this, consider again Sentence (28):

(28)   *Bill said that Mary is sick.*

According to the Orientation relation, S_2 would be interpreted as simultaneous with S_1; this interpretation follows from the principles of Orientation, as Present tense has the value of simultaneity. But, of course, this is not the interpretation of (28). The complement of (28) is taken as simultaneous with ST and not with S_1.[11]

The Orientation relation holds within and across sentences that have the same tense. Sentences with different tenses are related by Orientation only under rather special conditions. They must be part of the same sentence, and the lower tense must not be present.

The principles of Sharing and Orientation account for temporal dependencies between sentences of English. In temporal dependency, one sentence is anchored to a time in another sentence rather than to ST. Multiple readings may arise when an adverb can be interpreted as anchored to more than one time, and vague readings arise when an RT is unspecified.

[11] The rules that relate sentences to semantic representations must be established separately for each language. In languages other than English, embedded presents do not necessarily have the interpretation of simultaneity with ST. Hindi, for example, is such a language; I am indebted to an anonymous reviewer for this information.

4.3. Stating the Principles of Sharing and Orientation

I consider briefly how best to account for temporal dependency by interpretive rules. A question arises because of cases where two TEs have different tenses. These cases behave differently from those where the TEs have the same tense, and therefore require special mention of some kind.

Past and Present tenses are interpreted according to different principles when they are embedded under Present and Past respectively. If a Present tense embedded under Past, it is taken as simultaneous with *ST*. If a Past tense is embedded under Present, there are 3 possible interpretations: The Past may be oriented to the higher tense, to *ST*, or to another sentence.

If temporal dependency were accounted for with two general rules, provision would have to be made for sentences in which the TEs have different tenses. Rather than complicating two rules so that they can apply in all cases, I suggest that Sharing and Orientation should be stated to apply only to TEs with the same tense. Two additional rules would deal with embeddings involving different tenses.

There are several advantages to this treatment. It makes relatively simple the statement of the Sharing and Orientation principles. The principles will apply between and across sentences, a generalization that would not be possible in the other treatment (recall that Orientation does not hold across sentences if the TEs have different tenses). Orientation would automatically be prevented from applying to a Present tense embedded under Past. There are other peculiarities of embedded Pasts (see Section 5) that could be incorporated into the system without disturbing its generality.

Presents embedded under Pasts will be handled by a special rule that interprets them as anchored to *ST*. No performative sentence is involved. A second rule will deal with Past tenses embedded under Presents, interpreting them as oriented to the higher tense under the appropriate syntactic conditions. Not only do the suggested rules maintain relative simplicity, they also reflect the fact that relations between TEs of the same tense are more general and flexible—in fact, different—than relations between TEs of different tenses.

5. TEMPORAL ANAPHORA AND SYNTACTIC CONSTRAINTS

In the interpretation of temporal dependency, information from one temporal expression is used in the interpretation of another temporal expression. In other words, the interpretation of one TE is dependent on the interpretation of another. This formulation brings out a fundamental similarity between temporal and pronominal dependency. Both can be seen as a type of anaphora.

In fact, temporal dependency has all of the properties of anaphora, according to a definition of anaphora by Hankamer (1976). The definition is this:

(36)   Given surface segments of A and B in a sentence or discourse, B is anaphoric to A if:
       a. A and B are disjoint;
       b. The reading of B and the reading of A have identical subparts; and
       c. If A is varied both readings vary, but if B is varied the reading of A remains constant.

In the Sharing relation, the anchor TE is A and the dependent TE is B. They have identical subparts, namely the tense and adverb of A; the readings vary just as specified in (c). In the Orientation relation, the tense and adverb of A also function as identical subparts for both A and B. In Orientation, they specify OT for the lower sentence; in Sharing, they specify RT for both sentences.

Although temporal dependency can be considered a type of anaphora, there are some obvious differences between temporal and pronominal anaphora. The most important for this discussion is that pronouns are not anchored to a reference point as temporal expressions are. An interpretation of coreference is never obligatory, and pronouns may be interpreted without anchors. Rather, coreference is possible under certain conditions; as is well known, if a pronoun both precedes and commands a noun phrase, the two cannot be interpreted as coreferential.[12]

One might expect that surface structure would limit temporal anaphora as it limits pronominal anaphora. In the examples of temporal dependency discussed so far, surface structure has been held constant, with the anchor TE both preceding and commanding the dependent TE. I now ask whether and how the surface structure position of TEs affects the interpretation of temporal dependency, that is, of temporal anaphora. If temporal anaphora is sensitive to the surface structure properties of precedence and command, the rules of interpretation must take this fact into account. One reason for investigating the question is to look for data that is essential to the correct statement of interpretive rules. A second reason is that such an investigation provides an avenue for comparison of pronominal and temporal anaphora. By studying the way structural variation

---

[12] In a particularly interesting treatment of coreference, Lasnik (1976) proposes that interpretive rules need specify only those cases where an interpretation of coreference is impossible.

affects temporal anaphora, then, I expect to answer the following two questions:

1. Must interpretive rules for temporal anaphora be sensitive to the surface structure properties of sentences?
2. Does temporal anaphora have the same pattern of interaction with surface structure as pronominal anaphora?

The effect of surface structure on interpretation was studied by varying the structures in which TEs occurred. Both the relative position of TEs and the type of syntactically dependent sentence were varied systematically. The variations were assessed for different types of temporal expressions and for different types of temporal adverbs. For each variation, I asked whether a given TE could be interpreted as semantically dependent on the other TE. The results of these variations provide answers to the two questions raised here.

5.1. Structures

The sentences investigated had two TEs, each consisting of a tense and a time adverbial, one in an embedded sentence. Their structures were varied as follows:

1. TYPE OF EMBEDDING: complement, relative clause
2. TYPE OF TE: (a) both TEs establish RT, same tense
             (b) both TEs establish RT, different tense
             (c) one TE establishes RT, one does not
3. TYPE OF ADVERB: Deictic, Clock-Calendar, Dependent

5.2. Variations

The syntactic properties under investigation were precedence and command. Therefore each structure was varied in four ways, so that a given TE appeared in all possible positions relative to the other TE. The variations are given (37). For perspicacity, one TE, the putative anchor, appears in boldface throughout. The letters at the left give the relation of one TE (TE_x) to the other (TE_y); P stands for precedence, C for command, n for neither.

(37)   PC $_S(\mathbf{TE_x}_S(TE_y))$ P $_S(_S(\mathbf{TE_x})TE_y)$
         C $_S(_S(TE_y)\mathbf{TE_x})$ n $_S(TE_y_S(\mathbf{TE_x}))$

The variations all resulted in grammatical sentences. In some cases TE_x could be interpreted as an anchor for TE_y; this was the interpretation I

was testing for. Two other interpretations arose that must be distinguished from this first one. Sometimes both TEs were interpretable as anchored to *ST* rather than to each other, for instance:

(38) *Mary confided to me on Sunday that Bill arrived on Tuesday.*

This sentence has an interpretation in which both Sunday and Tuesday
are computed from *ST*; neither of the TEs is anchored to the other. Such
cases are ignored in what follows. Other cases involve dependent TEs
that cannot be interpreted as anchored to the second TE in the sentence;
such sentences are semantically incomplete. An example of this is:

(39) *John was marrying in 3 days a woman he met on Wednesday.*

The only interpretation considered after each structural variation was the
first one, which involves temporal anaphora.[13]

5.2. Results

The general answer to the first question raised earlier is yes: Temporal
anaphora is sensitive to surface structure. The answer to the second question is no: Temporal anaphora does not pattern like pronominal anaphora.
I present and discuss the results of the structural variation, and, at the end
of this section, compare pronominal and temporal anaphora. I will show
that, in spite of their differences, they are sensitive to similar structures at
the semantic level.

The effects of precedence and command are different for (*a*) sentences
with relative clauses and complements; (*b*) different types of TEs in sentences with relative clauses; (*c*) Dependent adverbs versus other types of
adverb; (*d*) sentences in which the TEs have different tenses. The discussion of the results is organized according to these topics.

5.2.1. Sentences with Complements

For these sentences, TE_x can be interpreted as an anchor for TE_y only
if TE_x commands TE_y. The relation of precedence between the TEs plays
no role in the interpretation of temporal anaphora. This holds for all three
types of TEs, for both Deictic and CC adverbials.

I suggest that the explanation for this pattern is semantic. The TE of the
matrix sentence has the entire sentence in its scope, and this fact is deci-
sive for temporal anaphora. Two semantic relations are involved: the rela-

---

[13] Adverbs of each type, and *RTs* (Past, Present, and Future) were also varied in all of the
structures. I omit much of the detail in the presentation of the results.

tion between a TE and the sentence it is associated with, and the relation between matrix and complement sentences. First, note that tense is traditionally considered a sentence operator, with an entire sentence in its scope. In the analysis presented in this chapter, the composite tense + adverb functions as a sentence operator. Second, in a sentence with a complement, the complement is within the scope of the matrix (for discussion, see recent model-theoretic treatments of such sentences).[14] Therefore, the TE of a complement sentence is within the scope of the matrix sentence and, in particular, of the matrix TE. Intuitively speaking, when one element functions as anchor for the second, it has the second within its scope. If this is correct, it would be impossible for a complement TE to function as anchor for a matrix TE; the relation would involve a semantic contradiction.

Semantically, then, the constraint affecting sentences with complements can be stated in terms of scope: If TE_x is within the scope of TE_y, it cannot function as anchor for TE_y. The following examples illustrate; TE_x is in boldface throughout, and is considered as the putative anchor for TE_y in all the examples presented here.

(38)   TEs: both *RT*, same tense[15]
  a. (PC) *The Secretary **will announce on Tuesday** that he resigns in 3 days.*
  b. (C) *That the Secretary resigns in 3 days **will be announced on Tuesday.***
  c. (P) *That the Secretary **resigns on Tuesday** is being announced in 3 days.*
  d. (n) *The Secretary announces in 3 days that he **will resign on Tuesday.***

Testing the interpretation of these examples, we ask whether the boldfaced TE can be interpreted as anchor for the second TE. Such an interpretation is possible for (a) and (b). In (c) and (d), however, both TEs are interpreted only as anchored to *ST*. The pattern is the same for the other types of *RT*:

(39)   TEs: one *RT*, one non-*RT*
  a. (PC) *The engineer **realized on Wednesday** that the satellite was being launched in 3 days.*
  b. (C) *That the satellite was being launched in 3 days was **realized** by the engineer **on Wednesday.***

---

[14] See, for example, Thomason (1974) and Partee (1976).
[15] Examples involving the possibility of reanchoring with complement clauses have verbs of communication because such verbs are the most likely to allow reanchoring.

    c. (P)   *That the satellite **exploded on Wednesday** was being announced in 3 days.*

    d. (n)   *The office was announcing in 3 days that the satellite **exploded on Wednesday**.*

(40) TEs: both *RT*, different tenses

    a. (PC) *The Secretary **will announce at midnight** that he burned the documents at 11:00.*

    b. (C)   *That the Secretary **burned the documents at 11:00** was announced at midnight.*

    c. (P)   *That the Secretary **will burn the documents at 11:00** was announced at midnight.*

    d. (n)   *The Secretary announced at midnight that he **will burn** the documents **at 11:00**.*

The examples illustrate the constraint stated earlier. Notice that the constraint does not rule out a complement TE that anchors to *ST*; nor does it rule out a complement TE in one sentence functioning as anchor for a TE in another sentence. The second situation is illustrated in (41); the complement TE, which functions as anchor, is in boldface.

(41)   *That the treaty **would take effect on Tuesday** was announced at noon today. People predicted that it would be abrogated in three days.*

5.2.2. Sentences with Relative Clauses

These sentences differ in the interpretation of dependency according to the types of TE that appear. Temporal anaphora in sentences with relatives is sensitive in different ways to the factors of precedence and command. When both TEs in a sentence can establish *RT*, precedence determines dependency: The first TE anchors to *ST* and the second may be interpreted as dependent on the first. When one TE is intrinsically dependent and the other establishes RT, both precedence and command are important. The dependent TE anchors to the other, unless the dependent TE both precedes and commands the other. When the TEs have different tenses, command determines dependency as in sentences with complement clauses. I shall suggest a semantic explanation for this variety of pattern after discussion of each type.

(42) TEs: both *RT*, same tense

    a. (PC) *Sally **married last April** a man who won a fellowship in May.*

    b. (P)   *The man who Sally **married last April** won a fellowship in May.*

    c. (C) *The man who Sally married in April* **won** *a fellowship* **last**
               May.
    d. (n) *Sally divorced in April a man who* **married** *Teresa* **last May**.

In these examples, (a) and (b) have the dependency relation we are looking for: The boldfaced TE may be taken as anchor for the other TE. In (c)
and (d), however, TE_y can only be taken as anchored to ST and not to
TE_x.

Precedence is the important factor here, and it functions to maintain the
normal anchoring property of the first TE in the sentence. Anchoring is
therefore more important than command in sentences with TEs of this
type. (Note the contrast with sentences that have complements, in which
command is the only important factor.) The second TE can anchor to ST
as usual but it can also anchor to the first TE.

To test whether precedence determines the interpretation of sentences
of this type, consider a reordering of (42c). Sentence (42c) does not allow
temporal anaphora between TE_x and TE_y. If precedence is crucial to an
anaphoric interpretation, fronting the adverb should allow it. Sentence
(43) is a reordered version of (42c):

(43)   **Last May** *the man who Sally married in April* **won** *a fellowship*.

Sentence (43) does have an interpretation of temporal anaphora, supporting our contention that precedence is the determining factor.

The next examples have an intrinsically dependent TE and a TE that
establishes RT. Their interpretation is different from those of the preceding examples.

(44)   TEs: one RT, one non-RT
    a. (PC) *John* **met on Thursday** *the woman he was marrying in 3*
              days.
    b. (C) *The woman who John was marrying in 3 days* **arrived on**
             Thursday.
    c. (P) *A woman John* **met on Thursday** *was leaving in 3 days*.
    d. (n) *John was marrying in 3 days a woman he* **met on Thursday**.

In these examples, the boldfaced TE can function as anchor for the other
in (a)–(c), but not in (d).

Here for the first time we encounter the syntactic pattern exhibited by
pronominal anaphora. The interpretation of dependency is blocked when
the putative antecedent, or anchor, is both preceded and commanded by
the other form. Sentence (44d) allows only an incomplete interpretation
because there is no RT. These examples show that temporal anaphora
patterns like pronominal anaphora when the differences between them are
removed; in previous examples, semantic structure and the anchoring

properties of TEs determined possible interpretations. At the end of this section I suggest a reason for the fact that precedence and command together block dependency for both temporal and pronominal anaphora.

The next examples have TEs with different tenses.

(45) TEs: both *RT*, different tense
  a. (PC) *Mary **will marry next Thursday** a man who joined the For- eign Service on Wednesday.*
  b. (C) *A man who joined the Foreign Service on Wednesday **will marry** Mary **next Thursday.***
  c. (P) *A man who **will join** the Foreign Service **next Thursday** mar- ried Mary on Monday.*
  d. (n) *Mary married on Wednesday a man who **will join** the For- eign Service **next Thursday.***

The Past *RT* can be interpreted as anchored to the Future *RT* only if it is commanded by the Future *RT*.

It was noted in Section 4 that when TEs have different tenses their patterns of interpretation are unlike those with TEs of the same tense. The sentences of (45) are a further case in point. An explanation for the behavior of TEs with different tenses awaits further research on the relation between semantic and structure structure.

5.3. Distinction between Relative Clause and Complement Temporal Anaphora

I turn now to a more general discussion of the difference between temporal anaphora in sentences with relative clauses and with complements. The former depend on the type of TE, whereas the latter have a consistent pattern of interpretation.

Both relative and complement clauses involve the surface syntactic relations of precedence and command. They differ, however, in their semantic relations to the matrix clause, and I suggest that this is the explanation for the different patterns of interpretation uncovered here. Semantically, a complement clause is within the scope of the matrix clause: Syntax mirrors semantics. The semantic relation between a relative and its main clause, however, is different. In semantic structure, a relative clause has sister scope with the main clause; this is the model-theoretic version of the intuition that relative clauses are independent in a way that complement clauses are not.

Because the TE in a relative clause is semantically independent of the main clause, it is available as anchor for the TE of the main clause. However, such a TE is subject to other constraints: It must have the appropriate anchoring properties and must have the appropriate precedence and command relations. These considerations explain the variations noted earlier.

5.4. Sentences with Dependent Adverbs

None of the results reported thus far hold for TEs with Dependent adverbs, if the TEs have the same tense. Sentences with Dependent adverbs allow an interpretation of dependency between TEs regardless of their surface structure position. The following examples illustrate:

(46) Complements—TEs: one *RT*, one with Dependent adverb
    a. (PC) *The Secretary **announced on Tuesday** that he (had) resigned the day before.*[16]
    b. (P) *That the treaty **expired on Thursday** had been announced the day before.*
    c. (C) *That the Secretary had resigned the day before **was announced on Tuesday**.*
    d. (n) *The Secretary had announced the day before that the treaty **expired on Wednesday**.*

(47) Relative clauses—TEs: one *RT*, one with Dependent adverb.
    a. (PC) *The Secretary **discussed last Tuesday** the treaty he signed a day earlier.*
    b. (P) *A woman John **talked to on Wednesday** was leaving three days later.*
    c. (C) *The treaty that the Secretary was signing a day later **was unveiled on Tuesday***
    d. (n) *John had married three days earlier the woman he **divorced on Tuesday**.*

All of these examples can be interpreted so that the boldfaced TE is the anchor for the other TE. Sentences with different tenses are omitted here; they pattern like the other examples of sentences with different tenses, rather than like the examples of (46) and (47). This is another reason for the separation of such cases, to be advocated in Section 6.

These examples show that Dependent adverbs anchor to a TE that establishes *RT* in the same sentence, regardless of the relation between the two TEs. The sentences of (46) differ from those examined before in that the relation of command is not a factor. The sentences of (47) differ from those examined before in that the relations of precedence and command are not factors that affect the interpretation of dependency between the TEs.

---

[16] Some of the interpretations of sentences such as those of (46) and (47) may differ for the dialect that does not require *have* to indicate anteriority.

Recall that the Dependent adverbs differ from others in that they never establish RT; furthermore, they require an explicit anchor to be fully interpreted. The semantic and syntactic constraints observed earlier apply to expressions that would under some circumstances anchor to ST. Perhaps because they never establish time reference independently, Dependent adverbs are not sensitive to these constraints.

6. SUMMARY DISCUSSION

This study of syntactic variation shows that temporal anaphora is sensitive to syntactic structure. Two of the types of TEs discussed have patterns of interpretation that differ significantly from the others: Temporal expressions with Dependent adverbs are not constrained and require an explicit anchor for complete interpretation; when TEs have different tenses, the possible interpretations are constrained.

For the other structures, a generalization can be given at the semantic level that accounts for many of the facts that have been brought out. An interpretation of dependency is possible for TEs if the anchor TE is not within the semantic scope of the other TE. When this condition is met, as in relative clauses, the anchoring properties of the TEs and the precedence relation determine actual interpretations. That semantic structure takes precedence over anchoring is shown by the constraints on sentences with complements. In such sentences the first TE cannot anchor to ST if it belongs to a complement clause.

It is interesting to note that this generalization must be made at the semantic level. Syntactically, the pattern of temporal anaphora varies considerably. The reason for this variation is that syntactic structures do not always correspond to semantic structures. Although both relative clauses and complements are commanded by their matrix clauses, the former have sister scope with their matrix clauses and the latter are within the scope of their matrix clauses.

Yet to be explained are the sentences with relative clauses in which the relations of precedence and command determine temporal anaphora, with temporal anaphora being blocked if a putative anchor TE is both preceded and commanded by another TE. I will argue that such cases are predicted by the semantic constraint given earlier, because they correspond to semantic structures in which one TE is within the scope of another.

6.1. Temporal and Pronominal Anaphora

Both temporal and pronominal anaphora are blocked under the same conditions: when one expression precedes and commands the putative anchor expression. I suggest that the reason for this blocking is the same in both cases, and that it has do with semantic structure. It is apparently a general fact of English that when an expression precedes and commands another, the other is within its semantic scope. And when element A is within the scope of element B, it cannot serve as anchor for element B; to have both relations at once is impossible, for they involve a semantic contradiction.

What I am suggesting is that the syntactic structure of precedence + command corresponds to a semantic structure I will characterize as within-scope. Thus (48a) is a syntactic reflex of (48b):

(48)   a.   Syntactic structure: $_S(TE_{xS}(TE_y))$
          b.   Semantic structure: $(TE_x(TE_y))$

Such a correspondence is assumed in much recent work on coreference, in which surface structures are related to logical form.

The correspondence between structures like (48a) and (48b) explains why sentences with relative clauses such as (44d) do not exhibit temporal anaphora. Although relative clause has sister scope with a matrix sentence, the structure of (44d) corresponds to a within-scope semantic structure, and it is this structure that blocks anaphora.

Abstracting away from the differences between pronominal and temporal anaphora, they are seen to be constrained by the same very general semantic structure. Such a structure has many syntactic realizations, so that many different syntactic structures are affected by the constraint. For instance, complement clauses correspond to within-scope syntactic structures, and so do deictics such as temporal and pronominal expressions that are commanded and preceded by other deictics.

The next area to investigate in temporal anaphora might well be sequences of sentences in narrative and other discourse. Further differences between temporal and pronominal anaphora will surely be brought out by such an investigation. For instance, temporal anaphora can occur across sentences, if a dependent TE precedes its anchor. The corresponding type of pronominal anaphora, however, is prohibited. Compare for instance (49) and (50).

(49)   *John was leaving in three days. Bill told Marsha the plans last Sunday.*

(50)   *He was leaving in three days. John was making a trip to the Orient.*

The first TE in (49) can be taken as anchored by the second TE, although they are in different sentences; but the pronoun in (50) cannot be taken as anaphoric to John in the following sentence (except perhaps in certain special situations involving a shift in point of view).

ACKNOWLEDGMENTS

I would like to thank Emmon Bach, Jorge Hankamer, Lauri Karttunen, and Stanley Peters for discussions connected with this chapter. I also thank Annie Zaenen and an anonymous reference for many helpful comments on the chapter.

REFERENCES

Hankamer, J. (1976). The semantic interpretation of anaphoric expressions. *Georgetown Roundtable Proceedings*, Washington, D.C.: Georgetown University Press.

Lasnik, H. (1976). Remarks on coreference. *Linguistic Analysis*, **2**, 1–22.

Partee, B. (Ed.). (1976). *Montague Grammar*. New York: Academic Press.

Reichenbach, H. (1947). *Elements of Symbolic Logic*. New York: The Free Press.

Smith, C.S. (1976). *A theory of auxiliary have in English*. Distributed through the Indiana Linguistics Club.

Smith, C.S. (1977a). The vagueness of sentences in isolation. *Papers from the 13th Regional Meeting, Chicago Linguistics Society*. Department of Linguistics, University of Chicago.

Smith, C.S. (1977b). How context contributes to the interpretation of sentences. Discourse group of the AERA, *Proceedings*. Los Alamitos, California: SWRL Research Corp.

Smith, C.S. (1978). The syntax and interpretation of temporal expressions in English. *Linguistics and Philosophy*, **2**, 43–100.

Thomason, R. (Ed.) (1974). *Formal Philosophy: Selected papers of Richard Montague*. New Haven: Yale University-Press.

SOME EVIDENCE FOR A BRANCHING-FUTURES SEMANTIC MODEL

PHILIP J. TEDESCHI

1. INTRODUCTION

An adequate semantics for natural language must include consideration of problems of temporal reference. Although some sentences in natural languages are "eternal" sentences [e.g., Sentence (1)], most sentences are not [cf. Sentence (2)]. An adequate truth-theory for natural languages will evaluate the truth-value of sentences with respect to a possible world and time, not just with respect to a possible world. In order to analyze temporally indeterminate sentences, the model must include a time coordinate as well as a possible-world coordinate.

(1)   *The sun rises in the east.*

(2)   *There was an ice-storm in Providence last winter.*

Temporal reference is encoded in several ways in natural languages. A tense system, morphological or periphrastic, may indicate a chronological ordering relationship with respect to the moment (or interval) of utterance, or with respect to some independently established reference point. An aspectual system may describe a temporal quality of an event in terms of its inception, continuation, completion, duration, repetition, *etc*. Finally, a system of temporal adverbs may specify a chronological ordering,

239

Syntax and Semantics, Volume 14
Tense and Aspect

a temporal quality of the event, or the exact temporal reference. In this chapter, temporal adverbs are not considered: tense–aspect systems are the primary concern. Although many of the example sentences have generic readings in addition to event readings, the generic readings are ignored.

Following a general discussion of tense operators, a branching model is described and the evaluation of basic tense operators with respect to this model is detailed. Consideration of certain problems with respect to the analysis of the progressive and other aspectual operators leads to an argument (primarily due to Dowty, 1977), for the use of a branching, as opposed to linear, time model for the analysis of natural language aspectual operators. The evaluation of conditionals in this model is then considered. Finally, a simplification of the pragmatic analysis of *before* brought about by this model is discussed.

2. TENSE OPERATORS

Tenses have been analyzed semantically as a type of sentential operator, whose interpretation involves order relations on a time axis. Although the natural language tense–aspect systems used for indicating the time reference of an utterance can be quite complex, logicians and many linguists who are concerned primarily with Indo-European languages have assumed that there are three semantic tenses—past, present, and future—and that the past and future tenses are sentential operators whose interpretation depends on an order relation on the set of times and on a specified origin time. Although other language families may require expanding the set of tenses, I believe these three will remain central. In English, of course, there are two syntactic tenses, present and past, as well as a modal, *will*, or a periphrastic modal, *be going to*,[1] that function semantically as the future tense.

In order to devise a semantic analysis for English tenses, we must decide whether the future modal should be given an analysis parallel to the analysis of the present and past tenses (as in the linear tense logics presented in Rescher and Urquhart, 1971) or whether an analysis parallel to the analysis of the logical/epistemic modals would be preferable; that is, we must decide whether it is languages like French or like English that have a surface structure closer to semantic representation.

---

[1] I will not treat the periphrastic future as I am not sure that *be going to* should be treated as a variant of the future tense. See Binnick (1971, 1972) for some of the distinctions between the modal future and the periphrastic future.

Tenses are analyzed as sentential operators because of their interaction with quantifiers and other independently established sentential operators. For example, Sentence (3) has two readings: one in which the tense has scope over the quantifier and one in which the quantifier has scope over the tense operator.

(3)   *All seedlings will become trees.*

That is, the set of seedlings under consideration may be the set of those now existing (quantifier has wide scope) or the set of those seedlings that will exist at some future time (tense has wide scope).[2] Note that the same ambiguity is present in past tense sentences as well as future tense sentences and that the ambiguity is predictably not present in present tense sentences [cf. Sentences (4a) and (4b)]. The ambiguity is not due to the modal nature of *will*. Thus assuming that quantifiers are sentential operators, the tense operators must be sentential not VP operators.

(4)   a. *Everyone expected John to be there.*
      b. *All trees are growing tall.*

The scope ambiguities that could be predicted given an analysis of both tenses and negatives as sentential operators do not occur, however, as is illustrated by Sentence (5).

(5)   *John won't go to the store tomorrow.*

Sentence (5) only has one interpretation: "It is not the case that at some future time (point or interval) contained within the interval 'tomorrow,' *John goes to the store* is true." It does not have the interpretation "At some future time contained within the interval 'tomorrow,' it is not the case that *John goes to the store* is true." Sentence (5) can be falsified by noting that there is a time during the interval "tomorrow" in which John does go to the store. The form with the future operator having wide scope would give the correct result if its interpretation were "At all times in the interval 'tomorrow' it is not the case that *John goes to the store* is true." This interpretation of the future operator clearly produces wrong predictions for nonnegative future sentences like Sentence (6) and, hence, is not tenable. Further, the double negative sentence

(6)   *John will go to the store tomorrow.*

(7)   *It is not the case that John won't go to the store tomorrow.*

---

[2] If *exists* is treated as temporally independent, the two meanings will, of course, collapse to one. In this particular case, I intend for *exist* to mean something like *now alive*. The observation here is from Ladusaw 1977.

only has the interpretation that John will go to the store sometime tomorrow, not the interpretation that for the entire interval "tomorrow," *John goes to the store* is true. That is, the logical form of Sentence (7) is always (8a) and never (8b); hence *will* interacts with negatives in the same way that *can* does, as opposed to the way that *must* does.[3]

(8)   a. $\sim \sim Wp$
       b. $\sim W \sim p$

There are other expected scope ambiguities, given a sentential-operator analysis for tenses, that do not occur. As Ladusaw (1977) has pointed out, we do not find all of the ambiguities that are predicted by an operator analysis of tenses and an NP-lowering device (such a device is utilized in both Montague grammar and generative semantics as exemplified by McCawley 1972). Sentences (9a)–(9c) do have the predicted scope ambiguity. For example, in Sentence (9b) there are two readings: in one the unicorn is walking at the time of the speech act, in the other the unicorn is walking at the time in the future at which it is found. Sentences (9d)–(9f) do not exhibit a scope ambiguity. If we assume that the perfect is not merely a past tense operator and that present perfect sentences are syntactically present tense sentences, the lack of ambiguity in these sentences is predictable.

(9)   *John will find the unicorn that* $\begin{cases} \text{a. *has walked.*} \\ \text{b. *is walking.*} \\ \text{c. *will walk.*} \end{cases}$

        John has found the unicorn that $\begin{cases} \text{d. *has walked.*} \\ \text{e. *is walking.*} \\ \text{f. *will walk.*} \end{cases}$

Ladusaw (1977) proposes a modification of Montague's PTQ (1973) framework along the lines suggested in Cooper 1975. Ladusaw proposes treating the perfect as an aspectual auxiliary specifying priority.[4] He pro-

---

[3] In Sentences (8a) and (8b), the symbol "$\sim$" represents the negative operator; the symbol W, the future operator. The negative operator always has wide scope with respect to *will*—as it also does with *can*, but not with *must*. Sentence (i) only has the reading in (ii) and not the reading in (iii), unlike Sentence (iv) which can have the reading in (v), where p is "John leaves," P is "permitted," and O is "obligated."

(i)   *John can't leave.*
(ii) $\sim Pp$
(iii) $P \sim p$
(iv)   *John must not leave.*
(v) $O \sim p$

[4] Neither Ladusaw nor I have really formalized a semantic analysis of the perfect operator. As noted earlier with respect to possible ambiguities created by having an NP-lowering

poses a sequence-of-tense rule to explain why Sentences (10b) and (10c) have only one reading corresponding to the case in which the present tense operator commands the past tense operator in the base structure; whereas Sentences (10a), (10d), and (10e) have three readings.

(10)   *Mary saw the unicorn that* {
a. *walked.*
b. *is walking.*
c. *will walk.*
d. *was walking.*
e. *would walk.*

The sequence-of-tense rule only applies to base-generated subordinate present tenses; it would not apply to an embedded present tense that was lowered to its embedded position. For example, the three readings for Sentence (10a) would come from the following three sources: a higher past tense sentence lowered to complement position, a base past tense complement, and a base present tense complement to which the sequence-of-tense rule has applied. The three readings have the time of walking before, after, or simultaneous with the time of seeing, respectively. Sentence (10b) can only come from a source with the present tense sentence higher than the matrix clause into which it is lowered. Because the present tense sentence is not embedded in the base structure, the sequence-of-tense rule would not apply. This argument is predicated on having a tense logic system in which the time of reference for an embedded tense is derived from the embedding tense not from the time of utterance. The time of utterance would only be used to determine the reference time of the highest tense operator.

3. BRANCHING FUTURES

The next question to consider is what kind of a model we should use to interpret tense operators. Usually a model for interpreting tenses has consisted of a set of points of time (or time intervals), T; a linear order "$<$" on T; and a preferred point (or interval), *now*. The two tense operators, P and W (past and future), have usually been given an interpretation on the order of the one in (11) (cf. Rescher and Urquhart, 1971).

---

device, the present perfect functions as a present tense, but with respect to truth-criterion the present perfect and the past tense seem to be equivalent. The perfect will be ignored in this chapter, but it is clear that what is needed is an analysis of the perfect both as a present tense and as an operator in some ways equivalent to a past tense, but not participating in possible NP scope ambiguities.

(11)   a. $P\alpha$ is true at *now, n*, iff there is a t in T such that $t < n$ and α is true at t.

     b. $W\alpha$ is true at n iff there is a t in T such that $n < t$ and α is true at t.

3.1. Truth Evaluated over Intervals, Not Points, of Time

There are some interesting questions about the iteration of tense operators that depend on the particular axiomatization of the expression "α is true at t," but these questions are not discussed here. Instead, we will take up another question—the question of whether truth should be evaluated with respect to a point or an interval of time. Traditionally, temporally indeterminate sentences have been analyzed with respect to points of time. Recently several authors investigating temporal phenomena in natural languages have treated the index as ranging over intervals rather than over points.[5] One argument, due to Taylor 1974, as reported in Cresswell 1977, for using an interval-based semantics results from consideration of sentences such as (12):

(12)   *John polishes all of the boots.*

Taylor claims that Sentence (12) can be true of an interval even though there is no subinterval of that interval in which John is polishing all of the boots, that is, he is polishing a set of boots one at a time. I do not have intuitions about Sentence (12) except for the generic reading and the programmed-future reading, neither of which is the reading Taylor wants us to consider. We can note that, if this argument is correct, later arguments presented to support a sentential-operator analysis of the progressive, the perfect, the aspectual predicates in terms of scope ambiguities may fall apart, as the ambiguity used to argue for a sentential operator could be due to evaluation of the embedded sentence over an interval.

The adverbs *tomorrow, for one minute, in a minute, etc.* refer to an interval of time, so that we independently need a notion of truth with respect to an interval of time. If we assume that truth is evaluated with respect to points of time and try to define truth at an interval in terms of truth at points in the interval, an interesting problem arises. If we are evaluating a sentence with respect to an interval established by a temporal adverb, we can note that there are processes and actions which when true of an interval can be true of all of the points in the interval, true of most of the points, or true of some but not necessarily most of the points. There are also events that relate to the interval as a whole—that is, if the event occurs in an interval, it does not occur in any subinterval of that interval.

---

[5] These authors include Cresswell (1977), Dowty (1977), and Johnson (1977).

For events like the one in Sentence (13d), we can further note that there is always an associated process—*baking* in (13d)—which is true of all, most, or some of the points of the interval. The various cases of truth of sentences at intervals are illustrated by the sentences in (13⁶).

(13)   a. *Mary washed her face for 2 minutes.*
       b. *Susan wrote a letter in 10 minutes.*
       c. *I drank beer for 2 hours yesterday.*
       d. *John baked a cake in 2 hours yesterday.*

We assume that truth at an interval should be taken as a primitive, rather than truth at points, because of the difficulties inherent in defining truth with respect to intervals given truth with respect to points. We need not define truth at a point; rather we consider truth at intervals about the point whose measure is less than the psychological threshold of perception of measure for evaluations normally carried out at points.[7]

The linear model presented in (11) for the analysis of tenses is adequate for a semantic analysis of tenses but inadequate for the an analysis of certain aspects. Arguments for a nonlinear model based on analysis of aspects are presented in what follows. The model reduces in the case of the semantics for tenses to a linear model, that is, the semantics for the tenses will not allow us to distinguish between the two models. The model is a branching-futures model—a model in which the past is linear but the future branches.[8] Thus future contingent statements can be represented if any language processes so require.

----

[6] As Dowty (1977) noted, it does not seem to be the case—as Rescher and Urquhart (1971) maintained—that there are actions and processes that really require truth at every point of an interval. For any action a context can be found in which a native speaker would say that the action occurred even though there were minor interruptions of the action in the interval. Sentence (13a), which is Rescher and Urquhart's example of a predicate requiring truth at all points of an interval, would certainly be judged true of an interval in which there is a minor interruption of the action (e.g., Mary rubbed soap out of her eye for a few seconds during the 2 minute interval of washing her face).

[7] Thus truth with respect to a point of time will not be defined. For mental change-of-state predicates, *realize, discover, etc.*, we will assume that the interval of evaluation is always less than the measure threshold. Those predicates usually analyzed as point predicates (punctual predicates) will be analyzed in terms of an interval sufficiently small so as to be perceived as a point in time. The actual measure of such an interval is, of course, pragmatically as well as physically determined.

[8] Branching futures are certainly reasonable in epistemic terms. The interesting question is whether future tense sentences have a truth value or not. Following most modern philosophers, I will assume determinism,—that is, there is a distinguished future branch (the actual future). Future tense sentences will always be assigned a truth value with respect to the history (world–time set) of reference. Our lack of intuition with respect to future tense sentences should be captured in an epistemic system, not in the logical system. The model to be developed in what follows (and formalized in the Appendix) is similar to the model developed by Thomason (1970) with an extension to interval-based truth.

3.2. Branching-Futures Model

Basically, a branching structure is an infinite extension of a tree structure (see Appendix A for a formal definition). Assume that (14) represents
a finite branching structure. Heuristically, a single point on (14) represents a state description of a world at a moment of time. We define the
branching structure (in the Appendix) via restrictions on an order relation
E.[9] The order relation E is not assumed to be linear but it is assumed to be
backwards-linear. The relation is a partial relation on state descriptions,
not an order relation on the set of times. For any point on the structure
there is a uniquely definable past, that is, a linear past. In the Appendix, it
is assumed that the set of times, T, is metrizable; a nice, smooth metric is
introduced and used to define intervals in the standard manner; the order
relation E is related to the standard order relation induced by the definition of a metric. We define a history as a linear maximal chain on the
structure. A specific history is represented by the bold line in (14). Having
defined intervals with respect to the metric and histories with respect to
the structure, we define intervals with respect to specific histories. For a
given history h and a given interval $t = (x_1, x_2)$ (where x_1 and x_2 are real
numbers), define the h-interval, t_h as the set $\{x \in h : x_1 < \delta(x) < x_2\}$ where
δ is the metric.

(14)

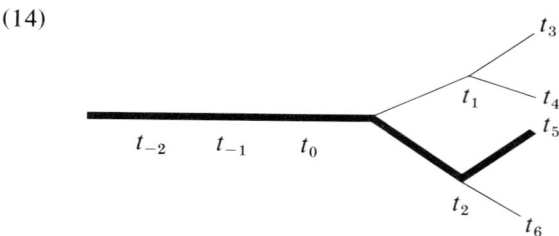

Let the set H_t be the set of all histories that contain the interval t_h, that
is, $H_t = \{g : t_h \text{ is a } g\text{-interval}\}$. For example, on (14), $H_{t_1} = \{\{t_{-2}, t_{-1}, t_0, t_1, t_3\}, \{t_{-2}, t_{-1}, t_0, t_1, t_4\}\}$.

We define a classic valuation of formulas at an interval with respect to a
history. As every history is a linear path on the branching structure, the
valuation is linear. For every formula α of a tensed propositional logic,
the valuation V^h assigns a truth value for each h-interval, and there is a

---

[9] Following standard conventions, the symbol "$<$" will be reserved for linear order relations; the symbol "E" (earlier than), is used here to distinguish between the order relation
on events that defines the branching structure. It will be assumed that the distance function
which maps the branching structure into the real-number line will preserve the relation E,
that is, the order relation that could be introduced via the metric is the same as the order
relation E restricted to a branch (i.e., a history).

valuation V^h for every history h.[10] That is, for every formula α and every h-interval t_h, $V^h(\alpha, t_h) = \{^1_0\}$. We then define a supervaluation, V, as follows:

(15) $V(\alpha, t_h) = 1$ iff $V^g(\alpha, t_h) = 1$ for all $g \in H_{t_h}$
           $V(\alpha, t_h) = 0$ iff $V^g(\alpha, t_h) = 0$ for all $g \in H_{t_h}$
           $V(\alpha, t_h)$ is undefined otherwise.

In particular, if $\alpha = W\beta$:

(16) $V(W\beta, t_h) = 1$ iff for all $g \in H_{t_h}$ there is a t'_g g-interval, such that $t_h < t'_g$ and $V^g(\beta, t'_g) = 1$
           $V(W\beta, t_h) = 0$ iff for all $g \in H_{t_h}$, there is no t'_g, g-interval, such that $t_h < t'_g$ and $V^g(\beta, t'_g) = 1$
           $V(W\beta, t_h)$ is undefined otherwise.

We can thus consider the truth of future statements bivalently with respect to specific histories and we can define contingent-future statements with respect to the supervaluation. A future statement α is contingent if $V(\alpha, n)$ is undefined. Although we do not need the supervaluation for analyzing the tense system of English, we may find it helpful for describing the logical, modal system. One feature of the super valuation is that the law of the excluded middle is preserved.

4. LINGUISTIC EVIDENCE FROM ASPECTUAL PREDICATES

In what follows, arguments are presented to show that a branching-futures model provides a more adequate model for the analysis of aspectual phenomena than a linear model. Evidence is presented to show that a more intuitive, unified analysis of counterfactual and factual conditionals can be defined given a branching model. A unified pragmatic analysis of factual, indeterminate, and counterfactual *before*-clauses also provides some evidence for the branching-futures model.

---

[10] Although it is somewhat debatable whether we actually have intuitions about arbitrary sentences over arbitrary intervals, I am assuming that for a specific sentence at a particular interval we do have truth-value intuitions. That is, for a sentence like *John is walking* evaluated at an interval in which John both walks and does not walk at subintervals, I am assuming that we can decide whether the sentence is true at the entire interval or not. Assuming that truth is defined only with respect to intervals—that is, that truth at an interval is primitive—we need not specify how a sentence is true at an interval when it is both true and false at subintervals of the interval.

4.1. Imperfectives

The first phenomenon that provides evidence that a branching-futures model might yield a better semantic interpretation than a linear model is the "imperfective." In English a certain class of predicates [Vendler's (1967) accomplishment predicates] when embedded under aspectual predicates or when in the progressive function semantically like the imperfective aspect in, for example, the Slavic languages. The sentences in (17) do not entail the achievement of the relevant encoded accomplishment. That is, Sentences (17a), (17b), (17c), and (17d) do not entail Sentences (18a), (18b), (18c), and (18d), respectively. This is in contrast to Sentences (19a), (19b), (19c), and (19d), which do entail the relevant past tense activity sentences—Sentences (20a), (20b), (20c) and (20d), respectively.[11]

(17)   a. *John was smoking a box of cigars.*
       b. *Mary was running a mile.*
       c. *John began to walk to school.*
       d. *Mary continued to write a symphony.*

(18)   a. *John smoked a box of cigars.*
       b. *Mary ran a mile.*
       c. *John walked to school.*
       d. *Mary wrote a symphony.*

(19)   a. *Susan was running.*
       b. *Tom was eating.*
       c. *John began to walk.*
       d. *Sue continued to run.*

(20)   a. *Susan ran.*
       b. *Tom ate.*
       c. *John walked.*
       d. *Sue ran.*

The use of aspectual predicates or the progressive with accomplishment predicates does IMPLICATE that the accomplishment will be achieved. The sentences in (21) illustrate the suspension of this implica-

---

[11] Frequently this entailment is described in terms of a present perfect sentence or a future perfect sentence, for example, from *Mary is running* one (or both) of the following is (are) entailed: *Mary has run* and *Mary will have run*. As I do not have an analysis of the perfect, I will continue to somewhat naively describe this entailment in terms of the past tense. Given a semantic analysis of the perfect as a past tense operator, which does not participate in possible NP scope ambiguities due to a syntactic analysis as a present tense, the entailment and nonentailment of the present and future perfects in the relevant cases is consistent with my analysis of the progressive.

ture. We can note that the predicate STOP predictably does not have this implicature and does not entail the achievement of the accomplishment although it does entail the relevant activity sentence—that is, Sentence (22) is unacceptable. Sentence (23) does not entail Sentence (24), though Sentence (25) does entail Sentence (26).

(21) a. *Tom was writing a letter but he was interrupted before he could finish it.*
      b. *Mary began to write a symphony but she was interrupted before she could finish it.*
      c. *Zeb continued to walk to school but he was interrupted before he got there.*

(22) **John stopped writing a novel but he was interrupted before he could finish it.*

(23) *Sue stopped smoking the cigar.*

(24) *Sue smoked the cigar.*

(25) *Jane stopped running.*

(26) *Jane ran.*

The analyses of both the aspectual predicates and the progressive involve a sentential operator. Riddle and Tedeschi (1974) have presented syntactic and semantic arguments that the aspectual predicates should be treated as one-place sentential operators. Consider the following sentence:

(27) *John began to run.*

It is fairly clear that aspectual predicates should be semantically analyzed as one-place predicates. Perlmutter (1970) presented an argument, based on the like-subject constraint, that *begin* is a predicate with two homophonous forms: transitive and intransitive. If the like-subject constraint is redefined as a constraint that Equi must apply then the arguments for a two-place *begin* disappear. To argue against the like-subject constraint we noted that *seem* and *appear* could be embedded below like-subject verbs so Perlmutter would have to posit transitive *seem* and *appear* as well as transitive *begin*. Further, sentential adverbs and other logical operators can be embedded below like-subject verbs and Perlmutter's argument would force us to posit transitive sentential adverbs and logical operators, given a higher-operator analysis of sentence adverbs and logical operators.

Cresswell (1977) uses Sentence (28) to argue for a sentential operator analysis of the progressive.

(28)   *Every boot is being polished.*

Cresswell argues that we have to allow *every boot* to occur in the scope of the progressive operator to get the reading in which the boots are being polished sequentially. He further maintains that Sentence (28) is ambiguous: On one reading, all of the boots are being polished at once; on the other, the boots are being polished successively. Similarly, in Sentence (29):

(29)   *Someone is polishing every boot.*

Cresswell notes that it need not be one person who is doing the polishing, so that *someone* can occur in the scope of *every* while *every* occurs in the scope of the progressive. Hence the progressive is a sentential operator.

Note that with progressives analyzed as sentential operators a negative always has wide scope. Sentence (30) only has an interpretation on the order of "It is not the case that there is an interval t' containing the interval of evaluation t such that John builds a house is true at t'," rather than "There is an interval t' containing t such that it is not the case that John builds a house is true at t'."

(30)   *John isn't building a house.*

The illustrations in (31a) and (31b) represent the two interpretations. The analysis of the progressive given in (32) is essentially that presented in Scott 1970 and in Bennet and Partee 1972.

(31)

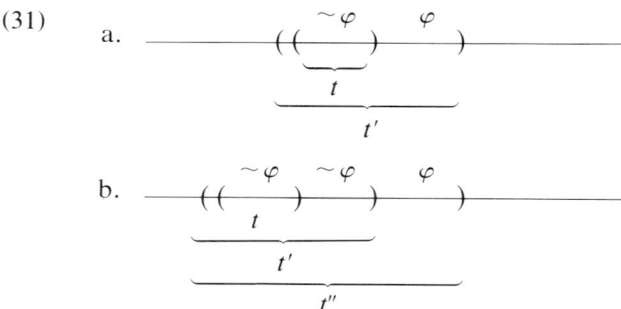

(32)   PROG(ϕ) is true at the interval t iff there is an interval t' containing t such that ϕ is true at t'.

The second interpretation of Sentence (30), where the *not* has narrow scope with respect to the progressive operator, would counterintuitively allow (30) to be true *now* if John does not build a house in a 10 minute interval but does build the house in a slightly larger, say 11 minute, interval [cf. t' and t'' in (31b)]. It can similarly be argued that aspectual predicates and progressives always occur in the scope of the tense operators. Given an operator analysis of the English perfect, it could be shown that progressives are within the scope of the perfect when they co-occur.

The interpretation of the progressive operator given in (32) does not work in the case of the progressive of accomplishment predicates (and of those achievement predicates that can occur in the progressive). The interpretation in (32) would predict that Sentences (17a) and (17b) would entail Sentences (18a) and (18b), respectively. Sentences (33a) and (33b) illustrate the fact that the implicature of the accomplishment can be suspended, that is, it is not a semantic entailment relationship.

(33) a. *Jane was writing a symphony when she died.*
      b. *Karen was reading the Silmarillion when she was interrupted.*

The implicature that the achievement will be realized in accomplishment sentences in the progressive can be explained in terms of some sort of Gricean pragmatics. By using Gazdar's (1976) formalization of implicatures due to Grice's maxims of Quantity and Quality, we can claim that Prog(ϕ) implicates ϕ and that Prog(ϕ) entails ϕ where ϕ is an activity sentence. As, in Gazdar's system, entailment is a higher-order relation than implicature, the implicature is canceled in the case that ϕ is an activity sentence. Hence we can associate a suspendable conversational implicature with nonactivity sentences and still allow for a nonsuspendable implicature — that is, an entailment — with activity sentences.

4.2. Arguments for a Branching-Futures Structure

Dowty (1977) and Riddle and Tedeschi (1974) present several arguments for a branching structure based on possible analyses for progressives and aspectual predicates, respectively. Dowty considers the analysis of the progressive presented by Bennet and Partee (1972), which is similar to the analysis presented by Scott (1970). Dowty's arguments against this analysis are similar to the arguments that have been presented here against the analysis in (32). Dowty maintains that, in Sentence (34), the existence of a circle is a possible outcome of John's activity, but not necessarily the actual outcome.

(34)   *John is drawing a circle.*

He proposes an analysis of the progressive as a mixed temporal–modal operator as in (35).[12]

---

[12] The semantics for the progressive given in (35) is assuming a standard model with a set of possible worlds and linear time. Truth is defined relative to a specific world and a specific time.

(35)   PROG(ϕ) is true in w at time t iff $\exists$ a t' such that t is a subinterval
          of t' and $\exists$ a world w' exactly like w at all times preceding and
          including t such that ϕ is true in w' at t'.

One immediate problem with this analysis is that it predicts that the sentence

(36)   *John is running.*

is true in a world w at an interval t in which John does not run but which is
a subinterval of a larger interval t' which is such that in some world w'
John runs is true at t'. To remedy this problem, Dowty adds a meaning
postulate to his system; the postulate ensures that an activity sentence
true at an interval is true at an initial and a terminal proper subinterval of
that interval.[13]

The crucial part of this formulation of the truth of the progressive is the
notion "exactly alike." Although this concept is intuitively satisfying and
seemingly central to any temporal–modal operator analysis of the
progressive, it does not prove to be readily defensible. Trivially, if the language has a future operator, then the two worlds cannot have all sentences that refer to the future of the designated moment of time up to
which they are identical have exactly the same truth-value; otherwise
they would be identical. Intuitively, however, the notion "exactly alike"
seems to imply that specific sentences evaluated with respect to the two
worlds should have identical truth-values up to the moment prior to which
the worlds are identical. If we assume that all future events can be expressed by some futurate sentence, then the futures of the two worlds
must also be identical.

One possible solution to this problem, which Dowty (1977) recognized,
is to follow Montague's (1968) approach and define an auxiliary formal
language exactly like the basic formal language but without tense and aspect operators. Then we could say that a possible world w is exactly like a
world w' up to time t iff the interpretation assigns the same truth value to
all expressions of the auxiliary language with respect to both of the worlds
up to the time t. As Dowty notes, this technique does work for a formal
language; for English semantics, however, merely removing the tense operators is insufficient. There are quite a number of other basic expressions, including adjectives like *future*, adverbs like *in the future, tomor-*

---

[13] Terminal and initial subintervals are defined as would be expected. For an interval, t_h,
which is mapped by the metric into (x_1, x_2), an interval, t'_h, is an initial subinterval if it is
mapped into (x_1, y) where $y < x_2$, and is a terminal subinterval if it is mapped into (y, x_2)
where $x_1 < y$ (as defined, the subintervals are proper). This meaning postulate will be further
discussed in what follows.

row, *next*, and some verbs like *postpone, progress, occur, happen,* which would also have to be removed from the auxiliary language. Consider Sentences (37a)–(37d); these sentences all encode at t the occurrence of an event at a time subsequent to t.

(37) a. *The arrival is postponed until tomorrow.*
      b. *The presentation occurs as scheduled at 10:00 tomorrow.*
      c. *The party starts when the guest-of-honor arrives.*
      d. *The event is progressing to its expected conclusion.*[14]

We may have to examine all of the nonlogical constants of the language to determine which expressions depend crucially on time for their denotation. If we are trying to define a model-theoretic semantics for English, we cannot exclude all temporally dependent expressions from our formal language. We can note that we could not define a semantics for the progressives of any predicates like *happen, occur, postpone,* and *progress,* which we have removed from the formal language to use the notion "exactly alike" for the semantics of the progressive. For these predicates there is no way to guarantee that anything occurs in the world of reference when they are true in a larger interval in some other possible world.

With a branching-futures model, the problem of using the notion "exactly alike" disappears. If we could consistently postulate the notion "exactly alike," the resulting semantic model would be equivalent to a branching model, as two worlds identical up to a point would be indistinguishable except by referring to their histories after that point.

5. THE SPECIFIC BRANCHING-FUTURES MODEL

To define the truth of the progressive in a branching model at an interval t, we need merely consider histories that contain t as an interval; all such histories will be "exactly alike" up to that interval as they are the same chain up to that interval. We consider histories whose branch point with the history of reference is later than t to define a semantics for the progressive. Dowty's analysis, adapted to the notation developed earlier in the chapter, is given in (38).

(38) $V^h(\text{PROG}(\phi), t_h) = 1$ iff $(\exists g \in H_{t_h})(\exists t'_g)$ with t_h a g-subinterval
        of t'_g such that $V^g(\phi, t'_g) = 1$.
        0 otherwise.

---

[14] The sentences in (37) are intended as rough representations of possible English sentences in which a future event can be encoded without using the future tense. In general, the adverbs in the sentences in (37) can be deleted in proper contexts without losing the future reference of the sentences.

There are problems with Dowty's analysis though it is on the right track. We cannot say that the progressive of a sentence is true at a time t if there is some larger interval extending into the future of t at which the tenseless sentence is true. If the sentence is not a contradiction and if we allow a complete system of possible futures, there is always such an interval. The semantics in (38) would always assign 1 to arbitrary progressive sentences.

To avoid the problem inherent in Dowty's analysis but to preserve the manner in which his analysis deals with the imperfective, we can appeal to Lewis's (1973) concept of a similarity metric. Using this metric we can claim that the progressive of a sentence ϕ is true in an interval t iff, if in the most similar set of futures in which there is a history in which the causing action continues in an interval t' containing t and causes the result that ϕ encodes, then in all histories in the set in which the causing action similarly continues, the result ensues.

(39) $V^h(\mathrm{PROG}(\phi), t_h) = 1$ iff $(\exists S \in \$) (\exists g \in S) (\exists t'_g \in H_{t_h})$ (t_h is a g-subinterval of t'_g and $V^g(\psi, t'_g) = 1$ and $V^g(\chi, t'_g) = 1$ and $(\forall j \in S) (\exists t''_j \in H_{t_h}$ with $|t'_g| \le |t''_j|) (V^j(\psi, t''_j) = 1 \supset V^j (\chi, t''_j) = 1))$
         0 otherwise

where $\$$ is the partition of the set of possible futures with respect to the interval t by the similarity metric, ψ is the causing action, and χ the result.[15]

The analysis in (39) claims that the semantics of the progressive is not independent of pragmatics. It claims that the progressive is true if the "causing action" leads to the "result." Both of these concepts are pragmatically determined for most processes and events, however. In general an action or event has many causes. The cause singled out by the speaker–hearer from the many potential causes as THE cause of an action or event is clearly pragmatically determined. Similarly, in some cases the result itself may be pragmatically determined.[16] The speaker–hearer expects a particular action to lead to a particular result. It is this expectation that allows the use of the progressive. For example, consider Sentence (40) in the context of an elderly composer who has contracted an incurable cancer.

---

[15] Further, if ϕ is an activity sentence, $\phi = \psi$ and if ϕ is an accomplishment or achievement sentence, $\phi \equiv \psi$ CAUSE (COME ABOUT χ) where ψ is an activity sentence and χ is a stative sentence encoding the result.

[16] One possible context in which the result is pragmatically dependent was mentioned at the conference. Consider the case in which an artist is drawing either a horse or a unicorn. A speaker's judgment of which depends on his beliefs about the artist's intentions; the truth of *He is drawing a horse* would depend on the speaker's belief about the result state.

(40)   *Mr. R. is writing a symphony.*

We can still truthfully utter (40) of this composer even though the "normal," most likely course of events is that he will not live to complete the symphony. Neither the speaker of (40) nor the referent need expect that the symphony will ever be concluded to truthfully utter Sentence (40). Our intuition, rather, is that if the causing action, in this case the composing, were able to continue for a sufficiently long period, the accomplishment would come about.

One possible criticism of this analysis can be stated heuristically as follows: Consider Sentence (41); can it not be that for an interval t_h, there is a history $g \in H_{t_h}$, such that t_h is a g-subinterval of t'_g where *I walk a mile* is true while it is also the case that *I walk* is false in t_h and in all other intervals in h in general? Consider the diagram in (42) for a schematic representation of this case.

(41)   *I am walking a mile.*

(42)

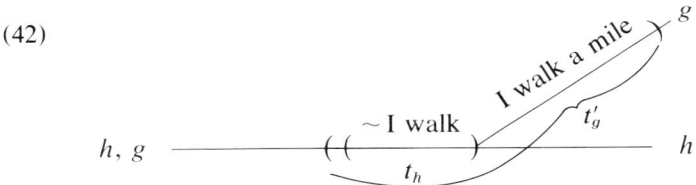

The interval t_h would be relatively small compared to t'_g. The meaning postulate proposed earlier for a similar problem can be extended to this case. Dowty (1977) proposed a further meaning postulate for accomplishment sentences which states that there is an equivalent formula associated with all accomplishment sentences of the form φ CAUSE (COME ABOUT χ) where φ is an activity sentence and χ is the result state. Whenever the progressive of an accomplishment sentence is true at an interval, there is a corresponding progressive of a causative true at that interval; the meaning of cause guarantees that the causing action is also true for that interval. As the cause is an activity sentence, the first meaning postulate applies and the causing action is true at an initial subinterval of t_h. With regard to Sentence (41) this guarantees that *I walk* is true at t_h.

6. CONDITIONAL SENTENCES IN A BRANCHING MODEL

If we consider the case of conditional sentences, a branching-futures model matches our intuitions more closely than a linear model. Our intuitions about the analysis of counterfactual conditional sentences like Sentence (43) indicate that we are considering truth relations with respect to a possible, albeit unrealized, future of a past time.

(43)   *If Hubert had disagreed with LBJ, he would have become president.*

We evaluate counterfactual conditional sentences as if we returned to the past and looked at possible futures with respect to that past. Considering conditional sentences in general, we find an interesting problem with respect to defining truth at an interval for conditional sentences. This problem must be resolved before we can consider questions concerning the analyses of factual and counterfactual conditional sentences.

6.1. Cresswell's Model

A first approximation to a semantic analysis for indicative conditional sentences with respect to an interval was presented by Cresswell (1977). Ignoring temporal relations, his analysis is the following:

(44) $V^h((if\ \varphi,\ \psi),\ t^h) = 1$ *iff if* $\exists t'_h$, subinterval of t_h, such that $V^h(\varphi, t'_h) = 1$, then $\exists t''_h$ subinterval of t_h, such that $\not\exists x \in t'_h\ \forall y \in t''_h\ y < x$ and such that $V^h(\psi, t''_h) = 1$.
0 otherwise.[17]

6.2.1. FACTUAL CONDITIONALS

This semantics is too simplified even for factual conditionals, as in the case of "eternal" sentences evaluated at points it reduces to material implication. Stalnaker (1968), Cooper (1968), Stalnaker and Thomason (1970), and Tedeschi (1976) have argued that material implication is inadequate for the semantic analysis of natural language conditionals. An alternative semantics can be given in terms of a possible-worlds, time-coordinate model or a branching-futures model that has the advantage of presenting a unified semantic analysis of factual and counterfactual conditional sentences. First, two problems have to be considered: (*a*) should conditionals be evaluated as in (44); that is, should we consider subintervals of the interval of evaluation; and (*b*) how do sentential operators behave with respect to conditionals.

Consider Sentence (45). It can be argued that there are three readings

---

[17] Cresswell eventually develops another analysis of conditionals which uses a branching model; this model will be discussed in what follows. He does maintain this semantics, (44), as central to his later semantics, that is, the notion of truth at an interval even using a branching model follows the semantics in (44).

for this sentence: two in which the events are sequential and one in which the events are simultaneous.[18] Cresswell (1977) claimed that the semantic representation of Sentence (45) on the sequential readings is something like (46a) and that the representation for the simultaneous reading might be (46b).

(45)   *If Bill planted beans, then he planted peas.*

(46)   a. $P\varphi \to P\psi$
        b. $P(\varphi \to \psi)$

Heuristically, the semantics in (44) claims that a conditional is true of an interval iff, whenever its antecedent is true at a subinterval t', its consequent is true of a subinterval t'', which ends no earlier than the subinterval t'.

First, note that the logical form in (46a) is already consistent with having the two events simultaneous. The ordering of the subintervals at which the antecedent and consequent are true does not affect the relative ordering of the intervals at which the tenseless counterparts of the antecedent and consequent are true. The logical form in (46b) presents a redundant case. Further, the form in (46b) does not guarantee simultaneity of the two events; a case in which the antecedent of a conditional is true in an initial subinterval of the past interval in which the conditional is evaluated while the consequent is true in a disjoint terminal subinterval of the same past interval can be assigned truth by the semantics in (44). The logical form in (46b) is consistent with two of the three possible orderings of the events whereas (46a) is consistent with all three orderings. The truth of conditional sentences should be evaluated with respect to intervals as a whole. We should not try, as Cresswell does, to capture in the semantic analysis the intuition that the antecedent of a conditional usually precedes its consequent. This intuition, just like the intuition that the first conjunct precedes the second in a conjunction, belongs in the pragmatics, not in the semantics, of complex sentences. Grice (1967) argued that the apparent temporal ordering of antecedent and consequent clauses in conditionals and of conjuncts in conjunctions is due to a pragmatic implicature; in Tedeschi 1976, further arguments supporting Grice's position with respect to conditionals were advanced.

To address the second question, we need to note a peculiar syntactic-semantic fact about English. For many sentential operators, English sentences of the form "If A operator C" are ambiguous; the two readings semantically have the forms $O'(A' \to C')$ and $A' \to O'C'$ where A', C',

---

[18] Actually in the formal sense of "reading" I believe there is only one reading for this sentence. Reading is being used here in a linguistic sense of "possible meaning."

and O' are the semantic representations of A, C, and the operator, respectively. For example, consider Sentences (47a) and (47b).

(47)   a. *If we are doing arithmetic base nine, then necessarily $8 + 3 =$*
           2.
       b. *If the sidewalk is wet, it must have rained.*

These sentences are reasonable only on the interpretation represented by the logical form in (48a); there is an absurd reading represented by the logical form in (48b).

(48)   a. $\Box(\varphi \to \psi)$
       b. $\varphi \to \Box\psi$

With negatives a related phenomenon occurs; Sentences (49a) and (49b) are synonymous.

(49)   a. *It is not the case that if God exists, His name is Sun Moon.*
       b. *If God exists, His Name is not Sun Moon.*

In Stalnaker (1968), Cooper (1968), and Tedeschi (1976), arguments are presented that the negation of a conditional $\sim(If\, A,\, C)$ should be equivalent to the conditional $If\, A,\, \sim C$. Hence Sentence (49b) only has one reading; the two possible readings are equivalent. With performatives a similar phenomenon occurs [cf. Sentences (50a) and (50b)]. We would probably want to derive Sentence (49b) from (49a) through an adverb-raising (or fronting if you prefer) process just as we would derive one reading of Sentence (50d) from (50c). With performatives a sentence on the order of Sentence (50d) has only one reading; adverbs generally do not modify performatives.

(50)   a. *I bet that if Cauthen's horse isn't scratched, he $\begin{Bmatrix} will\ win \\ wins \end{Bmatrix}$ the*
           race.
       b. *If Cauthen's horse isn't scratched, I bet that he $\begin{Bmatrix} will\ win \\ wins \end{Bmatrix}$ the*
           race.
       c. *I bet that tomorrow Cauthen $\begin{Bmatrix} will\ win \\ wins \end{Bmatrix}$.*
       d. *Tomorrow, I bet that Cauthen $\begin{Bmatrix} will\ win \\ wins \end{Bmatrix}$.*

Tense operators exhibit a similar phenomenon. Consider Sentence (51). As we have already noted, Cresswell claimed that there might be three readings for this sentence, represented by the logical forms in (52a) and (52b).

(51)   *If John planted beans, he planted peas.*

(52)   a. $P\varphi \rightarrow P\psi$
         b. $P(\varphi \rightarrow \psi)$

We have noted that the representation in (52b) is redundant and that it makes the wrong predictions. The interesting cases are sentences like those in (53) where we have the situation "*If A,* operator *C.*" My intuition is that these sentences only have the reading represented by (54b); the reading in (54a) does not seem possible.[19]

(53)   a. *If John's throwing a party, his wife left him.*
         b. *If the experiment is running, today's work was successful.*

(54)   a. $P(\varphi \rightarrow \psi)$
         b. $\varphi \rightarrow P\psi$

Further interesting cases occur when we consider the future tense, as the future tense does not appear in the antecedent clause of conditional sentences. Jespersen (1964) noted that the logical and epistemic modals do not occur in the antecedent clauses of conditional sentences; this is shown by the sentences in (55).

(55)   a. **If John must realize that Mary is here, he'll leave.*
         b. **If John'll discover the answer, he'll get an A.*[20]

First, note that this constraint is not a semantic constraint, as the verbal

---

[19] I cannot interpret the time of occurrence of the present progressive sentence in the antecedent as prior to speech time for either (53a) or (53b).

[20] Achievement predicates have been used in the antecedent in these examples primarily because achievement predicates, and statives in general, do not co-occur with deontic modals so that one possible reading of the modal in the antecedent is removed. Note that the deontic modals can readily command exactly those achievement predicates that have a progressive form (without extreme twisting of context), as shown by Sentence (i). Volitional *will* functions something like the deontic modals; in a matrix sentence volitional *will* is unacceptable with achievement predicates, but both volitional *will* and deontic modals are acceptable with active predicates in antecedent clauses [see Sentences (ii) and (iii)].

(i)   a. *You must* $\begin{Bmatrix} die \\ arrive\ at\ 10{:}00 \end{Bmatrix}$.

       b. *He is* $\begin{Bmatrix} dying \\ arriving\ now. \end{Bmatrix}$.

(ii)   **You* $\begin{Bmatrix} will \\ must \end{Bmatrix}$ *realize that Mary is here.*

(iii)   *If you* $\begin{Bmatrix} will \\ must \end{Bmatrix}$ *drive to school, at least take the small car.*

There is a dialect split here, though. Some informants readily accept modals in antecedent clauses with both stative and achievement predicates.

periphrases of the logical and epistemic modals can occur in the subordinate clause [Sentences (56a) and (56b)]; though the adverbial periphrases cannot [Sentence (57)].

(56) a. *If John has to realize that Mary is here (as you've established), he'll leave.*

  b. *If John's gonna discover the answer, he'll get an A.*

(57) **If ⟨necessarily⟩ John ⟨necessarily⟩ realizes that Mary is here ⟨necessarily⟩, (then) he'll leave.*

Sentences (58) and (59) have at least four readings, three of which correspond to the three readings given Sentence (51) by Cresswell.

(58) *If John plants beans, he'll plant peas.*

(59) *If John is planting beans, he'll plant peas.*

If both events are interpreted as future, they can be sequentially ordered or simultaneous. Cresswell's approach can be extended to the future case and would assign the three semantic representations in (60) to the four readings.[21]

(60) a. $W(\varphi \rightarrow \psi)$
  b. $W\varphi \rightarrow W\psi$
  c. $\varphi \rightarrow W\psi$

The arguments presented for past tense sentences apply mutatis mutandis to the future tense situation given an assumption that the future tense operator does not lower into the subordinate clause or that it is deleted when it is present. The form in (60b) already includes the case represented by (60a) and, further, (60a) does not guarantee simultaneity of the two events.

6.3. Counterfactual Conditionals

Finally consider the case of counterfactual sentences. Cresswell follows Lewis's (1973) analysis of counterfactual conditionals; the counterfactual is essentially treated as unanalyzed with respect to tense in this approach. Lewis postulated a similarity relation on the set of possible worlds; a relation through which the set of possible worlds is partitioned into spheres of equally similar worlds with respect to a world of reference.

[21] This extension of Cresswell's semantics really is a "straw man" case. He does present a more reasonable alternative semantics for conditionals using an approach following the Lewis and Stalnaker models presented in what follows. His analysis does reduce to something like the straw man case presented here in the indicative case, however.

A counterfactual conditional sentence with respect to a world of reference is true when the consequent clause is true in all worlds in which the antecedent is true in the most similar sphere of worlds to the world of reference which contains at least one world in which the antecedent clause is true. When we try to consider sentences like (61)

(61)   *If Germany had invaded England, they would have won the war.*

with respect to a temporal axis, we find that the notion of worlds being "exactly alike" up to some time enters into our concept of spheres of similar worlds. To evaluate a sentence like Sentence (61), we assume that we are in a world like the actual world up to the validity of the antecedent and the validity of any other propositions that are needed to maintain consistency. That is, we generally assume that the world has basically the same history as the actual world up to a point where the two diverge to allow the antecedent to be true.

If the notion of worlds "exactly alike" up to a time is crucial to using a similarity relation on world–time pairs, then the arguments presented against a linear system in the section on the progressive apply equally well here. Although I have no arguments to establish that this notion is essential to understanding the similarity relation when this relation is extended to world–time pairs, I believe that it will prove to be so.

We can try to present an analysis of counterfactual conditionals by noting that a sentence like (62) suggests an analysis in terms of tense operators.

(62)   *If John would have been chosen, we would have problems.*[22]

Cresswell's original analysis of past tense conditionals extended to this case suggests the three semantic representations in (63) for this sentence.

(63)   a. $PW\varphi \to PW\psi$
        b. $PW(\varphi \to \psi)$
        c. $P(W\varphi \to W\psi)$

We could assume that for counterfactual conditionals we would evaluate the antecedent and consequent in the most similar futures in which the antecedent is true.

If we assume, as Cresswell did, that the antecedent and consequent

---

[22] Although some grammars claim that (62) is ungrammatical, I find this form to be the prevalent form for counterfactuals in my dialect. Sentences like (i) and (ii) seem relatively formal to me. N. Francis (personal communication) claims that this is a geographic phenomenon.

(i)   *If John had been chosen, we would have problems.*
(ii)   *If John were chosen, we would have problems.*

should be evaluated at possibly different subintervals of the interval of evaluation for the conditional sentence, we can show that the logical forms in (63a) and in (63c) are untenable. The structure in (64) illustrates the problem with the form (63a).

(64)

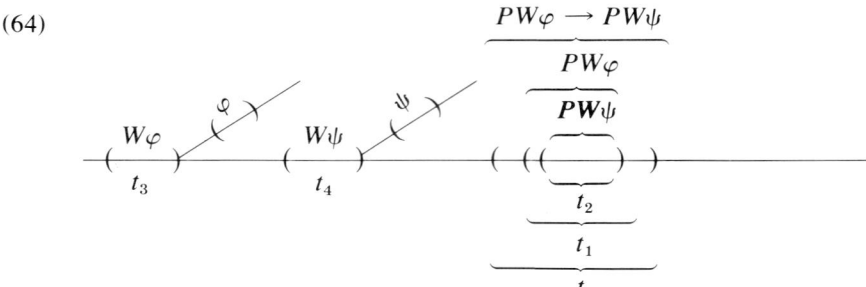

Suppose the conditional is true in the interval t, the antecedent in the interval t_1, and the consequent in the interval t_2. There is an interval, t_3, in which $W\varphi$ is true and $t_3 < t_1$ and there is an interval, t_4, in which $W\psi$ is true and $t_4 < t_2$. Without loss of generality, assume t_1, t_2, t_3, and t_4 are ordered as in (64). If the propositions φ and ψ are then evaluated with respect to alternate possible futures, the semantics can assign truth when φ and ψ are not evaluated with respect to the same history. The causative or pseudo-causative connection which generally relates antecedent and consequent disappears. If, in some possible future of t_3, John is chosen, and, in some distinct possible future of t_4, we have problems, Sentence (62) would be evaluated counterintuitively as true. A similar argument applies to the form in (63c); the diagram in (65) illustrates the crucial case.

(65)

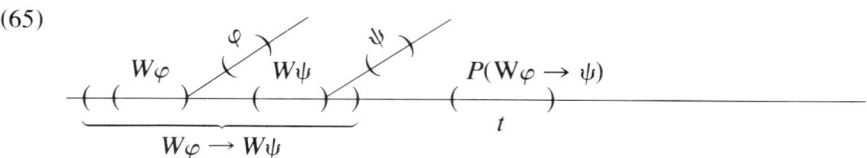

Again evaluation with respect to subintervals does not force the evaluation in the future to select the same future.

With this simplistic extension of Cresswell's semantics for conditionals, we would thus have to argue that the logical form in (63b) is the only possible representation for counterfactual conditionals. It seems counterintuitive to have past tense conditionals analyzed as in (66), future tense conditionals as in (67), but counterfactual conditionals as in (68).

(66) $P\varphi \rightarrow P\psi$

(67) $W\varphi \rightarrow W\psi$

(68) $PW(\varphi \rightarrow \psi)$

Why should the counterfactual, which already is receiving special treatment in terms of alternate futures, require a distinct type of logical form in terms of tense operators?

Instead of adapting this workable but unsatisfying approach to counterfactual conditionals, we can adopt Stalnaker's (1968) and Lewis's (1973) approaches to a branching-futures model. In addition to allowing the basic semantic representation of sentences like (62) to be the form in (63a), paralleling the past and future cases, this semantics will allow a unified treatment of factual and counterfactual conditional sentences. First, assume that there is a similarity relation defined on possible histories with respect to an interval in a history. That is, the relation will partition the set H_{t_h} when considered with respect to the interval t_h; not the entire branching structure. We are thus assuming that the similarity relation introduces a partial order on the set of possible histories with respect to an interval, as we will need the notion most similar neighborhood to be well defined.[23] The semantics for conditionals, then, is proposed in (69).

(69) $V^h(\varphi \rightarrow \psi, t_h) =$ 1 iff $V^g(\psi, t_g) = 1$ for all $g \in S$ such that $V^g(\varphi, t_g) = 1$ where S is the most similar neighborhood to h in which there is a history g' such that $V^{g'}(\varphi, t_{g'}) = 1$
                          0 otherwise.

Considering counterfactual conditionals, Cresswell also defined a semantics using the Lewis–Stalnaker approach. He uses a branching model to try to capture Lewis's notion of similarity: The degree of similarity is determined by the relative nearness of branch points. His semantics depends on this use of similarity as well as on the notion, discussed earlier, of true at subintervals of intervals. Clearly in a branching model two histories that branched in the distant past can differ only minimally. Nearness of the branch point is not equivalent to similarity.

7. BEFORE-CLAUSES IN A BRANCHING MODEL

Zaenen (1977) has argued that the counterfactual *before* also presents some evidence for the use of a branching-futures model. Consider the sentences in (70).

---

[23] This is a fairly strong assumption; it means that the similarity relation exhibits the greatest-lower-bound property.

(70)   a. *Mary ate before Henry did.*
       b. *John stopped climbing before he reached the top.*
       c. *Sam died before he finished his dissertation.*

Sentence (70a) receives a preferred interpretation in which the event in the *before*-clause occurs, Sentence (70b) is neutral with respect to the occurrence of the event in the *before*-clause, and Sentence (70c) requires that the *before*-clause event did not occur. Contrary to previous analyses of *before,* Zaenen proposed a unified analysis of factual, neutral, and counterfactual *before.* As is the case with *if,* there are languages that use distinct forms for factual and counterfactual *before*-clauses; in particular, many languages use a subjunctive predicate in the neutral and the counterfactual case. Thus, the existence of a single form in English is no argument that a unified analysis is necessary.

Note that the factual *before*-sentence, Sentence (70a) does have readings that are consistent with neutral or counterfactual interpretations. The truth of the *before*-clause can be linguistically suspended as in Sentence (71); further, the truth can be contextually suspended.

(71)   *Mary ate before John did* $\begin{cases} since\ John\ is\ fasting\ today \\ if,\ in\ fact,\ he\ ever\ ate \end{cases}$.

This possibility of suspension suggests that the implicature of the *before*-clause should be treated as a pragmatic implicature, not as part of the semantics of *before.* If we assume Gazdar's (1976) formalization of some of Grice's (1967) conversational implicatures, we can define the implicature of the truth of the *before*-clause as a presupposition of *before* which is a presupposition in the factual case but is suspended in the neutral and counterfactual cases. The semantic analysis of the *before*-sentences would merely require that the matrix sentence is true and that the subordinate sentence has not been true up to and including the time at which the matrix sentence is true; a formalization appears in (72). The presupposition set of *before*-sentences would include the function in (73) according to Gazdar (1976).

(72) $V^h((\varphi\ before\ \psi), t_h) = 1$ iff $V^h(\varphi, t_h) = 1$ and there is no t'_h with
          $V^h(\psi, t'_h) = 1$ and such that there is an $x \in$
          t'_h with $x < t_h$ and $t'_h \nsubseteq t_h$.
          0 otherwise.[24]

[24] In the semantics in (72), a *before*-clause sentence is true if the two events overlap but the matrix event begins to be true prior to the subordinate event. Actually my intuition about the overlapping cases is not very strong. We may want rather to define a semantics in which the *before*-clause sentence is true only in the cases where the matrix event is completed before the subordinate event, false when the subordinate event is completed first, and leave

(73) $f(\varphi before \psi) = \{K\psi\}$

This analysis of *before* is completely consistent with a linear model. The argument for the branching-futures model does not arise through defining the semantics for *before;* rather, it arises when we consider the formal pragmatics. The information value of the *before*-sentence is equivalent to a sentence like *The event A has occurred and the event B has not occurred.* If we assume Grice's maxim of Quantity, we have to explain why we utter *before* sentences instead of information-value equivalent conjunctions.

Zaenen argues, first, that—unlike most of the presupposition cases that Gazdar discusses—suspension of the presupposition of so-called factual *before* requires no linguistic context. She considers the case of a future matrix clause and notes that Gazdar's presupposition function is too strong. Consider Sentence (74).

(74)   *Mary will eat before John.*

We need not KNOW that John in fact will eat to properly use this sentence. Knowledge is too strong a requirement; the utterance of Sentence (74) does not require that the speaker, not necessarily consciously, KNOW that *John will eat* will become true after *Mary will eat* becomes true.

Zaenen argues that the crucial relationship between the matrix and subordinate clause which is not captured by the semantics in (72) is that, if the world follows the expected normal course of events, the matrix event will occur prior to the occurrence of the subordinate event. That is, in all futures that follow the "expected" normal course of events, the matrix clause event occurs and then the subordinate clause event occurs. We assign truth to (74) via the semantics in (72) using only the history of reference; we assign acceptability to (74) only if all futures in which the world follows the "expected" course of events, the matrix event occurs, and then the subordinate event occurs. Although Zaenen has not formalized

---

a truth-value gap otherwise. With basic activity sentences, however, it seems fairly clear that this is the wrong approach. Consider Sentence (i).

(i)   *Mary was walking before John was.*

Clearly this sentence can be true if both John and Mary are still walking. The problem occurs with accomplishment sentences. Consider Sentence (ii).

(ii)   *Chris built a house before Marion did.*

The clauses are true over intervals. The semantics in (72) claims that (ii) is true if Chris built a house in an interval t_h and if Marion did not build a house in an interval that began earlier than t_h and which is not a subset of t_h.

the notion "expected" normal course of events, it is clear that a branching model is needed to capture the pragmatics. Of course, counterfactual *before*-clauses are acceptable without this pragmatic requirement; they are the case of suspension of the expected pragmatic conditions.

8. SUMMARY

To summarize, a linear-time-axis model is sufficient for the semantics of tense in English. Certain aspectual phenomena, however, require a branching-futures model. To properly analyze the progressive, inceptive, and continuative of accomplishment and achievement predicates, the notion "worlds exactly alike up to a time t" is needed. This notion is incoherent in a linear model, but coherent in a backwards-linear model. A unified semantics for factual and counterfactual conditionals that accords with intuition about evaluating conditionals can be defined on a branching-futures model but not on a linear model; the notion "exactly alike" also enters into the evaluation of most counterfactuals so that the argument given for aspects applies here also. Finally, a unified semantics for *before* crucially requires a branching model to define a formal pragmatics.

APPENDIX: DEFINITIONS FOR BRANCHING-FUTURES MODEL

BRANCHING MODEL: A branching-futures structure is an ordered planar graph with a transitive, irreflexive, antisymmetric, backwards-linear (a relation R is backwards linear iff for all x, y, z, xRz and yRz implies that either xRy, $x = y$, or yRx) ordering relation E.

For simplicity it will be assumed that the graph is rooted and connected (however, as L. Carlson pointed out to me, if we want to consider the semantics for sentences like *If the entire past had been different, ...,* we would have to drop the requirement that the set be connected). None of the arguments presented in this chapter and none of the interpretations given various semantic forms depend on either of these assumptions.

BRANCH: A subset B of a branching-futures structure T is a branch iff for every x and y in B $\{z: z \in B \text{ and } zEx \text{ or } z = x\} \subseteq \{z: z \in B \text{ and } zEy \text{ or } z = y\}$ or $\{z: z B \text{ and } zEy \text{ or } z = y\} \subseteq \{z: z \in B \text{ and } zEx \text{ or } z = x\}$ and, further, if $x \in B$ and there is a $y \in T$ such that xEy, then there is a $y \in B$ such that xEy. Essentially a branch is a maximal linear chain on the structure.

HISTORY: A history is a branch on a branching-futures structure that is used for natural language semantics.

It will be assumed that the branching-futures model used for semantics is metrizable. This assumption is again for simplicity; it is not crucial to any of the arguments or evaluations of truth discussed in the chapter. Any set, of course, is metrizable; we are assuming that a metric that preserves the order relation E can be defined on the branching structure.

Let T be the branching model and let $\delta: T \times T \rightarrow R^+$, where R^+ is the set of nonnegative real numbers, be a nice, smooth metric defined on T (note that δ is only a partial function, $\delta(x, y)$ is defined only if x and y are comparable with respect to the order relation E). Let $y \in T$ be the root of T, define $\delta_y: T \rightarrow R^+$ as follows: $\delta_y(x) = \delta(x, y)$ (note that δ_y is a total function as all points are comparable with the root). We will assume that the order relation induced on T by δ_y and the standard order of the reals is the same as the relation E. Such an assumption—that is, that a metric δ can be defined so that δ_y does induce the relation E—is fairly easy to prove as E is linear restricted to histories. Here we are crucially using the assumption that the structure is rooted, but partial functions with respect to various origins could be used to define the same notion; again, the assumption is not crucial to our semantics, it is introduced for notational simplicity.

With respect to a particular branch h, we define the open interval t_h to be the set of points on h mapped onto $t = (x, y)$, that is, $t_h = \{z \in h : x < \delta_y(z) < y\}$ and, similarly, the closed interval $t_h = \{z \in h : x \leq \delta_y(z) \leq y\}$.

To drop the metrizability assumption, we assume that there is a separate linear set of points, a time axis, and assume a linear order on that set. We then would define a set of partial functions mapping the linear time axis onto branches of the branching structure in such a way as to preserve the order relation E. That is, the order relation induced by the partial function on a history is the relation E, restricted to that history.

The branching structure itself can be defined strictly by considering the ordering relation; intervals can be defined as linear chains. Following this approach, we would have to show that the partial functions preserve intervals. We do need to be able to compare the intervals in order to use a Lewis–Stalnaker type semantics for conditionals. We need to be able to say that an interval t_h is in some way equivalent to an interval t_g in another branch. I have opted for using a metric on the branching structure rather than defining the structure more generally and using properties of the structure and of the linear continuum to achieve the same results.

ACKNOWLEDGMENTS

I would like to thank the students in my model-theoretic semantics course at Brown University for their patience with earlier drafts of this chapter, students and faculty members at the University of Michigan, and Barbara H. Partee, Östen Dahl, James McCawley, Annie Zaenen, and Polly Jacobson. Their discussion and comments have led to many revisions of this chapter. Of course, the author is completely responsible for all remaining errors. I would also like to thank the three reviewers for their many insightful comments.

REFERENCES

Bennet, M., and Partee, B. (1972). *Toward the logic of tense and aspect in English*. Unpublished manuscript (available through the Indiana University Linguistics Club).

Binnick, R. (1971). *Will* and *be going to*. In Papers from the Seventh Regional Meeting of the *Chicago Linguistics Circle*. Department of Linguistics, University of Chicago. Pp. 40–50.

Binnick, R. (1972). *Will* and *be going to, II*. In *Papers from the Eighth Regional Meeting of the Chicago Linguistics Circle*. Department of Linguistics, University of Chicago. Pp. 3–9.

Chomsky, N. (1957). *Syntactic Structures*. The Hague: Mouton.

Cooper, R. (1975). *Montague's Semantic Theory and Transformational grammar*. Unpublished doctoral dissertation, University of Massachussets, Amherst.

Cooper, W. (1968). The propositional logic of ordinary discourse. *Inquiry*, **11**, 295–320.

Cresswell, M.J. (1977). Interval semantics and logical words, unpublished manuscript.

Dowty, D. (1977). Towards a semantic analysis of verb aspect and the English 'imperfective' progressive. *Linguistics and Philosophy*, **1**, 45–77.

Gazdar, G. (1976). *Formal Pragmatics for Natural Languages: Implicature, Presupposition and Logical Form*. Doctoral dissertation, University of Reading (available through the Indiana University Linguistics Club).

Grice, H.P. (1967). Logic and conversation. Unpublished manuscript (Reprinted in P. Cole and J. Morgan (Eds.), *Syntax and Semantics 3: Speech Acts*. New York: Academic Press. Pp. 41–58).

Jespersen, O. (1964). *Essentials of English Grammar*. University of Alabama Press, University, Alabama.

Johnson, M. (1977). *A Semantic Analysis of Kikuyu Tense and Aspect*. Unpublished doctoral dissertation, Ohio State University.

Ladusaw, W. (1977). Some Problems with Tense in PTQ. *Texas Linguistic Forum*, **6**, 89–102.

Lewis, D. (1973). *Counterfactuals*. Edinburgh: Blackwell.

McCawley, J.D. (1971). Tense and time reference in English. In C.J. Fillmore and D.T. Langendoen (Eds.), *Studies in Linguistic Semantics*. New York: Holt, Rinehart, Winston. Pp. 97–114.

McCawley, J.D. (1972). A program for logic. In D. Davison and G. Harman (Eds.), *Semantics of Natural Language*. Dordrecht: Reidel. Pp. 498–544.

Montague, R. (1968). Pragmatics. [Reprinted in R. Thomason (Ed.), *Formal Philosophy*. New Haven: Yale University Press.]

Montague, R. (1973). On the proper treatment of quantification in ordinary English. [Reprinted in K.J.J. Hintikka, J.M.E. Moravcsik, and P. Suppes (Eds.), *Approaches to Natural Language*. Dordrecht: Reidel. Pp. 221–242.]

Perlmutter, D. (1970). The two verbs *begin*. In R.A. Jacobs and P.S. Rosenbaum (Eds.), *Readings in English Transformational Grammar*. New York: Ginn and Co. Pp. 107–119.

Prior, A.N. (1968). Now. *Nous*, **2**, 101–119.

Rescher, N., and Urquhart, A. (1971). *Temporal Logic*. Springer-Verlag.

Riddle, E., and Tedeschi, P. (1974). *Some aspects of temporal aspectual predicates*. Presented at the 49th Annual Meeting of the Linguistic Society of America, New York.

Sag, I. (1972). On the state of progress on progressives and statives. In C.-J.N. Bailey and R.W. Shuy (Eds.), *New Ways of Analyzing Variation in English*. Washington, D.C.: Georgetown University Press. Pp. 83–95.

Scott, D. (1970). Advice on modal logic. In K. Lambert (Ed.), *Philosophical Problems in Logic*. Dordrecht: Reidel. Pp. 143–173.

Smith, C. (1978). The syntax and interpretation of temporal expressions in English. *Linguistics and Philosophy*, **2**.

Stalnaker, R. (1968). A theory of conditionals. In N. Rescher (Ed.), *Studies in Logical Theory*. Pp. 98–112.

Stalnaker, R., and Thomason, R. (1970). A semantic analysis of conditional logic. *Theoria*, **36**, 23–42.

Taylor, B. (1974). *The Semantics of Adverbs. Unpublished doctoral dissertation, Oxford University*.

Tedeschi, P. (1976). *If*: A study of English conditional sentences. Doctoral dissertation, University of Michigan (in *UMPIL*, **2**:3, 1–95).

Thomason, R. (1970). Indeterminist time and truth-value gaps. *Theoria*, **36**, 264–281.

Twaddel, W.F. (1963). *The English Verb Auxiliaries*. Providence: Brown University Press.

Vendler, Z. (1967). *Linguistics in Philosophy*. Ithaca: Cornell University Press.

von Wright, G.H. (1968). An essay in deontic logic and the general theory of action. *Acta Philosophica Fennica*, fasc. 21. Amsterdam: North-Holland.

Zaenen, A. (1977). *A proposal for a unified treatment of "before."* Paper presented to a workshop on tense and aspect, University of Massachusetts, Amherst, Summer 1977.

THE SEMANTICS OF THE PROGRESSIVE

FRANK VLACH

1. INTRODUCTION

This discussion is of the same general kind as Bennett and Partee 1972 and Dowty 1977; that is, it is intended as a contribution to the task of providing something like a Montague grammar (Montague, 1972) for a fragment of English that contains real English tenses, including the progressive. In Scott 1970, Bennett and Partee 1972, and Dowty 1977, truth conditions set out for the progressive are topological (in the case of Dowty, close enough to topological) in the sense that the set of instants at which the progressive of a sentence ϕ is true is claimed to be a function of the set of intervals at which ϕ is true. I argue that the truth conditions for the progressive cannot be topological and that the notion of a PROCESS is central to any correct account of the progressive.

This discussion is carried out informally, with nothing defined rigorously, so it might be worth emphasizing that I do not mean by this to depart from the standards of formal precision advocated by Montague. On the contrary, this chapter is part of my own attempt to construct a formally precise system containing as full as possible an account of English tenses. But before the formal syntactic and semantic rules for the progressive can be written down, it is necessary to have some idea of

271

Syntax and Semantics, Volume 14
Tense and Aspect

what facts these rules are meant to explain, and this chapter is an attempt to find some of those facts. One of the benefits of the construction of a logically rigorous system is that it forces a more exact investigation of the facts the system is meant to account for.

2. TENSELESS SENTENCES

If all the tenses are sentential operators, as I believe, then there must be a fundamental level of tenseless sentences in order for there to be any sentences at all. These tenseless sentences will be indicated by putting the main verb in the infinitive (with *to* omitted, e.g., *Max build a house*).[1] By calling these sentences "tenseless" I mean only that they contain no tense operators.

This tenseless form, the basic form to which the progressive operator and other operators apply, is sometimes identified semantically with some form of present tense (nonhabitual, reportive), but the only requirement that must be made of the tenseless form is that all the tenses can be represented as operators on it. It is most reasonable, then, to let the tenseless form have whatever truth conditions it needs to have in order to fulfill its function, rather than to identify it with some predetermined English tense. In other words, we should figure out what the tenseless form is by figuring out what it has to be.

Truth conditions for complex sentences can be given only if truth conditions for tenseless sentences are specified first; and truth conditions for tenseless sentences, in turn, can only be given relative to the semantic class to which they belong. For the purposes of this discussion, sentences are divided into four classes, following Vendler 1967. These are the classes of stative sentences, process sentences, accomplishment sentences, and achievement sentences. The fact that preceding accounts of the progressive tend to fit one or more of these semantic classes much better than the rest indicates that these classes must be kept firmly in mind throughout any further investigations of the progressive.

This classification is made by Vendler as a classification of verb phrases,[2] but is best made as a classification of sentences, given that subject noun phrases as well as verb phrases affect the classification. For ex-

---

[1] Or, if the main verb has no infinitive, the first person present indicative will be used.

[2] Vendler does not quite put it this way, but I think this is a fair interpretation. In any case, Vendler does not see it as a classification of sentences.

ample (see Sections 2.2 and 2.3), just as *Max build a house* is an accomplishment sentence and *Max builds houses* is a process sentence, *Max fly to Boston* is an accomplishment sentence and *Tourists fly to Boston* (the tenseless sentence, not the "habitual" present) is a process sentence (cf. *Tourists are flying to Boston*). It may be possible to classify verb phrases in a derivative way: An achievement verb phrase, for example, is one that forms an achievement sentence when prefixed by a noun phrase denoting an individual (as opposed to a set).

I will briefly discuss the four classes and the truth conditions for some simple tenseless sentences of each class.

2.1. Statives (*Mary love Max, Max be here, Mary be running*)

The property of statives exemplified by Sentence (1)

(1)   *Max was here when I arrived.*

is the most important for the semantics of tense; I will take it to be the defining property of statives. In order for (1) to be true, Max must have been here for some period preceding and extending up to the time of my arrival. This is in sharp contrast to the situation for the other three categories. *Max ran when I arrived, Max polished his shoes when I arrived,* and *Max died when I arrived* indicate that the running, polishing, or dying took place at the time of or slightly after my arrival, not before.

I adopt the following definition of a stative sentence:

(2)   A sentence ϕ is stative if and only if the truth of (Past ϕ) *when I arrived* requires that ϕ was true for some period leading up to the time of my arrival.[3]

This behavior of statives with *when I arrived* seems to hold for other point adverbials (e.g., *at 3:00*) as well.

---

[3] Alex Mourelatos has pointed out that sentences of the kind required for this test are odd with statives not involving *be* (e.g., *Max understood Kant when I arrived, Max trusted Mary when I arrived*). My feeling is that these sentences are grammatical and have the truth conditions specified in (2), but are odd because the probably long-term nature of the state involved makes it peculiar to stress that the state held at one particular instant. Semantically similar sentences with *be* are also odd: *Max was tall when I arrived.* Mourelatos has also noted that these sentences are better when *already* is added: *Max already understood Kant when I arrived.* I think pragmatic reasons can be given for this that are consistent with my claim about why the sentences are odd without *be*.

It is important to notice that sentences in the progressive are stative according to (2).[4]

(3)   *Max was running when I arrived.*

Sentence (3) indicates that Max was running for some period preceding and extending up to the time of my arrival.[5]

It is widely recognized that statives do not take the progressive. When an apparent stative occurs in the progressive, as in *John is being stupid,* it is said to be used in a nonstative sense. If progressives are statives then there is an explanation for the fact that statives do not take the progressive. The function of the progressive operator is to make stative sentences, and, therefore, there is no reason for the progressive to apply to sentences that are already stative.[6]

Suppose Max arrives here at 2:00 and leaves here at 3:00. Then the tenseless sentence *Max be here* is true at every instant between 2:00 and 3:00 and also true for every subinterval of [2:00, 3:00].[7] *Max be here* is not

[4] It seems that my claim that progressives are statives is a radical one, but I have seen no evidence against it, and there is other evidence (partly circumstantial) in its favor:

1. The main verb is *be*. What other construction with *be* is nonstative?

2. One of the historical antecedents of the progressive is a construction involving a locative preposition (see Section 5). Comrie (1976, pp. 98–103) and Anderson (1973) point out that the progressive in quite a number of totally unrelated languages has syntactic features in common with locatives. Locatives are statives. If progressives are not statives, why do they have so much in common with locatives?

3. Attempts have been made to define stativity in terms of semantic facts about the sentence (or verb phrase) in isolation (e.g., Comrie, 1976, pp. 48–51) but it seems that any successful attempt of this kind must include progressives among statives, due to the equivalence of such pairs as *Tweetie is flying* and *Tweetie is in flight.*

4. Progressives do not take the progressive. *Max is being running* is not a sentence. Failure to take the progressive is often the only hard criterion given for stativity. Bennett and Partee (1972), for example, characterize stative verb phrases as "verb phrases which do not take the progressive form." Despite this, they do not seem to believe that progressives are statives; yet their discussion on p. 35, for example, would be greatly simplified if this were recognized.

[5] It might be thought that Max also has to be running after my arrival, but Dowty's example (Dowty, 1977) *John was watching television when he fell asleep* makes this doubtful.

[6] Something like this is said in Palmer (1974, p. 73).

[7] If t and t' are instants and t is before t', then

(i) $[t, t']$ is the set of instants between t and t' (inclusive)
(ii) (t, t') is the set of instants between t and t' (exclusive)
(iii) $[t, t']$ is a closed interval
(iv) (t, t') is an open interval

Closed intervals contain a first and a last instant. Open intervals contain neither. The instant t is identified with the interval $[t, t]$, so that every instant is an interval. It is assumed that time is continuous.

true at or for any other intervals so far as the particular one-hour visit in question is concerned. I think that this stipulative definition of truth conditions for tenseless statives has a certain plausibility, but, like the corresponding stipulations for other classes of tenseless sentences, it stands or falls on what it, in conjunction with the rest of the theory, predicts about the truth conditions of actual tensed sentences of English.

The notion of truth for an interval depends on the notion of truth at an interval, and is meant to connect up to English in such a way that, for instance, *Max has been here for an hour* is true (on one reading) if and only if there is a past one-hour-long interval *I* such that *Max be here* is true for *I*. Truth for an interval is thus in a way the interpretation of *for* in its temporal use. This notion is vague in English and I will not attempt to make it exact, but it is something like this:

(4)   The sentence ϕ is true for the interval *I* if and only if ϕ is true at a set of subintervals of *I* which are more or less scattered all over *I* in such a way that there are no large gaps between the subintervals of *I* at which ϕ is true.

The required number of subintervals and permitted size of gaps are in practice heavily dependent on pragmatic factors. For instance, *Ralph taught for a year* can be true despite the fact that Ralph did not teach during the three-month summer vacation. *Ralph attended the meetings for a year* can be true even if the meanings were monthly or even quarterly, but not if they were held weekly in December only.[8] Notice also that attendance at four meetings is sufficient for the truth of *Ralph attended the meetings for a year* if there were only four or five meetings, but not if there were fifty.

---

[8] Perhaps this is the point for a brief discussion of truth with respect to intervals. In the preceding paragraph two distinct notions were mentioned: truth at an interval and truth for an interval. There is also (at least) a third kind of truth with respect to intervals—truth in an interval. These three concepts are meant to bear a close relation to English adverbials of time. Thus *Max reached the top at 2:00* is to be true if and only if *Max reach the top* is true at the relevant past 2:00; *Max has been here for an hour* is true (on one reading) if and only if there is a past one-hour-long interval *I* such that *Max be here* is true for *I*; *Max built a house in 1972* is true if and only if *Max build a house* is true in the interval 1972.

The notion of truth at an interval has generally been assumed to be the basic notion; truth in an interval has not been considered, and truth for an interval has been conflated with truth at an interval, as in the Bennett and Partee definition of the progressive. It is not obvious, though, that truth at an interval is the basic notion. The goal before us is a recursive definition of truth with respect to intervals. I think it has been implicitly assumed that truth at an interval is the notion that will be defined recursively, and that the other two notions can be defined, if they are necessary at all, in terms of truth at an interval. Nevertheless, we know nothing that makes this certain. Any of the three notions could be the one that occurs in the

2.2. Processes (*Max run, Max stand, Max push a cart, Mary abuse Max, Max sell cars*)

Suppose Mary starts running at instant 2:00 and continues running until 3:00, when she stops. Then tenseless *Mary run* is true at every instant between 2:00 and 3:00. The topology of the truth conditions for tenseless process sentences is the same as that for tenseless stative sentences. The difference between the two (in this respect) shows itself only in context, as mentioned in the preceding section. The close connection between truth at an interval and English tense adverbials with *at* disappears for process sentences.[9] In the preceding *Mary run* example, *Mary run* is true at 2:30, but *Mary ran at 2:30* is false, or at least an odd way to say what is more usually expressed by *Mary was running at 2:30*. *Mary ran at 2:30* is more likely to mean that Mary started to run at 2:30. Later on we will find reason to believe that, for process sentences, the progressive is equivalent to the tenseless form.

Despite the lack of connection between truth at an interval and *at* adverbials, it must be said that *Mary run* is true at every instant between 2:00 and 3:00 in order to retain the connection between truth at and truth for an interval, and in order to account for the equivalence of *Mary ran for an hour* and *Mary was running for an hour*.

2.3. Accomplishments (*Mary run a mile, Max sell some cars, Max push a cart for an hour*)

If Mary starts running a mile at 3:10 and finishes at 3:16, then *Mary run a mile* is true at the interval [3:10, 3:16] and not at or for any other interval, so far as that run is concerned. Mary would have to run a mile on

---

recursive definition of truth, or it could be that two or more of these notions must be defined together in a simultaneous recursion.

I believe that (4) is correct for most English sentences of the appropriate semantic categories, but there is a problem about sentences with adverbs like *regularly*. Consider the sentence *Max came here regularly for a year*. In order for *Max come here regularly* to be true for a year-long interval *I*, it is not necessary that *Max come here regularly* be true at a set of subintervals of *I* (indeed, it does not seem to make sense that *Max come here regularly* should be true AT any interval). The regularity holds over the year, not necessarily over parts of the year. This suggests that the truth conditions for *regularly* should be something like

(i) φ *regularly* is true for *I* if and only if φ is true at regular intervals throughout *I*.

This definition, of course, would be part of a recursive definition of truth, and, therefore, if it is necessary to have such a clause for *regularly*, then both truth at an interval and truth for an interval must play a part in a recursive truth definition for English.

[9] Actually, the connection seems to hold in the simple form (φ *at 3:00* is true if and only if φ is true at 3:00) only for achievement sentences.

more than one occasion for *Mary run a mile* to be true for any interval [see (4)].

It might not be entirely obvious that *Mary run a mile* should not be true at every instant between 3:10 and 3:16. An intuitive explanation might be that Mary can not run that many miles in 6 minutes, but in the end the only way to decide the question is to test out its consequences for the truth conditions of actual tensed sentences. For example, the truth conditions for the perfect are such that *Mary has run a mile* is true at an instant *t* if and only if *Mary run a mile* is true at some interval previous to *t*. Given this, it follows that *Mary run a mile* cannot be allowed to be true at any subinterval of [3:10, 3:16] that does not extend up to 3:16, because then *Mary has run a mile* would be claimed to be true at some instant before 3:16; that is, before Mary finishes running the mile.

Only accomplishment sentences can be true at noninstantaneous intervals. The idea is that an accomplishment sentence asserts that an event of a certain kind takes place, and the tenseless accomplishment sentence is true at the interval that begins when the event begins and ends when it ends. As with process sentences, there is no direct connection between truth at an interval and *at* adverbials. Instead, the connection has to be with *in* adverbials—*Max built a house in 1972* is true if and only if *Max build a house* is true at some subinterval of the interval 1972. English seems to have no concise adverbial that says an accomplishment takes place at an interval.[10]

2.4. Achievements (*Mary win, Max die, Max arrive, Max finish building the house*)

Suppose we are talking about a foot race. Then *Mary won at 3:00* is true if and only if the relevant past 3:00 was the instant at which Mary crossed the finish line ahead of everyone else. If *Mary won at 3:00* is true, then 3:00 is the only interval *t* (in this case, of course, an instantaneous interval) such that *Mary win* is true at *t*. This property of being true at isolated instants only is the defining property of achievement sentences.

3. SOME OBSERVATIONS ABOUT THE PROGRESSIVE

None of the following facts seem particularly surprising at first glance but some have proven difficult for the natural and reasonable-looking

---

[10] This may suggest that *in* adverbials are more fundamental than *at* adverbials. Further support for this can be found in Cresswell (1977, p. 5), where the recursive clause for *every* could be greatly simplified by stating it in terms of truth in an interval rather than at an interval.

theories of Scott (1970), Bennett and Partee (1972), and Dowty (1977), so that there is good reason to consider them problematic.

The truth conditions suggested by Scott, Bennett and Partee, and Dowty are listed here for reference:

(5)   (Scott)   Prog[ϕ] is true at an instant t if and only if ϕ is true at every instant in some open interval containing t.

(6)   (Bennett and Partee)   Prog[ϕ] is true at an instant t if and only if ϕ is true at an interval I containing t such that t is not an endpoint of I.[11]

(7)   (Dowty)   Prog[ϕ] is true at an interval I (in the actual world) if and only if there are an interval I' and a possible world w such that I is a proper subinterval of I', ϕ is true at I' in w, and w is exactly like the actual world at all times preceding and including I.

Sections 3.1–3.6 present six facts about the progressive, together with some comments about how well these facts fit the truth conditions given in (5)–(7).

3.1 Equivalences between the Progressive and the Tenseless Form with Duration Adverbials

There are certain equivalences between constructions with and without the progressive, involving processes and iterated accomplishments and achievements. So far as I have been able to tell, *Max ran from 3:00 to 4:00* has the same truth conditions as *Max was running from 3:00 to 4:00*. Also, suppose Max enters a certain contest weekly. Then *Max won for a year* and *Max was winning for a year* have the same truth conditions. A theory of the progressive ought to predict this equivalence.

3.2. The Imperfective Paradox

Max is building a house can be true even if Max is never going to complete the house. There is nothing contradictory about *Max was building a house when he died*. Notice that this applies only to accomplishments and achievements—we can have *Max was building a house but he never built*

---

[11] This definition is meant to hold both for accomplishments and processes, and therefore conflates what I believe to be two totally distinct notions—truth for an interval, which makes sense only for processes and states, and truth at a noninstantaneous interval, which makes sense only for accomplishments. Truth for an interval must be defined in terms of truth at an interval, as in (4), but truth at a noninstantaneous interval is just as basic as truth at an instant. Dowty also fails to distinguish these (Dowty, 1977, p. 50).

it, but we can not have *Max was running but he never ran*. This fact about accomplishments and achievements was called the "imperfective paradox" in Dowty 1977. The Scott and Bennett and Partee analyses fail on this point, and Dowty introduces possible worlds other than the actual one in order to avoid it.

3.3. Progressives of Achievement Sentences

Dowty initially claimed (in Dowty, 1972) that there are no progressives of achievement sentences, and later maintained (Dowty, 1977) that such progressives are rare. Despite this, there seems to be nothing odd or unusual about such sentences as *Max is dying, Max is winning,* or *Max is reaching the top.*[12]

The reason these sentences are problematic is this: Suppose Mary starts the race at 3:10 and finishes, winning, at 3:16. Then there will be a third instant *t* between 3:10 and 3:16 such that Mary pulls ahead at *t* and stays ahead until 3:16. As a matter of actual usage *Mary is winning* is true at every instant between *t* and 3:16, but *Mary win* is true only at the instant 3:16. This is a counterexample to any theory that says that the progressive of ϕ is true only at instants that are contained in intervals at or for which ϕ is true, as do the theories of Scott and of Bennett and Partee.

This problem is apparently first fully taken notice of in Dowty (1977), where some effort is devoted to its solution. Nevertheless, an examination of Dowty's argument reveals that according to his analyses *Max is dying* is either true from the moment of Max's birth or else is never true.[13]

The problem would dissolve if the progressive in

(8)   *Mary was winning, but she didn't win.*

were a futurate progressive as in *The Celtics are playing tomorrow*. It has often been noted that the futurate progressive involves, in some not very

----

[12] The idea that progressives of achievement sentences are rare may be due to an initial concentration on such mental achievement verbs as *recognize,* which are odd in the progressive. On the other hand, see Comrie (1976, p. 47). I do not share Comrie's intuition about *reach the summit* and *die*.

[13] There are three analyses of [BECOME ϕ] in Dowty 1977: According to (11), p. 52, *Max is dying* would be true from Max's birth, as Dowty realizes. According to (11'), p. 53, with clause (3) interpreted as a felicity condition, *Max is dying* is true, but infelicitous, from Max's birth (Dowty speaks, on page 58, as if it would be false in this case, but surely the failure of felicity conditions results in infelicity, not falsehood). According to (11') with clause (3) interpreted as a truth condition, *Max is dying* is never true. This assumes a two-valued logic; if there were truth-value gaps (a possibility mentioned by Dowty), then *Max is dying* would still be true from Max's birth in the first two cases, and in the last case it would be true only in the interval when Max is no longer alive but not yet dead.

well understood way, the notion of planning, scheduling, or predeter-mination. It is this that makes *The Celtics are winning tomorrow* or *Max is dying tomorrow* so odd. These sentences, because of the adverb *tomor-row*, have to be genuine futurate progressives and therefore suggest that the Celtics game is fixed or that Max has decided to die tomorrow. The progressive in (8) has no such implications on the most natural reading. It is possible to interpret the progressive in (8) as a futurate progressive, but this is decidedly the less likely interpretation, so that the problem re-mains.

3.4. Progressives Lack the Subinterval Property

Someone walks into a theater, points to an empty seat and asks "Is someone sitting here?" The question being asked can only be whether anyone is sitting there for the evening; it is obvious that no one is sitting there at the moment. The speaker, so to speak, knows that the sentence *Someone is sitting here* is false at the moment of speaking, but does not know whether that sentence is true for the interval of that evening. The sentence can be true for the interval but not true at a moment contained in the interval.

A sentence ϕ is said to have the subinterval property if and only if whenever ϕ is true for an interval I it is also true at every instant in I (and therefore true for every noninstantaneous subinterval of I).[14] The example just given shows that the sentence *Someone be sitting here* does not have the subinterval property.

To take another example: Suppose Max sold cars for one week only in the year 1976 and had lunch every day that week from 12:00 to 1:00. Then *Max be selling cars* is false for the interval 1976;[15] if it were true for that interval, then *Max sold cars for a year* would be true. *Max be selling cars* is true for the week in question, as *Max was selling cars for a week* is true. *Max be selling cars* is false for every lunch hour and every subinterval of every lunch hour, as *Max was selling cars from 12:00 to 1:00* was false at, say, 3:00 in the afternoon on every day on which Max sold cars.

The problem about the subinterval property does not arise immediately from the Scott or Bennett and Partee analyses of the progressive, because for them the truth of progressives is defined initially only at instants. Dowty's analysis works on noninstantaneous intervals directly in such a way that progressives have the subinterval property, which must of course be avoided.

[14] This definition differs from the original (Bennett and Partee, 1972, p. 17) for reasons I have given in Note 13.
[15] That is, it is not the case that it is true for the interval 1976.

3.5. Progressives of Accomplishment Sentences

From the fact that an accomplishment sentence ϕ is true at an interval I it does not follow that the progressive of ϕ is true at every instant in I, or for every noninstantaneous subinterval of I. It does not even follow that the progressive of ϕ is true for I.

For example, suppose Max started building a house at the beginning of 1972, worked on it throughout January, left it half finished until December, and then worked on it throughout December, finishing it at the end of 1972. In that event *Max build a house* is true at the interval 1972, but *Max was building a house in June 1972* is false,[16] and so is *Max was building a house for a year.*

The analyses of Bennett and Partee and of Dowty are in direct contradiction to this. This is surprising in Dowty, as he notices (Dowty, 1977) that one can spend an hour at an activity ''even though one did not engage in the activity at literally every moment within that hour [p. 50].'' He might just as well have said ''even though one was not engaging in the activity at literally every moment within that hour.''

3.6. Iterated Achievements and Accomplishments

An analysis of the progressive ought to account for the two senses of the sentence

(9)   *Max was winning for a year.*

One sense of (9) has already been mentioned. Suppose Max is competing in a contest that lasts a number of years and for which a continuous ranking of participants is maintained. Then (9) is true if Max was ranked first for a year. The other sense of (9) is the iterative sense. Suppose that a certain contest was held weekly, and that Max won it every week or nearly every week for 52 weeks. In that case (9) is true in the iterative sense.

One key feature of the latter case is that (9) can be true only if Max

---

[16] This may require qualification. I do not think that this sentence is ambiguous, but its truth depends partly on factors not specified, for example whether it was the case in June that Max intended to complete the house.

There is a degree of latitude in what counts as part of the process of building a house, and this would be determined partly by context. If Max is a carpenter (the best case for my claim), then the process of building a house would naturally be construed as consisting only of hammering, sawing, *etc.* If Max is the owner or the contractor, the process might be taken to include such things as repaying mortgages, thinking about plans and alterations of plans, and simply intending to finish the house. These things might continue through the period when the house was left half built.

actually won a lot of the contests. In fact, in this sense (9) seems equivalent to *Max won for a year.* If Max never won a contest but was winning each contest at some time in its duration, then (9) is false on the iterative reading, even though *Max be winning* is true on the noniterative reading at lots of closely spaced intervals throughout the year.[17]

4. TRUTH CONDITIONS FOR THE PROGRESSIVE

I will now try to construct more adequate truth conditions for the progressive. I begin by considering process sentences, which are the easiest. From this point onward I will consider iterated achievements and accomplishments to be processes (and not to be accomplishments or achievements), as they share with other processes the possibility of being true at a lot of points within an interval and also being true for the interval itself. A sentence that would otherwise be an achievement or accomplishment sentence becomes a process sentence when what is in question is its repeated truth throughout an interval. Thus *Max win* is a process sentence when it occurs as a constituent of *Max won for a year.*

4.1. Progressives of Process Sentences

Truth conditions for progressives of process sentences can be given quite simply, as follows:

(10)   If ϕ is a process sentence, then Prog[ϕ] is true at t if and only if ϕ is true at t.

To begin with, this definition has the advantage that it makes *Max was running for an hour* equivalent to *Max ran for an hour* and it makes (9) (iterative) equivalent to *Max won for a year.*

---

[17] Various writers (I am acquainted mainly with Mourelatos, this volume) have drawn analogies between process verb phrases and mass nouns (designating entities that are divisible, in the sense that a part of a stretch of running or a mass of water is still a stretch of running or a mass of water), and also between accomplishments or achievements and count nouns (designating indivisible entities). English bare plurals (e.g., *dogs* with no article) may form a third category, designating entities divisible up to a point. A bunch of dogs can be separated into two bunches of dogs, but the process cannot be continued indefinitely. Similarly, a stretch of winning (in the iterative sense) can be separated into two stretches of winning, but the process is not continuable.

These analogies can be continued further. Emmon Bach has suggested that *Max ran for an hour* means that there was an hour full of Max's running. An hour full of running is naturally assumed to be without gaps, like a bathtub full of water. A year full of winning (iterative) has got to have gaps, like a street full of policemen.

Further justification of this account of the progressive depends essentially on an argument concerning the interaction of stative sentences and point adverbials like *at 3:00* or *when I arrived*. As has already been noted, *Max was running when I arrived* entails that the running occurred at least in part before my arrival. *Max ran when I arrived* entails that the running occurred after my arrival.

Now assume the following:

1. The construction

(11)   Past φ *when I arrived*

is topological; that is, the truth value of (11) depends only on the set of instants at which and intervals for which φ is true.

2. *Max be running* is true for any interval *I* if and only if *Max run* is true for *I*.

3. (a) *Max be running* is Prog [*Max run*].
   (b) *Max was running* is Past [*Max be running*].
   (c) *Max ran* is Past [*Max run*].

Suppose in addition that *I arrive* is true at 3:00 and that *Max run* is true for some interval *I* beginning at 3:00 (or perhaps slightly after 3:00). Then, as a matter of actual usage, *Max ran when I arrived* is true (at 3:30, say). Now by Assumption (2) *Max be running* is true for *I*. By Assumptions (1) and (3) it then follows that *Max was running when I arrived* is true, which is incorrect as a matter of English usage. Therefore, if the system is to make accurate predictions about English usage, one of the three assumptions must be given up.

I cannot prove that it is impossible to give up Assumptions (2) or (3), but I have found them both essential to a coherent semantic account of the fragment of English I have been working with. Assumption (3) is hard to avoid; it might be held that Past or Prog or both are verb phrase modifiers rather than sentence modifiers, but this would still allow essentially the same argument. It might be thought easier to get around Assumption (2), but how then is the equivalence of *Max ran for an hour* and *Max was running for an hour* to be accounted for?

It remains only to give up the first assumption and conclude that the truth value of (11) must depend on something besides the temporal truth pattern of φ.

Another key fact is that (11) is topological when φ is restricted to stative sentences and also when φ is restricted to nonstative sentences. Point adverbials behave in one uniform way with stative sentences and in another uniform way with nonstative sentences. I suppose this is best regarded as a contextual ambiguity of all point adverbials, with the proper meaning to be determined by the stativity or nonstativity of the sentence to which the adverbial applies.

On this view, the progressive operator turns sentences into stative sentences, and the defining characteristic of stative sentences is their way of interacting with point adverbials.[18] This is not just one fact about the progressive; this is what the progressive is FOR. If this is right then every difference between progressives and nonprogressives should be explained by the fact that progressives are statives.

This interaction of the progressive with point adverbials is the substance of Jespersen's excellent discussion of the progressive as "a temporal frame encompassing something else" (Jespersen, 1954, pp. 178–180), as Jespersen's examples indicate.

It also must lie behind the Scott truth conditions for the progressive, which ensure that *Max is walking* is not true at the first instant (if any) at which *Max walk* is true. On the double analysis of point adverbials, which I have argued is necessary on independent grounds, there is no need to adopt Scott's definition of the progressive or to complicate matters in any similar way.

There is another related argument in favor of this theory of the progressive. If the interaction of progressives with point adverbials were to be explained by a special analysis of the progressive such as those of Scott, Bennett and Partee, or Dowty, then there would have to be some separate feature built into the grammar to explain why nonprogressive statives behave just like progressives in this respect. Because this behavior is common to stative sentences in general, it ought to have an explanation that applies to stative sentences in general.

4.2. Progressives of Achievement and Accomplishment Sentences

The analysis given for processes will not work for achievements and accomplishments, of course, because on that analysis *Max be winning* could not be true at any time before *Max win* is true.

To begin with, we are faced with the fact that any correct truth conditions for the progressive operator applied to accomplishment and achievement sentences must be in a certain sense nontopological; that is, the set

---

[18] There are various facts about the behavior of the progressive in a continuing narrative that may or may not have to do with interaction with point adverbs, but at least have to do with meaning in context as distinct from in isolation.

of instants at which Prog[ϕ] is true cannot be a function of the set of instants and intervals at which ϕ is true.[19]

A topological definition cannot work for achievement sentences. Suppose *Mary win* is true at 3:00 and *Max die* is also true at 3:00. Then there are likely to be a time *t* before 3:00 at which *Mary be winning* is first true (or *Mary be not winning* is last false)[20] and a similar time *t'* for *Max be dying*. Obviously *t* and *t'* need not be the same; Max could have started dying before Mary started winning. But if a topological definition were correct, then *t* and *t'* would have to be the same, since the set of instants at which *Max be dying* and *Mary be winning* were true would have to be identical, both being the value of the same function for the same argument.

David Lewis, as quoted in Dowty 1977, makes the suggestion that "PROG[ϕ] should be defined as true in case ϕ will be true in that possible world most similar to the actual world in which 'the natural course of events' obtains." This suggestion is rejected by Dowty (though he says it "may be correct") because he sees "no way of making 'natural course of events' precise in model-theoretic terms."[21] I see Lewis's idea as a big step in the right direction, at least so far as achievement and accomplishment sentences are concerned. The *Max be dying–Mary be winning* counterexample does not apply to it, and it requires of the possible world in which ϕ is true that it bear a specific relation to the actual world.

The most obvious modification that must be made to Lewis's account concerns the limitations of the natural course of events. It is not the entire natural course of events that must continue uninterrupted, but some sort of restriction to the state and actions of the subject of the sentence. Suppose Max is crossing the street (he is halfway across, making progress toward the other side with the intention of getting there), but unknown to

---

[19] The definitions of Scott and of Bennett and Partee are topological in this sense. The definition in Dowty 1977 is nontopological because of his introduction of possible worlds, but it is topological if restricted to those cases in which the sentence to which Prog is applied is true at some future time in the actual world. The counterexample given in what follows will apply to Dowty's definition as well as to the others.

[20] This qualification is due to the mathematical fact that an interval *I* need not have a first member, but if *I* does not have a first member then there must be a last point preceding the interval.

[21] I cannot see the force of this objection. For one thing, many English constructions are not precise, and to make them so is to give an inadequate account of their meaning. Lewis's semantic account of counterfactuals (Lewis, 1973) is given in terms of similarity. Lewis notes that similarity is a vague notion, and depends on what aspects of things one is interested in; these facts about similarity help to explain the behavior of counterfactuals (Lewis, 1973, pp. 91–95).

Max a bus traveling at 30 miles per hour is an inch away from hitting him. The fact that the preceding is a wholly consistent description shows that ϕ need not become true in the natural course of events in order for Prog[ϕ] to be true. In the natural course of events the bus will hit Max and he will never cross the street; it would be not only unnatural but a miracle for *Max cross the street* to become true. For the progressive of ϕ to be true it is not necessary that ϕ's becoming the case later be natural, predictable, expected, probable, likely, or even (perhaps) physically possible. The bus's hitting Max is not an interruption of the natural course of events; it is the natural course of events, but it is an interruption of something.

Another objection to Lewis's definition is shown by the following example: Suppose Max gets up in the morning and begins putting on his clothes, intending to go to work. According to Lewis's definition *Max be going to work* is true. His intentions, force of habit, his current actions all indicate that he is going to get to work as usual; in the natural course of events he will do so. In spite of all this, *Max be going to work* is not yet true. He has not started to go to work yet.

The exact restriction necessary here, needless to say, is not easy to find. A restriction involving the proximity of the required outcome in time or in the causal sequence of events is not only difficult or impossible to state; it is also doomed in advance by counterexamples. Consider the bus in the case just described where Max is crossing the street. *The bus is hitting Max* is not true (excluding the futurate sense), but the truth of *The bus hit Max* could hardly be closer, either in time or in the causal sequence of events.

5. ANOTHER APPROACH TO THE PROGRESSIVE

There is another line of attack on the progressive that is suggested by its historical development. One of the antecedents of the progressive was a construction

(12)   *John is* $\begin{Bmatrix} on \\ at \\ a\text{-} \end{Bmatrix}$ *hunting.*

It seems that the earliest of these forms used *on* or *at*, which were later shortened to *a-* and finally dropped altogether, resulting in the modern form of the progressive. In the old form *on* or *at* was a preposition and *hunting* a gerundive noun phrase, the name of the process or activity.[22]

---

[22] This is indicated by the possibility of using the preposition with nongerundive noun phrases as in the historical antecedent of *asleep* (=*at sleep*).

The preposition is now forgotten and *hunting* is no longer a noun phrase in this context, but the modern progressive has at least very nearly the same meaning as the older construction. The right meaning is arrived at by reading the preposition as something like *engaged in* or *in the process of*.

This older construction could be used with processes, accomplishments, or achievements, as in the sentences in (13).

(13)   *John is at* $\begin{Bmatrix} running \\ building\ a\ house \\ dying \end{Bmatrix}$.

Thus, assuming there to be a common meaning for the preposition *at*, there ought to be an idea *in the process of* which would be common to the meaning of all progressives, and an examination of the progressive with the three types of sentence tends to confirm this. *John is running* means *John is in process of running*, *John is building a house* means *John is in process of building a house*, and *John is dying* means *John is in process of dying*. Looked at from this point of view, the problem for a unified analysis of the progressive is that John's running is a process that goes on when *John run* is true, John's building a house is a process that goes on at certain times within the interval at which *John build a house* is true, and John's dying is a process that goes on before *John die* is true.

As described in Section 4.1, the operator Prog, when applied to process sentences, had only one effect—to change the process sentence into a stative, which amounts to changing the interaction of the sentence with certain adverbials. Obviously that interpretation for Prog will not do for achievement and accomplishment sentences, but the changing of a process sentence into a stative is central to the meaning of the progressive, so I introduce an operator Stat which does just that and nothing else.

In addition, if ϕ is a sentence of the form NP VP, I will let Proc[ϕ] be a name denoting the process of NP's VP-*ing*, if any.

Given these two definitions, the operator Prog can be defined in general as follows:

(14)   Prog[ϕ] if and only if Stat[Proc[ϕ] goes on]

I believe this definition to be correct as far as it goes, but no truth conditions have yet been given for the progressive, because nothing has been said about when Proc[ϕ] goes on. For process sentences, (14) will reduce to [Prog[ϕ] if and only if Stat[ϕ]]. For accomplishments and achievements, in order to determine at what times the progressive is true, it still remains to say when the corresponding process goes on.

There are pragmatic reasons why all of this turns out as it does. The operator Stat applies only to process sentences, and, whatever type of sentence ϕ is, the progressive of ϕ says that Proc[ϕ] is going on. However, Proc[ϕ] does not have a uniform semantic characterization in terms of the truth conditions for ϕ. Rather, for each of the three classes of sentences ϕ, Proc[ϕ] is a process naturally related to the truth conditions for ϕ. The case for process sentences is most straightforward; a process sentence is true when a certain process is going on, and Proc[ϕ] is then the process that goes on when ϕ is true. This is why (14) reduces to [Prog[ϕ]] if and only if Stat[ϕ]] for process sentences. For achievements and accomplishments the situation is more complex. In each of these cases Proc[ϕ] cannot be the process that goes on when ϕ is true, because there is no such process. For achievements and accomplishments, Proc[ϕ] is a process that leads to the truth of ϕ. We can say that a process P leads to the truth of ϕ if and only if the continuation of P would eventually cause ϕ to become true.[23]

5.1. Accomplishment Sentences

The process of John's building a house, or Proc [*John build a house*], is a process that leads to the truth of *John build a house*. It is a process that consists of hammering nails, sawing wood, and such. It cannot be characterized simply as the process that leads to the truth of *John build a house*, because there are a variety of such processes (one is the process of John's finishing building a house). It might be possible to characterize it this way:

(15)   If ϕ is an accomplishment sentence, then Proc[ϕ] is that process P that leads to the truth of ϕ, and such that if ϕ is to become true at I, then P starts at the beginning of I and ends at the end of I.

5.2. Achievement Sentences

Achievement sentences give rise to the most difficulty for an analysis of the progressive. All the analyses of the progressive mentioned so far (and also Bennett, this volume) fail radically for achievement sentences, because it is impossible to specify in topological terms truth conditions that

---

[23] I had originally intended to state this definition along the lines of David Lewis's suggestion for the progressive as

P leads to the truth of ϕ if and only if ϕ will be true in that possible world most similar to the actual one in which P continues.

This has the unfortunate consequence that nearly any process that is going on leads to the truth of *The sun set*. A similar problem exists for Lewis's truth conditions for the progressive and for Dowty's. It seems that causation is the necessary concept here, however it is to be analyzed in terms of possible worlds.

allow the progressive of ϕ to be true before ϕ is true, but not indefinitely before. So far, what I have said about achievement sentences entails only that, for each achievement sentence ϕ of which Prog[ϕ] is sometimes true, there is a process P that leads to the truth of ϕ (and therefore goes on before ϕ is true) such that Prog[ϕ] is true just when P goes on. It remains to specify process P for achievement sentences.

Unfortunately the following example (suggested to me by Östen Dahl) makes it appear that no such specification can be given in a uniform way for all achievement sentences. Consider these four sentences:

(16)   *Max die.*

(17)   *Max's life end.*

(18)   *Max be dying.*

(19)   *Max's life be ending.*

In the case in Section 4.2 where the bus is about to hit Max, (19) is true but (18) is false; yet whatever process is leading to the truth of (17) must also be leading to the truth of (16). This shows that, for achievement sentences, Proc[ϕ] cannot simply be the process that leads to the truth of ϕ. In view of the apparent identity of intension of (16) and (17), it also at least suggests that the difference between Proc[*Max die*] and Proc[*Max's life end*] must be explained in terms of something besides the intension of (16) and (17).

It seems that there is a large class of what I will call typical achievement sentences, of which (17) is a member but (16) is not. These sentences often contain verbs like *finish, complete, end,* and *arrive* that have to do with reaching a point, either literally or figuratively. The significant thing about a verb ϕ of this class is that there is an obvious and easily specified accomplishment A such that to ϕ is SIMPLY to finish A; to arrive there is to finish going there, to reach the summit is to finish climbing to the summit, and so on. It may be possible, for any achievement, to represent it as the completion of some accomplishment, but for typical achievement sentences the accomplishment is a natural one in something like the sense in which there are natural classes as opposed to artificial ones.

For typical achievement sentences, Proc[ϕ] is the vaguely defined last part of the process that leads to the accomplishment of which ϕ reports the completion. This last part is simply some final portion of the process, which may or may not be qualitatively different from what precedes it. If there is a qualitatively distinct final part, then the progressive is likely to mean that this final part is going on. To say that a ship is arriving may be to say that it has entered the harbor, or that it has begun procedures for docking, or something of the sort; to say that a piece of furniture is being finished is to say that the finish is being applied.

There is considerable justification for saying that to die is not SIMPLY to finish living one's life, so that (16) is not a typical achievement sentence. The Oxford English Dictionary says that *die* is the proper word "especially for the cessation of life by disease or natural decay." I would modify this and say that *die* suggests an end of life due to the more-or-less gradual failure of the body's natural functions, whatever the cause. This process of gradual failure is the one reported in (18). One whose body simply blinked out of existence could hardly be said to have died, even though life was ended. The case for someone instantly vaporized by a nuclear bomb is to some extent similar. One could construct a series of increasingly appropriate cases for the use of *die*, beginning with hydrogen bombs and ending with long illnesses.

If this is right then not all processes that lead to the truth of (17) lead to the truth of (16), and certainly not characteristically to the truth of (16). The implications of this for the case in Section 4.2 where the bus is about to hit Max are obvious.

Perhaps there are other verbs like *die*, which report the completion of some accomplishment as a result of some characteristic process. If so then possibly, for any achievement sentence ϕ whose main verb is of this semantic class, Proc[ϕ] is the process that characteristically leads to the truth of ϕ.

There is a class of achievement sentences that do not report the completion of any accomplishment and such that there is no process that characteristically leads to their truth. Presumably for this reason, progressives of sentences in this class are unusual. *I am astonishing Max* is distinctly odd, although *I am doing something that will astonish Max* is acceptable. Some other mental verbs, like *realize*, belong with *astonish*, as do some verbs that designate instantaneous physical events, like *explode* and perhaps *hit*.

Progressives of sentences involving the verb *win* are particularly puzzling, especially in view of the fact that those involving the verb phrase *finish first*, which semantically ought to be like *win*, are typical achievement sentences. *Mary win* and *Mary finish first* seem to say nearly the same thing, but Mary has to be finishing (i.e., engaged in running the last part of the race) in order to be finishing first, whereas she can be winning even near the beginning of the race. These facts suggest that progressives of such sentences are to be treated as idiomatic.

Even if they are idiomatic, there is the question of the meaning of such progressives. It has been suggested that *Mary is winning* means simply that Mary is ahead; but Mary is not winning when she is faltering and pursued by the still-fresh world record holder, even if she is ahead. It looks as if the notion of leading to the truth of *Mary win* is still central. Also, the fact that rampaging buses are still irrelevant indicates that it is something other than the natural course of events that must lead to the truth of *Mary win*. As a first approximation, *Mary is winning (the race)* is true at *t* if and only if the situation at *t* is such that the process of Mary's running the race will, if continued, lead to the truth of *Mary win*.

6. SUMMARY

All topologically specified truth conditions for the progressive must fail. Any correct account must make central use of the notion of a process. The process that must be going on in order to make the progressive of a sentence ϕ true is always a process that is connected with the truth of ϕ. If ϕ is a process sentence, then the process that goes on when the progressive of ϕ is true is the same one that goes on when ϕ is true. If ϕ is an accomplishment or achievement sentence, then the process that goes on when the progressive of ϕ is true is always one that will lead, if continued, to the truth of ϕ.

ACKNOWLEDGMENTS

I am indebted to Emmon Bach, Barbara Partee, to other members of the University of Massachusetts, Amherst Departments of Linguistics and Philosophy, and to Max Cresswell and Alex Mourelatos for a variety of helpful suggestions, challenges, clues, *etc.*

REFERENCES

Anderson, J. (1973). *An Essay Concerning Aspect*. The Hague: Mouton.
Bennett, M., and Partee, B. (1972). *Toward the logic of tense and aspect in English*. System Development Corporation, Santa Monica, Calif. (Available from the Indiana University Linguistics Club.)
Comrie, B. (1976). *Aspect*. Cambridge: Cambridge University Press.
Cresswell, M.J. (1977). Interval semantics and logical words. In C. Rohrer (Ed.), *On the Logical Analysis of Tense and Aspect*. Tubingen: TBL Verlag Gunter Narr.
Dowty, David (1972). *Studies in the Logic of Verb Aspect and Time Reference in English*. Department of Linguistics, University of Texas, Austin.
Dowty, David (1977). Toward a semantic analysis of verb aspect and the English imperfective progressive. *Linguistics and Philosophy*, **1**, 45–77.
Jespersen, O. (1931). *A Modern English Grammar on Historical Principles*, Part IV. London: Allen and Unwin.
Lewis, D. (1973). *Counterfactuals*. Cambridge, Mass.: Harvard University Press.

Montague, R. (1972). The proper treatment of quantifiers in ordinary English. [Reprinted in R. Thomason (1974).]

Palmer, F.R. (1974). *The English Verb*. London: Longman.

Scott, D. (1970). Advice on modal logic. In K. Lambert (Ed.), *Philosophical Problems in Logic*. Dordrecht: Reidel.

Thomason, R. (Ed.). (1974). *Formal Philosophy: Selected Papers of Richard Montague*. New Haven: Yale University Press.

Vendler, Z. (1967). Verbs and Times. In Z. Vendler, *Linguistics in Philosophy*. Ithaca: Cornell University Press.

SUBJECT INDEX

CONTENTS OF PREVIOUS VOLUMES

Contents of Previous Volumes